A World Full of Women

Martha C. Ward
University of New Orleans

Allyn and Bacon
Boston London Toronto Sydney Tokyo Singapore

President: Bill Barke
Vice President, Social Sciences: Susan Badger
Series Editor: Sylvia Shepard
Editorial Assistant: Jennifer Normandin
Marketing Manager: Joyce Nilsen
Production Administrator: Elaine Ober
Production Coordinator: Thomas E. Dorsaneo
Editorial-Production Service: Menagerie Design & Publishing
Text Designer: Andrea Miles
Cover Administrator: Suzanne Harbison
Composition Buyer: Linda Cox
Manufacturing Buyer: Aloka Rathnam

Library of Congress Cataloging-in-Publication Data
Ward, Martha Coonfield
    A world full of women/Martha C. Ward.
    p. cm.
    Includes bibliographical references and index.
    ISBN 0-205-16992-9
    1. Women's studies. 2. Feminist anthropology. I. Title.
HQ1180.W37 1995
305.42—dc20   95-9022
                                                                              CIP

Printed in the United States of America
10 9 8 7 6 5 4 3 2 1   99 98 97 96

Dedication

A *World Full of Women* is dedicated with respect, love, and gratitude, to:

Jo, Meg, Beth, and Amy

Marlowe, Moselle, Tommie Louise, and Nell

Heidi, Meg, Mary, Nancy, Emalene, Elizabeth

June and Jane and Jane

Orissa, Kay, Katy, Donna, Nancy, Corinne, Beth, Ann, Betsy, Gayle, Christine, Alvina, Tommie, Doris, Toni

Rayna, Faye, Annette, Weesie, Suzanne, Jill, Michele, Marcia, Patty, Patti, Mary, Brigitte, Olga

Maggie, Rebecca, Erin, Caitlin, Missy

Sylvia, Laura, Jennifer, Andrea, Naomi

Seraphia, Shirley, Susan, Alice, Pam, Joyce, Alma, Jane, Naomi, Mary, Kay, Margaret, Tina, Emily

Coralie, and Grace

Contents

Reviewer Acknowledgments

We would like to thank the following reviewers for reading the manuscript and responding so eloquently: Paul Bohannan; Candice Bradley, Lawrence University; Dona Davis, University of South Dakota; Ellen Gruenbaum, California State University of San Bernardino; Penn Handwerker, University of Connecticut; Homes Hogue, Mississippi State University; Jane Lancaster, University of New Mexico; Nancy McKee, Washington State University; Claire Renzetti, St. Joseph's University; Mary Jo Schneider, University of Arkansas; Ann Weber, University of North Carolina at Ashville; Karen Wedge, Women's Studies Program, Colorado State University.

Photo Credits:

Introduction

elcome to a world full of women. This book has two goals: to explore and validate woman-centered experiences, and to illuminate the common grounds of being female on Planet Earth.

You will find many voices for or about women. These include examples from ethnography, autobiography, biography, journalism, research, or other sources that explore the varieties of female experience. You will meet anthropologists and other scholars who do fieldwork and critical research. We will highlight women's lives, including some secret parts, and underscore strategies, negotiations, and maneuvering rather than static social structures. This book does not exclude men; it simply puts women in the foreground.

The foundations of the book are firmly woman-centered and gently humanistic. I hope to speak to people who are not anthropologists or whose fascination with the field has only started. I treat women as bicultural creatures who live in at least two different worlds. As a result, women may be strategists or actors in our own lives on a stage we did not invent. Sometimes we cooperate with each other in resistance, and sometimes we participate in systems of domination.

Many theories and positions come into play. I have longstanding friendships with Charles Darwin, Karl Marx, Margaret Mead, many theorists, some postmodernists, and few modernists, as well as structuralists, functionalists, materialists, and those who think best in symbols and myths. As with other friends, I have spent many hours in their company and appreciate the insights they give me about the world. However, I have no intention of eloping or setting up housekeeping with any of them. You will, of course, find their fingerprints throughout the book. There are many theoretical debates in anthropology about gender, gender ideologies or feminism, and many ways to look at women and our lives around the world. Please feel free to add your own interpretations, friendships, experiences, and intellectual commitments, and to use the books and articles cited to follow your own direction.

Much of the book is **ethnographic.** Ethnography literally means "a portrait of a people," that is, research on groups of people, generally ordinary people in cultures different or distant from one's own. The discipline of anthropology started as a small science, a group of researchers who assumed responsibility for studying small-scale, preliterate, or preindustrial societies. In those days, everyone called such groups "primitive." Their lives were thought to be less complicated than people who lived in "civilizations." This little social science coincided with the rise of colonial empires throughout the world and what everyone perceived as an enormous rate of social and cultural change. The subject matter of anthropology seemed to be disappearing rapidly. Anthropologists tended, therefore, to take an odd view of time and space; we spoke of before contact with the West and after contact with the West. Talk about ethnocentrism!

Anthropology grew out of the European and specifically the Victorian world-view, in which women were "naturally" subordinate, inferior, and taken for granted. It had a clear masculine bias. With a few dramatic exceptions, much of the research tended to ignore, misinterpret, or trivialize the lives of women: When people believed that "women's place was in the home," they could not see much else. So women were invisible. And the best strategies of survival probably did not involve drawing ourselves to anyone's attention! So much of women's lives in our own and in other cultures has been hidden.

Many traditional anthropologists only saw women in the role they were believed to be playing right here at home: supporting and nurturing men, dutifully following orders, working at home raising children, gossiping, preparing food, and so forth. They did not even see women in other roles: women whose deepest emotional relationships were with each other; middle-aged women who came into their power so easily that no one noticed they were in charge; married women who supported husbands and children but who could not claim the tributes of that labor; women who cooked or cured but were never addressed as chef or doctor; women who both mothered and fathered, and who, denied formal access, found radical, resistive, and restorative private routes to sensuality, spirituality, artistry, or professionalism.

At the same time, the discipline of anthropology has incorporated more women than the other social sciences. From the beginning, anthropologists emphasized direct personal experience and fieldwork, a lengthy and life-changing type of research. Over the last hundred years many women have done fieldwork. In fact, women may have advantages in fieldwork settings. Today anthropologists do research in our own neighborhoods as well as across the planet. Today we add women to the human experience.

Old Words and New Realities

The names for various cultures and social divisions in the world are a problem. We can no longer comfortably refer to the First World (Europe, the United States, and other Western democracies), the Second World (Communist-bloc countries), and the Third World (countries mostly in the southern hemisphere who invented this term for themselves to avoid the labels of developing or underdeveloped). At the same time, we speak of the Fourth World, or the growing consciousness of tribal peoples who may share more with each other than with the dominant political systems. Concepts like "the West" or the "Free World" may exclude "the Other," people who are somehow different, exotic, pagan, female, or poor. At the end of this extraordinary century, most people have a new sensibility about gender, to the differences between women's lives and "a man's world."

Caught up of necessity in our habits, our languages, and our outlooks, we sometimes cannot see beyond our own cultural patterns. So I want to reach out to your sense of being a citizen of the planet, connected or tied to women regardless of our cultural differences. At the same time, I want to honor those cultural differences.

A number of terms or words are used for women's condition in the world: sexism, patriarchy, sex or gender stratification, sexual asymmetry, male dominance, female subordination, gender segregation, paternalism or paternalistic dominance, and women's oppression. The meanings are clear. They indicate a form of social inequality based on gender; we know these conditions vary in intensity from place to place and time to time in complex ways. I am not using these terms in any technical or cleverly theoretical sense. I'm not even going to argue that these phenomena really exist. They just do.

We also have a set of terms to describe our goals and hopes for changing these conditions. We speak of feminism, feminist consciousness, women's rights, women's movements, women's emancipation, consciousness-raising, and women's liberation. A great many books and articles, some of which I included in the bibliography, throw light on these concepts. However we use these terms, we are speaking out about awareness, our sense of working together, and our shared commitment to an alternate vision of the future.

These themes will cross and crisscross in many complex ways. I have found it impossible to find words, labels, or terms that will please everyone in every context. The glossary includes terms used in the text, with some interpretations.

Where J'm Coming From

In the international women's movement, women tell each other that "the personal is political." We have learned from each other that our stories count for more than our feelings, our opinions, or our observance of the rules. We know that no writer or researcher can claim complete objectivity or can be honest if we separate ourselves from what we say. This is no longer the age of disembodied experts who speak authoritatively from high places. So you should know something about the person who is speaking with you on these pages.

I have taught anthropology at the University of New Orleans (UNO) since 1969. I wrote up and taught the first official women's studies course in the state of Louisiana. At that time, such a seditious act was possible only because I was "chairman" of my department. Indeed, this was also the climax of my career as an administrator. Since then, I have hit the glass ceiling a number of times.

But the university's loss of my energies as an administrator is probably my gain as a person. In the mid-1980s, a group of faculty women at UNO started a Women's Studies Minor Program and a Women's Center; their dedication and collegiality inspired this book. In addition, I spend every other summer in Europe, teaching, traveling, doing fieldwork, directing UNO's international summer school in Innsbruck, Austria, or running a field school at a twelfth-century castle in the magnificent mountains of northern Italy.

I grew up in a wonderful, loving family in a fundamentalist Christian community in small-town Oklahoma. Fleeing that quiet life at the first opportunity, I escaped into the institution of marriage, the study of anthropology, and the city of New Orleans. My husband and I put each other through a series of graduate degrees. My first fieldwork was in a rural parish on the Mississippi River studying how African American children learn and use language. I also listened to women talk about having babies, getting sick, preparing home remedies for each other, and living as females.

In the early 1970s, my husband and I spent almost two years doing research in medical ethnography in Pacific Micronesia, on a magnificent tropical island named Pohnpei (today the capital of the Federated States of Micronesia). I fulfilled my dream of doing fieldwork in a faraway place. It was simultaneously scary, boring, sweaty, confusing, exhilarating, and addictive. And I got pregnant.

Becoming a mother changed me. My life in the early 1970s became a series of what *MS. Magazine* calls "clicks," that moment when something shifts forever inside us. A vice-chancellor at UNO said, "Women don't look feminine when they carry briefcases." Click. My university health insurance refused to pay for my daughter's birth because they claimed that I neither had nor was a faculty wife. The hospital refused to admit me because my husband was a graduate student and their blanks could not be stretched to include me as head of household. Click. I could not get credit in my own name, and under the head and master laws in Louisiana could not own property under any name or vote in my "maiden" name. Click. My husband said, "I like the dessert my sister served us. Get the recipe for it." My brothers said, "While you're up, get me the mayonnaise." Click. I realized I would protect my daughter with my life; that meant I had to take care of myself first. Click. A well-loved relative revealed the sexual abuse her father had hoped to conceal. CLICK. A pregnant friend was beaten by her husband and the baby died. CLICK. Friends, relatives, and students were raped, stalked, beaten, and battered. CLICK. CLICK.

Yes, of course, I am a feminist. I am also happily divorced, a proud mother, a loving daughter, a good sister, a passionate anthropologist, a voter, a homeowner, and I can claim many wonderful people as friends. I write about and do research on the politics of reproduction, early childbearing or adolescent pregnancy, family planning, AIDS, and health-care delivery systems, particularly for poor women. And I teach anthropology.

No, the discipline of anthropology is not perfect. We don't have all the answers and we are just learning to ask some of the eternal questions. I am, however, indebted to the life-changing research on a world full of women done by my colleagues in anthropology and other disciplines. For myself, I claim only the legacy of a woman to grow older and tell her collected stories.

Some Books Which Changed Our Lives

Early in the decade of the 1970s, a number of books came out that heralded an explosion of knowledge, debate, and revelations for and about women. In the last quarter-century, we have seen an exponential growth in visibility and understanding about women's lives. That generation of research centered on three basic questions: (1) How is gender built, assembled, forged, or constructed in a myriad of cultural settings? (2) When and where and how, if ever, did women have status and power? (3) What do the voices of women sound like when we emerge from our silences?

Many anthropologists feel these early books and the studies that followed revolutionized our discipline. Here is a short sampling. A list of related, relevant, and readable books is similarly included at the end of each chapter.

Michelle Rosaldo and Louise Lampheres's collection of articles, *Women, Culture and Society,* (1974), is probably the classic statement for the generation of how we can view women in human society. It set out the theoretical range and many of the definitions for women's studies and for anthropology. Rayna Reiter's 1975 book, *Toward an Anthropology of Women,* is a still-valuable collection of articles. It remains one of the most-cited and most influential series of statements about women in anthropology we ever had. And in 1975 Shirley Ardener published her first collection of innovative and carefully reasoned articles, *Perceiving Women.*

Kay Martin and Barbara Voorhies wrote *Female of the Species;* it came out in 1975. This book was a responsible, practical, and down-to-earth comparative view of women in various societies. They handled thorny topics such as biology and culture or gender ideologies so well that the rest of us could rest on their triumphs. In the same year, Ernestine Friedl brought out *Women and Men: An Anthropologist's View.* This book has been widely used, particularly by people who are not anthropologists, for its calm, careful, caring approach. Her basic view is that the technological levels of human societies constrain the relationship between the sexes (sex roles, as we used to say).

Ethnographies usually have a longer shelf life than theory books. Two books, in particular, enlarged our anthropological visions in this era as we began to see women as actors and producers rather than items of exchange. Jane Goodale wrote *Tiwi Wives* in 1971 and a new edition came out in 1994. On the northern coast of Australia, in a group of hunters–gatherers, women just followed the elaborate kinship and marriage rules. At least that's what anthropologists and Tiwi men thought until Jane came along. Meanwhile, Carol Stack was writing *All Our Kin* (1974). This book is about some matrifocal African American domestic units that taught anthropologists something new about family, households, partnering, and survival strategies.

Chapter One

"What's for Dinner Honey?"

Work, Food, and the Facts of Life

J n the tiny coastal village of Grey Rock Harbour in Newfoundland, where residents earn their living in the precarious, cold, hard work of ocean fishing, one woman inquires of another, "How are you today?" Her neighbor replies, "My nerves is some bad." Another woman stirs her boiled caribou stew and concentrates on her husband fishing from a small boat in rough seas. "It grates on my nerves," she says. "I worries some awful when he's out and the weather turns." A friend compliments her. "After the life you've led, my dear, you can't expect much more from your nerves."

Some Newfoundlanders say that men don't have nerves, that men can't feel much. Others say they have heard about men who had nerves. But chiefly, as everyone knows, women have nerves. One woman summarizes: "I worries about the worst happening. That's what nerves is."

Ethnographer Dona Lee Davis conducted this research on nerves in icy Newfoundland. She notes, "It is the women, who carry the burden of worry, who deserve nerves. Her lot in life is harder than the male's. Nerves belong in the emotional, affective realm, the domain of women" (Davis 1989:74). This work is part of the work of being married, of husbanding resources, of being a housewife. Worry is one of the ways women work. We are **Women the Worriers.**

This chapter is an affirmation of some things you already know about women. For example, women work, have babies, and provide food for ourselves and others. The typical or model woman on this planet works for a living; she also does the work associated with family life—however these may be defined for her. The chapter centers on two operating principles, or what I call the facts of life. The first is about women and work, the division of labor by sex or gender. The second questions the ownership of women and the concepts of women as property. Each fact of life offers some dramatic examples. Last we will look at the great "what's for dinner" debate within the discipline of anthropology. All of these concepts—women and work, women as property, and the "what's for dinner" debate—are part of the larger and very real concept of women's culture.

Women's Culture

Being a human female is quite different from being a **woman.** The latter is a cultural category. Women are not just biological organisms with physical traits different from males of the same species; women are embedded in complex social, cultural, and personal histories. We have feelings, attitudes, role expectations, and identities to which we have been assigned, acquired along the way of growing up, or taken up deliberately.

So different are the lives, work, and bodies of women and men that it is safe to say we live in two different worlds. In fact, it is helpful to think of human societies as divided into two cultures, his and hers. In that sense, women are **bicultural.** This means women are born into a culture that men rarely enter and few know about. Women learn the rules of our own half of the world as well as those of the other half because we move in and out of the male world regularly. Here is a definition of **women's culture:**

The term has also been used in its anthropological sense to encompass the familial and friendship networks of women, their affective ties, their rituals. It is important to understand that woman's culture is never a subculture. It would hardly be appropriate to define the culture of half of humanity as a subculture. Women live their social existence within the general culture. Whenever they are confined by patriarchal restraint or segregation into separateness (which always has subordination as its purpose), they transform this restraint into complementarity and redefine it. Thus, women live a duality—as members of the general culture and as partakers of woman's culture. (Lerner 1986:242)

The concept of women's culture is useful, but it does not mean that all women are automatically sisters or that the political agendas of one group of women are the same as the agendas of a different group. Indeed, most of us live in more than just two cultures or subcultures.

Human beings transcend sex or biology with gender. We assign social roles and determine how people defined as females will act, dress, speak, get married, or be friends with others; the same is true for males. These are basic **gender roles.** Then human beings assign symbols and spell out the social meanings to being male or female. These are called **gender ideologies;** they include the prescriptions and sanctions for what is considered appropriate female or male behaviors, and cultural rationalizations or religious explanations for the social and political relationships that are believed to exist between the genders.

The basic point is that gender is a **construct.** Through time and in adaptation to their environment, groups of people construct, build, forge, or fabricate what they think women are really like and what they believe men are really like. Looking across human cultures, it is clear that what is "naturally" feminine, either in roles or in personalities, is a matter of local conventions. It is very difficult to put the blame or the credit on biology or on culture exclusively. Our behavior and belief systems are the complex interaction of many factors—social, organic, random, historical, chance, or mischance.

Fact of Life Number One: Women and Work

Women work for a living. In every human society that anthropologists ever studied, people divide the work they have to do between women and men. This is called the **sexual division of labor,** the assignment of the survival tasks of the society according to gender. Men get some of the jobs and women get some of the jobs. A few jobs may be done by both sexes. Generally, people feel strongly that their way of dividing up work is the best way or the "natural" way. Generally, some other group does it differently. That this division of work may be neither equal nor equally rewarding is quite beside the point.

Here is an amazing fact: Everyone from conservative male sociobiologists to radical Marxist feminists agrees that the sexual division of labor is fundamental to being human. Work divided by gender is somehow a true statement about the human condition. This will be the last time for such easy agreement in this book. At the same time, these people do not agree on *why* the sexual division of labor is true. Some say God, religion, nature, science, or mothers make us live this way. And no one concurs on *how* to translate this agreement over the sexual division of labor into decent and life-affirming social policies. In fact, there is no widespread agreement that human beings even need such policies.

The basic point to understand here is that all women work. All mothers or wives have jobs. That these may be invisible or unrewarded is immaterial. That they may be acknowledged or ignored, easy or life-threatening, is totally beside the point. Women still work.

Some jobs are "women's work" and others are defined as "men's work." The catch is that these tasks are not the same from group to group. For example, in cultures along the Sepik River in New Guinea, people eat flour made from sago palms. Someone must cut, haul, and process the trunk of the palm tree for the soggy flour it reluctantly yields. In some of the groups along the dramatic river, only men do this work. There people say, "Of course, it is naturally men's work." Downriver or upriver, women gather to strain the flour out as people in that group remark, "Naturally, this is women's work."

Gathering Work

Anthropologists think that the spacing of children and the customs of raising children are everywhere adjusted to the kinds of work women customarily do. In classic gathering–hunting societies, for example, births are rarely closer than three to four years apart. Babies nurse for long periods. A female cannot easily carry a pregnancy, a nursing baby, and a toddler, or any two of the above, and still carry out her work in gathering. Do not think that her job is unimportant or that she will automatically be excused because child care comes first. Her first job is gathering. Arrangements around raising children will adjust to her work.

Women as mothers in such societies are not the exclusive caretakers of small children. In fact, this labor is generally shared between a number of women in ways structured by kinship and networks of friendships. There are also ways for men to assist. Bearing and raising children will depend on how the energies of adult women are used in subsistence and other economic or social tasks. Women in societies that depend on hunting and gathering or foraging space the time between pregnancies and organize child care around the work they have to do. The spacing of births in hunting–gathering cultures is not an accident; it is one of the clearest examples we have of how women manage work.

Homework

The following description of the sexual division of labor in Grey Rock Harbour will feel familiar to most readers. This describes the traditional relationship of work and gender in peasant farming and fishing cultures until quite recently.

Despite the physical separation of the sexes, the family remained important. Nuclear and extended family networks were extensive and defined local social organization. Kinfolk could be counted on for support when times were hard. Marriage was universal and was considered essential for entry into full adult status. There was no divorce. Couples married in their midteens, started their families early, and looked forward to a life of fishing or work at the fish plant. Flexible hiring patterns at the local fish plant make it easy for women (and men) to schedule wage labor around family obligations. (Davis 1993:461)

The equalitarian ethic in Grey Rock Harbour was, "We'll help each other out, but we all come up together or we don't come up at all." Most men fished; most women ran households. Men and women equally worked at the fish processing plant. Every person was expected to be a hard worker. Other tasks filled their extra time; women knitted and men built or repaired their equipment. Figure 1.1 illustrates this old division of labor, one similar to many traditional peasant, fishing, farming societies around the world. Note that women do 100 percent of women's work, men do 100 percent of men's work and only some overlap is shared.

Figure 1.1
An Old-Fashioned Model of Work and Gender

Piecework

In Turkey, where ethnographer Jenny White conducted her research, women may spend up to fifty hours per week producing goods for export. When women and their families moved from the rural areas to the city to find jobs, they started doing piecework, handwork, or finishing work on products destined for the world market. One such woman, Hayriye, skillfully embroiders nightgowns, blouses, head scarves, and doilies for neighbors and friends and nightclothes for trousseaus. Occasionally, she knits sweaters for a merchant. He pays her by the piece. She speaks:

> At holidays work piles up so I do the urgent ones first. I am a housewife and how much I can stitch depends on the time I have left over from housework and my other duties. (White 1994:111)

Hayriye and her peers insist on making a distinction between labor and work. They do the labor and give the products out. But this is not a job or employment. "I am busy," they say. Busy means doing housework, tending children, or helping kinfolks and neighbors. Among themselves they maintain the fiction that they are not working; they are merely staying busy.

> This allows them to avoid the onus of being considered a woman who has economic dealings with strangers, a woman who has to "work," demonstrating that her husband is not able to support his family financially. This latter dishonors the family as a whole, including the women. . . . This allows them to contribute financially, while remaining reconciled with the moral standards of the traditional family. This conflation of labor with a woman's traditional identity is one of the factors that keep production costs low and profits high for distributors, intermediaries, merchants, and exporters. (White 1993:130)

In their view, women who work among strangers outside their homes cannot be good wives or moral Muslims. But economic circumstances are difficult in the cities; family survival may depend on more than a man's salary. So men work at more than one job. Women and children bring in extra income through piecework.

At the same time, women affirm and cement their membership in community life through sharing and exchanging labor. They do not keep track of the time spent or calculate hourly wages and piece rates. They put the work down and pick it up again as the day unfolds; they may finish up another woman's piece during some spare time. Within these networks, women pool money with each other rather than in pensions, health insurance, or social security. The crocheting, knitting, embroidery, and stitching are also investments in the financial and emotional support a mother can expect from her grown children. They call this "milk debt." So a woman's son may be a more important man in her life than is her husband; it may also mean that she has internalized a kind of gender ideology others call the patriarchy.

These Turkish women would say that they do **kin work,** not piecework. To them, piecework or sewing in workshops is not work but an expression of group identity, solidarity, and redistribution that sustains their families in tough economic times. The fact that men and women alike devalue women's work creates a pool of cheap labor for the world market and provides consumers in the West with what we think of as bargains in handmade table cloths, hand-stitched clothing or boutique sandals and purses (among many similar items). But women still work even when work operates on the logic of kinship rather than on the logic of capitalism.

Sex Work

Another model for looking at women's work is found in prostitutes' rights organizations around the world. Women "in the life" or "in the trade," that is, women selling sex, maintain that prostitution is not always forced servitude or sexual slavery. They say that prostitution or sex work is not a crime, a sin, or a vice. It may be a career choice as well as a legitimate and necessary social service. These women assert that sex workers have a right to work in conditions they themselves control. For them, the power in prostitution is the chance to choose, to set the terms of sexuality, and to demand substantial payment for their time and skills.

> *Prostitution, by definition, is the exchange of sexual services for money. Some prostitution is forced, and forced prostitution is clearly rape combined with kidnapping and perhaps brainwashing. At the other end of the spectrum, there are women who make a clear decision to work as prostitutes, a few because they enjoy sex and have no qualms about enjoying sex as work. Most women who work as prostitutes, I think, do so out of economic motives—the hourly pay is better than that paid for most of the work women are allowed to do. Some get to like the work as they become skilled at it. Other women hate it from beginning to the end. And still others like some aspects of the job while hating parts of it. (Delacoste and Alexander 1987:15)*

This example is not about whether prostitution should exist or not; nor does it concern moral judgments about people who sell sex. It is only about how some groups of women define the marketing and sale of sexual services as work. The box "A Sample of Prostitutes' Rights Organizations" lists some names of the international organizations sex workers have formed. These operate as unions, guilds, or professional associations for sex workers worldwide.

A Sample of Prostitutes' Rights Organizations

The most famous prostitutes' rights group in the United States is:

COYOTE	Call Off Your Old Tired Ethics

Other groups in the United States include:

CAT	California Advocates for Trollops
DOLPHIN	Dump Obsolete Laws; Prove Hypocrisy Isn't Necessary
FLOP	Friends and Lovers of Prostitutes
HIRE	Hooking Is Real Employment
HUM	Hooker's Union of Maryland
PASSION	Professional Association Seeking Sexual Identification Observant of Nature
PONY	Prostitutes of New York
PUMA	Prostitutes' Union of Massachusetts Association
SPARROW	Seattle Prostitutes Against Rigid Rules Over Women
U.S. PROS	
Hooker's Hookup	

Organizations in Other Countries

PLAN	Prostitution Laws Are Nonsense (Great Britain)
ECP	English Collective of Prostitutes (Great Britain)
ICPR	International Committee for Prostitutes' Rights (Amsterdam)
De Rode Draad	The Red Thread (Netherlands)
De Roze Draad	The Pink Thread (Netherlands)
CORP	Canadian Organization for Prostitutes
Austrian Association of Prostitutes	
Australian Prostitutes Collective	
National Association of Prostitutes, Brazil	
Lysistrata	Cologne, Germany
Kassandra	Nuremberg, Germany
Messalina	Munich, Germany

Source: Adapted from Valerie Jenness, *Making It Work* (1993)3–4.

Marriage Work

When we follow the sexual division of labor as a fact of life to its logical conclusion, then we see marriage as a form of work. If a man is a "breadwinner" and his wife "keeps house," then they have a sexual division of labor. They have an agreement or contract about sharing work. Advice books for women emphasize that being married is hard work. "You have to really work at it," they say. Students say, "We're taking some time off to work on our relationship." At a cocktail party, a man may ask of a woman, "What kind of work do you do?" She replies, "I'm just a housewife." Either or both may think, "This is not really work." But it is. In fact, collecting welfare may be a form of work where the government acts like a husband. Unpaid or unrecognized, it's still work.

The contemporary view of marriage and women's work in the West centers on assumptions of equality and an equalitarian division of labor. Figure 1.2 illustrates this model of how work is supposed to be distributed in modern families. Men do their share of the work (for example, 50 percent), and women do their share (the other 50 percent). Unlike women's and men's work in traditional societies, the tasks are interchangeable in modern settings. Both genders are supposed to do the same jobs, whether in the workplace or at home. However, this idea of equivalency or equality does not offer much crosscultural comparison. It is only recently evolved in the American middle class.

Figure 1.2
A Modern Model of Work and Gender

Work and Revolution

After the Socialist revolution in Russia, Lenin, the ideological father, decreed that women must work for wages if they wanted to be equal to men. As he noted in a newspaper interview,

> *Housework is the most unproductive, savage and most arduous work a woman can do. . . . Women must participate in common productive labor. . . We are setting up model institutions, dining rooms and nurseries, that will emancipate women from housework. And the work of organizing all these institutions will fall mainly to women. (Pravda 213: Sept. 25, 1919)*

Under Lenin's new socialism, Russian women would be paid as wage laborers for the same work they did for no pay before the revolution. But his socialist ideals never materialized. The state did not provide day care, laundry, or food preparation. Wives continued to do that work in addition to working for wages. The same thing is true now that Communism is dead and the Soviet Union disbanded.

As of this writing, no country or economic system in the world has solved the problem of valuing women's domestic work. The capitalist solution pays only lip service to motherhood, expecting women "to stay at home." No socialist country has been able to organize large-scale socialized domestic services. There has been no liberation from what Lenin called "household bondage and petty individual housekeeping." None of these systems provide adequately for the economic problems of divorce or widowhood. Worse, they assume that all women find satisfaction in domestic work, do it "naturally," and are always available to do it.

The current American middle-class solution to this age-old dilemma is to affirm the belief that women and men are equally responsible for child care and domestic work. By contrast, people in many countries are shocked at the demand for day care in capitalist countries; staying at home with their children would be an unimaginable luxury. In fact, in traditional societies or in socialist societies, there was never a category of women's work Americans call "staying at home."

It's Off to Work We Go

The work that human beings do falls into four categories: production, reproduction, status enhancement, and morale building. Although both men and women do all these kinds of work, we do them to a very different drumbeat. We are rewarded and recognized in separate ways. Women's work in these spheres feels and looks quite distinct from men's work.

The first kind, **work as production,** generates goods, money, wages, or income of some kind. Generally, we associate this kind of work with men. People tend to call this "real work" or "going to work." The work of women in production is often seen as only an extension of household work. An example is a woman selling her handmade, homemade, or homegrown products in local markets. These economic activities in the **informal sector** are usually not listed in statistics about productivity or regulated by national laws. Jobs in the **formal sector** or the official part of the economy are thought of as real productive work.

Then there is the **work of reproduction.** This is having babies and raising them. Overwhelmingly associated with women, these tasks are often more undervalued and underpaid than is the work of production. Moreover, the work of reproduction is routinely broadened to include extensions of "housework" such as home gardens, subsistence farming, food preparation, preservation, and storage, as well as caring for those who are like babies, sick people, old people, or helpless people.

The third kind of work is what we might call the **work of status enhancement.** These activities promote prestige and social worth—however they are defined. This kind of work includes leisure activities and volunteer work that not only integrate but enhance the status of a husband or family. Conspicuous consumption, effective consumerism, and social climbing are still work and are often highly valued. Among the upper classes all over the world, wives of prominent (rich) men organize large-scale events like charity balls. A wife is a public acknowledgment of a husband's ability to afford a "nonworking" wife. She may arrange other status-enhancing activities, such as dinner parties, rounds of seasonal festivities, or the debutante seasons. The latter are training grounds for daughters as status-enhancers, as future wives, and as fodder for parental ambitions. Sometimes women in these social circles are widowed, divorced, abandoned, or bankrupt. They may have "to go to work" and find paying jobs using the same abilities they developed as wives.

Although the activities of status enhancement are often valued as entertainment or special events, their importance as work—skilled, necessary, and time-consuming—is largely invisible.

The last major type is **work as morale, caring, repairing, and integration.** These tasks are overwhelmingly assigned to women. Inevitably, they include feelings, emotional responsibilities, and social obligations that start with parents, husbands, and babies and flow directly into public life. This kind of work includes arrangements for crucial and regular rituals and religious observances and the care of elderly and disabled people or other nonworkers as well as children. Women visit, write notes, call others, and plan weddings, family reunions, or holiday celebrations. Women often create community, build bonds that hold groups of people together, and provide crucial services to others in times of trouble. This is the work of integration. While men frequently have titles, positions of authority, and salaries attached to this kind of work, women usually work through their networks without pay simply because the work is there to be done.

By taking on the burden of worrying over their menfolk at sea, women in Grey Rock Harbour, Newfoundland, are valued in their communities for easing the dangers and deprivations of maritime life and freeing the men to fish. Women as Worriers are found throughout the world. Nerves, stress, anxiety, it's still work. Someone has to do it!

Value, Valued, and Valuable

Many women naively believe that if women's work is so vital to human survival and comfort, then we should be treated accordingly. Our work is valuable and the reward should correspond to the importance of our contributions, we protest. Alas, women's work is not always **valued.** In fact, there is often no system for placing a value on female labor. For example, look at the concept called **use value.** This means that products made and services rendered within families are not sold and do not have a monetary value. They have a "value" only in private domestic settings. This contrasts sharply with **exchange value work** which is the production of commodities or services for sale in the marketplace. When goods or services are exchanged for money or other financial considerations, then people say they have value.

The underlying economic principle is this: The ability to distribute, exchange, and control valuable goods and services to people who are not in our own domestic unit buys whatever we treasure—status, time, privacy, power, prestige, income, or goodies. This is true in each and every human group. Just working hard within our domestic units is only that: just working hard within our domestic units. This work, however hard, exciting, or crucial to survival it may be, does not automatically translate into power, control, status, or money. If women produce wonderful services or objects and cannot market them or keep the proceeds, then there is little or no exchange value or power. This principle also applies to the products of women's bodies. After all, the term "labor" refers to birthing an infant. This is also why sex workers claim that offering sex in return for marriage is much the same as selling it in a free market.

But the control or power any woman has over the process and the product of her labor varies greatly between cultures. As many have observed, in most societies men seem to have greater rights than women to distribute goods outside their domestic networks. So the best question is not about how hard women are working; ask instead if women control access to the resources they need. Resources typically include education, employment, child care, legal standing, land ownership, the freedom to marry and divorce, and access to the tools of survival or the means of production, as Karl Marx called them.

A related example of the sexual division of labor and work assigned by gender is the **family wage ideologies.** Family wage laws and practices, developed in nineteenth-century industrializing, capitalist societies, and are still a fundamental part of gender ideologies in the West. The premise is that a male worker (as head of a household) is hired and paid enough to support his wife and their children. Females (for example, young single women) who work the same jobs are not paid the same as men. Presumably, they do not have to support families. Married women are assumed to have access to their husband's income; they are said to be working at home for him. If wives take wage-labor jobs, it is seen as supplementing their husbands' income. This cultural formulation of the sexual division of labor has been enormously instrumental, even seductive, in western European and North American societies. You may recognize the impact of this gender ideology on your own salary and life.

Women don't just work; we are often overworked and invisible. Our work is taken for granted. Low wages, lack of support services, and the **double day** or the **second shift** are probably the most characteristic pattern for women's work on the planet. In the double day, women do child care and household and domestic duties in addition to agricultural work and full-time or part-time wage-labor jobs. Figure 1.3 diagrams these workloads.

Fact of Life Number Two: Own, Owned, Owning, and Ownership

Fact of Life number 2 is a question: **who owns her body?** The principle is that someone, somewhere, in most human groups, inevitably believes that he or she can, does, or should control the bodies of women. Ruling groups, gatekeepers, policy makers, the power elite, the patriarchy, tribal elders, religious authorities, relatives, kinfolk, cults, congresses, commissions, or committees, in whatever form they take, tend to worry about controlling women's bodies. Their concerns generally come to light in the areas of sexuality and reproduction. Please note, this is not predictably an issue of men controlling women. Women often participate in systems of controlling each other; this has been a difficult phenomenon for feminists and the women's movement to explain.

Figure 1.3
The Double Day or the Second Shift

Everywhere on the planet, women's bodies are restricted and controlled in ways men's bodies are not. Men's bodies are much less subject to rules than women's bodies are. Every human society has elaborate covert and overt rules women are supposed to observe. Some groups have taboos, for instance, about breast–feeding in public, mentioning menstruation at certain times or places or in certain company, eating special foods, not eating special foods, or not going into sacred places. There are rules for proper attire in public, covering heads, hair, faces, breasts, hands, feet, sitting in a designated spot or not sitting in a designated spot. Taboos abound. The evidence for this principle is amazingly extensive.

The reasons for excluding women from full public participation or enforcing peculiar customs vary, but they usually sound something like this: Women are too emotional. Women don't really know what they want. Women are a source of danger and pollution. Women cause a lot of trouble between men. Being around women is just too tempting, too exciting or too provocative for men to handle; therefore women need to be restrained. It is extremely common around the world for men to believe that sexual contact with a woman somehow weakens them. Men, they say, should not have sex when preparing for, engaging in, or recovering from important masculine enterprises, such as hunting, trading expeditions, warfare, ceremonials, or sports activities. According to this reasoning, women are unclean or polluted, profane, not sacred. Therefore it makes perfect sense to exclude women from assorted male activities.

In a number of human cultures, the problem is women who somehow fall outside established categories. Widows, divorced women, or teenage mothers may have no defined status, no place, or no position. What happens to a woman who wants to control her own sexuality or her own income? Circumstances vary, but the principle remains: Who is she if she is not connected to a man or to legitimate kinship groups?

There are many examples throughout this book about women as property or about defining the ownership of women. Here are five brief, bold illustrations of this fact of life.

Laws on a Pillar

Hammurabi's Code is the first set of laws ever written down in human history. It formed the basis for legal systems in the Middle East, ancient Israel, and other cultures of this important historic region. During the life of King Hammurabi, from 2067 to 2025 B.C., lawmakers ordered stonemasons to carve 270 laws on a stele or upright stone pillar (no symbolism implied). Approximately 100 of these laws dealt with the problems of keeping women in line, assigning ownership and responsibility for them, and defining the boundaries of their sexuality.

These and similar laws reveal their fundamental question: How can we tell the difference between decent women and indecent women? So many of these laws prescribed elaborate codes of veiling. For example, Middle Assyrian Law number 40 ruled that wives, daughters, and widows of ranking men must be veiled on the street. A concubine who went into the street with her mistress must be veiled. A sacred prostitute whom a man married must veil herself, but one whom a man did not marry must have an uncovered head on the street. Slaves, harlots, and unmarried women must go unveiled as a sign of their status. Any woman who violated these rules was punished, and sympathetic men who failed to report a "veiled harlot" or helped a woman evade these restrictions were also punished severely. Tribunals or courts could take away a woman's clothing, although not her jewelry; they could flog or beat her with staves or rods and pour pitch on her head.

The basic distinctions for women under these ancient laws was not whether they were slave or free, young or old, rich or poor. The characteristic embedded in these early legal systems was between respectable women—that is, domesticated women under the protection and in the sexual service of one man—and disrespectable women, public women, or women not under one man's protection and sexual control.

The customs of female modesty, seclusion, and veiling we call **purdah** came into being during this period in the Middle East and southern Asia. The word means "curtain" and today refers to the practices of seclusion for women in Islamic and Hindu cultures. This includes screens placed in households to prevent men from seeing women or the veils used for the streets and other public places or other forms for enforcing standards of female modesty. Practices of purdah and seclusion produce **harems.** The word means "forbidden" in Arabic and today identifies one part of a household as the residence of women. The term is also extended to all the women, mothers, sisters, wives, concubines, daughters, female entertainers, slaves, or servants who reside there.

Feet Like Lilies

A vivid example of the omnipresent principle of controlling women's bodies is the old Chinese practice of binding little girls' feet. A woman's bound feet, her "three-inch golden lilies," were often her greatest assets. Poets wrote that women walked on their tiny feet like tender young willow shoots in a spring breeze. Here is a quote from writer Jung Chang, who discusses her grandmother.

> My grandmother's feet had been bound when she was two years old. Her mother, who herself had bound feet, first wound a piece of white cloth about twenty feet long round her feet, bending all the toes except the big toe inward and under the sole. Then she placed a large stone on top to crush the arch. My grandmother screamed in agony and begged her to stop. Her mother had to stick a cloth into her mouth to gag her. My grandmother passed out repeatedly from the pain.
>
> The process lasted several years. Even after the bones had been broken, the feet had to be bound day and night in thick cloth because the moment they were released they would try to recover. For years my grandmother lived in relentless, excruciating pain. When she pleaded with her mother to untie the bindings, her mother would weep and tell her that unbound feet would ruin her entire life, and that she was doing it for her own future happiness. (Chang 1991:24)

Why did the Chinese practice this custom? It is said that a concubine of an emperor invented the practice a thousand years ago. It is said that men found the sight of women hobbling on tiny feet and embroidered silk shoes very erotic. At a young girl's wedding, the bridegroom's family would publicly insult or criticize any girl whose feet were more than four inches long. A bride enduring the contempt of her in-laws often blamed her mother, who had not done her duty properly.

Bound feet would certainly deter wives or daughters from running away, and would also prevent them from doing most kinds of work. Peasant women who worked in the fields or carried heavy loads had large feet that were unsightly and ugly by Chinese standards. From a contemporary viewpoint, it seems reasonable to infer that having a wife with tiny feet was some kind of status symbol; this interpretation means that bearing pain and inflicting it on one's daughters was a type of work.

Death by Fire

On the great subcontinent of India, at various times and in various classes or castes, women died in fires; the custom is called **sati.**

> The word sati (now in common parlance) refers to the burning of a widow on her husband's funeral pyre in a rite that is seen as a mani-festation of extreme loyalty and virtue. However, in the original Sanskrit meaning, the word "sati" means a virtuous or a chaste woman. Over the last three centuries the phrase "committing sati" has been commonly used to describe a widow's immolation. A woman who perishes thus is said to have "become a sati." The next step is usually the deification of the widow who has died. (Narasimhan 1990)

Young girls were frequently married to much older men who could be expect-ed to die long before their child bride. Then the question for such societies was what to do with the widow. Can she be returned to her natal family? Hardly. What assets does she bring to another marriage? None. Why didn't she just become independent, take lovers, and forge her own life and status? Because she doesn't have a job when her husband is dead. There is no **social space** defined for her. In defense of this custom, I have heard it claimed that young widows want to honor their husbands in this fashion, something beyond "until death do us part." It is said the respect and holiness they achieve after death is far greater than the benefits of living. I have also heard that someone slipped drugs to these marital sacrifices before the torch was lighted. Ultimately, the custom can be evaluated in the light of the status of women in India, customs favoring child betrothal, bans on widow remarriage, and the lack of education for women.

Missing Genitals

In at least twenty-six countries in Africa and the Middle East, many young girls undergo surgery on their genitals. This is called **female genital surgery** or female genital mutilation. Some people use the term circumcision for this surgery because it seems to parallel the operation on men (usually as newborns) in which the foreskin of the penis is removed. Sometimes only the clitoris or the clitoris and part of the lips of their vulvas are removed, and sometimes the sides of the vulva are stitched together and only a small opening is left. See **clitoridectomy** and **infibulation** in the glossary. Estimates for females who have undergone this surgery range from 80 million to 90 million in Africa alone. Perhaps 4 million to 5 million girls, commonly two to seventeen years of age, are circumcised each year. Mothers and midwives perform the operations on young girls. The operation may result in painful urination, intercourse, and childbirth, or chronic infections and permanent scarring.

Why? There are many songs, myths, stories, and centuries of traditions about these practices. The custom may well be 6,000 years old, but there seem to be no ultimate reasons for its existence. Some say that a woman will remain unmarried or childless if she is not excised. This ties the customs to finding a husband and thus a social identity and social acceptability. One of the reasons commonly given for the practice is Islamic custom; it is said to be written in the Koran, an obligation of the devout like prayers or spiritual cleansing. However, no clear cut command exists in the scriptures. Another set of reasons centers on the issue of female pollution. The clitoris is believed to be dirty or dangerous. Some folktales tell of a clitoris that had teeth and devoured men's penises, or of a clitoris that grew and grew. It is possible to interpret these stories as fear of women, women's sexuality, women's bodies, a fear that leads to forms of control.

Blood on the Sheets

Another important ideology about gender takes roughly the same shape in many parts of the world. Anthropologists call it "the **virginity complex**." The glossary provides a dictionary definition of **virgin** for purposes of background.

> *In an extraordinarily wide range of societies in the world one finds a peculiar "complex": ideologically it is held that the purity of the women reflects on the honor and status of their families; and the ideology is enforced by systematic and often quite severe control of women's social especially sexual behavior. One sees this pattern manifested among peasant societies in Latin America and around the entire Mediterranean area, among pastoral nomadic tribes of the Middle East and southwest Asia, among the castes of India, and among the elites of China. (Ortner 1993:257)*

The virginity complex more or less translates to the idea that the start of sexual life equals the start of married life. Young girls must be mystically pure and sexually inexperienced.

In some cultures, girls are killed, maimed, sold into slavery, or otherwise severely punished if, somehow, they are not found to be virgins. It is widely reported from circum-Mediterranean cultures that knowledgeable older women provided a bride with a vial of chicken blood to stain the bridal sheets, which her family members displayed from the honeymoon balcony on the next morning. There are many stories or beliefs in human society about virgins used as sacrifices, virgins as possessing curative powers, virgins as commodities, or virgins as saints.

In cultures with a virginity hang-up, the chief ideas are: Men are directly responsible for women's behavior. A woman's kinsmen are only defending her from the known habits of other men, and at the same time defending family (read male) honor. The ideal woman is both mother and virgin. Typically, we find a separation of sex from reproduction and a lot of symbolic idealization. Mothers enforce the codes of dress, modesty, chaperonage, language, eye contact, and social situations. They say something like, "It's for your own good," or "You'll thank me later for making you do this." Given the situation, these mothers are probably right. They are doing what they know, what they themselves survived, and the best job under the circumstances. Please note, the virginity complex coupled with the ideologies of romantic love have been the ideals of marriage enforced by religions and national governments in the West for many hundreds of years. This coupling has a powerful resonance for many of us raised in this system.

Anthropologists have many explanations for this odd complex and its persistence or distribution. The question of controlling female sexual purity is ripe for symbolic interpretations—of which there are many. There are also economic arguments: In some kinds of property-holding groups, women are valuable resources like cattle, land, pastures, or water, and have to be similarly managed. In fact, the virginity obsession often looks like women as personal property and marriage as the legal contract or bill of sale. Many of the explanations frame the problem in terms of males interacting with other males or the feelings of shame and dishonor when daughters, sisters, and wives are not "pure." People in some cultures insist that without rigid controls over young girls, men would fight or compete with each other too much or take their sisters or daughters as wives. In fact, most of these theories assume that female sexuality has to be controlled. The issue is simply the best way to do it. When all is said and done, however, these extensive rules and ideologies simply do not apply to men anywhere in the world.

In chapter 10 we will return to these sets of customs and the questions they raise about "who owns her body." Meanwhile, the emotionally laden questions about women's bodies and their ownership will echo in each chapter.

The Great "What's for Dinner" Debate

Imagine this scene: In a suburban backyard in the United States, some husbands are preparing meat over a fire; they are said to be cooking or barbecuing. Women and children are in and out. They are carrying things, fixing salads and desserts, setting the table, or getting drinks. They are said to be helping out. This picture mirrors contemporary domestic disputes over who does household work and who gets the credit, as well as one of the all-time great debates in anthropology. The debate centers on who fixed dinner during millions of years of human evolution: men or women. At stake in this debate is understanding human origins as well as how human beings live together in contemporary societies.

During the last 5 million years or so, our ancestors turned from apes into human beings. As scientists and popular culture portrayed this transition, women's place was clearly marginal. Researchers in the past projected Western belief systems about "the little woman" and "staying at home" onto the past. They used evolutionary slogans like "the naked ape," "the killer ape," "men in groups," "man the hunter," "man the toolmaker" or the ever-popular "caveman." In their sexual division of labor, men brought home the bacon and women cooked it. In some accounts, women apparently hung around the campfire cooking meat, grateful for every morsel, available for sex and bearing little hunters of the future. In the 1970's, anthropologists like Adrienne Zihlman and Nancy Tanner began to challenge this viewpoint.

> The presently popular "hunting hypothesis" of human evolution
> argues that hunting as a technique for getting large amounts of meat
> was the critical, defining innovation separating early humans from
> their ape ancestors. This view of "man the hunter" has been used to
> explain many features of modern Western civilization, from the
> nuclear family and sexual division of labor to power and politics.
> But as more and more data have accumulated in recent years, and as
> approaches to them have changed, the notion that early "man" was
> primarily a hunter, and meat the main dietary item, has become
> more and more dubious. Consequently, interpretations of early
> human social life and the role of each sex in it must be reevaluated.
> (Zihlman 1978:5)

The great debate began when a generation of (mostly) female anthropologists noted that our ancestors probably survived because of the unsung collecting and gathering activities of women. These professionals claimed that females shared food with their own offspring before sharing with males. In fact, anthropologists claimed that early hominids had no idea of being husbands and wives at all. Moreover, some of the first major advances in technology came from females, and sex was not the primary organizing principle of these groups. The idea of pegging our evolution as a species to "woman the gatherer" was a revolutionary theory about evolution.

A Set of Recipes

Rather than rearguing the case, I have reconstructed sample meal plans or menus from two periods of human evolution: Early and Transitional Hominids and *Homo erectus*. The menus in the box "Evolutionary Cuisine" reflect the best

Evolutionary Cuisine

Early Human's Salad Bar

This menu comes from Early Hominids who lived in the savannahs of eastern and southern Africa from roughly 5 million to 1.5 million years ago. Everything was served raw. Cooking with fire had not been invented.

Main Course: Nuts, birds' eggs, roots, tubers, beans, leaves, gum, sap, berries and fruits in season, greens, insects, worms, grubs, termites. 90 percent of the meal.

Raw Meat Appetizer Tray: Opportunist and gathered goodies, delicacies include small mammals, birds, reptiles, fish, shellfish, slow game, dead or dying animals, and infants of species such like antelope, pig, giraffe, or baboons when available. Bone marrow or the contents of animal heads and stomachs are delicious additions to this menu. 10 percent of the meal.

Season with honey, rock salt, or puree of worms and insects.

Ancestral Pot Luck Dinner

The first members of our own genus, *Homo erectus*, used these recipes from 1.5 million years ago to about 100,000 years ago in the tropical and temperate zones of Africa and Eurasia. New technologies in fire making, advanced scavenging, and simple hunting as well as social advances in cooperation, sharing and the sexual division of labor provided some very tasty and nourishing meals for our ancestors.

Main Course: Stew or soup made with vegetables, bird bones, roots, nuts and foods from the Salad Bar and Raw Meat Appetizer Tray plus other gathered foods as available. Add leftovers and herbal seasonings. 80 percent of the meal.

Outdoor Barbecue: Sizzling deer haunch, roasted rabbit, shellfish, wild boar, ox or cattle ribs. 20 percent of the meal.

scholarship and research available. As the meal plans make clear, food-getting is work. The menus are powerful arguments for many tools, sharing and other social skills, wide variability in diets, and extensive knowledge of local environments. They make no argument for idleness by either men or women.

Most people are accustomed to reading recipes, gathering food by shopping, thinking about food, or feeding children and other people. We know that food is basic to survival and that food carries as much symbolic and practical significance as any activity humans do. In fact, anthropologists categorize human cultures by the foods people eat and how they get them. That is why we speak regularly in this book about hunting and gathering, horticultural and agricultural societies, or working for wages to purchase food.

A generation of research on nonhuman primates shows that they gather food individually and rarely share it with each other. Each individual must find most of its own food for itself each day. In sharp contrast, all known contemporary foraging groups divide subsistence tasks by gender and age. So at some point, our ancestors invented the idea of sharing the work of food-getting. Think of these transitions in terms of recipes. A salad, for example, contains a number of ingredients put together rather flexibly. Mixing food together like this enhances the nutritional value for everyone. But no one person could gather and prepare his or her own bowl of salad each day. The same is true for soups and stews. Just imagine preparing a rich vegetable soup or stew for one person from scratch each day. Now imagine helping someone make a soup and sharing from a large pot. That's the difference.

Sharing Food

Decades of anthropological research now indicate that females were activists and innovators in the technology of gathering. They shared food first with their offspring, then with biological kin and others, including grown males. During the transition period from being apes to being humans, females were at the social center of group life. Females formed lifelong bonds with their children, who had lifelong bonds with their mother and with each other as siblings. Those who learned to share in this mother-centered setting probably had a better diet and other survival advantages.

> It is women who bear babies and nurse infants. Above and beyond such physical nutritional stress on females, it was also early women who had the most responsibility for the survival of the next generation. Mothers' sharing of food with offspring—well documented for both chimpanzees and humans—meant that the gathering innovation made the utmost sense. (Tanner 1981:268)

Sophisticated new research and analysis of contemporary foraging groups over the last thirty years reveals the complexity and contributions of gathering. Our ancestors ate plant foods. They used plants for making medicines, drinks, clothes, equipment, and tools. At the same time, females carried and nursed an infant almost continually for three to four years, did a lioness' share of food-gathering, and 90 percent of child care. A woman often walked miles carrying an equivalent of 75 percent of her body weight in baby, firewood, gathered foodstuffs, or other raw materials. Women contributed dietary proteins, clubbed turtles, and collected eggs and insects. Women made systematic observations about the availability of game or tracks and reported back to the men. Anthropologists know that women hunted as well and gathered small game and fish. Mothers often, as they still do, left small children in the care of kinfolk, sister-like cooperatives, brothers, or other adult males. Males also gathered, for themselves and in groups. The menu from our ancestral hominids indicates that protein foods were as much gathered foods as hunted foods. Fishing and hunting were always less predictable and varied in importance from group to group.

Anthropologists believe that the first form of food sharing, even before the sexual division of labor, was a mother giving food to her child. Women as mothers gathered and shared food with children who were no longer nursing. This means that the primary bond in early hominid groups, the most omnipresent and stable social unit in early societies, was a woman and her offspring. This unit is usually called the **matrifocal unit** or **matrifocal family.** Matrifocal means "mother-centered." This was the first kind of sharing; the second kind was between siblings, brothers and sisters with a common mother. As we shall see, anthropologists have also studied matrifocal families in monkeys, apes, or other primates, as well as in many human cultures. Mother-centered kinship is an extremely significant pattern on the planet.

The notion that sex was the first or primary bond in primate or hominid life or that husband–wife teams are the building blocks of evolution are only fantasies. Sexual partnerships such as monogamy and marriage are secondary social inventions. There were mothers as we know them, but not fathers, husbands, or wives.

Tools with a Feminine Twist

Our ancestors, judging from all available research, used basic tools such as anthropologists have documented in contemporary hunting and gathering groups: digging sticks and tools or containers for carrying things. Unfortunately, objects made of stone survive better than tools or objects made of wood, skins, bone, fibers, or other perishable organic materials. So scientists emphasize stones. In fact, some scientists in the past seemed only to see tools as weapons and only men as toolmakers or tool users.

More and more anthropologists, however, see women in the role of tool inventors. The best example is the simple act of carrying things. For starters, females carry babies in all nonhuman primate groups and in all human cultures. Slings for carrying infants are found in most human societies, so this is probably one of the earliest and most profound applications of tool use. Contemporary foragers use skin bags, fiber nets, or woven baskets for carrying food, wood, and other objects for long distances. Today humans make thousands of kinds of containers. We buy them, give them as gifts, and rely on them for numerous tasks: purses, pocketbooks, pockets, knapsacks, backpacks, shoulder bags, handbags, tin cans, paper bags, plastic sacks, boxes, baskets, briefcases, cosmetic cases, and brown paper packages wrapped up in string. These are major inventions. Frankly, I think women should just claim credit for inventing the concept of containers for carrying and celebrate the incredible crafts that followed.

Hunting, Gathering, and Being Human

Sharing, gathering, and carrying shaped human life. A woman gathered foods from a source she knew about; then she exchanged some for a foodstuff she had not found. One day she gave foodstuffs to relatives who couldn't go out foraging that day; on another day she prepared a soft, easy-to-chew dish for an old person or an easily digestible dish for a sick person or a child. This lifestyle required an amazing amount of knowledge, of practical intelligence; in fact, anthropologists know that horticulture and agriculture grew out the increasingly skilled gathering or foraging complexes of our early ancestors.

Given the specialized nature of hunting, anthropologists think this complex developed rather late in the evolutionary picture. Hunting, however, as an image of male activity and a contribution to group survival, offers an enormously powerful image. The impact of this model for male lives in our own culture is easily felt. To many, it is more glamorous than a complimentary view of survival and adaptation through cooperation, sharing, and eating vegetables.

The simplistic view of "man the hunter" overlooks the fact that no man, however heroic, can prepare and eat a whole animal. In contemporary hunting societies, hunters owe others and pay them in flesh. A man has responsibilities to groups in his mother's clan, his father's clan, his mother-in-law's clan, and so on. Meantime, someone must prepare other foodstuffs and process the hide into leather.

With the discovery or domestication of the energy of fire, cooking as we know it was invented. In addition to salads, our ancestors could eat soups or stews. The potluck principle has been a key to human survival. People contributed what they had and fed themselves and several others better than they could do it alone. Like us, our ancestors fed sick people, old people, women with newborns, injured men, and little kids.

Overall, gathering–hunting societies show us a portrait of women as active, mobile individuals who carry heavy loads and contribute a major source of food to their families. They organize and share food, make and use tools. At the same time, they carry and bear infants, lactate, and care for children. Increased sociability, sharing of resources, structured giving, and ordered social relationships would have contributed to growth and survival. Shared food is good for everybody. In fact, in some fashion or another, the metaphors of shared food around a fire are at the heart of every human religion.

Years of careful research on the Bushmen of the Kalahari Desert in Africa reveal that women's gathering activities contribute between 60 percent and 80 percent of their total diet. Ironically, this information was first published in a book called *Man the Hunter* (Lee and DeVore 1968). People liked meat and talked about it a great deal, but the majority of their diet as measured, counted, and weighed was plant food and small edible creatures. In other foraging populations anthropologists have studied, gathering may account for up to 90 percent of the diet; usually it produces over 50 percent of what people eat.

As part of a research team, anthropologist Marjorie Shostak did field work in the Kalahari desert of southern Africa (Botswana). There she listened to and recorded the life story of Nisa, a woman who was born into one of the last gathering–hunting cultures, the !Kung Bushmen. Here Nisa discusses food and her memories of childhood. The fathers brought animals home for everyone to eat. She loved meat dripping with fat.

> *We lived, eating the animals and foods of the bush. We collected food, ground it in a mortar, and ate it. We also ate sweet nin berries and tsin beans. When I was growing up, there were no cows or goats. . . . Whenever my father killed an animal and I saw him coming home with meat draped over a stick, balanced on one shoulder— that's what made me happy. I'd cry out, "Mommy! Daddy's coming and he's bringing meat!" My heart would be happy when I greeted him, "Ho, ho, Daddy! We're going to eat meat!" Or honey. Sometimes he'd go out and come home with honey. . . . Sometimes my mother would be the one to see the honey. The two of us would be walking around gathering food and she'd find a beehive deep inside a termite mound or in a tree. (Shostak 1983:87)*

Contemporary foraging or nomadic peoples provide us the only realistic model we are ever going to have for how our ancestors lived. The gathering–hunting way of life persisted 4 million to 5 million years as we evolved. Starting about 50,000 years ago, sophisticated hunting and gathering groups, who were emotionally and anatomically like us, moved confidently into all of the continents and spaces in the world. About 12,000 years ago, some groups learned how to cultivate and harvest plants and care for domestic animals as sources of food. They settled down on farms and in villages; in some parts of the world cities developed. This striking new relationship to the environment is called the **Neolithic Revolution.** This key transition in food-getting had extraordinary implications for women's work and daily lives.

How people in human societies earn their living tells us a great deal about how women and how men live in that society and what kinds of work they do. Anthropologists use a continuum to define how societies earn their living; this is the key piece of knowledge about any group. The continuum of cultural divisions runs from our ancestors, all of whom were gatherers and/or hunters, to those of us who live now in complex, multicultural, postindustrial nation–states.

So what have anthropologists learned? The most equalitarian groups we know about are probably hunting and gathering groups. Do women and men do exactly equal work and get treated the same way? No. They do not have equality, just relatively equalitarian traditions and a sexual division of labor. In actual fact, no known groups allow one gender to be idle or excused from the basic work of survival. Yesterday as today, both females and males share the work of food-getting. The box "What's for Dinner Honey?" is a folktale about the sexual division of labor collected from storytellers in the peasant societies of northern Europe. If you are familiar with this folktale, you will note that I have taken some liberties with it. You too are free to interpret or rewrite it as you like.

A Folktale
What's for Dinner Honey?

Once upon a time, a couple lived on a farm. They quarrelled constantly about the work they had to do on their homestead. Each claimed that her or his labor was the most difficult and that the other one was not properly appreciative. Finally, when there seemed no other way to settle the issue, the husband and wife agreed to trade tasks for an entire day.

Early the following morning, the wife arose and went out to plow the fields and make hay. When she returned that evening, her muscles were sore and her hands had new blisters. But she had enjoyed her quiet, simple day outside in the fields. She was fiercely hungry; the leftovers from breakfast and the small lunch her husband packed for her had not been enough. As she stepped through the carved wooden door of their cottage, she called out, "What's for dinner honey?"

But instead of dinner, she faced a disaster! Feathers coated in honey clung to the rafters. The cat, who should have been in the barn catching rats, crawled from the overturned butter churn, licking her paws with glee. Chickens cackled as they laid eggs on the mantel; they cackled as the eggs rolled off and broke on the floor. Ducks left their droppings and droolings as they marched across her handmade white quilt. From somewhere, the mooing of an unmilked and unhappy cow filled the air. The bread dough had not risen and the beer she was brewing had spilled. Flax fibers, soaking as the first stage in making linen cloth, were strewn damply about the dirty floor. Her garden was not weeded and something had happened to the fruits and vegetables she was preparing for winter. But worse, her husband, tied by his foot, hung upside down in the chimney, his face covered by her best apron and his head only inches away from a pot of uncooked soup teetering above the dead fire in the hearth.

"Don't ask," he moaned. "I've had a very bad day." Before she released him, she satisfied herself that he had a new appreciation for her work and her work skills. Then she began to clean up enough to fix dinner for them. They lived and worked together for a very long time after that.

Interpreting Food, Work, and the Facts of Life

Today, in Grey Rock Harbour, Newfoundland, women no longer worry about their men at work fishing. That way of life ended in the late 1970s when the fishing industry collapsed. Men are now land-bound. A combination of policies from the Canadian government and a changing ecology have resulted in chronic unemployment, the loss of a work ethic, and what the women call "ruined men." There is conflict and hostility between men and women. One man says, "You want to know about women in Grey Rock Harbour? They've changed, let me tell you. Newfoundland women now are possessive, jealous, and everything you do is wrong, wrong, wrong." A woman responds,

> *The young unmarried men you'll find at the club all the time now.*
> *They're of an age for it but I think they will never grow out of it. . . .*
> *Most of these guys will remain single because no woman will marry a*
> *drunk. These days you're better off alone. (Davis 1993:470)*

Men now stay at home; they have invaded the domains of women. They spend dreary daytime hours at local bars and some turn to confrontational bravado. Women don't need the romantic and idealized job of worrying any longer; they don't have to be helpmates to earn a living. They are advantaged competitors for the few jobs available, which they can do as well as the men can. Divorce, extramarital activities, single mothering, and expensive TV dinners, unheard of in traditional times, are now common. Women are now "unhusbanding" their resources because marriage has few survival advantages for them. The sexual division of labor changed as the means of earning a living changed.

I once heard Margaret Mead say that women's work is about giving birth and giving death. In some human societies today, and certainly most of them in the past, women delivered babies for each other and laid out the dead for burial. Women were often the most visible mourners as well as the sources of information and knowledge about these transitions. But when economic circumstances changed, it became possible to charge something for these services. When a person could charge for the services of delivering babies or burying the dead, men got the jobs. The work became visible, valuable, and paid. The services were produced outside rather than inside the domestic networks. Then women "lost" their jobs. Or as two other anthropologists say,

> *One generalization that appears to hold true crossculturally is that*
> *women are responsible for those tasks essential to survival: making*
> *sure the family is fed on a daily basis; protecting it from the elements*
> *through care of the household; and producing and caring for chil-*
> *dren. Men, on the other hand, are allocated the "glamorous" tasks*
> *that enrich the cultural life of the group: hunting, making war, main-*
> *taining ritual relation with supernatural entities, storytelling, and*
> *conducting the affairs of government. Yet, the duties of men are*
> *defined as "important" and the affairs of women are defined as*
> *"trivial," beneath the notice of men. (Womack and Marti 1993:10)*

Women, living in two or more cultural worlds, seem to have an extraordinary variability and variety. Few generalizations apply for everyone. Motherhood, for example, is a biological possibility for females across human cultures. But being "maternal" or mothering as work has wide interpretations. In some cultures, motherhood is said to be the central fact of a woman's life; a woman offers self-less devotion and complete identification with her children. In other cultures, women who get pregnant and have babies exhibit a practical, get-serious attitude and emphasize their economic roles over their nurturant ones. In order to see how individuals and personalities can exist within their various cultural settings, we now turn to chapter 2 and two of our "foremothers," Ruth Benedict and Margaret Mead. They helped invent the concepts of culture and cultural relativism, and challenged forever any fixed notions of "feminine" or "masculine."

A Few of the Many Books You May Want to Read

At the end of each chapter are some suggestions for additional readings. In 1991 Micaela di Leonardo edited a theoretically sophisticated collection of essays that brings feminist anthropology and analysis up to date: *Gender at the Crossroads of Knowledge: Feminist Anthropology in the Postmodern Era.* Another excellent collection of papers edited by Faye Ginsberg and Anna Lowenhaupt Tsing (1990) applies anthropological insights and methods to issues in contemporary American culture. In this book, *Uncertain Terms: Negotiating Gender in American Culture,* the authors use gender, class, and race in families, workplaces, and public institutions to make their radical, caring, and vivid points. An edited volume by Sherry Ortner and Harriet Whitehead (1981), *Sexual Meanings: The Cultural Construction of Gender and Sexuality,* helped anthropologists and feminists articulate how gender is constructed. Most anthropologists I know have a favorite article from this book.

Seeing women's work in prehistory and women studying prehistory are both fairly recent happenings. Archaeologists are beginning to provide innovative and much-needed work. The following volumes are particularly helpful. Joan Gero and Margaret Conkey (1991) edited a volume called *Engendering Archaeology: Women and Prehistory.* Or look at Cheryl Claassen's *Women in Archaeology* (1994), which examines the profession of archaeology and the specific contributions of women as scholars. Francis Dahlberg's *Woman the Gatherer* (1981) and Nancy Tanner's *On Becoming Human* (1981) were two of the books that caused some of the trouble and offered some answers about women, work, and prehistory.

There are many books about work, food, or women in contemporary American society. I would start with Arlie Hochschild's *The Second Shift: Working Parents and the Revolution at Home* (1990). This is the single best book

I know on the sexual division of labor in the United States married middle and working classes. The basic point is that a rather harsh reality for women does not match the rosier gender ideologies reported by both wives and husbands. On a different note, Joan Jacob Brumberg's *Fasting Girls: The Surprising History of Anorexia Nervosa,* explores the cultural meanings of appetite in women's lives from medieval ascetics to twentieth-century adolescents. Or you might contrast food with clothes in Ruth Barnes and Joanne Eicher's collection of articles on clothes, *Dress and Gender: Making and Meaning* (1993). The concept of "housewives" haunts women's studies. Start with Glenna Matthews' *"Just a Housewife": The Rise and Fall of Domesticity in America* (1987).

Margery Wolf wrote *A Thrice-told Tale: Feminism, Postmodernism, and Ethnographic Responsibility* (1992). This is a personal exploration by an ethnographer of the puzzles posed by postmodernism and feminist critiques of doing ethnography. The author takes one event from her fieldwork in Taiwan and tells and retells the story from three points of view. This reflexive book helps us understand the difference between fiction and ethnography.

The very special collection edited by Annette Weiner and Jane Schneider, *Cloth and Human Experience* (1989), honors women's work around cloth, clothing, the production of fabrics, and the reproduction of people, society, and ideologies in material goods. The emotional, spiritual, anthropological, and historic associations of fabrics, women, and weaving are one of the golden threads you will be able to pick up throughout this book.

Chapter Two

Love and the Work of Culture

In the autumn of 1922, two women met in a classroom at Columbia University in New York. The instructor, Ruth Fulton Benedict, was a shy, awkward person with a tendency to stutter, a tentative speaker whose hearing problems were not apparent. Ruth was registered as an older, or what we now call nontraditional or reentry student, and she was working as a teaching assistant for Dr. Franz Boas, who had founded the first department of anthropology in the United States. She often wore the same dress to work on successive days because men were allowed to wear the same suit without comment.

In her class was a self-confident and energetic undergraduate named Margaret Mead, a psychology major trying out her first anthropology class. Gradually, Ruth opened up the ideas of anthropology to Margaret; she said, we have nothing to offer but an opportunity to do work that really matters.

> *Ruth, on her side, was warmed by Margaret's admiration and saw her, fifteen years younger, at least at first, as somewhat of a daughter to be helped with problems and career choices. Often deeply depressed, she appreciated Margaret's outgoingness, her sunny personality, her energy, her intensity toward living. Though they were attracted to each other by differences, both were fanatically tolerant freethinkers with a radical bent of thought and both were of superior intelligence and attracted to intelligence in others. Both thought ideas important and valued creative, original thinking. Both felt a need to be useful, to make a difference in the world. (Caffrey 1989:187)*

More Than Personal Lives

This chapter centers on some core concepts in anthropology and the methods of fieldwork and ethnography. Here we will talk about culture, culture relativism, male and female, feminine and masculine, and normal and deviant, as cultural categories. The personal lives and professional careers of Margaret Mead and Ruth Benedict form the scaffolding that supports these topics.

At the heart of this chapter are stories about women and men who live in dramatic cultures on the Sepik River in New Guinea. They are the players in Margaret Mead's most debated and yet most enduring contribution to studying women, a book called *Sex and Temperament in Three Primitive Societies*. Many of us who teach about gender turn to this book. It informs, provokes, and illuminates. Mead went into the field to study what she called the social personalities of the two sexes. Today scholars tend to use the term gender. But she found that her fieldwork and data shed even more light on differences in the temperaments or personalities of individuals.

Margaret Mead's and Ruth Benedict's basic questions live on. How can we reconcile the obvious biological differences between the sexes on the one hand and ourselves as individuals with temperaments or personalities on the other hand? Everyone has a sex, or what we now call gender, which we share with others in the same category. But each one of us also has a temperament—what we

Ruth Benedict during her field study on Native American cultures. Summer of 1927.

now call personality—in which we may look like, feel like, or act like people in another gender are said to be. Mead felt that "temperament" or personality ranks higher than biological sex in influencing or affecting who and what we are as adults. People can be typically gentle, assertive, aggressive, or nurturing. The culture and subculture we are born into will, however, reward or discount these traits unevenly.

One of the primary organizing principles in human societies is gender. So people within one group say, "This is just the way women are." Yet people in another area will say exactly the opposite, "That is just how women are." Sex roles or gender codes can differ in amazing ways. Yet we know that biology is everywhere the same.

Does this mean there is some absolute bottom line or a universal set of rules about gender? How "should" males act? How "should" females act? How do girls grow up to be what we define as women, as "feminine"? How do boys grow up to be what we call men, to act "masculine"? What if people in our own culture don't act the way our cultural definitions say they should? What if people in other cultures don't behave the way we in this culture think women and men should "naturally" act? Where do the misfits, the abnormal, and the deviates fit in? Who makes up these categories?

Both Mead and Benedict wrote for ordinary people, in a readable and popular style. Some anthropologists have criticized them heavily for this defection. But the

Margaret Mead in the
Admiralty Islands in 1954

major themes of their work remain, particularly when we study women. Human beings are more than just a collection of our ideas or thoughts. We are also our autobiographies or our biographies. It may be particularly important for women to study how other women live, whether we are lovers, professionals, wives, mothers, or making sago flour on the Sepik River.

The Personal Is Professional

Ruth Fulton had attended Vassar College and thrived in its all-female atmosphere. After several years of teaching and social work, she married an engineer named Stanley Benedict. As one of her biographers notes:

> *After three years of emotional turmoil, of internal struggles over conforming or not conforming to society's expectations of her as a woman, of hesitancy over what to do in the world, and the frustrations of what she was allowed to do, she surrendered. She fell head-over-heels in love and the whole world changed. (Caffrey 1989:74)*

Ruth hoped, as have many women, that love, a husband, and a baby or two would grant a measure of calm and the answers to her tormenting questions. But no babies came, and her suburban marriage soon proved to be a suffocating trap. Her idea of wedlock was a meeting of two equals, sharing thoughts and feelings. But Stanley Benedict wanted a wife to play homemaker, to take care of his house, and to put him first in her thoughts and actions. Ruth felt betrayed, and observed privately that she had to work hard to avoid the unconscious moments where she might carelessly end her life. She was often depressed; she called her mood swings the "blue devils."

In anthropology, however, Ruth Benedict found an intellectual community who tolerated differences and offered alternatives to the restrictions of American culture. More to the point, Ruth Benedict found women who had created a place for themselves in this new discipline. She was ready in her own gentle way to throw off her religious background, Victorian morality, husband, and other social conventions, in order to embrace this source of understanding and meaning.

As an undergraduate, Margaret Mead was in a group of lively students called the Ash Can Cats; they planned activities that felt sophisticated, daring, even radical or liberated. At the same time, she had been engaged for years to a man studying for the Episcopalian ministry. Margaret Mead had grown up in a liberal, academic family in which her paternal grandmother, Martha Mead, was her granddaughter's conscience and the only person whose opinion about Margaret's proposed career in anthropology mattered.

At some point, Ruth Benedict and Margaret Mead moved from being mentor and student to colleagues and friends, and then to lovers. Remember that both of these women grew up with traditions of passionate and romantic love between women. Women in those days wrote each other letters full of love poetry, hugs, kisses, embraces, and news of the latest baby, husband's health, or church socials. Deep emotional involvements and erotic attachments between women seemed innocent and nonthreatening. But in the years after World War I, the idea of same-sex romances changed. Deep love required making love or having sex. Romantic friendships between women sounded like lesbianism, and this frightened the establishment.

In the poetry Benedict and Mead wrote, and in their personal and professional lives, separately and together, they explored the meanings of alternative standards. Both worked with and respected men who voiced strong judgments about "unnatural acts" and "personal sex problems." So they talked about being deviate or being a misfit within one's own culture. For example, they decided that

> *women who loved women, dubbed Lesbians by society, were healthy when they accepted their love as an alternative standard to that of the mainstream. Women-loving women became unhealthy when they internalized society's condemnation of them and the sinfulness of their love. (Caffrey 1989:198)*

Benedict wrote that there were no universally valid definitions about what was abnormal; so-called deviates were only people for whom their culture had no appropriate categories, rewards, or names. Today what they said seems obvious to contemporary women working out the questions of "our sexual identities." It was not so obvious at that time. These themes remain one of their enduring legacies to anthropology and to an understanding of how individuals live within the culture assigned at birth.

Husbands, Lovers, and Fieldwork

In 1923 Margaret married her fiance, Luther Cressman, in the Episcopal chapel where at the age of eleven she had defied her agnostic parents to be baptized. Mead kept her own name and her lifelong affiliation with the church. The couple settled into a student marriage. They had a plan: no children until they both finished school, then a large parsonage, a frugal lifestyle, and six children. Luther and Margaret would serve a parish, a country rectory—he as minister, she as minister's wife. He liked her friends and the new discipline of anthropology she was learning.

But, in fact, Luther was drifting out of church work and Margaret was writing poems with suggestive imagery: "denied the power to bloom," and "throttled by sullen weeds I die." So in 1925 they agreed to do separate things with their marriage and their respective careers. She wanted passionately to do fieldwork, to test herself in the rigors and dramas of exotic places amidst people unlike herself. She also needed to finish and publish her dissertation.

In order to do fieldwork, Mead had to negotiate with her husband, her father, and her advisor, Franz Boas. She also had to teach herself many practical skills and raise money to finance her trip. As usual, Ruth assisted her. Boas thought Mead was too high-strung and emotional; no women had traveled so far away alone. But he also knew she was absolutely determined to go, and so he urged her to study how teenage girls grow up and pass through adolescence in another culture. He wondered if there were predictable stages when teenage girls were passive, submissive, bashful, strongly rebellious, sullen, or capricious. He enjoined her to look at the crushes and extremes of romantic love among adolescent girls. He set up the primary research questions and told her to stick to observing individuals and patterns.

Boas and Mead agreed that she could go to Samoa, a legendary and beautiful island chain in the South Pacific. So she made preparations, packed clothes, cameras, notebooks, and lamps, endured inoculations, and developed the psychological tests she wanted to administer. In her grant application, she noted a need for anthropological investigation in a virgin field, as it were. No one had ever studied "feminine reactions and participation in the culture of the group." She craved to see how individuals and individual psychology responded to the general patterns within a culture.

On the long journey to Samoa, Margaret Mead stopped off in the Southwest to visit Ruth Benedict, who was doing her own groundbreaking field research there. They visited the Grand Canyon together and there apparently began an affair, or continued one already begun.

Mead's Samoan fieldwork was a success. She established a rapport with the girls and a degree of empathy that male fieldworkers could not hope for and which even today tells a kind of truth about their lives. She was, however, very lonely. A fellow passenger on the long return boat trip was a fascinating psychologist from

New Zealand. Reo Fortune was going to England after having completed fieldwork among a group of dour sorcerers called the Dobu on islands off the coast of New Guinea. Hungry for intellectual challenges and the English language, Margaret Mead and Reo Fortune talked nonstop through the many weeks of slow boat travel. With anguish, Margaret realized that she was falling in love with a genuinely unsuitable person, "unlike anyone I had ever known." He was younger than she, fiercely ambitious, possessively jealous, and quite inexperienced with women or the wider world.

Margaret's life at this point reads like a novel or a soap opera. This was her first trip to Europe and, as she records in her autobiography, she was pulled between two men, the intensity of fieldwork, the shipboard conversations, and her own feelings. Her husband, Luther, met her as the boat docked. At the same moment, she parted from Reo in confusion. Then she and Ruth met for another glorious holiday week—this time in Rome. Margaret commented on how beautiful Ruth looked to her; Ruth, shy and modest, was always embarrassed when Mead or others remarked on her beauty. Meanwhile, both women were married, and Margaret was trying to decide whether to continue with Luther, her husband, or Reo, a fascinating lover in her mind.

Once back in the United States, Ruth and Margaret wrote poetry to each other. Margaret was Ruth's teaching assistant. They were also lovers, collaborating on projects, and supporting each other through books, career development, and marital maneuverings. Mead took a job as assistant curator at the American Museum of Natural History in New York. She wrote a technical monograph on Samoan kinship, a few papers, and a little book she entitled *Coming of Age in Samoa.* Mead reported in her autobiography (which is often unrevealing, even misleading, but always riveting), that a doctor told her that she could never have children. So she reassessed her life plans and decided to marry Reo, a man whom she believed would be radically unsuited for fatherhood but an exciting partner for field research. She and Luther parted amicably and with respect.

More Love, Husbands, and Fieldwork

So in 1928, at the age of twenty-seven, Margaret Mead departed with her second husband for her second field trip, this time to the island of Manus off the coast of New Guinea. She had wanted a man with whom to do joint research. Throughout most of New Guinea, culturally based antagonisms between males and females were so strong that no single field worker could possibly hope to understand the other gender and as a result would miss half of the culture. In Manus Mead studied childhood; she created new techniques for studying children, invented new fieldwork methods, and laid the groundwork for a lifetime of commitment to telling the story of how this particular group changes before our very eyes.

When Mead returned to her museum job, she discovered that the little book on Samoa had become a best-seller and she a famous author! She had answered Boas's questions: The teenage girls of Samoa did not experience the same pressures and struggles Americans take for granted. She wrote that the transition through adolescence for Samoan girls *represented no period of crisis or stress, but was instead an orderly development of a set of slowly maturing interests and activities. The girls' minds were perplexed by no conflicts, troubled by no philosophical queries, beset by no remote ambitions. To live as a girl with many lovers as long as possible and then to marry in one's own village, near one's own relatives and to have many children, these were uniform and satisfying ambitions. (Mead 1973:87)*

She was particularly impressed that Samoan teenagers lacked the craziness of romantic or obsessive love, or the notion that one boyfriend or one husband will fulfill a woman and make her whole. Margaret was pleased to find an alternative approach to the problems bound up with ideas of monogamy, exclusiveness, jealousy, and undeviating fidelity.

Her field trip and research in Samoa have been dissected by many scholars; they remain a major legend in anthropology. But the book was not just about teenage girls on a tropical island. In a simple and profound way, this book offered an antidote to notions of racism and fascism growing in Europe, forces of hatred that would culminate in World War II. Mead said that culture shapes our lives more than biology does. Human cultures have the capacity to change and to allow for many different expressions of personalities. The book said that human beings are not assigned to a place or a position by biology, which can never be changed and for which we may be judged or killed (as in the Holocaust that followed). We are not just the sum of our genes, but the products of belief systems, collective experiences interpreted over time and filtered through value systems that she and her colleagues later called **ethos.**

Margaret and Reo rented a small apartment and spent the next two years working, writing up their respective fieldwork into new books, finishing a field stint among the Omaha Indians and making preparations for both of them to return to New Guinea. In her autobiography, she talks about the nature of their domestic life living in New York just as the stock market crashed and the great depression hit. Reo was British, and she attributed disagreements in their marriage largely to their differences in nationality or cultural background.

Reo did not like to see me doing the housework, which he did not intend to help me with; yet he felt it was a reproach to him that I had to do it at all. As a result, I became expert at tidying up on Sunday morning while appearing to give complete attention to what he was saying. I would wait for a pause in the conversation to slip out and spread one sheet or wash one cup and then appear again. In this way I managed to get the necessary things done so unobtrusively that later, when Gregory Bateson visited our camp on the Sepik, he remarked that he had never seen me perform a domestic task. (Mead 1972:207)

Today Reo's attitude might be attributed to his being a man trained and socialized in male attitudes and privileges. Contemporary women might give Margaret advice on getting him to help in the house or taking equal responsibility. At any rate, the Mead–Fortune household had its own sexual division of labor and gender roles of the kind Mead was so eager to study in others.

Sex and Temperament

From 1931 to 1933, Margaret Mead and Reo Fortune mounted an anthropological expedition to the Sepik River region of New Guinea. The map shows Mead's fieldwork sites in the southwest Pacific and a closeup of the Sepik River cultures. What happened during this trip is an incredible story about four cultures, three anthropologists, two genders, and one river. This story is enormously significant to what anthropologists know about women, men, and culture. In fact, the story has achieved its own mythic status in the history of science.

The Sepik River is a land of mosquitos, crocodiles, cannibals, and floating corpses, Mead would write. People ate tasteless flour laboriously processed from sago palms, yams, bananas, and other produce from their garden plots and fish from the Sepik and its tributaries. Until the Australian government imposed a colonial peace a few years earlier, the peoples of the river region had been cannibals and headhunters. But memories and the social organizations that supported these activities remained potent. People constructed narrow dugout canoes with carved prows, villages raised on stilts over flooded river plains, and men's houses with painted gables filled with exquisite art. Sepik peoples' striking and dramatic "prim-

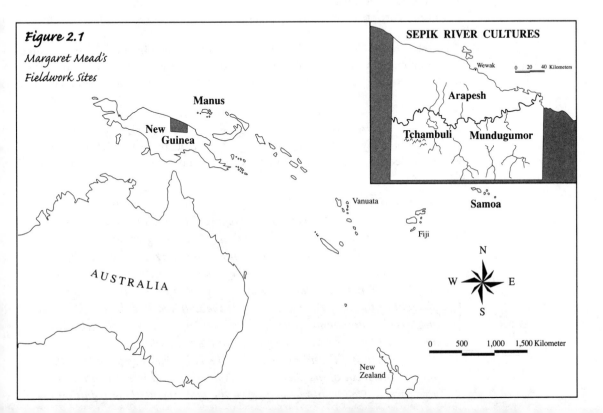

Figure 2.1
Margaret Mead's Fieldwork Sites

itive art" complements their ceremonies and rituals, which appeared to worship, subvert, or invert the differences between females and males. In common with much of New Guinea, these small, intact cultures seemed to play with elaborate permutations of being male or female.

In the first group Mead studied, the Arapesh, both men and women acted in a mild, parental, and responsible manner—like the stereotypes about females at various times in human history. In the second group, the Mundugumor, both men and women were fierce, sexually charged, assertive, and loud—a view some people hold about males from time to time. And in the third, the Tchambuli, men gossiped about each other and worried about their hairstyles, pretty costumes, or whether any women would marry them. The women in this region of beautiful dark lakes were competent and no-nonsense business managers. These three groups showed Mead that a culture may impose personalities and patterns on one gender or both genders that are only a subset of the whole spectrum of possibilities available to human beings.

The Arapesh

When they first arrived in New Guinea, Margaret and Reo were not certain where to go or which group to study. They hired carriers from the interior to help them up the slippery trails and across the rivers; these workers even had to carry Margaret because her ankle was broken. The decision was made for them when their carriers simply stranded them, with six-months' supplies, in a mountain village.

In the steep hills above the flood plain of the Sepik, level land is scarce. Collecting enough firewood and food is difficult. The women carry loads of sixty to seventy pounds suspended from their foreheads, often with a nursing baby in a bark sling or bag. Precious pigs die easily and yams grow poorly in shallow tropical soils. Mead described the sexual division of labor as a necessity for survival. Men were freer to assume authority, a necessary but evil responsibility. Men worked desperately hard to keep the dangerous secrets of the men's houses; women were excluded from ceremonies to protect them and unborn children from malignant spirits.

> When the Arapesh are questioned as to the division of labour, they answer: Cooking everyday food, bringing firewood and water, weeding and carrying—these are women's work; cooking ceremonial food, carrying pigs and heavy logs, house-building, sewing thatch, clearing and fencing, carving, hunting, and growing yams—these are men's work; making ornaments and the care of children—these are the work of both men and women. If the wife's task is the more urgent—if there are no greens for the evening meal, or a haunch of meat must be carried to a neighbour in the next village—the husband stays at home and takes care of the baby. He is as pleased with and as uncritical of his child as is his wife. . . . And in recognition of this care, as well as in recognition of the father's initial contribution,

if one comments upon a middle-aged man as good-looking, the peo-
ple answer: "Good looking? Ye-e-s? But you should have seen him
before he bore all those children." (Mead 1963:39)

Mead called the Arapesh cooperative, oriented to the needs of the next generation, gentle, responsive, carefully parental, and willing to subordinate themselves
in caring for those who were younger and weaker. She noted that the Arapesh
would probably find the Western notion of parenting and paternity repulsive.
They said that a man and a woman cannot make a baby from a moment of passion or a simple act of intercourse. Rather, sex is the strong purposeful work of
feeding and shaping a baby during the early weeks in its mother's womb. Since
the child is the product of both father's semen and mother's blood, combined in
equal parts in the beginning weeks, both parents must work diligently to make the
child both desire. This arduous labor begins when menstruation ceases. When this
hard work is done, intercourse is strictly forbidden and a wide array of taboos are
placed on the mother to protect the unborn child and insure a safe delivery.

An Arapesh man is strategically involved with various phases of his wife's
labor. Immediately after birth and the careful disposal of the afterbirth, he brings
her a bundle of soft absorbent leaves to line the little net bag in which the baby is
suspended through its waking time, curled up as though still in its mother's
tummy. He brings water to wash the baby and sweet smelling leaves to keep evil
influences from the hut. Putting his wooden pillow (which men use to protect
their hair styles) beside his resting wife, he is "in bed having a baby." Together
they fast and perform small rituals to help their baby grow safely. His maternal
and nurturant tasks continue in diminishing degrees through the baby's first year
of life. Arapesh parents observe what we call a **postpartum sex taboo:** They don't
have intercourse with each other or with others until their baby is walking
around; then it is strong enough to withstand its parents' renewed sexuality.

Mead's descriptions of mothers nursing their babies are one of the most
authentic and enduring images from *Sex and Temperament*. The emotional con-
tent of the culture for her came through in these ordinary moments. Always a
skillful observer, she related how mother and infant nursed together to how men
and women have sex later in life. She tells how Arapesh mothers, like mothers
everywhere, have to go back to work at some point. By the time her child is walking, it may be too heavy for a mother to carry on long trips to her garden. So she
may leave it with its father or her sister or mother. When she first leaves the baby,
it cries. When she returns, however, she spends an equal time in playing with and
nursing the child.

This is an experience that the mother enjoys as much as the child.
From the time the little child is old enough to play with her breasts,
the mother takes an active part in the suckling process. She holds her
breast in her hand and gently vibrates the nipple inside the child's
lips. She blows in the child's ear, or tickles its ears, or playfully slaps
its genitals, or tickles its toes. The child in turn plays little tattoos on
its mother's body and its own, plays with one breast with its hands,
plays with its own genitals, laughs and coos and makes a long, easy

*game of the suckling. Thus the whole matter of nourishment is made
into an occasion of high affectivity and becomes a means by which
the child develops and maintains a sensitivity to caresses in every
part of its body. It is no question of a completely clothed infant
being given a cool hard bottle and firmly persuaded to drink its milk
and get to sleep at once so that the mother's aching arms can stop
holding the bottle. Instead, nursing is, for mother and child, one
long delightful and highly charged game, in which the easy warm
affectivity of a lifetime is set up. (Mead 1963:42)*

But what about Arapesh individuals who do not conform to these cultural patterns she described? Mead was deeply concerned about people who did not "fit in" their culture; the term she used was "deviant." If the Arapesh insisted that everyone was gentle, maternal, and not sexually aggressive, then they would have trouble with others who did not fit these patterns. In fact, Mead said that ego-centric, possessive, or jealous women suffered most from their deviation from the norms of Arapesh society. They were likely to act out violently because there were no boundaries or acceptance for them as part of the continuum of human culture.

But Margaret Mead left the Arapesh disappointed. She had not found temperamental differences between women and men. So how could she examine the differences between the sexes if both had roughly the same temperament or social personality?

Moreover, Margaret and Reo had other frustrations. Her bad ankle kept her confined to the unstimulating Arapesh while her restless and volatile husband went off on trips. It is clear from her autobiography that she found Arapesh values of nurturing over aggression compatible with her own personality, while her husband found them particularly shapeless and offensive. She attributed their marital troubles to differences in their respective temperaments. Reo, it seems, was equally disgruntled with both the Arapesh and his wife.

The Mundugumor

Their second field site was equally arbitrary. Margaret and Reo looked on a map and selected the nearest group accessible by water, patrolled by the government but not visited by missionaries. The river-dwelling Mundugumor were in sharp contrast to the Arapesh. Both males and females acted like stereotypes of men we would probably like to avoid. In fact, until the early 1930s, the Mundugumor had been cannibals and headhunters.

Mead called both men and women of the Mundugumor virile, actively masculine, positively sexed, jealous, violent, hard, and arrogant. She witnessed many episodes of angry defiance, mutual hostility, and ruthless individualism. She said they could be charming but hypocritical.

The Mundugumor lived on high, fertile land between swift and treacherous tributaries of the Sepik River. Their neighbors and trading partners spoke of them as ferocious and reckless, and avoided crossing their lands. Rich by Sepik standards, the Mundugumor waterways were filled with fish, and with little effort, their gardens produced plenty of sago palms, coconut trees, and yams. The Mundugumor did not have to cooperate with each other to live well.

> *Upon the basis of women's work, the men can be as active or as lazy, as quarrelsome or as peaceful, as they like. And the rhythm of the men's life is in fact an alternation between periods of supreme individualism, in which each man stays at home with his wives and engages in a little desultory labour, even an occasional hunting-excursion with his bow and arrows, and the periods when there is some big enterprise on foot. The competitiveness and hostility of one Mundugumor for another are very slightly expressed in economic terms. They quarrel principally over women. (Mead 1963:186)*

The rules of Mundugumor kinship and marriage were elaborate and harsh. In fact, they appeared made to be broken at the earliest opportunity. In their best-possible kinship system, every man was supposed to acquire a wife by giving his sister in return for some other man's sister. But this principle never worked well. First of all, men wanted more than one wife; they also wanted to marry younger women who should have been properly married to a man in their sons' generation. So men competed with their sons for women because these young men wanted to use their sisters to make their own marriage alliances. Fathers used their daughters to make matches for themselves.

But Mundugumor women as sisters or daughters were never docile or cooperative in the marital schemes of their fathers or brothers. Furthermore, mothers plotted for themselves and against their daughters! A good Mundugumor mother wanted to see her daughter out of the way, replaced by a daughter-in-law living under her control. The best strategy of these two women was to become allies against their respective husbands. For obvious reasons, a Mundugumor woman preferred to have sons; a man preferred to have daughters.

The same atmosphere of jealousy and hostility prevailed after marriage. A man whose wife announced her pregnancy was a marked and unhappy man. He had to observe many public taboos while his peers taunted and teased him. He resented his wife and cursed the contraceptive magic which had so clearly failed him. A pregnant woman was deprived of sex and worried that her husband would desert her or take another wife altogether.

Mead wondered how any infant survived Mundugumor babyhood. Her discussion of nursing as the crucible for adult personality makes her points very forcefully.

> *Mundugumor women suckle their children standing up, supporting the child with one hand in a position that strains the mother's arm and pinions the arms of the child. There is none of the mother's dallying, sensuous pleasure in feeding her child that occurs among the Arapesh. Nor is the child permitted to prolong his meal by any playful fondling of his own or his mother's body. He is kept firmly to his major task of absorbing enough good so that he will stop crying and consent to be put back in his basket. The minute he stops suckling*

> *for a moment he is returned to his prison. Children therefore develop
> a very definite purposive fighting attitude, holding on firmly to the
> nipple and sucking milk as rapidly and vigorously as possible. They
> frequently choke from swallowing too fast; the choking angers the
> mother and infuriates the child, thus further turning the sucking situ-
> ation into one characterized by anger and struggle rather than by
> affection and reassurance. (Mead 1963:196)*

Poor Mundugumor babies. They were not comforted with their mother's
breasts; they were put in scratchy, harsh baskets until they learned to kick their
way out of them. Once out of their baskets, they had to cling strongly to their
mother's hair and make lots of noise to gain even the minimal attention necessary
for survival. Mothers resented their smallest illness, accident, or weakness. Blows
and cross words marked their weaning. They were surrounded by rules, a series
of prohibitions: Don't go in the houses of your father's other wives and ask for
food; don't cry or demand attention; don't wander out of sight, and so on.

It is not surprising that sex for Mundugumor adults potently mirrored their
childhood experiences. Children who fought for every drop of milk and every
ounce of nurturing would be unlikely candidates for romance, docility, or cooperation with parents' plans for arranged marriages. So girls put on their best jewelry
or grass skirts and boys watched for the slightest sign of opportunity. The following quote is an obvious complement to her discussions about breast feeding.

> *The love affairs of the young unmarried people are sudden and highly
> charged, characterized by passion rather than by tenderness or
> romance. A few hastily whispered words, a tryst muttered as they
> pass on a trail, are often the only interchange between them after they
> have chosen each other and before that choice is expressed in inter-
> course. The element of time and discovery is always present, goading
> them towards the swiftest possible cut-and-run relationship. . . .
> Foreplay in these quick encounters takes the form of a violent
> scratching and biting match, calculated to produce the maximum
> amount of excitement in the minimum amount of time. To break the
> arrows or the basket of the beloved is one standard way of demon-
> strating consuming passion; so also is tearing off ornaments, and
> smashing them if possible. (Mead 1963:215)*

What would happen, Mead asked, to a Mundugumor couple who somehow
invented long, languorous lovemaking, to a Mundugumor man who rejoiced in
his children's growth, or to a Mundugumor woman who cuddled and comforted
her crying child? Too bad. They would be defined as deviates in Mundugumor
society. While such individuals did not cause trouble in their communities, they
were outsiders nonetheless. Who would marry a man who wished to be loyal or
parental, or a woman who suckled a foster child?

The Mundugumor called some individuals "really bad men." They had more
than their share of wives; some they stole or bought from neighboring groups;

some they cheated their sons out of or traded their daughters for. These men garnered allegiance from younger, less established men who jockeyed for power. At the same time, the bad men conspired secretly to betray these opportunistic alliances. The Mundugumor men worked together only when headhunting and eating their enemies at the victory feasts. But such men were not deviates; they were only exaggerations of the expected.

The three months among the Mundugumor were troubled and discouraging for Mead. For starters, the group did not throw any light on her central theme of showing the contrast between female and male temperament since both sexes were so aggressive and assertive. As in the Arapesh, there were no behavioral styles that seemed to separate women and men. She hated the way they treated children and used them in conflicts between the parents. The village flooded regularly and the mosquitos were even more hostile and aggressive than the Mundugumor.

Judging from her autobiography and their letters from the field, it is also clear that Margaret and Reo were getting on each other's nerves. She notes: "Reo was both repelled and fascinated by the Mundugumor. They struck some note in him that was thoroughly alien to me, and working with them emphasized aspects of his personality with which I could not empathize" (1972:206). When she was ill with malaria, her husband offered no sympathy or assistance. When he was sick, he raged, fought the sickness, and climbed mountains.

The couple had an odd division of labor, which strained their marriage and seriously affected the results of their research. Reo assigned Margaret to study mothers, children, and language, topics that were not important to him. Everything else was his. So she would "do gender" and he would do the official ethnography. But their distribution of work created more problems.

> In the middle of our stay I discovered that Reo, who had insisted that he alone would work on the kinship system, had missed a clue. . . . I felt that if he had not drawn so rigid a dividing line between his work and mine, we would have been able to put the material together much sooner. . . . It was a flat contradiction of good scientific practice. I did not mind a division of labor based on what Reo wanted to do, in which I was left to do whatever he thought was least interesting, as long as the work got done. (Mead 1972:205)

So Margaret and Reo decided to leave this troubled field site. The government patrol boat took them upstream in time for Christmas. With the kind of luck, good and bad, that had so marked this trip, the boat deposited them on the doorstep of an English anthropologist named Gregory Bateson, who had been working in a dramatic culture called the Iatmul. This group set their tensions between the sexes into elaborate dances and ceremonials, using cross-dressing with costumes and makeup, and mock and ritual homosexuality.

The Tchambuli

"You must be tired," Gregory said to Margaret tenderly as he pulled out a soft chair for her. She melted. Everything about this new anthropologist and the village was a relief for the aching ethnographer.

So Mead and Fortune decided to stay and finish their fieldwork with a group called the Tchambuli. They were neighbors to the Iatmul and had many similar practices. Both groups had splendid artistic traditions and complex cultures. Both lived in settled villages and traded fish with bush dwellers who made sago flour, the other staple of their diet. For both groups, women fished for a living and retained sole control of the disposition and marketing of their catches. Women manufactured large, woven mosquito-proof sleeping bags traded throughout the Sepik.

The Tchambuli lived on a blue-black lake. Small, sharp hills rose beyond the indistinct shores of the lake. In Mead's time a road wound near the lake margins. Men's houses, thirty to forty feet long, with painted, carved gables and figures of bird-men at the ends, lined the road. Paths ran from the ceremonial houses up the rocky hillsides to the women's houses. These were built to last three or four lifetimes and house three or four families.

For Mead, the Tchambuli dwelling house revealed the solidarity and solidity of women. Women, competent, collegial, and certain of themselves, occupied the center of the house. Men sat at the edges near the doors, uneasy, wary, ready to bolt back into their ceremonial houses. There they gathered their own firewood and cooked their own bachelor meals. While the women fished and wove, the men practiced dances, prepared extravagant costumes of feathers, fibers, and shells, or arranged each other's curls.

To men, the thing that mattered most in life was art. Every man knew at least one art: carving, weaving, painting, dancing, music, costume-making, drama productions, and the creation of a graceful pattern of social relations that allowed the unadorned women to draw sustenance and return to their work or trading activities. The women tolerated and even appreciated the games, dances, and theatricals the men staged. But the dance was valuable, not the dancer.

The relationships of Tchambuli men to each other were delicate. By contrast, men related to women as the most solid and predictable element in their lives.

> *As a small child, he was held lightly in the arms of a laughing casual mother, a mother who nursed him generously but nonchalantly, while her fingers were busy plaiting reeds into sleeping-baskets or rain-capes. When he tumbled down, his mother picked him up and tucked him under her arm as she went on with her conversation. He was never left alone; there were always some eight or ten women about, working, laughing, attending to his needs, willingly enough, but unobsessively. (Mead 1963:248)*

Tchambuli women weaned their children in the same careless, casual manner as they nursed them, stuffing their mouths with sweet delicacies to stop their crying.

Mead concluded that Tchambuli women had what she called dominance. She pointed out that the group practiced both patrilineal descent and polygyny (having two or more wives). These customs would seem to be oppressive or degrading to women. Yet these women had real power. While men bickered and reconciled, the women quietly carried on with their work. Mead spoke of women as impersonal, vigorous, and efficient.

The Tchambuli view of sex and sexually active females was firmly illustrated in the problem of what to do with young widows.

> *A young widow is a tremendous liability to a community. No one expects her to remain quiet until her remarriage has been arranged. Has she not a vulva? they ask. This is the comment that is continually made in Tchambuli: Are women passive sexless creatures who can be expected to wait upon the dilly-dallying of formal considerations of bride-price? Men, not so urgently sexed, may be expected to submit themselves to the discipline of a due order and precedence.* (Mead 1963:258)

Women, it is clear from her description, exercised their own choices for a mate despite patrilineal clans, polygyny, and a shallow mystique of arranged marriages.

Do not, however, be misled. Assuming that Mead presented a proper perspective on what she witnessed, women's freedom to ignore the rules of patriliny and arranged marriages still produced jealousy, conflicts, and soap opera dramas. For boys, there was a deeper discontinuity; a young man had no real training for his future role. By contrast, girls were thoroughly and practically trained in handicrafts, fishing, and the responsible, practical lives of women. The young men Mead saw in this society were confused; she says they were more maladjusted than any other group she had known. The patrilineal system justified a young man's wish or need to dominate, to initiate marriage choices, and to dictate economic decisions. But for reasons that are clear only in a later historic context, a man could not do these things. So some young men grew angry, violent, and neurotic. This was the primary example of deviancy she noted for the group.

Situations on the Sepik

Meanwhile, the anthropologists were having a crazy time. During part of this period, the three of them worked together in a tiny eight-foot by eight-foot mosquito room. Relentlessly, they analyzed themselves, each other, and their respective cultures. Then they added the four Sepik cultures they studied and others they had known. The three of them talked continually about their work, their theories, and the implications of their findings for studying a topic such as marriage. Bateson lacked the methodological sophistication of the American researchers, but Margaret and Reo lacked his theoretical elegance. From all existing accounts, the events and feelings of this time changed their lives profoundly and probably the discipline of anthropology as well.

All were experiencing some depression in the field. Margaret and Gregory were beginning to build a deep communication that Reo could never share. Margaret was at the apex of a triangle; two men courted her, competed for her, and even coerced her on occasion. No wonder she wrote of the confused Tchambuli men living in a charged atmosphere of courtship and of energetic and competent women who chose at leisure.

> *The intensity of our discussion was heightened by the triangular situation. Gregory and I were falling in love, but this was kept firmly under control while all three of us tried to translate the intensity of our feelings into better and more perceptive field work. As we dealt with the cultural differences between Arapesh, Mundugumor, Tchambuli, and Iatmul, we talked also about the differences in temperamental emphasis in the three English-speaking cultures— American, New Zealand, and English—that we represented and about the academic ethos that Gregory and I shared. No part of this was irrelevant to our struggle to arrive at a new formulation of the relationships between sex, temperament, and culturally expected behavior. (Mead 1972:217)*

None of them, as they saw it, fit the classic gender roles for their respective cultures. At various times in their writings and in conversations with each other, Mead, Benedict, and Bateson identified themselves as "cultural misfits." Mead certainly did not fit the stereotype of the American wife and mother nor the image of a career women with no children. Bateson was brilliant but uncertain what to do with his intelligence. In her writings, Benedict often expressed a sense of herself as a person living so far from the cultural norms or expectations that only anguish and unhappiness would result. She wished she had lived in a time more in tune with her personal characteristics.

So the people of the Sepik were not the only ones testing the possible configurations of gender. Benedict's best-seller, *Patterns of Culture*, argued forcefully for accepting the many ways humans learn to love each other. Margaret Mead brought her own temperament and sex into the field with her. Bateson's work on the transvestite or cross-dressing ceremonies of the Iatmul people who live in the same area would become a classic and lead to some formative work on schizophrenia, cognition, and the boundaries of human thought. For Mead and Bateson, this was the beginning of an extraordinary collaboration; a personal and professional journey that had enormous impact in anthropology and beyond. As Margaret's third and last husband remarked to their daughter,

> *It is not accidental that when Margaret was on the Sepik, struggling with the question of diversity in herself and in her ways of loving, she was formulating the contrasts between three New Guinea peoples who dealt very differently with maleness and femaleness, with assertion and creativity. (Bateson 1984:160)*

Daughters of Sex and Temperament

In the years that followed the publication of *Sex and Temperament,* many readers had trouble believing that within a 100-mile area of a remote and magnificent river region Mead conveniently found three societies that perfectly illustrated her points. During her lifetime, she was criticized forcefully for this book; she called it "my most misunderstood book." As she said in one of the many reprintings of *Sex and Temperament,*

> *It is difficult to talk about two things at once—sex in the sense of biologically-given sex differences, and temperament in the sense of innate individual endowment. I wanted to talk about the way each of us belongs to a sex and has a temperament shared with others of our own sex **and** others of the opposite sex. In our present-day culture, bedeviled by a series of **either-or** problems, there is a tendency to say, "She can't have it both ways, if she shows that different cultures can mold men and women in ways which are opposite to our ideas of innate sex differences, then she can't also claim that there **are** sex differences." (Mead 1963:ii. The emphasis is hers.)*

Mead always insisted that the sites selected for their three phases of fieldwork were only good luck. Ultimately, each was a theoretical bonus. As we shall see a little later, later ethnographers tend to back her up on these points.

In addition to this influential book on gender and personality, Mead published five volumes on the Arapesh. Few anthropologists have left such a record, and this one remains unsurpassed and unchallenged. Bateson's work on the Iatmul also complements and validates her work. And, fortunately, we have the fieldwork of contemporary anthropologists, Nancy McDowell in the contemporary Mundugumor (now called the Biwat) and Deborah Gewertz among the Tchambuli (now called the Chambri). So we can ask these anthropologists and the host of excellent ethnographers who do fieldwork in this area: Was Margaret Mead losing it on the Sepik? Did she know what she was doing? Can we trust her conclusions? What can we really learn from studying sex and temperament in such settings?

Anthropologist Deborah Gewertz went to the Sepik River to do fieldwork in the early 1970s with the Chambri (Tchambuli). Although she was primarily concerned with trade and exchange networks, Deborah knew that she would be working in a group that had become an icon in women's studies. After all, Margaret Mead had labeled the women of Tchambuli "dominant."

Deborah concludes that Mead was essentially correct in what she saw, but she didn't stay long enough or have the viewpoint at that time to see the Chambri embedded in a long history of which 1933 was only a piece. Mead studied the Tchambuli as the group had just returned to the shores of the beautiful lake after a twenty-year exile in the hills above. While Mead was there, competition between males decreased temporarily while they rebuilt their base, the men's houses, the male rituals, and the symbolic equipment: slit drums, costumes, art, and musical instruments. It is no wonder the men seemed strained and watchful, worried about marital prospects, or that they appeared preoccupied with artistic productivity and building activity. The women had already rebuilt their barter market system, trading fish for sago in the complementarity that ensured their food supply. So the women appeared "dominant."

According to Deborah Gewertz, Mead did not take complex regional histories into account nor push her own brilliant methodology to its fullest conclusions: She should have noted that women can move throughout a hierarchy without changing into men. Women can move through time taking on different attitudes and practices without losing basic functions. Sex roles (or gender roles) have enough flexibility to use in adjusting to changing circumstances. We cannot just label a group of women as dominant or submissive. Instead, we may find an underlying pattern of relationships that persists through time and provides us a range of negotiations for a complex variety of social situations.

With the blessings of Mead, anthropologist Nancy McDowell reworked the field notes from Margaret and Reo's sojourn among the Mundugumor in 1932 and compared them to her fieldwork with the group (now called the Biwat) in the early 1970s. Nancy concludes that "Mead's ethnographic skills, as well as her powers of observation and perception, were exceptional and clearly superseded the theory she espoused" (McDowell 1991:77). Unlike Mead, however, Reo Fortune never wrote up his notes from this trip. Margaret did some of them for him (as many academic wives have done for husbands); but the rest in his handwriting are useless.

> There are indications that they were not fully sharing data with each other. Fortune's notes are fragmented, disorganized, and practically unreadable. The theoretical paradigms within which they worked led them to ask only certain kinds of questions and neglect others. Mead's American cultural anthropological approach led her to assume that human culture was far more simple than it really was, that it could be encapsulated by particular themes or as "personality writ large," and she fell victim to oversimplification. (McDowell 1991:290)

Margaret Mead and ethnographers who followed her put a great deal of emphasis on women's economic powers. Bateson did not even notice the economic roles and autonomous activities of the women; he saw them only in complementary relationships with men, their fathers and husbands. Gregory Bateson recognized that women and men do not always follow the rules or conform to anyone's stereotypes.

> For the most part, the [Iatmul] women exhibit a system of emotional attitudes which contrasts sharply with that of the men. While the latter behave almost consistently as though life were a splendid theatrical performance—almost a melodrama—with themselves in the centre of the stage, the women behave most of the time as though life were a cheerful cooperative routine in which the occupations of food-getting and child-rearing are enlivened by the dramatic and

exciting activities of the men. But this jolly, cooperative attitude is not consistently adopted in all contexts, and we have seen that women occasionally adopt something approaching the male ethos and that they are admired for so doing. (Bateson 1958:148)

He found that women occasionally took assertive roles in warfare, in the dancing grounds, and with husbands who could not or would not compete with other men.

What do we learn from these researchers? We see that gender roles are not fixed, rigid, or defined for all time. Sex roles are not divinely assigned nor inherent in something we call "nature." They are flexible; they can be used as problem-solving devices. For example, the Arapesh believed that women should avoid the yam gardens because the yams did not grow well around females; both women and gardens were believed to be protected by this belief. By contrast, Mundugumor couples took advantage of a similar mindset and deliberately copulated in other people's gardens just to ruin them.

What Mead called sex roles are only a script, not a prescription. She quoted Ruth Benedict, who said culture is "personality writ large." In Benedict's view, writes Mead,

It is possible to see each culture, no matter how small and primitive or how large and complex, as having selected from the great arc of human potentialities certain characteristics and then having elaborated them with greater strength and intensity than any single individual could ever do in one lifetime. (Mead 1934:v)

Their view of culture as a pattern or configuration of homogenous and integrated elements, often linked with a unified theme, lacks the dimensions of contemporary theories. Now anthropologists think that culture is never simple, uniform, or well-integrated. It is a messy, complicated, and often contradictory set of differences or oppositions that may exist side-by-side within the same group claiming the same territory, history, or worldview. This is why, today, we can talk of a female culture and a male culture within complex and contradictory ethnic, national, and world cultures.

Mead published *Sex and Temperament* in 1935; in the same year, Gregory Bateson completed *Naven,* his still-stimulating study of Iatmul culture. And in 1935 they married and went to the island of Bali in Indonesia to begin their first, last, and most extraordinary collaboration.

Beyond the Sepik

The Mead–Bateson collaborative research in Bali was probably far ahead of its time, involving systematic observations and an innovative use of photography. But for purposes of our story, the key event was Margaret's unanticipated pregnancy. There she was, thirty-eight years old. Her English husband had been called up for the war just beginning. In a forthright and organized way, she took charge of her pregnancy and delivery. She taught a young pediatrician, Dr. Benjamin Spock, about comparative styles in child-rearing and the importance of breast–feeding. She showed a film on births in New Guinea to those attending her birth.

Gregory and Margaret were delighted with their newborn daughter, Mary Catherine, called Cathy. In the mellowness of breast–feeding the baby she had never expected to have, Margaret was full of empathy for young mothers and grateful for the advantages she had.

> *I had nothing to do except keep my milk up and feed and hold the baby. I did not have to go anywhere, I had no housework to do, no uneasy husband to placate, no worries about money—in fact, I faced none of the problems that can make the first baby so difficult for an inexperienced young mother. But I was trying to do something, consciously and in a new way, that combined our best knowledge and my own observations of mothers and babies in many cultures. (Mead 1972:306)*

She acknowledged the desperation of many young mothers, isolated and afraid, lacking experience, support, or confidence, even sinking into depression.

One has the feeling reading her autobiography that Mead was constructing her life as she went along. She was building it out of pieces of people she studied and admired, bringing other people, friends, and husbands, into her life, enriching theirs at the same time. Her daughter comments:

> *In* Blackberry Winter, *Margaret again and again uses metaphors that suggest her sense of herself as directing a play, as a producer, assembling and placing a particular constellation of people. (Bateson 1984:111)*

The households she constructed after Catherine's birth are a major case in point. Although Margaret was always sensitive to the lives of wives and mothers in American nuclear families, she herself did not wish to create such an arrangement. Mead thought that nuclear families were too isolated or limiting. As she grew older, she did not want to own or clean an apartment or house or do any domestic tasks beyond salad making; she always lived with close friends in assorted households and hired assistants in the museum where she worked.

Catherine had a nanny, the nanny had a child. Catherine's father was away most of the time. So Catherine grew up in the households of loving and responsible people, in the families of others. She created extended households, although not an extended family in the genetic sense. As Margaret notes in her autobiography, mothering was not a full-time occupation for her. In fact, it would appear from her autobiography that she and Gregory spent little time alone with their child. It is also clear that each parent had close ties with Catherine throughout their lives. In fact, their only child did not grow up "weird," disturbed, or neurotic. Catherine had a number of mothers in this arrangement; she knew her biological mother was loving but different from the American norm. This is an important example for any who perceive American culture as monolithic or one-dimensional or who think only one family style will work.

Intimacy and the World Stage

Margaret Mead continued to puzzle out the meanings of gender and to speak out about women and children throughout the rest of her long career. She taught at Columbia University and worked for the American Museum of Natural History. She was finally promoted to curator in 1964. Although neither institution gave Mead the status or the salary she probably deserved, they offered her flexibility and the much-valued freedom to work as anthropologist-at-large.

Most of her advances and royalties went into the Institute for Intercultural Studies, which gave grants to young anthropologists and supported research, public service and the discipline of anthropology in numerous ways. Margaret Mead was mentor to dozens and dozens of young anthropologists at key turning points in their careers. She called for a woman's viewpoint in anthropology long before we knew it had a male-centered bias. As feminism and a female-centered viewpoint became established, she reminded us to remember the men. She brought large numbers of women in the calling of anthropology and refused to listen to protests about discrimination. She would say, "Don't complain about women's status or problems. Just get to work."

All of Margaret Mead's husbands were anthropologists. Each was involved with the questions of how to relate their personal lives to their work as anthropologists. Mead met and liked the women her ex-husbands married and helped the three men at many stages in their careers. As one of her friends remarked, "Margaret was always a gentleman." Margaret sustained an intimate life throughout her adult years with a man and with a woman. While this double pattern satisfied her, it required a certain secrecy and thus a certain isolation. As her daughter, Catherine, notes in her own autobiography,

> Margaret worked hard and incessantly to sustain relationships, caring most about those in which different kinds of intimacy supported and enriched each other, the sharing of a fine meal, the wrestling of intense intellectual collaboration, the delights of lovemaking. . . . The intimacy to which Margaret and Ruth progressed after Margaret's completing of her degree became the model for one axis of her life while the other was defined in relation to the men she loved or married. (Bateson 1984:117)

But Ruth Benedict died in 1948 and Margaret's marriage to Gregory Bateson was gradually dissolving in the same period. Gregory, more than anyone else, resented Margaret's management of his life and eventually left her, moving far away. That was not part of her life plan, and she grieved the loss for a long time. They remained friends, colleagues, and co-parents. For Margaret, intense conversations and collegial involvement were linked to lovemaking; this theme appears again and again in her writing.

In 1975 Margaret Mead wrote an article for her regular column in *Redbook* magazine and talked about bisexuality. She defined it and defended it without identifying herself publicly. The time has come, she says, to view this as normal. That a person is capable of loving members of both sexes should not be such a taboo subject nor such a strange phenomenon. She talks about cultures in which boys or girls go through a stage of relating almost exclusively with each other. They fall in love and have deep physical attractions. She spoke of times in history when people experimented with a great variety of personal relations in politics, art, music, drama, and intellectual projects, crossing barriers of race, sex, and age.

> *Changing traditional attitudes toward homosexuality is in itself a mind-expanding experience for most people. But we shall not really succeed in discarding the strait jacket of our cultural beliefs about sexual choice if we fail to come to terms with the well-documented, normal human capacity to love members of both sexes. . . . What is new is not bisexuality, but rather the widening of our awareness and acceptance of human capacities for sexual love. (Mead 1975:30)*

When Margaret married Reo (a jealous and straitlaced type) and went into the field for two years, her physical relationship with Ruth ended. But the separation of marriage and travel did not alter their intellectual intimacy. Theirs was a spiritually permanent relationship. Margaret, however, cared about the consequences of living openly with a women and desired to protect her public image and professional position. She might see herself as marginal or a misfit; but she never intended to become a social outcast.

For Ruth, however, her relationship to Margaret was the touchstone of her life. From the start of their deepest friendship until the end of her life, Benedict was what she called "a woman-loving-woman." In the early 1930s, Ruth Benedict separated from her husband and found the first of two women who lived with her and shared her life and spiritual sensitivities until her death in 1948. Benedict's writings from that time on talked about redefining the categories of abnormal and normal; she spoke out strongly about the absurdities of treating homosexuality as an illness. She pointed out cultures that treated homosexuals as healers or leaders, or allowed alternative gender roles. She wrote about the Native American customs in which men wore women's clothes and did women's work. "Normal," in her view, was relative to the culture in which a person lived.

Her masterwork, *Patterns of Culture,* was an instant success. Some have called it "a paradigm shift," which means its radically new perspective forever changed the collective worldview. It replaced the absolute standards of morality and harsh value judgments of the nineteenth century with the enduring concept of **cultural relativism.** If cultural standards are relative to place, time, and people, then all of us can reevaluate the relationships between men and women in our own society. She made a very clear statement about biology: If women are weak, this is because we have learned to be or are expected to be, not because our biology has predetermined our weakness. She used her own field experiences in the American Southwest and those of her colleagues from around the world (including Reo Fortune's work on Dobu) to show how matrilineal cultures differ from the patrilineal model of Euro-American societies. The book and its radical message moved beyond anthropology and other intellectual circles into popular consciousness. At its core was a profound feminist vision that has become, in effect, the coin of the realm. Ordinary people, not just anthropologists, now talk about particular cultures and the patterns that give their lives meaning.

Her book caused serious arguments among anthropologists. Some felt that it threatened the status of the discipline as a science. Some said it was too humanistic, too fuzzy, too literary, too subjective, too simplistic. The book was, of course, one of the inspirations for Mead's *Sex and Temperament* and other studies who talked about the "approved personalities of each sex." Out of these two books came an entire school of anthropology, the study of culture and personality, as well as reaction against this kind of theory and research. But these are stories for another day.

Conclusion: Their Last Great Work

World War II and Margaret's child-care responsibilities prevented more field work after 1940. So Mead and Benedict gathered a host of dynamic colleagues to work on a project they called Research in Contemporary Cultures or "the study of culture at a distance." They formed a research team of scholars and citizens from many places in the world and did ethnography without the fieldwork. Well-funded, they believed that their work had national significance and would be their contributions to winning the war and establishing the peace to follow. They developed innovative and interdisciplinary methods with an emphasis on complex modern civilizations grounded in cultural relativism and the culture and personality approach. The most famous book to come out of this massive governmental and professional collaboration was Benedict's classic study of Japanese national character, *The Chrysanthemum and the Sword*.

The project probably did not change the course of American anthropology nor did it enter popular awareness as their earlier works had done. Nonetheless, there are reasons to look at this venture today. Their project addresses questions that women in contemporary social movements regularly ask. If women organized and controlled the institutions that seem to control us, would the world be a different place? A better place? Do women structure people and activities differently than men do?

Mead and Benedict would answer yes. In their project there were no hierarchies, no pyramids of status, no ladders of success. There were only co-equal circles. Conveners took responsibility for getting groups together. The only titles they used marked types of responsibility, not types of prestige. Volunteer or paid, beginners or professionals, part-time or full-time, everyone worked together and gave away power to get results. They did not even have a central office. Ruth Benedict thought of this as a synergy in which the framework and goals of the group complemented and enhanced individuals and their contributions. They treated interpersonal relations, not formal structure, as the foundation of productivity. This meant that raising a family, being a parent, spouse, or lover, were rewarded; these activities were considered relevant to the project and accorded prestige! They talked about fostering diversity, accepting dissonance or diversification, and the creative use of chaos.

This project, as was everything Ruth Benedict touched in the last period of her life, was gently but firmly feminist. As president of the American Anthropological Association, she said that insight and intuition are as important to the nation as are the findings of science. She also believed that societies that honored maternal principles had greater peace and balance. In her publications she emphasized women's values and a woman's perspectives.

Both Mead and Benedict practiced warm ties of interdependence cemented with rituals, shared meals, all-night conversations, and physical intimacies. They contrasted these activities with war. War, they said, is not an innate or biological response of human beings. It does not result from some instinct, some gene, or some drive. It is not "natural for mankind." Instead war, for all its terrors or triumphs, is purely cultural. It is only another, albeit murderous, social institution. If this is true, they said, then human beings can change; we can choose to "study war no more." We could teach each other and raise our children to adopt other cultural and psychological means to avoid conflict and destruction. Naive by our standards, yes, but influential throughout the world and beyond their lives.

From Samoa to the end of her life, Margaret Mead focused more intensely on women, children, growing up, and the fundamental questions of gender than any other anthropologist or social scientist has ever done. She introduced these topics into our national discourse and into international arenas and forever challenged and changed our ways of seeing.

In the next chapter, we continue these themes as we look at how women in human cultures have marked our passages through biology and the life cycle.

So Many Books: Where Can J Start?

Start with autobiographies and biographies. The best ones on Ruth Benedict are by Margaret Caffrey, *Ruth Benedict: Stranger in this Land* (1989) and Judith Modell, *Ruth Benedict: Patterns of a Life* (1983). Of course, Margaret Mead wrote two biographies herself, *An Anthropologist at Work: The Writings of Ruth Benedict* (1959) and *Ruth Benedict* (1974).

Margaret Mead's own autobiography is fascinating: *Blackberry Winter: My Earlier Years* (1972). So is her daughter's autobiography, which is combined with biographies of her famous parents: Mary Catherine Bateson, *With a Daughter's Eye: A Memoir of Margaret Mead and Gregory Bateson* (1984). Three other sources to read about Mead are Jane Howard's biography, *Margaret Mead: A Life* (1984); Rhoda Metraux's *Margaret Mead: Some Personal Views* (1979); or the *American Anthropologist* of June 1980 (vol. 82, no. 2) entitled, *"In Memoriam: Margaret Mead."*

Some related books worth reading include Mary Catherine Bateson's *Composing a Life* (1989). Here she treats the lives of five extraordinary women as works in progress, creative compositions, and empowering improvisations. There are two extremely informative collections about the lives and careers of women in anthropology. Their patterns of professionalism, mothering, love, and the work of culture, are particularly interesting. Ute Gacs, Aisha Khan, Jerrie McIntyre, and Ruth Weinberg edited *Women Anthropologists: Selected Biographies* (1989). Peggy Golde edited *Women in the Field: Anthropological Experiences* (1986).

Chapter Three

Blood and Milk

Biocultural Markers in the Lives of Women

The Navajo People of the American Southwest tell of a spirit named Changing Woman. She is enigmatic; young at one time, old at another, and then young again. She is the mystery of reproduction and birth; sometimes she is the earth's mother. Changing Woman decrees fertility and sterility and has elaborate mythic ties to Sun, Moon, the Holy People and to the power of rainmaking.

The ceremony for Changing Woman at her first menstrual period was the first ever performed and the model for all to follow. The great epic tale about the creation of the world instructs the Navajo how to honor menstruating girls in a four-day ritual called Kinaaldá. The Navajo, the largest group of Native Americans in the United States, practice matrilineal kinship, tracing descent through the female line. This may be one reason why they honor the biological beginnings of womanhood with a celebration.

Where Biology and Culture Meet in the Bodies of Women

In this chapter we will discuss the intersections of biology, our life cycle as females, and the cultural constructions of these processes. The juxtaposition of biological processes with social imperatives, or **biocultural markers,** are the core of women's existence on the planet. It is probably here that woman's lives differ most substantially from men's lives. This is the arena where authorities (of whatever kind) place their most substantial controls on women. These transitions in women's lives are also rich, deep sources for strong feelings and spirituality. These passages link women across political boundaries and cultural differences.

We will start with first menstruation, or **menarche,** and the social constructions called **maidenhood.** Then we will go on to the end of menstruation and reproduction, **menopause,** and the social constructions of middle age. We will discuss the **"life stream,"** the potentials for conceptions, pregnancies, and births, and ways and reasons to understand, alter, or control this stream. The "life stream" concept helps us understand that arbitrary breaks and definitions for women's reproductive lives are cultural artifacts. We end with comparative childbirth practices and **lactation,** or producing milk for nursing babies.

In most human societies, pregnancy and childbirth, if not menstruation and menopause, are treated as major life passages. They may be transformative experiences or a source of status or recognition. These moments represent a kind of growth or initiation that only women experience. Menarche as biological experience is universal; but social recognition takes many forms. Some are public; some are private. Some are controlling and others feel liberating. All human cultures recognize the biological meaning of menstruation. But not all human cultures honor the coming of age of young girls as do the Navajo.

Moonstruck Maidenhood: Taboo and Meaning

In recent years many scholars (including a large number of women) have looked at menstruation, menstrual symbolism, and the diversity in cultural approaches to menstruation. New contributions of human reproductive biology have led us to question the received wisdom of the past or the Western medical-scientific belief systems. Crosscultural studies demonstrate the enormous ranges of meanings attributed to this phenomenon.

In many times and places, menstrual blood has been considered dangerous and defiling; it could somehow contaminate or harm men, babies, plants, food or the group as a whole. Menstruating females pollute others. So precautions, rules, and customs, or **menstrual taboos,** regulate contacts with such women.

Here are a few examples of events menstrual blood is said to cause: It stops fermentation in winemaking and cheesemaking; poisons men in intercourse; frightens away deer or other prey; attracts bears and other predators; cures medical conditions such as epilepsy, eye problems, open sores, intestinal parasites, rabies, or liver problems; or sours milk and causes rising bread to fall. In some cultures, it is believed that the possibility of menstrual blood on the ground makes it dangerous for men to walk on streets or paths, and certainly under balconies where women may be walking overhead.

> *Many menstrual taboos, rather than protecting society from a universally ascribed feminine evil, explicitly protect the perceived creative spirituality of menstruous women from the influence of others in a more neutral state, as well as protecting the latter in turn from the potent, positive spiritual force ascribed to such women. In other cultures menstrual customs, rather than subordinating women to men fearful of them, provide women with means of ensuring their own autonomy, influence, and social control. (Buckley and Gottlieb 1988:7)*

Positive myths and metaphors of life force, generativity, and fertility use menstrual blood as a symbol. Menstrual blood is said to be used in witchcraft or in the manufacture of various kinds of love charms and potions. Sometimes there is protection from evil in the uses of menstrual blood. What this shows most profoundly is that menstrual taboos are arbitrary, symbolic, and "culturally constructed." They make sense only in context. There is no crosscultural evidence that menstruation is everywhere considered unclean, that women uniformly feel shame or pain, or that menstrual blood repulses men.

One popular interpretation of menstrual taboos is that they oppress women, and that the isolation of a woman during her period is evidence of her low status. The problem with such theories is that they rarely come from menstruating women themselves. It is men who have by and large defined menstruation as polluting. Ethnographers typically report what men have said about menstrual periods.

Anthropologists have been fascinated with a widespread type of taboo, the seclusion of women in "menstrual huts." Imagine how these customs would sound today if an early generation of anthropologists, missionaries, or travelers had labeled them "menstrual sanctuaries." Unfortunately, we have no detailed studies of the lived experiences of women themselves in these places, and the customs have largely disappeared. In 1931 anthropologist Ruth Underhill recorded the experiences of a Papago woman named Chona. Chona's story of her menstrual hut is told in the box below.

Was the little house solitary confinement or rest and recreation? Some accounts suggest resentment; but others hint that women enjoyed a communal break from men and work. Most women can imagine taking out five or six socially sanctioned

Chona's Little House

When I was nearly as tall as my mother, that thing happened to me which happens to all our women though I do not know if it does to the whites; I never saw any signs. It is called menses. Girls are very dangerous at that time. If they touch a man's bow, or even look at it, that bow will not shoot any more. If they drink out of a man's bowl, it will make him sick. If they touch the man himself, he might fall down dead. . . . Our mothers watch us, and so mine knew when it came to me. We always had the Little House ready, over behind our own house. It was made of some branches stuck in the ground and tied together at the top, with greasewood thrown over them to make it shady.

Chona could crawl in her little house but she could not stand up. Her mother brought her food without meat or salt; her father gave her a sharpened stick to scratch her head with.

It was a hard time for us girls, such as the men have when they are being purified. Only they give us more to eat, because we are women. And they do not let us sit and wait for dreams. That is because we are women, too. Women must work.

So she walked far up the mountain to bring water and firewood back before daylight. The old woman who was supervising the work of ritual seclusion told her to work hard in order to find a good man to marry. Her mother came before dawn of the fourth day and made her bathe in icy cold water. Then her mother washed Chona's hair with soapweed fibers so it would never turn gray and cut it. In the month that followed, until the moon completed its rounds, the people in the village danced and sang and honored the girl who had been to the Little House for the first time.

Source: Ruth Underhill, *Papago Women* (1979), 57. Data collected from 1931 to 1933.

days a month to nap, meditate, talk, weave, or just mope around. In some times and places, women systematically used rules of seclusion for spiritual or economic enhancement, even for nonmarital love affairs. Sometimes there were ritual powers associated with female seclusion practices. Menstrual customs do not simply discriminate against or suppress women.

Experiences of menstruation vary between cultures. In some foraging or peasant groups where women breast-feed for three or four years, have low-fat diets, heavy physical labor, or many pregnancies, they may have few or no periods (**amenorrhoea**). For various reasons, human females may begin menstruation late in their teens and stop early in their life cycle. Under these circumstances, having a period is worthy of some ritual notice. In some human groups, menarche does not mean that ovulation begins simultaneously. Even girls whose periods have started cannot conceive for a number of years; this is called **adolescent infertility**. By contrast, teenagers in Europe and North America begin both their periods and the possibilities of becoming pregnant at quite young ages. Cultural responses will be quite different under these circumstances.

The time between the beginning of menstruation and actual adulthood (however defined) is important to the social lives of females. It is customary in anthropology to call this period **maidenhood,** or the culturally constructed period between menarche and marriage, motherhood, or other socially constructed adult statuses. Not one human society ignores this period. People in all human groups worry about and try to regulate female sexuality or the consequences of it during this time. Every single human society has cultural rules and customary strategies for controlling young girls at this time. At least they try.

Anthropologist Victoria Burbank went to Australia to see how adolescent girls in a community called Mangrove made this transition through maidenhood. This is one of the first ethnographic studies on teenagers since Margaret Mead went to Samoa.

> At one time it appears that the Aborigines of Mangrove attempted to regulate female sexuality, as least as far as adolescent females were concerned, by marrying them off before they were sexually mature. Thus ideally, by the time a female was likely to be interested in sexual activity and could reproduce, she had been placed with a male that her community deemed an appropriate sexual partner and father of her children. (Burbank 1988:7)

Today, the Australian government, supported by missionaries and social workers, have banned early marriages and infant betrothals. Now the teenage girls of Mangrove want to choose their own husbands. They often manage to exert personal choices by having sex with boyfriends and getting pregnant. The elders are predictably upset that young women no longer observe traditional laws about marriage.

In all societies, however, maidenhood is the time to learn and practice the social skills of adulthood. The length of maidenhood and the amount of restraints vary. If girls are engaged before birth and married before menarche, as in traditional Aboriginal Australia, they never have a maidenhood. In complex Western societies, girls may enter puberty at twelve or thirteen and not marry until their late twenties (if ever). Others have babies before they finish high school. A teen's viewpoint of the regulation of sex and reproduction looks very different than a traditionalist's does. There is often amazing incongruity between teenagers' strategies for maximizing maidenhood and what adults want them to do. This is particularly true in complex societies such as ours.

Social controls are heaviest for females in maidenhood, regardless of how long this phase lasts, how much young girls conform or struggle, or which society we are talking about. Males, on the other hand, have no events that correspond to menarche and may experience a great deal of freedom after childhood.

Prime Time or Dirty Old Ladies

At a point in the middle of the female's lives, menstrual cycles end. Generally **middle age** is that phase defined by the universal physiological changes of **menopause.** So women are no longer bearing children or living with that potential. In some cultures, women in this stage are known as **crones, matrons,** or wise women. The changes that happen to women do not parallel or have counterparts in men; if they do, no one can discern them.

Research on women getting older is often fueled by pro-male and pro-youth biases. Ethnographers tend to ignore or take for granted the presence and activities of midlife females. But comparative research offers a better picture of this stage.

> First and foremost, this is the time in which a woman enjoys her greatest power, status, and autonomy. In some cultures this increase in power and status is gradual; in others, there is a sharp break with earlier requirements for women's seclusion and deferential behavior. Second, both in societies that sharply oppress young women and those that have egalitarian gender ideologies, the freedom, prestige, and authority of women increases at middle age and comes closer to that of men than it did in earlier years. So, whether it is seen in relation to a woman's own life or in relation to the lives of men of her culture and generation, middle age is a woman's prime. (Sacks 1992:2)

In many cultures, the restrictions that encumber younger women fall away. Typically, a woman no longer has to defer to a husband, a mother-in-law, or other senior relatives. She can travel, talk back, and be bawdy, outrageous, or independent. In some cases, she can safely take a lover; in other cases, she is relieved never to have sex again. She can drink too much, use forbidden language, or dress in a way that pleases her. The whole complex of obligations or taboos surrounding fertility (menstrual management, birth control, or the possibility of pregnancy) drop away. The displays of respect are now her dues as once she paid them.

Moreover, middle-aged women gain control over other people and have social or economic authority. Often women do administrative work, organizing and delegating to others. Good examples are the societies where middle-aged women have serious power over food production, processing, preparation, preserving, and ultimately, over food distribution. Observers may overlook her authority and see only the work of young women, daughters-in-law, nieces, or daughters. In societies with strong rules of separation for males and females, middle-aged women pick brides for kinsmen and act as go-betweens for marriage arrangements. These tasks carry power and traditionally belong to menopausal females.

In some societies, the high status and subtle power of being a mother-in-law are the reward for middle-aged women. What a women lacked in influence over her husband she can have over her grown son. In societies where young girls are betrothed to older men, an aging woman may come into her personal and structural power at the time her tired husband is losing his. The best examples of structural autonomy for middle-aged women come from patriarchal groups, particularly those who have fairly strict separation for the sexes. Traditional China, India, and the Islamic Middle East are prime examples. Maidenhood and the early years of marriage are times when controls are the heaviest in such societies; these fall away as women age.

Better still, middle-aged women often aspire to leadership or achievement in politics, religion, or medicine. They often become midwives, healers, or holy women of many kinds. When a woman is pregnant, nursing, or managing husband and children, she predictably does not have either time or energy for ritual roles. So one of the virtues of middle-age is that female fertility is separated from female sexuality; this is the opposite of adolescence. New forms of sensuality or spirituality may emerge. This is why aging females are widely linked to occult or psychic powers.

Middle age is also a time of striking individuality. Women often develop novel personalities and find unpredicted paths. Some say midlife women become androgynous, sexually bimodal, or that women become men or like men. David Gutmann (1987) calls this time, "the Big Bang," the eruptive energies released when women no longer work as full-time parents and wives. Margaret Mead called it "menopausal zest."

Not all women, however, encounter this time as positive growth. The potential for and general increase in power may be destructive as well as sacred; for some it may be accompanied by severe depression. Women without the support of male kin, husbands, sons, or alternative forms of economic security predictably suffer.

Anthropologist Judith Brown asks, "Why don't we seem to experience positive changes for middle-aged women in the United States?" Although there are many entrepreneurial and energetic midlife women on the one hand, we know of many depressed or struggling women on the other. Her answer is that American life-passage for women is very different from other societies. We have few restrictions on ourselves in our early years, so there is less to look forward to. Adult children may live far away and our lives are no longer linked to each other for growth and survival. Other social institutions and specialists (mostly men) do the food growing, processing or medical care and healing; it is difficult to develop a career in these fields at midlife. It is clear that the managerial roles open to midlife women in other societies are not available in most Western societies. Some observers suggest that the admiration of and quest for perpetual youth in American culture further reduces middle-aged women's options. As Judith Brown says, "The crosscultural evidence suggests that our society may be wasting the potential of its middle-aged women" (Kerns and Brown 1992:27).

New research on industrialized societies like Canada, Japan, the United States, or other places defies any conventional wisdom of middle-aged women as passive, predictable, sick, or empty-nesters. The crosscultural data indicates enormous diversity, creative responses, and resistance to medical models or other social scripts. Many women refuse to accept the limitations of cultural codes, husbands, or biology.

The only universal experience of menopause is the end of periods. Feelings, emotions, bodily states, and specific symptoms like hot flashes are not universal. They are constructed from authority figures, other women, and assigned cultural meanings. Researcher Yewoubdar Beyene compared the experience of menopause for rural Mayan Indians of Yucatan Mexico and rural Greek women. The only symptom Mayan women reported was the end of periods; they did not report anything that resembled the "power surges" North American women emphasize. Indeed, they looked forward to a symptomless menopause they associated with youth and freedom. On the other hand, the Mayan women were poorly nourished, had poor overall health, and had spent their reproductive years in early and repeated pregnancies.

By contrast, the Greek women she studied married later, used birth control, and had fewer children and better health. They experienced some of the conditions we are told about: hot flashes, cold sweats, irritability, depression, but considered them normal. Anthropologist Margaret Lock compared middle age in Japan and North America. Japanese women are very sensitive to their body states, but they did not have the range of symptoms American women report. Lock notes that Japanese women are adopting the negative and biomedical views of menopausal pathologies imported from the West. In both cultures, the overriding issue appears to be contested viewpoints about what kind of people aging women are.

Desire and Control

Between menarche and menopause are about three decades of potential reproduction for women. So this section is about the ways women across human cultures modify or control the reproductive life stream. When we talk about women constructing our lives, one of the major plots or subplots in the drama is managing our fertility—whatever that may mean to an individual woman at a specific time.

Why do people want control over their bodies, the products of sex and the life stream of reproduction? What are the major motivations? Ethnographic and historic literature as well as our personal experiences reveal the following reasons: Women want to get pregnant. Women don't want to get pregnant. Women want child spacing. Women and men want temporary or permanent sterility. Women want to stop a pregnancy from proceeding. Women want to relieve barrenness. Women and men want to enhance lovemaking or to cure impotence. Women and men want babies when we want them and no babies when we don't want them.

So how do humans achieve control over our bodies, the products of sex, and the life stream of reproduction? The ethnographic and historic sources are clear: Humans beings have widespread and ancient ways of contraception, abortion, and infanticide. These methods are universal. So the reigning principle or fact of life is: People want control over the life stream and we will do *anything* we have to get it. Call this the Do Anything principle.

Techniques and Methods

I used to believe that birth control somehow started with the Pill and that my generation was the first to really know about contraception and good sex. I assumed that people in the past just had babies without thinking about it, perhaps acted unconsciously or unscientifically or just followed the rules. But now I know that contraception

> is a social practice of much greater historical antiquity, greater cultural and geographical universality than commonly supposed even by medical and social historians. . . . Men and women have always longed for both fertility and sterility, each at its appointed time and in its chosen circumstances. (Himes 1970:xii)

The first written accounts in human history mention methods of birth control. These include the earliest scriptures of the great religions, and the first law codes or medical texts. In ancient times, groups of men debated intensely about motivations and methods for controlling fertility. The anthropological literature is filled with references to these practices from all over the globe. In all my fieldwork experiences, from islands in the Pacific to urban teenagers in the United States, and in all of my personal friendships or anthropology classes, I hear stories about what women do.

Women who have periods, pregnancies, miscarriages, and stillbirths, as well as the burdens of childlessness or too many children, talk to each other. We share information, stories, and trial-and-error methods, in secret if necessary. It is clear that so-called "primitive" peoples knew about and used contraceptive techniques. It is clear from all the ethnographic and historic accounts we have that human desire for controlling the life stream is universal; it transcends place or time. As historian John Riddle remarks of women and the desires for control in antiquity,

> I suggest that their knowledge was primarily transmitted by a network of women working within the culture of their gender and that only occasionally was some of it learned by medical writers, almost all of whom were men. (Riddle 1992:16)

Basic birth control methods involve modifying or avoiding vaginal intercourse by technique or timing, taking something by mouth, or using some means of blocking the "eye" of the cervix—or all of the above. These methods demonstrate a working, practical knowledge of reproductive physiology. That none of these techniques works perfectly or predictably is quite beside the point. They will work some of the time. All of them imply practical intelligence and the desire for control. There is also an abundance of what we think of as magical reasoning and unproven remedies. These cannot be dismissed as superstitious or unscientific; they indicate a search for and organization of knowledge and useful actions. Furthermore, many of the so-called old-wives remedies are effective; they are often only older versions of what any one can buy in a drugstore or pharmacy.

Recipes and Recommendations

Consider the numerous ways in which human beings have modified or avoided vaginal intercourse. One of the most consistently reported is "pulling out," withdrawal before ejaculation, or in its Latin form, **coitus interruptus.** One ancient rabbi recommended, "During the twenty-four months after the birth of a baby, the husband must thresh inside and winnow outside." Some teenagers in New Orleans whom I have interviewed think that they have invented this new, sophisticated, and safe technique of birth control.

Sexual variations such as oral and anal intercourse avoid completed vaginal intercourse. Times of tabooed intercourse are commonly reported after the birth of a baby or during sacred or ritual times. **Post-partum sex taboos,** the rules against having intercourse while nursing a child, might last two to five years. Abstinence, or sexual practices without vaginal intercourse, are highly effective contraceptives.

Knowing how to time intercourse to avoid the fertile period is also an ancient practice. All the historical, anthropological, and old wives' literatures contain references to periodicity, that is, safe periods based on the moon and women's menstrual cycles. People sometimes have the timing wrong; in fact, the knowledge of ovulation and the "safe period" has been known for less than fifty years in American society. Many contemporary parents, for example, cannot tell our own kids when that period is. Many so-called "primitive" groups calculated it accurately.

Contraceptive recipes widely reported from cultures around the world involve ingredients found in most ordinary households. A common recipe recommends this: Cut a lemon in half, squeeze it, and insert it as a cervical cap. Lemon juice or citric acid is probably a more effective spermicide than lactic acid, the basis for our contemporary contraceptive jellies.

Similar recipes over the last 7,000 years recommend a wide variety of oily, astringent, acidic, gummy, or fibrous substances, alone or in combination. The bark and nuts of many kinds of trees provide tannic acid, an astringent vegetable compound that is a remarkably effective spermicide. Vinegar or acetic acid, yogurt, honey, salt, butter, and buttermilk are also reported from China, India, or the Middle East. The housewives of history made tampons or contraceptive suppositories out of lint, cotton, wool, silk, seaweed, or other common household fibers and absorbent substances. Any household spermicide could be used with a tampon or as a douche for washing out the vagina. These were relatively effective and easily available.

Sponges as a birth control device are noted regularly in historic accounts over the last 6,000 years. Any housewife might have natural sponges in her possession. She simply soaked the sponge in an ordinary household spermicide and placed it against the eye of the cervix, where it absorbed semen, killed sperm, and prevented impregnation. In Europe, women acquired sponges as gifts at marriage from experienced older women or from lovers. In some periods, it was against the law to use them or even to own them. A sponge moistened with lemon juice is one of the most effective and ancient contraceptive measures in the entire range of indigenous or folk medicines.

Old recipes consistently mention alum (colorless, odorless, water-soluble crystals that have astringent or drying properties). Alum has dozens of domestic uses, such as pickling fruits and vegetables or dying cloth and tanning leather. Alum was a common household chemical for thousands of years and is often cited as useful in contraceptive sponges or applications to the vagina to cause the eye of the cervix to close before intercourse.

Counterparts of contemporary cervical caps or diaphragms abound in the literature. Women in northern Europe using softened beeswax pressed in a cap against the cervix. In the Corn Belt of the United States, where hogs are raised, lard was used the same way. Prostitutes in Japan placed a disk of oiled tissue paper made from bamboo against the eye of the cervix. There are many suggestive accounts of devices like buttons, stones, or gems placed in a woman's uterus; such items acted as IUDs or intrauterine devices.

Through the ages, both women and men were advised to avoid simultaneous orgasms. Or women were counseled to jump up after intercourse, sneeze, or shake themselves assertively. It seems obvious to us that many techniques were based on magical reasoning, such as being very still during intercourse, holding one's breath, or avoiding orgasm. Expelling the semen by violent bodily movements such as jumping up and down, sneezing, and coughing, are regularly reported; I have also heard these methods extolled among American teenagers.

There are literally thousands of accounts of women drinking teas or taking something by mouth to control fertility. These come from every continent and from all types of observers, travelers, missionaries, colonial health officials, ethnographers, and many others. The oral methods used throughout antiquity and in many places today operate as both **abortifacient** and **emmenagogue.** These terms refer to anything that establishes regular menstrual cycles. Oral methods work to "make the blood come down," as some women in Louisiana say. Women knew ways to prevent implantation or bring on a period late in coming. These may also end a pregnancy in its early stages. Under these circumstances the line between birth control and abortion is blurry. What one drinks or eats achieves the desired result, that is, regular menstrual periods. Other teas or potions were chosen for their sterilizing properties or to help a woman conceive when she wanted to.

These data are confusing to those who perceive abrupt boundaries between preventing a pregnancy and ending a pregnancy, between wanting and not wanting a child. But historic and ethnographic accounts make no sharp distinctions between contraception and abortion. The Greek physician, Soranus, author of the first text on gynecology, illustrates this point in the box on page 68.

Greek Physician Soranus Speaks: Second Century A.D.

For if it is much more advantageous not to conceive than to destroy the embryo, one must consequently beware of having sexual intercourse at those periods which we said were suitable for conception. . .

Yet if conception has taken place, one must first, for 30 days, do the opposite of what we said earlier. In order that the embryo be separated, the woman should have [more violent exercise], walking about energetically and being shaken by means of draught animals; she should also leap energetically and carry things which are heavy beyond her strength. She should use diuretic decoctions which also have the power to bring on menstruation.

Source: Soranus, *Gynecology* (1965), 63,66.

In German folk medicine, teas of marjoram, parsley, or lavender are recommended for regular periods. Cherokee women desiring to remain sterile permanently were told to chew and swallow the roots of spotted cowbane for four consecutive days. Ancient Jewish rabbinic teachings speak of drinking a "cup of roots" to induce sterility. Arabic literature, some of the most extensive existing records, cited teas of sweet basil, weeping-willow leaves, pulp of pomegranates and alum, myrrh, rue, hellebore, or tampons impregnated with peppermint juice, pennyroyal, leek seeds, pepper, bindweed, and others.

Women in the Appalachian mountains of the United States and the Rajasthan state in India rely on the seeds of Queen Anne's lace, or the wild carrot plant, to keep from getting pregnant. Hippocrates, another Greek physician, swore by these seeds, which taken orally, establish a regular menstrual cycle. Pennyroyal is another plant widely cited as an abortifacient among women in the United States. Pomegranate, myrrh and the plant, Artemisia, named after Artemis, goddess and protector of childbirth, are also antifertility potions. Rue prepared as a tea is a traditional abortifacient and emmenagogue in many places in Latin America (Browner and Ortiz de Montellano 1986; Newman 1985; Riddle 1992).

All the literature contains reasons or motivations people have for controlling fertility. The grounds include a woman's poor health, repeated miscarriages or stillbirths, or her physical inability to care for a baby. Girls of tender years, women of advanced years, or those whose marriages were not on firm emotional or financial grounds are candidates for contraception. See the box on page 69 for anthropologist Hortense Powdermaker's discussion of the island of Lesu.

Women of Lesu, Melanesia

Fear of pain at birth is one reason for not wanting a child, and one woman who had had one child told me that she then ate the sterility leaves because she did not want to go through the birth pains again. Several other women told me they did not want children because it interfered with their dancing, which forms so large a part of ritual life, and which they so thoroughly enjoy. Still another reason advanced was that it interfered with their having sexual relations. No woman would ever admit this as her own reason, but some of them gave it to me as the motive for other women not wishing children. These were the only three reasons for not desiring children that I was able to secure, and it must be remembered that these women were in the minority. The larger number of women said that they had never eaten sterility or abortive leaves, and had no desire to. As has already been said, when a child is born nothing could exceed the affectionate care bestowed on an infant by his mother and the whole family. There are thus the two contradictory sentiments, desire for and rejection of motherhood existing side by side in the same society.

Source: Hortense Powdermaker, *Life in Lesu* (1933), 243. Collected in field trips, 1929–1930.

Many treatments mentioned are used with affirmations, prayers, and chants. They are often related to love potions or involve rituals of cleansing. Frequently, the same means are used to attract and keep a lover as to attract and keep a baby. Some of the techniques may have been more available to privileged women than to poorer women. Nonetheless, even the simplest kitchens or workrooms had the basic ingredients. We must carefully note that all the techniques had counterparts for those who had not conceived. The literature on control is just as much about wanting babies as it is for not wanting babies.

Some women in every human culture know about being barren. If the only route to adulthood, social status, physical safety, or personal worth is by having children, these are truly women who will try anything. Couples without children subjected themselves to tests, trials, or divinations to find the source of their infertility and thus a cure. The variety of ways to create a much-desired pregnancy involve the same use of plants, fruits, concoctions, potions, and rituals as preventing a pregnancy does. In a common form of magic worldwide, women make a doll or surrogate baby and carry it beneath their clothes. They may stage a delivery, wrap it in baby clothes, build a cradle, and sing to it. It is common to petition goddesses of fertility or saints associated with pregnancy and birth.

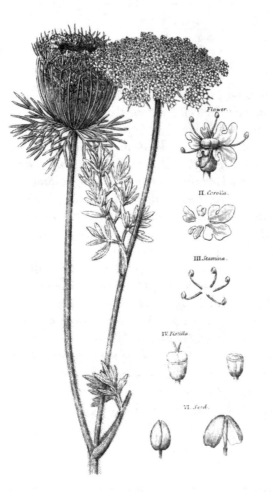

At many times and in many places, women chewed up or brewed the seeds of Queen Anne's Lace, the wild carrot plant, to prevent or end their pregnancies.

Keeping a pregnancy intact and having a safe delivery of a live and healthy baby also require attention and assistance. In Western traditions, the best medicines for preventing miscarriage was thyme, feverfew, and sage. Anglo-Saxon women who had suffered a miscarriage would step over the grave of a dead man and recite:

Be this my aid 'gainst hateful slow birth;

Be this my aid 'gainst dour monstrous birth;

Be this my aid 'gainst hateful misbirth. (Sha 1990:97)

These methods for controlling the life stream are not magic, superstition, or folklore. To the contrary, they argue for advanced knowledge of the properties of plants, for clever herbal gardens, and for practical gathering in marshes, forests, and fields. These methods speak of experimentation and knowledge transmitted verbally from generation to generation, as easily lost as painfully gained. Even so-called "folk beliefs" or "old wives' tales" illustrate knowledge and a desire for understanding and autonomy. It is entirely possible that in many places and many periods in the past, women knew more than they are credited with or than we know today.

If you think some of these recipes sound uncomfortable, tricky, or dangerous, then concentrate on this principle: "Women will do *anything*." Think about using so-called modern techniques. Or think about the alternatives.

Abortion

Many people are surprised to learn how universal abortion has been through human history. The sense I have from studying the historic and anthropological literature is that "they" (society, religion, husband, or family) usually want some kind of control. At the same time, "she" (a pregnant female) also wants control. Sometimes these motivations and desires coincide. Sometimes they do not. The alternatives and strategies at this point are the material of high drama. "They" could lock her up, marry her off at gunpoint, kill her or the baby, give the baby away, or threaten her with exile, stigma, or eternal damnation. "She" could commit suicide, do something in secret, lie, run away, conform, get married, or give the baby away.

On the island of Pohnpei in Micronesia, where I once did fieldwork, a pregnant woman may decide to have an abortion. She may feel that she is too young, having too much fun, and not yet ready to be a mother. Her friends and relatives might say, you should give the baby to us. Adoption on this island, as in much of the Pacific, is common and carries no stigma for women. Indeed, it is regarded as a positive contribution to others who do not have the babies they desire. In the past, women used abdominal massage to end a pregnancy. The procedure is effective although painful. Such decisions were accepted with regret; they were probably rare.

Anthropologist George Devereaux examined ethnographies for 400 preindustrial societies (1976). Each of the 400 groups knew about or practiced abortion in some form. There were many techniques for abortion reported: hard work; lifting or carrying heavy objects; climbing; jumping; starving; shaking a woman; or placing hot things on her abdomen or somehow causing bleeding. Massage or pressure through the abdominal wall is reliably reported from a number of groups, and from all evidence is safe although uncomfortable. This may include leaning on hard objects, rolling around, constricting or squeezing the abdomen, or being pulled through a forked tree. The types of instruments that can be introduced into the vagina are limited only by imagination. Knitting needles or coat hangers have their sharp equivalents in many if not most human cultures.

Here again is the consistent blurring of categories or interventions along the life stream. In some societies, it is said that hard, repetitive work and lifting or carrying heavy burdens can bring on a miscarriage, a spontaneous abortion. Yet doing such work is normal for millions of women. What is planned? What is unavoidable but welcomed? Devereaux noted that miscarriages occur because of physical assaults, through the malice of magic sent against a pregnant woman, or through women's unconscious motivations. It is often difficult to tell the difference between a miscarriage and an abortion. Women may believe an abortion attempt has ended a pregnancy never established.

There are literally thousands of reports of effective teas or potions from all over the world (Newman 1985; Himes 1970). Herbal remedies and a broad pharmacopeia are too commonly mentioned to be discounted. They are forerunners of birth control pills, RU 486, and the morning-after pills. Sometimes these pharmaceuticals "make the blood come down"; sometimes they prevent pregnancy in other ways; and sometimes they temporarily or permanently prevent pregnancy. Rates of miscarriages (or spontaneous abortions) are high at various times, at various places and for certain women. Because of this, we may give more credit or place more hope in these methods than they deserve. Nonetheless, oral abortifacients and contraceptives are probably the oldest and most widespread of all the techniques for desire and control.

Infanticide and Social Birth

This is a hard topic. Most of us condemn the killing of infants and children as morally wrong or as acts done by people not like us. But scholars know that human infanticide is widely practiced, in many places, in many periods of time, by many people for many reasons. Infanticide seems to occur primarily when it aids one parent, both parents, or other children to survive better, or where the infant itself has little chance of survival.

Look at the legends about Oedipus Rex, Moses, and Romulus and Remus; they were male babies abandoned to die. Greeks in classical times, as have other human societies, did away with weak, deformed, or unwanted children. People in other societies killed one or both twins, babies born too close to another sibling, or one born in some unusual manner, for example, under the wrong zodiac sign. Margaret Mead says the Arapesh sometimes resorted to infanticide if food were scarce, if there were several children, or if the father had died.

In China, Japan, India, and other places, girls were killed, "thinned out" like rice fields. In Europe, in various periods and places, dead newborns were a common sight floating down rivers or left in parks. Orphanages were founded to take in these children. Newborn babies, alive or dead, are found abandoned in cities all over the world; newspapers regularly print such stories.

Parents in hunting–gathering societies used infanticide to space children and to adjust a woman's workloads. We know that overpopulation, famine or other disasters, and power politics may require the sacrifice of selected children. Infanticide appears to be more common when the mother is very young or when, like the old woman in the shoe, "she had so many children she didn't know what to do." This does not mean it is casual or painless.

Anthropologists regard infanticide as a way to alter the reproductive stream at a point before the infant or child has the status of a real person, however that is locally defined.

In most societies, including Christian societies, personhood is conferred on infants via birth ceremonies. Human infants do not become legal entities or social beings until some adult or group of adults (e.g., parents, godparents, kinsmen, religious practitioners) have named, purified and/or blessed them in a rite that says 'This child belongs to us.' By this ceremony adults admit infants into their group and assume the responsibility of supporting and raising the babies they claim as their own. (Minturn 1989:93)

So **social birth** is the event, ceremony, ritual, or marked point in time when an infant child takes on or is given a cultural identity. This is always different from biological birth. The deaths of weak, illegitimate, excess, deformed, and unwanted infants are not defined as murder when the infants have not yet been born into a social world.

Once again, the boundaries are not as we in the West have defined them. The point at which life begins has many cultural definitions. Some people in the world believe that birth is the beginning of regular life. Others say that conception is the marker; yet others refer to some point in the pregnancy. In some cultures, life begins only when the infant is formally named or ritually incorporated. In some places, life is said to begin only after the first day, the first week, the first month, or the first year—depending on the culture. Before the child is accepted as a full member of the society, infanticide is possible. After a commitment, it is not. Seen in this light, it is safe to say that people in some cultures regard infanticide as an abortion late in the reproductive stream. The social statuses of fetuses, newborns, and young children are always and everywhere locked to broad social contexts.

This observation is not new: a burgeoning literature illuminates the links between abortion, childrearing, women's status, social stratification, child welfare, ethnic and gender discrimination, and changing relations between the sexes. The process through which young human lives come to be valued is derived in part from these factors, but personhood is also a function of cultural divisions in the life cycle, attitudes toward death, the social organization of descent and inheritance, and social systems of authority and achievement. (Morgan 1989:97)

Who makes the decision? Birth attendants may decide in cases of physical or mental defects in the infant or when something is drastically wrong with the mother. Very often the family decides; but in the majority of cases, the father or the mother of the infant decides.

It is more common to throw away girl babies. Perhaps their families believe it is too expensive to raise them and give them a dowry or wedding. Perhaps the investment in nursing and feeding them would be better spent on older children or sons that might follow. Doing away with daughters may be done in such a covert fashion that the patterns show up only in statistics from the entire population. In many countries of the world, there is an excess of female infant mortality over male; that means that noticeably more females die in infancy and childhood than do males.

Anthropologists have also studied infanticide resulting from aggressive neglect, abuse, or circumstances where women have inadequate support from partners, family, or other sources. In many cases, parents favor some children over others. Where resources are inadequate, one child may be neglected or parents may fail to invest time, attention, medical care, or other resources in a child. Some children just "fail to thrive" or "lack the will to fight." Their parents say, "She is not for this world," or "He's just another angel baby gone to heaven." This lack of investment in children is common. Although outright infanticide is outlawed in most of the world, scholars tell us that neglect and abuse are abundant. As anthropologist Susan Scrimshaw notes:

> Perhaps the greatest tragedy of all in today's world is that modern contraceptives and even induced abortion have not sufficiently replaced infanticide as a means of fertility control. Further, infanticide has been superseded in many societies by abandonment, neglect, and differential care rather than methods of fertility control less costly in terms of lives and resources. . . . Ironically, the decline of infanticide may result in more suffering for older infants and children, and even adults, than when an infant's fate, be it life or death, was determined swiftly, early and irrevocably. (Scrimshaw 1984:462)

Some families are unable or unwilling to offer biological support and emotional support to children. Sometimes this kills as effectively, although more slowly, as exposure of infants to wild animals or numbing cold.

The beginnings and the ends of the life stream, the physical sensations and the emotions women experience are culturally rather than biologically defined. This is important. People in human cultures may reckon the beginning of pregnancy from ovulation, which provides the egg; from intercourse, which provides the sperm; from conception, which unites them; or from implantation, which gives the united parts a habitat. Women in many cultures reckon the beginning of pregnancy from a missed period, from the first felt movement, or from the moment they become aware of a spirit or ghost entering their bodies.

Comparative Childbirth

Childbirth, too, is far more than a physiological or biological event, far more than just a rite of passage for a woman or a day for a child to celebrate. Cultural values become awesomely visible at each human birth. Giving birth, however, is not just reproduction; it is **social production.** That means that each act of giving birth reproduces the society, the belief systems, and all the unspoken but powerful connections within that culture. Each birth carries the message: "This event shows how we do things in this culture and what we really believe about life and about each other."

Women throughout all human history and prehistory typically gave birth to babies in their own domestic surroundings and with the help of their friends, relatives, or other women with special experience and knowledge. This is a very important fact of life, but easy to forget. Most of us have not participated in such a birth and tend to project contemporary technologies, hospitals, and personal issues onto other cultures.

The first anthropologist to describe human births in crosscultural perspective was Brigitte Jordan. The following summary of births she witnessed in Mayan families living in Yucatan, Mexico, comes from her pioneering fieldwork on childbirth in four cultures. The midwife in this example is named Doña Juana; she is about sixty years old and the widowed head of an extended matrifocal household. The woman she aids in delivery is characteristic of the women Jordan and her colleague observed. The key point of this account is to see it as a social event, not a medical event.

Midwife and Mother

A pregnant woman in Yucatan sees her midwife several times during the pregnancy. They talk at length about her reproductive history, attitudes about birth, and who shall attend and assist. The midwife assesses her patient. What will be her attitude toward pain? Would she like traditional practices like prayers or burning rosemary to ward off evil spirits? The midwife gives the pregnant woman soothing massages, comforting touches, and helpful advice in the form of case histories and stories. Together they determine the approximate date of delivery.

Massage is the central event of the prenatal visit. As the midwife spreads oil on the woman's abdomen and massages her back, they chat and gossip. The midwife probes to feel the position of the baby's head; she explains why she is doing deep massage. Doña Juana, like many midwives around the world, believes that pregnancy is a normal state of things; she does not treat the mother-to-be as sick or her condition as a pathology.

Like many midwives around the world, Doña Juana does not do vaginal examinations; she believes that midwives should keep hands and everything else out of the birth canal. She is, however, an expert at shifting a baby that is not lying head-down. Sometimes a baby rests in a bottoms-down position (breech) or on its side (transverse). In a method called external cephalic inversion, a midwife can turn the baby with strong even pressure on the mother's abdomen. Then the infant's head points down. This procedure averts a Caesarean section, a hospital birth, a protracted labor or a dead baby, all undesirable outcomes for Mayan families.

A Mayan woman's first birth is at her mother's compound; the rest are in her own home. An area in the sleeping part of the compound is screened off and the other household activities go on about the birth scene. When someone comes to tell Doña Juana that a labor is underway, she grabs her equipment. Doña Juana greets the family and checks the mother, her contractions, feelings, and special needs. She gives her a massage; this feels good to the laboring woman and yields important information for the midwife about the position of the baby.

The midwife shows the laboring mother how to use a birthing chair, how to hold on to a rope, how to twine her arms around a husband's neck, and how to push hard when the time comes. Doña Juana says that every woman must find her own style. The midwife's function is only to help. In the later stages of labor, the woman stretches crosswise on the hammock. At the end, she decides her position.

Women in labor are entitled to the support of their husbands, their mothers, and often other women summoned to the birth, such as sisters, sisters-in-law, mothers-in-law, good friends, or godmothers. The women run errands, cheer on, scold, and offer physical as well as emotional support to the about-to-be-delivered woman. In Yucatan a husband is said to experience both the birth and his wife's pain rather than merely witnessing it. This is believed to lead him to **cuidar**, to care for, his wife after the birth. The verb is also a local euphemism for spacing the arrival of babies by abstinence or withdrawal.

A trusted person supports the woman's body and helps her push at the high point of contractions. Another person may rub her abdomen, legs, or back. If the labor slows down, the midwife may give the woman a raw egg to swallow; the vomiting that results usually enhances contractions. Someone may blow on her head to give strength through long contractions or help hold her nose and mouth shut for greater pressure during the pushes. Those in attendance chant with rhythm and words that rise and fall in time to the contractions. This is called "birth talk."

> *Having a baby is clearly regarded as work. The mother is always expected to do her part, though she may become discouraged, even somewhat panicked. Although the expectation is of a quick, fairly easy birth, at least some pain is recognized as a normal part of bearing a child. It figures in the birth stories that have been told all along, preparing the mother for what is to come. Consequently, she receives little sympathy if she complains. (Jordan 1993:38)*

A laboring woman may be reminded that the baby is at the center of the pain and that pushing hard is simply her job at that time. When the baby is "at the door" (its head begins to emerge), the midwife grasps it firmly. When the body emerges, she places the baby on the mother's lap. She announces its gender and watches until the umbilical cord is emptied of blood. Generally, she waits until the placenta is delivered completely before cutting the cord. The women sponge off the mother and help her rest comfortably back lengthwise in her hammock.

The midwife and birth attendants cauterize the stump of the umbilical cord with a candle flame. They bathe, dress, diaper, and swaddle the baby tightly. They say swaddling makes its legs straight and offers security like its home in the womb. Doña Juana will pierce the ears of a newborn girl for earrings. Because the mother is resting safely and the baby looks fine, the mood of the household is light. Their talk turns to practical matters, and those who are hungry will eat.

The period immediately after a birth is regarded in every human culture as liminal, suspended or potentially dangerous. It is certainly not an ordinary time. As a result, humans customarily do things that honor the event and avert the dangers, however these are defined. In Yucatan, spirits from the bush may bring harm to the mother and infant so they remain inside and take various precautions to keep the spirits at bay. The midwife checks every day or so; she sponges off the baby with warm water or oil and examines its navel, puts more alcohol on it to prevent the infant's illness or the death that can result from improper care of the stump.

Although she does not need to examine the mother, the midwife gives advice about nursing, especially to a first-time mother. Mayan mothers begin nursing minutes after their babies' births and nurse whenever the babies fret. Babies are held most of the time, first by their mothers and then by other family members. Bottle–feeding has increased in Yucatan, as in most places in the world, but is generally a supplement rather a replacement for the breast. On the twentieth day, the midwife gives the mother another massage and finishes it by binding her abdomen tightly with a long cotton cloth. The new mother can return to work.

More Facts of Life-Giving

The birth described above is a far more generic human and female experience than are technologically assisted hospital births in the United States. It testifies more to the norm or to modal events than anything most of us know or that doctors are taught in medical schools. So what can we conclude?

Fact of life: Birth practices are rigidly shaped. People have strong opinions about what should go on and what that means. We believe that certain practices are absolutely right; furthermore, the mother and baby are in danger if they are not done in the prescribed manner.

> It is therefore difficult to separate, within any given cultural setting, what is physiological necessity and what is social production. Doña Juana, for example, considers breaking the membranes dangerous and unnatural, while American obstetricians find this practice useful and routinely advisable in light of their conceptions of the physiology of the birth process. (Jordan 1993:45)

Women who help others in birth are another fact of life. In all human cultures, we find birth attendants and support systems. The crosscultural record is very clear; we cannot overestimate the benefits of caring human companionship during labor. There are specialists, like midwives or physicians, and nonspecialists, such as the laboring woman's family or friends. Sometimes helpers are called **doulas,** a Greek word meaning "a woman who serves women." A doula typically provides emotional support and expert guidance from mid-pregnancy through delivery and the adjustments afterward. The empathy, collaboration, active coparticipation, or colaboring of other women is believed in most human cultures to contribute to the safety and the special qualities of giving birth. A woman who has helped to birth a baby may be more willing to care for that child if something happens to its mother. Attending a woman through this sacred, liminal, scary, and suspended time probably helps her develop skills as a mother and contributes to her survival.

Another fact of life: Most of the humans who ever lived on this planet were born in a place we would call "at home." Where a birth takes place determines whether the woman can walk around during labor, can choose her own positions, can select the people present, can be with her infant at will, or whether professionals will make these decisions for her. The technology of birth for our species has involved only ordinary items found in any household. A sharp instrument to cut the umbilical cord has been the most important article of a midwife's kit throughout human history. Soft cloth or absorbent fibers are useful for cleaning. I point these facts out at some length because most readers of this book tend to think that hospital births are the normal thing, the safest thing, the best thing, the status thing, or the progressive thing to do.

So we could ask: What is the prevailing attitude about labor in any given culture? Is it "wait and see" or "Let's get this show on the road"? Does labor ebb and flow like the tides? If so, one does not hurry it. Or does labor progress in a mechanical momentum? If so, then failure to progress on a schedule is grounds for intervention. Who offers information, when, and what kind? How is pain defined? What do people really mean when they say "natural"? Is pain in childbirth decreed by some ancestral god; is it women's lot in life? Is pain avoidable? For example, American women seem to feel quite strongly about pain: in repeated studies, they opt for reducing pain to the point of not feeling it at all while remaining as conscious as medication permits (Jordan 1993:80).

Who owns a birth? Who has the power to make key decisions? Who is delivering the baby: the laboring mother or the medical specialist? The issue of birth position is probably the best example of how these questions get answered. For assorted reasons, the standard practice in American childbirth is the **lithotomy position:** The woman lies on her back with her legs in the air. Now that anthropologists have looked seriously at birthing practices around the world, we know that this particular position, almost an article of religious faith, is known only in the United States and in a few countries to which we have exported our medical standards. Laboring women do not seem to choose this position spontaneously. Combinations of lying down and squatting, sitting-lying down one side or the other, or semi-sitting with support of a helper or chair, are far more common. Some studies show that walking around and sitting up, changing postures frequently, and moving from one side to the other, eases and shortens labor and the passage of the baby through the birth canal. But the problems and disadvantages of the lithotomy position has not altered its prevalence. This peculiar cultural interpretation of how women give birth works against gravity, makes pushing much harder, and thus may result in irregular, weaker, less frequent contractions. The lithotomy position is most advantageous for the professional birth attendants and their machinery.

In the United States, a typical birth is in a hospital attended by a physician and other paid professionals whom the mother may or may not have met. The orientation is professional rather than personal, and involves increasing amounts of disputed and rather mysterious technology. The woman is a patient who signs over most of the decision-making power to hospital personnel. The physician in charge is concerned, among other things, about administering drugs for pain relief or for other conditions and the hospital policies that relate to deliveries. There is a sharp tendency to think of the patient as "being delivered" rather than as her doing the work of giving birth, and another tendency to think of pregnancy and birth as an illness, to make it a curable pathology. Anthropologists call this the **medicalization of childbirth.**

This is not to say that Mayan practices are automatically better, somehow more "natural," or should be imitated by others. It is to say, however, that they express the values of social production within that culture. Furthermore, they provide a sharp contrast to technologically assisted hospital births in other cultures.

Many anthropologists believe that being a midwife is the world's oldest job, craft, or professional specialization. We are not surprised that metaphors about birth and rebirth are profoundly part of mythology, spiritualism, and religious or healing practices everywhere in the world.

Breast or Bottle: The Big Controversy

In many circles worldwide, the controversies over feeding infants, breasts versus bottles, have become another example about women and the use or ownership of our bodies. As everyone knows, breast-feeding or nursing is in decline everywhere in the world. With international marketing and sales of lactational surrogates, more and more babies are fed with bottles, formulas, and purchased food. This contemporary situation contrasts sharply with traditional societies where all mothers nursed infants for lengthy periods. Embedded in these arguments are two competing viewpoints about women that I would like to summarize briefly.

The first is the "best for babies" approach. Members of the medical and international health establishments believe that breast-feeding prevents malnutrition and disease (Jelliffe and Jelliffe 1978). The World Health Organization recommends that mothers breast-feed for one to two years, adding two meals of solids by nine months. They note that breast milk is more sanitary than local water supplies and provides antibodies and immunity to diseases as well as providing "nature's most perfect food." Lactational surrogates, or prepared baby formulas in bottles, may not offer the same nourishment.

In this viewpoint, babies come first. Proponents of universal breast-feeding believe that educational campaigns are necessary to "encourage" or "motivate" women to nurse their babies. Women should not "return to work." They say that breast-feeding gives emotional and sensual gratification to both mother and child. Women have the equipment and the abilities for it. Nursing is good; women should do it routinely, regularly, and for a long time. Not nursing is somehow vain or selfish and such mothers, the campaigns hint, are inadequate or endangering their children's physical and emotional health. Romantics use soft, sensual images of motherly love and smiling babies. Practical people point to the immense financial savings for national economies when families do not buy formulas and baby food from international corporations. Surely, breast milk that is sterile, safe, and available is the best way, dare we say, the "natural way," to feed an infant.

Wait a minute, other people say. There is a second viewpoint in the breast–bottle controversy. Nursing is another kind of women's work. Looking only at the welfare of infants ignores the multiple roles of women. What about the effects of discrimination against women? Are nursing mothers treated better than other women? If not, then nursing may literally be a drain of limited resources. **Maternal depletion** is the term for severe breakdowns in women's health when they are chronically deprived of food or other necessary resources. Frequent pregnancies and prolonged nursing contribute to this condition. Pregnant or lactating women and female children simply get less to eat in many countries.

> *How safe is lengthy breast-feeding for the over-worked, underfed, multiparous mothers of many developing societies? What is the relationship between overwork, undernutrition, high fertility, lengthy breast-feeding and the high morbidity and low life expectancy of women in many developing countries? What consequences can a mother's ill health and early death have for the rest of her family? Is it possible that less breast-feeding might improve her life chances and those of her family? (Maher 1992:5)*

The key issue for survival of babies is the income of its parents; the key issue for survival for the mothers is access to resources, so she can survive to care for the baby. Studies show that babies stay well when their parents have a good income and what money can provide: piped-in water, toilets, sewers, garbage collection, adequate housing and medical care, and above all, education for its mother. The determining variable for survival is not whether the baby is breast-fed or bottle-fed; it is poverty, class, and women's abilities to negotiate.

Throughout most of history and in most places, women carried babies or made arrangements for them. Child care is the dependent variable; it is everywhere adjusted to any mother's work. For example, in places where women routinely sleep with their babies, they can nurse them all night. In Euro-American culture, conjugal requirements, and notions of hygiene, safety, privacy, and individuality, make sleeping with a husband the norm. This means weaning the baby or eliminating the night feeding as soon as possible.

Nursing is structured differently in cultures where people emphasize parents, children, and extended kin ties rather than couple ties. In these cultures, there are various idioms and social structures that emphasize "milk kinship," that is, those nursed by the same woman or the same set of women have special and reciprocal links to each other. This is often the idiom used to explain matrilineal clans. In these contexts, women who were sisters or friends nursed each other's babies in a kind of reciprocity.

The best evidence for nursing as another kind of women's work (valued or not) is **wet-nursing.** If a mother dies in childbirth or cannot (for a variety of reasons) feed her infant, she finds another lactating woman. Before nursing bottles and baby formulas, being a wet nurse was a job for women. Milk was a commodity and women's bodies were the means of production.

People in many countries spell out the duties of a woman to husband and children far more than they define the duties of a man to care for his children and his children's mother. Adult males are often privileged to more food, better quality food, or access and control of cash income. If feeding infants is women's work, then bottle-feeding or other substitutes may make economic sense. The cost does not come directly from a woman's body.

Breast-feeding, like having periods or giving birth, is not just a "natural" thing women do. It is not just biology. It is not only nutrition for infants. For example, many women reading this book have never spent time with a nursing mother, including their own. I talked with teenagers in New Orleans who were both charmed and embarrassed by the knowledge that breasts could be used to feed babies. They thought of breasts only in connection with sex. And what if nations counted breast-feeding as part of national productivity statistics and rewarded women for their work? What about the World Health Organization and other international agencies that promote breast-feeding but do not address the social and economic conditions that may make it impossible or dangerous to the health of mothers? Nursing is not the same experience for all women across all cultures at all times in history. So breasts and bottles are equally cultural.

Social Women in Biological Bodies:
Some Conclusions

The ideas in this chapter challenge the notion of "natural." There seems to be nothing in the life cycles of women that cultural forces do not influence, mediate, or transform. Indeed, the notion of "natural" often functions as a putdown of women in other cultures; somehow, all of us are "primitive" women. Some of us feel guilty if we do not or cannot conform. Moreover, women are often conscripted into motherhood, wifedom, and high fertility. We do not "naturally" fall into these conditions. Many women love nursing their babies. Others dislike it or do it in a perfunctory manner. Others want to nurse but cannot, for reasons that range from physiological to economic. Some women want babies; some don't. Most of us will do anything.

When we speak of women's lives we should ask, Who is taking care of this female person? Who is mothering the new mother, aiding the young maiden, or modeling aging? Women need advice and the company of other women at all stages of the life stream, before, during, and after pregnancy, for labor and delivery and during lactation. When women are placed at the center of the analysis, the life stream of reproduction has a new meaning. With all due respect to biology, women construct our lives from the raw materials of specific cultural habits, practices, structures, and accidents of history. There is a difference between saying "a baby has been born" and "a woman has just given birth" (Raphael 1975). Becoming a mother, or **matrescence,** is not just about having babies. It is about women's lives, about women's work, and once again, about who owns women's bodies.

The next chapter concerns females in primate societies, human and nonhuman. We will use weaning, sex, matrifocal families, and friendships to consider the contributions of innovative field research and open more questions about "nature versus nurture" in the lives of women.

Some Very Important Books to Read

The materials in this chapter only establish a starting place for learning about the women in our bodies. There is a vast literature in anthropology, in other disciplines, and in the popular press around these topics. Begin with Emily Martin's *The Woman in the Body: A Cultural Analysis of Reproduction* (1992). Martin neatly confounds medical science as she shows the different ways American women look at and feel about our bodies. Then turn to Faye Ginsberg's *Contested Lives: The Abortion Debate in An American Community* (1989), a balanced, sensitive, and award-winning book on women and the conflicts over abortion in the United States. Add a riveting book by Helena Ragoné called *Surrogate Motherhood: Conception in the Heart* (1994); this fascinating and fine-grained study shows how surrogacy is transforming the traditional meanings of motherhood in America.

One of the most meaningful areas in all of women's studies is childbirth and the medicalization or industrialization of births. The following are only a few of the books and studies in anthropology that use a comparative, biocultural, and female-centered approach to research and policy in childbirth practices. Robbie Davis-Floyd's *Birth as an American Rite of Passage* (1992) and the new expanded edition of Brigitte Jordan's classic, *Birth in Four Cultures: A Cross-Cultural Investigation of Childbirth in Yucatan, Holland, Sweden, and the United States* (1993), are probably the best studies in anthropology about the machinery and meaning of giving birth in contemporary and comparative cultures. Then consider the historical experience in the United States with Judith Leavitt's excellent book, *Brought to Bed: Child-Bearing in America* 1750-1950 (1986). Two special issues of leading journals in anthropology are also extremely helpful: Michael Lamb edited "Birth Management: Historical and Biocultural Perspectives," *Human Nature* (1993 and 1994); and Robert Hahn edited "The Anthropology of American Obstetrics," *Medical Anthropology Quarterly* (1987). Carol MacCormack has a new edition of her classic collection of articles about the cultural shaping of human fertility and childbirth: *Ethnography of Fertility and Birth* (1994).

To find out more about "child-survival," you can do no better than two books by Nancy Scheper-Hughes, *Child Survival: Anthropological Perspectives on the Treatment and Maltreatment of Children* (1987), and *Death Without Weeping: The Violence of Everyday Life in Brazil* (1992). The following books on breast-feeding are different but important approaches to one of the key biocultural arenas of women's lives. Vanessa Maher edited *The Anthropology of Breast-Feeding: Natural Law or Social Contract* (1992); and Dana Raphael, who is head of the Human Lactation Center, edited a now-classic volume, *Breast-Feeding and Food Policy in a Hungry World* (1979). Penny Van Esterik's *Beyond the Breast Bottle Controversy* (1989) is an excellent summary of this important debate about women.

John Riddle has written the best book in decades about women's medicine and reproductive control in ancient times: *Contraception and Abortion from the Ancient World to the Renaissance* (1992). Not having children when we want them is just as much an issue in women's lives as having too many or having them at the wrong times. For a distinguished comparative study of women's desire for control in another culture, I suggest Marcia Inhorn's *Quest for Conception: Gender, Infertility, and Egyptian Medical Traditions* (1994). To learn more about the ceremonies for Navajo women's coming of age, Charlotte Frisbee's *Kinaaldá: A Study of the Navaho's Girl Puberty Ceremony* (1967) is the source.

Anita Roddick of the Body Shop sponsored a beautifully illustrated and fascinating book called *Mama Toto: A Celebration of Birth* (1991); Carroll Dunham and the Body Shop Team are the joint authors. And last, finish off with a funny, amazing, painful, and always stimulating summary of what "experts" have told women about ourselves and our bodies by Barbara Ehrenreich and Deidre English: *For Her Own Good: 150 Years of the Expert's Advice to Women* (1978).

Chapter Four

Primates Are Us

Monkeys, Mothers, and "Nature"

J n 1973 anthropologist Jane Lancaster published an article called "In Praise of the Achieving Female Monkey." She said that females are worth noting and mothers matter. Given the climate of the time, that was a heartening message. In the article, Jane said that scientists were only ratifying their own folk beliefs when they talked about passive female behaviors or dominating male hierarchies. Like other primatologists, or people who study primates, she talked about the stability of matrifocal units, female coalitions, and the work that mothers do.

As a result of work such as Jane Lancaster's, there are two central motifs in this chapter:

First: A revolution in evolutionary biology and physical anthropology started in the 1960s when women began to study groups of apes and monkeys, societies of nonhuman primates. What did women as researchers do that was different from what men had done? What can we learn from their research?

Second: As a result of this new scientific consciousness, females in primate societies became the lively subjects of investigation, not just fixed objects in a male world. What can monkeys and apes teach us about being female on the planet or about being animals in complex and gendered environments?

To answer these questions, we will look at a generation of female scholars who did extensive long-term or longitudinal research on primates living in free-ranging groups. They developed sophisticated and innovative techniques of research and applied them to issues in evolution and contemporary life. Most important, these four decades of research have made females in primate societies visible. Past research tended to cast females in supporting roles, while males performed at center stage.

> *In part because nonhuman primates cannot be interviewed, it took years of patient observation to recognize that in most primate societies males come and go, playing only cameo roles, whereas females remain to carry the plot. (Fedigan and Fedigan 1989:42)*

Before the 1960s and a generation of female scholars, one of the most popular portraits of primate societies showed males in rigid hierarchies competing with each other for sex. Females dedicated themselves to the care of infants and the sexual needs of dominant males. Sex was the glue that held the groups together. Males needed it; females had it. Everything else followed.

Females were passive or squabbled among themselves. But for rigid and competitive male hierarchies, things would simply fall apart. Females were sexual receptacles or the primate equivalent of a stay-at-home helpmate for he-man the hunter. If primates were like this, it was thought, so were humans. Political domination was the "natural" way for males to act. Domestic passivity was the "natural" way for females to act.

Phenomena situated in "nature" or "in the wild" are good. Like certain breakfast cereals, they are healthy for you. If you resist or differ, you are "unnatural," probably sick in some way. You can locate many other models and myths in American culture as examples of this kind of "natural" reasoning. These views, quite frankly, looked like projections from television shows from the 1950s in the United States, Judeo-Christian myths of creation, or King Kong and Tarzan narratives.

It took years of patient observation to understand the hard work and social skills primate mothers exercise to raise their offspring or the friendship and cooperation males and females display.

Primatologists now say that members of most primate societies are biologically and socially related to each other through females of the group. They form **matrifocal units** or groups that center on mothers. These genealogies last through subsequent generations and form the stable core of group life. Of course, there is competition (the degree and significance varies according to whom we read). There is also intelligence, thinking, manipulation, strategies and feelings we are tempted to call love, jealousy, trust, affection, and grief.

The grand theory on which most of this research rested was, of course, Charles Darwin's. He wrote about the principles of natural selection, or the adaptation of animals to their environment; he wrote that the only ultimate survival was in producing offspring and raising them to adulthood so they could do the same thing. To him, the most telling features of evolution were males competing with each other for the sexual favors of females, and females choosing which male to favor. In the years since Darwin proposed this theory, the key element of females choosing mates somehow got lost. But a contemporary generation of scholars studying the lives of chimpanzees, baboons, and other primate species have restored female agency or action.

Today scientists in the field of evolutionary biology or physical anthropology use the theories of Charles Darwin to answer questions about human origins and the evolution of species. But applying theories of evolutionary biology to the meaning of gender generates controversies and sexual or biopolitics. In popular consciousness, we are often tempted to turn to "nature" to explain or justify human behavior. Women are particularly susceptible to this kind of interpretation.

So the goal of this chapter is to give you a solid framework buttressed by some fascinating examples about the words "natural" or "naturally." You will never again see "nature" in the same old way. Meanwhile, look for some central themes in the following examples drawn from chimpanzee and baboon societies: mothers and matrifocal units; sex and reproduction; friendships and social skills; and males and females at work, together and apart.

Studying Chimpanzees

Why start with chimpanzees? First, genetic analysis reveals the close kinship in evolution between chimps and humans. Second, chimpanzee social activities and behaviors may resemble our early ancestors. Third, and most important, watching animals is one of the best ways of confronting and getting beyond cultural biases. But fourth, the behavioral scientist with the most name-recognition in the world today is Jane Goodall.

Jane Goodall has been observing chimpanzee groups in Tanzania since July of 1960. No researcher has ever worked this long or presented an animal species as individuals with feelings and complex social behaviors. She was one of the first Western scientists to observe primates in what many call "the wild" or "natural" settings. Women who followed often worked under tough, arduous, even dangerous field conditions. Their long-term or longitudinal research provided insights that short field stays or studies of captive animals did not provide. Scholars like Goodall, who write for ordinary people, are often criticized in the profession. In fact, the *National Geographic Society* articles and documentaries about Jane were both popular and popularized. But her research was the first of its kind and the model for much more that was to follow.

Chimpanzees are great apes (not monkeys). They are **omnivorous,** which means they eat a wide variety of plant and animal foods. Chimps have tools. That is, they modify and use materials—such as leaves for sponges, twigs as probes to obtain termites, rocks and sticks as hammers to crack nuts. They eat meat when they can catch smaller animals. Individuals in small groups range over many square miles each day in search of food. They do not share food with each other in the way our early ancestors probably did with salads, potlucks, buffets, or picnics.

Chimpanzees have a flexible social organization called fission–fusion. This means that the composition of groups will vary from day to day.

> *Fusion and fission in chimpanzee society are carried to the limits of flexibility; individuals of either sex have almost complete freedom to come and go as they wish. The membership of temporary parties is constantly changing. Adults and adolescents can and do forage, travel, and sleep on their own, sometimes for days at a time. This unique organization means, for one thing, that day-to-day social experiences of a chimpanzee are far more variable than those of almost any other primate. (Goodall 1986:147)*

Individuals relate to each other in shifting and complex patterns of kinship and friendship. Chimps communicate with postures, gestures, facial expressions, and vocalizations in ways human observers are not even close to interpreting. These skills allow them to negotiate unique or complicated social situations.

Chimps, like other primates, concentrate their social life in the mothers and children and among siblings. These bonds endure for life. Female chimpanzees spend most of their lives either pregnant or lactating. They invest more time and energy in rearing offspring than males do.

Chimpanzees, like humans, practice **grooming.** Grooming is the intensely social activities of cleaning and handling each other's hair and skin; this keeps primates clean and gives pleasure. The groomer removes dirt, parasites, scabs, and other debris. This smooths thick, coarse hair and keeps wounds clean. The contribution of grooming to health is obvious. All primates, including humans, groom each other, our mates, and our offspring. Should anyone doubt the importance of grooming among *Homo sapiens,* they are advised to remember haircuts, manicures, squeezing our beloved's pimples, oils or sunscreens applied to each other's backs, or the mothers who straighten our collars and push a lock of hair from our eyes.

Jane Goodall

Jane Goodall was waiting tables in England and saving money to travel. She found a job in Kenya, East Africa, and contacted Louis B. Leakey, the famous paleontologist. He suggested that she study chimpanzees and arranged preliminary funding for her. He believed that women, even untrained ones, would bring much-needed sensitivities to field research.

So Jane and her mother went to Tanzania and set up camp in the Gombe Stream Reserve. For two years, she worked day after day with only occasional sightings of chimpanzees. But she persisted quietly until the chimpanzees became accustomed or habituated to her presence. Within four years she had acquired a chimp mentor named David Greybeard, started to accumulate systematic data and built the Gombe Stream Research Centre. Students began to come to the center to study chimpanzees and other animal species. Meanwhile, Jane had to finish a graduate degree and work to establish scholarly credibility in a tightly controlled and masculine academic world.

In those days, animals were not supposed to have feelings. Neither were scientists. Feelings were something only emotional women had. Jane argued with her advisers. She insisted that the chimps she observed did feel sad, happy, or afraid. Jane claimed that chimps set goals, made plans, and worked cleverly around the obstacles or opportunities presented to them. In her writings, she referred to animals by name and by the personal pronouns, "she" or "he." A chimpanzee was never "it."

Flo

Primatologists assign personal names to animals they observe. This practice allows them to follow individuals and their genealogies. Figure 4.1 shows the genealogy or family chart for a chimpanzee female named Flo. Chimpanzee and other primate genealogies are always traced matrilineally, that is, through the mother's line. This kind of kinship in human or nonhuman primates is also called **matrifocal**. The reasons for these terms will be apparent when we come to Flo's sex life.

Flo was an animal Jane describes as bulbous-nosed, ragged-eared, and ugly by any human standards.

> *Even in those days Flo looked very old. She appeared frail, with but little flesh on her bones, and thinning hair that was brown rather than black. When she yawned we saw that her teeth were worn right down to the gums. We soon found out that her character by no means matched her appearance: she was aggressive, tough as nails, and easily the most dominant of all the females at that time.*
> *(Goodall 1971:92)*

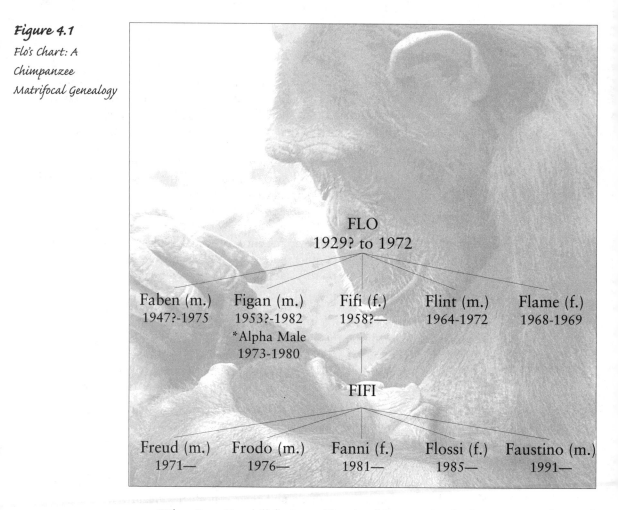

Figure 4.1

Flo's Chart: A
Chimpanzee
Matrifocal Genealogy

FLO
1929? to 1972

Faben (m.)	Figan (m.)	Fifi (f.)	Flint (m.)	Flame (f.)
1947?-1975	1953?-1982	1958?—	1964-1972	1968-1969
	*Alpha Male			
	1973-1980			

FIFI

Freud (m.)	Frodo (m.)	Fanni (f.)	Flossi (f.)	Faustino (m.)
1971—	1976—	1981—	1985—	1991—

When Jane Goodall first met Flo, the chimp mother had two sons, Faben and Figan, and a daughter, Fifi. Flo had begun to wean Fifi from nursing at her breasts. Chimpanzee mothers start to wean their infants when they are about four years old. Weaning is a major trial, a turning point for both mothers and infants in chimp society. A mother tries to prevent her child both from suckling and from riding on her back. She distracts her offspring with tickling or heavy play, but the little one often responds with temper tantrums. This stage of chimp growth is stressful, particularly to inexperienced mothers.

But Fifi had learned many skills from her mother and was ready for some independence. As chimp children do, Fifi wandered farther from her mother's protection as she played with other youngsters most of the day. Fifi started to eat a grownup diet, the kinds of food she watched her mother pick each day. Fifi no longer needed to ride on her mother's back as they traveled the mountain trails in search of food. She still jumped in her mother's lap when startled. They groomed each other daily.

When Flo was no longer nursing Fifi, she stopped lactating and came into heat, or **estrus**. This means that she was ovulating, and all other things being equal, could get pregnant at this point in her **estrous cycle.** Chimpanzee females have estrous cycles and menarche just like humans do. The difference, however, is that chimpanzee females have sex, indeed want to have sex, only during the period they are ovulating. This period of sexual desires and activity is fairly dramatic. The hidden agenda is that they can conceive at this time.

The skin of Flo's genital area swelled and turned a bright shade of pink. This sent out a signal to males: Flo was "in the pink." Ardent suitors knew that courting and mating could begin. Males saw the swelling; they often put out a finger to touch and then sniffed their finger. Adolescents and other low-ranking males followed Flo around, but in unrequited passion. Flo could pick and choose. She was extremely popular with the senior adult males, who vied with each other for her favors. Though intercourse itself lasts only ten or fifteen seconds, the public dramas of sex lasted for days. Jane Goodall once counted fifty copulations for Flo in a twenty-four-hour period. Despite her looks, Flo was a chimpanzee sex pot.

Chimpanzee females are generally "in the pink," pregnant, or lactating through much of their adult lives. Unless they are in the pink, however, they have no interest in sex. The literature on primates calls this attitude **sexually proceptive.** The term recognizes the active part females play in selecting, enticing, or rejecting certain males. Females conceive at the peak of the estrous cycle. So there is an evolutionary purpose for this dynamic combination of simultaneous sexual swelling, interest in sex, and ability to conceive. Together they enhance the chances for pregnancy. Completed pregnancies and effective child rearing, that is, rearing offspring who themselves grow up to reproduce, are the heart of what Darwin defined as successful adaptation and evolution.

The infant Flo conceived in this round of sexual adventures was named Flint; he is one of the best-described and observed babies in all the scientific literature. Neither scientists nor mother, however, will ever know the identity of his biological father.

Flo was an excellent mother. Her older sons romped nearby in the rough-and-tumble play of juvenile chimps. Fifi watched intently, ready to touch, groom, or hold the infant. Flint treated his mother's body as a playground. At Flint's first whoop of distress, Flo gathered him up and kissed him in the open-mouthed smooching chimps favor. She slept at night with him in a nest she built in a tree, and carried him against her chest during her travels, supporting him with one hand when he needed it.

When Flint was not quite five years of age, Flo came into estrus again. She was pink for only four or five days and Flint was not allowed to suckle. In the sixth month of her pregnancy, her milk dried up. During these periods as well as during her earlier attempts to wean him, Flint had acted like "a spoiled brat." He threw temper tantrums; he clung, he whimpered, he bullied her for attention. Flo tried to comfort and reassure Flint even as she encouraged him to give up his dependency. Flint appeared to accept the birth of a younger sister, Flame. But within a few months, he reverted to the clingy, irritated, and irritating brat he had been. When baby Flame was six months old, a flu-like illness swept the Gombe. Flo became ill and Flame died. Flint was once again the baby. Even at the age of six in chimp years, Flint clung, climbed on his mother, needed constant grooming, and slept with her at night. Flint had become what Jane called "a very abnormal juvenile."

The Dating Game

We cannot judge chimpanzee sex life by the standards of human society, particularly the dating customs of our own culture. It does, however, make sense in terms of evolutionary biology. Let us assume that females have different strategies than do males when it comes to sex and reproduction; call these **differential reproductive strategies** and **differential sexual strategies.** The basic idea which comes from the work of Charles Darwin, notes that each gender experiences results or consequences from having sex and makes an investment in being a parent. But the consequences or the investments are not the same for males as for females. Please note that Darwin and those who follow in his footsteps are talking about groups of animals, or species. They are not providing interpretations of individual behavior. This can get confusing.

Let's use Goodall's chimpanzees to illustrate these points about differential strategies.

What's a fellow to do? A male chimpanzee does not initiate sex. He must wait until the "pink ladies" are ready. Then he needs some techniques or a history of cooperation with a female. Sexual swellings are for male chimpanzees, a time of tension. They may tear down and wave tree branches. They may pick fights with each other for no apparent reason.

Sometimes a male chimpanzee manages to take a pink lady off into the woods for a few days together. They then are a **consort pair,** a temporary but exclusive mating relationship. This is sometimes called a pair bond or a consortship. Only in this way can a male keep an estrous female away from rival males. At the peak of her swelling, she is most likely to conceive. Exclusive access to her increases the likelihood that he is the father. If chimpanzees reasoned this out (and there is absolutely no evidence they do), then his strategy for getting her off alone is not only about sex. It is about reproduction from the male point of view. It is the kind of survival Darwin talked about.

Goodall and the researchers at Gombe report that all of the male chimps squired females on sexual getaways at some point in their lives. Often a male had to work very hard to take and keep a female on a consortship; others simply had good manners and better techniques. Some males were notably more successful than others. Some used aggressive and bullying tactics until they wore a female out. But once the pair left the group and mated, the male became docile or conciliatory. In customary behavior, chimps follow aggression or hostility with gestures of reconciliation. They make amends and restore social harmony. So perhaps consortships are a chimp equivalent of a honeymoon; perhaps they are also conducive to conception. That's what courtship is for.

Mothers and Daughters

An enduring result of primate research is the striking differences between mothering styles in individuals and the contribution that good mothering makes to succeeding generations. The closest relationship at Gombe is between a mother and her grown daughter. Until she is about ten years of age, a female will be separated from her mother only a few hours at a time. Her mother protects and supports her. In return, however, her mother may dominate and smother her.

Goodall says that most chimp females are relatively efficient at being mothers; this is similar to the concept of "good enough" or adequate that child-rearing experts talk about in the United States. She compares Flo's mothering style with another female, called Passion.

> *In the wild almost all mothers look after their infants relatively efficiently. But even so there are clear-cut differences in the child-raising techniques of different individuals. It would be hard to find two females whose mothers had treated them more differently during their early years, than Flo's daughter Fifi and Passion's daughter Pom. In fact, Flo and Passion are at opposite ends of a scale: most mothers fall somewhere between these two extremes. (Goodall 1990:33)*

The two daughters, Fifi and Pom, came into sexual maturity about the same time. After weaning, the beginning of estrus is the next major transition in the life of a female. Fifi and Pom were both sexually attractive and active for about ten days each month for two years, but neither got pregnant.

Fifi flourished in the bloom of adolescence; she learned how to be self-reliant without depending on the high status of her mother. She rejoined her mother for companionship between episodes of sexual availability and enjoyed grooming six-year-old Flint, playing with baby Flame, and gaining valuable maternal experience. Fifi was charmed by her new power.

> *Sometimes, when a male was, quite obviously, uninterested in what she had to offer, she would recline close by and, ever hopeful, stare at him. Or rather, stare at a certain portion of his anatomy that was, so far as she was concerned, disappointingly flabby. Once she went so far as to tweak the limp appendage—with highly satisfactory results! It soon became clear that the males regarded Fifi as a most desirable sexual partner. She did not have quite the sex appeal that Flo had once radiated—but in those days she was, after all, younger and less experienced. (Goodall 1990:35)*

Pom, by contrast, was a troubled teenager. Tense and anxious with males, she often leapt away screaming after intercourse. She seemed to lack the social skills which would endear her to sexual partners; thus she remained less popular than Fifi. Pom seldom went off alone with a male during her estrus. In fact, she and her mother, Passion, fought off and defeated such attempts by senior males.

So what was Passion's problem? Was she a bad mother? Cold and brusque with Pom, she had seldom played with her infant. Passion had pushed Pom onto her back long before the infant was ready for riding in that style. Passion had no close female companions; she herself was tense and edgy around males. Pom and Passion had a close bond and supported each other in community quarrels. The two of them backed each other up when either picked a confrontation with another chimp, male or female.

In May 1971 Fifi gave birth to Freud—named in honor of his mother's sexual exuberance during her adolescent years. Fifi was as relaxed and competent as her mother. Indeed, she lifted baby Freud with one foot and tickled him just as mother Flo had done. When at age thirteen Pom gave birth to infant Pan, she treated him better than she herself had been treated as an infant. Although Pom was more attentive and tolerant than mother Passion had been, she never developed the maternal proficiency or loving vigilance that marked Fifi's care of her infant.

In chimpanzee society, individuals may take on mothering roles even when they have not given birth. One daughter helped her mother, who had just borne twins. Another chimp, Gigi, was a large sterile female who cycled vainly into estrus every thirty days or so. She radiated sex appeal and basked in popularity. Her consorts performed valiantly, but she never conceived. After a time, she made friends with and acted as an older sister for Patti, whose mothering skills began to improve only after her third child was born. "Aunt" Gigi, in effect, adopted Patti's offspring, rescued them from their mother's intermittent neglect, and modeled vigilant, caring parenting for the hapless Patti.

Such fostering or **fictive kinship** appears common in chimp society, and its value for survival and adaptation is quite obvious. The research from Gombe contains many examples of older brothers or sisters looking out for younger ones after the death of their mother. It also points out once again the fact that being a mother is not a matter of instinct or "natural" impulses. Mothering is a learned and practiced set of behaviors. Some individuals who give birth are better at it than others. People other than biological mothers can and do perform these tasks.

Sons, Lovers, and Others

The advantage of years of fieldwork is tracking individuals through complex and shifting relationships or friendships. Jane Goodall's observations of chimpanzee social life make it clear that males and females have different life courses or cycles, that they are distinct individuals, and that they negotiate and interact in complex ways. Females, in estrus or out of it, prefer the company of some males to others. They will actively avoid other individuals. Both males and females have ongoing, active friendships with each other. The links between siblings are obvious throughout their adulthood. They often form close alliances after the death of their mother, for example. Two brothers may support each other in a bid for moving up the hierarchy. Brothers and sisters may groom each other or spend time in each other's company more frequently than they do with any other individuals.

But male chimps must break early from their mothers. Although a male may draw status from his mother and strength and insight from positive early social experiences, he still has to learn the skills of an adult male from other males. He must work his way around the loose dominance hierarchy, an ever-shifting matrix, dominating the females first and then his peers and age-mates before he can tackle the older males.

Fostering or fictive kinship appears common in chimp society.

The highest ranking male in a primate troop is called an **alpha male.** Such powerful or dominant males often act to suppress community conflicts. Alpha males will terminate otherwise destructive quarreling and promote strategies of social accord. Some males, however, seem to have no desire for being at the top. They may serve the alpha males in return for protection and a degree of tolerance when food and sex are available. Flo's son Figan, for example, was intelligent, well brought-up, and determined to make it to the top of the status hierarchy in his band. He worked on his charging display: He made his hair stand on end, shook heavy branches, slapped the ground, and stomped loudly. The threatening gestures and facial expressions are designed to impress rivals without resort to actual physical conflict. Audacity and persistence count for more than size or strength. Figan enlisted the support of his older brother, Faben, who seemed to be happy in his role as brother of an alpha. Thus Flo left a legacy of leadership through her sons—Figan, alpha male, and Faben, loyal supporter.

By contrast, a female in chimp society remains with her mother, her siblings, and the network of associations she was born into. She will learn by observing and participating how to care for an infant and what the sexual swellings mean. However traumatic weaning, a new sibling, or alpha rivalries are, the ultimate broken bond is a mother's death. When Flo died, Jane Goodall recorded the event and mourned a friend.

As I kept my vigil in the bright moonlight, I thought about Flo's life. For nigh on fifty years she must have roamed the Gombe hills. And

> even if I had not arrived to record her history, to invade the privacy
> of that rugged terrain, Flo's life would have been, in and of itself, sig-
> nificant and worthwhile, filled with purpose, vigour, and love of life.
> (Goodall 1990:31)

Flo is the only nonhuman ever to have an obituary in the *London Times*. When she died, Flint was eight-and-a-half years old. Under different circumstances, he would have been able to care for himself. But he was desolate. He visited the last nest they had shared and returned to the place where he had last seen her. Sick and refusing to eat, he curled up and died.

Jane Goodall saw in these individuals and their life stories what we think of as the "human" qualities of chimpanzees. Sometimes they show compassion, ambition, love, self-sacrifice, and sharing. However, it is dangerous to romanticize or sentimentalize chimpanzee life or to compare ourselves naively to other animal species. On occasion, and under conditions scientists are just starting to understand, chimpanzees hurt and kill each other. Females and males kill infants; adult males kill each other and adult females.

Studying Baboons

Baboons are monkeys and the most widely studied nonhuman primates in the world. In no danger of extinction, it is said that baboons outnumber human beings in Africa. They provide a primary model of how our ancestors lived on the savannahs of that continent. For decades, baboons in their rich varieties have been the major portrait of primate life for introductory anthropology classes.

Based on research done in the 1950s and 1960s, professors like me used to teach that baboons lived in male-dominated societies and had a clear-cut sexual division of labor. Like humans, some species even had harems. Aggressive, competitive males were the building blocks and cement, the structure and the stability, of their groups. But a generation of female primatologists in the 1960s and 1970s challenged the scientific validity of these notions. Here are three illustrative examples from the works of these women.

Maternal Care and Friendships

Jeanne Altmann was married to a baboon researcher and spent years watching baboons. Even before she earned her doctorate, she proposed observational methodologies and unbiased sampling techniques that are now standards in the field. She said that statistics, however sophisticated, are useless without a conceptualization of the problem. Her book on baboon mothers and infants emphasized the enduring conflict between females' productive and reproductive lives. Their work was a constant trade-off between maternal care or child rearing and the time and energy needed to forage for food. For example, youngsters wanted their mothers to carry, nurse, or amuse them endlessly; but mothers had to work. Once again we learn, if we needed this lesson, that females are involved first in tasks of subsistence or earning a living; then they arrange nursing, mating, or quality time with their kids.

Prior researchers, focused on topics such as food and sex, had missed a whole arena of possibilities, namely friendships, social skills and emotional qualities. Primatologist Barbara Smuts studied female–male friendships in baboon groups living in Kenya. She learned that

> *relationships between males and females transcend the narrow context of the sexual act. Flirtation, courtship, possessiveness, and jealousy are apparent in interactions between the sexes throughout all phases of the female reproductive cycle. Baboons are strongly attracted to members of the opposite sex independent of their immediate motivations to copulate. (Smuts 1985:231)*

If a woman is going to say that animals like baboons have an awareness of self and others, and live in complex systems of affiliation, then she better have convincing scientific methods. So Smuts developed rigorous procedures to measure friendship and sort relationships into categories she called Relatives, Friends, and Non-Friends. We know who Relatives are. What are Friends for? Friends groom each other and spend time in each other's company. This can be measured in terms of the frequency of mutual grooming and calculations of physical proximity to each other. Baboon Friends don't just have sex. They sleep together and spend time with each other. So sex and friendship are intimately twined.

What are the benefits of having a Friend? A male Friend protects a female and her vulnerable offspring. In doing so, he establishes a long-term alliance with the infants as they grow up.

> *What made Friends special was, most of all, the unusual quality of their interactions. Female baboons, in general, are wary of males. This is understandable: Males sometimes use their larger size and formidable canines to intimidate and bully smaller troop members. Females, however, were apparently drawn to their male Friends, and they seemed surprisingly relaxed around these hulking companions. The males, too, seemed to undergo a subtle transformation when interacting with female Friends. They appeared less tense, more affectionate, and more sensitive to the behavior of their partners. (Smuts 1985:61)*

A female favors her Friend as a mate when she is again in estrus. At other times she will spend long hours grooming her Friend. Becoming a Friend to an established female integrates a male in the social life of the group.

Primate Kinfolk

Shirley Strum went to Kenya to observe olive baboons, one group of which she called the Pumphouse Gang. But the baboons refused to cooperate. They seemed

Baboon societies have certain styles of child rearing, just as human or chimpanzee cultures do.

not to have heard about the scientific model for their lives. High-ranking males did not routinely monopolize sexy females. In fact, females often chose the losers in male contests to groom and befriend. Males often participated in caretaking friendships with youngsters; they acted like older brothers or "uncles." Females handled most disputes within their own hierarchies and family groupings. Both females and males had power. Confused and confounded, Shirley Strum spent months, then years, observing the baboons.

Strum puzzled about gender and personalities in the same way Margaret Mead, Ruth Benedict, Jane Goodall, and others have. Yes, baboon societies have certain styles of child rearing, just as human or chimpanzee cultures do. But individuals within the same troop or family are very different from each other.

Take Peggy, for example. Peggy had outstanding social skills; she was calm, solid, and assertive but not pushy. She was a forceful yet loving mother to her adult daughter, Thea, adolescent son Paul, juvenile Patrick, and infant Pebbles. By contrast, Thea had a troubled temperament. She relied on her mother to intervene for her in awkward social situations she herself had created. As Shirley Strum remarks, "Thea was, in fact, a bitch."

> *Thea was always poking her nose into other people's business.*
> *Whenever females or juveniles were involved in a tiff, Thea would be*
> *there in seconds, adding her weight sometimes to one side, some-*
> *times to the other, frequently almost schizophrenically switching*
> *sides unpredictably. She often managed to prevent the quarreling*
> *individuals from settling the argument. . . . I badly wanted to under-*
> *stand Thea's ambivalence toward her mother. What was she thinking*

*and feeling? What was driving her? What made her so different from
Peggy in her interaction with the other females? (Strum 1987:40)*

Thea's three daughters preferred grandmother Peggy's company. She groomed
them and spent so much time in their company that an inexperienced person
might believe they were Peggy's own. Peggy's high status and strong character was
an umbrella of protection for all the members of her matriline. Anyone who
messed with members of her family would have to deal with Peggy herself.
Although every adult male was larger and stronger, Peggy could get what she
wanted—a shady spot, a bit of food, or grooming—by moving in and waiting.
When Peggy sponsored a male, he was in with the group.

The core units of the Pumphouse Gang and other baboon groups were females
and their kinfolk. These matrifocal units have stable rankings. Peggy's unit or
matriline happened to outrank all the other matrilines. In fact, every member of
Peggy's matriline, male or female, infant or adult, enjoyed the fruits of this
female's high status. That a mother's status somehow covers her offspring and is
passed on is one of the most important insights we have from primate studies. But
primatologists are not sure why this is true or how it works.

More About Friendships

The research by Strum and others showed that females had long-lasting friendships with each other, an easy mutuality of sitting together, resting, sleeping, or
grooming. When they disagreed with each other, they worked things out. Female
baboons like Peggy also had friendships or "special relationships" with males.
Strum witnessed many friendships between females and males but none between
adult males.

The major fact of life for males in the Pumphouse Gang was mobility. For various reasons, they moved back and forth, in and out of other troops. Each time
they moved they had to work their way up. Newcomers used the only tactic at
their disposal, aggression. Males who lived with the troop for a short time developed social ties, so they fared better. But males who had lived with the troop the
longest had to develop serious social strategies. Males who used finesse rather
than force and subtlety rather than strength achieved much more in the long run.
Males who moved into a new troop fared best when they made friends with a
female. Then she championed his cause with others.

*The more I understood males, the clearer it seemed that they had a
hard life. Where did their size, strength and physical power get them?
. . . They had to reconstruct whole new lives for themselves after leaving behind all that was friendly, secure and familiar. Once in their new
troop, they had to recapture all they had lost: the social closeness, allies,
friends, experience and knowledge that ultimately constituted baboon
wisdom. Despite great effort and enduring patience, they ended up with
less than a female who had never left home could command simply
with a look, gesture or grunt. I felt sorry for males. (Strum 1987:126)*

Shirley Strum did not see what the theory predicted she would. Individual baboons had distinct personalities. There was no clear-cut male dominance. Aggression happened but rarely achieved anything. Rank among females seemed stable. Yet females were not in control, there was no primate matriarchy. Strum settled for the idea of "complementary equality." Females and males did separate things, had different jobs, and exchanged favors with each other. Both male and female baboons were involved in politics, peacekeeping, and caretaking. They practiced elaborate social reciprocity and complicated exchanges of favors and friendships.

Females were not powerless or passive no matter how busy they were in maternal care; in fact, their work as mothers conferred status. Wisdom, knowledge, and social skills were as important as strength or size. Allies, friends, and relatives were any individual's greatest asset.

In Darwinian terms, all these good habits contribute to reproductive success and survival. But baboons do not reason that way. Instead, they act as though friendships were central to a meaningful social life. They act with intelligence and reciprocity and they reap the rewards of their emotional investments.

Research such as this challenges notions like "the law of the jungle" and "dog-eat-dog" world. Aggressive competition and male domination are not the "natural" order of social life for primates. Instead we see the centrality of the mother–child unit, the capacity for friendships across age and gender lines, the need for social skills, and the two-bodied, bicultural worlds of females and males.

Studying the Human Nature of Women and Men

Many ideas flow from the decades of research only briefly presented here. I want to cover two.

The first one is that the sexual and reproductive lives of females and males are radically different. We are not mirror images; we are not equal. On the contrary, women and men have different agendas; each has separate interests and strategies.

The second point I want to make is that interpreting these differences and applying them in the cultural contexts we live in is fiendishly difficult. Let's examine the differences first.

What is the human nature of being female? Here is an explanation from evolutionary biology. Human females make eggs, one per month from menarche to menopause. If one month's egg is not fertilized, we have a period. If that month's egg is fertilized, we are pregnant, and may carry the fetus through a gestation period of ten lunar months and give birth to a tiny and very helpless infant. The baby develops slowly and requires feeding and extensive training in life-survival skills for approximately two decades. (This includes college!)

Females require access to necessary resources in the environment to rear these offspring to full adulthood, when they will begin the cycle for themselves. We organize such aid from mates, kinfolks, Friends, or cooperative nonrelatives. This is a form of work called **female parental investment** and may last through a meaningful segment of our life cycle. Females of the human species require lots of assistance in raising our young. Sometimes the trade-off in human cultures has been sexual access and assurance of paternity for males in exchange for protection and economic resources for females. Females may compete, not over the best-looking male, but over access to resources to sustain themselves and their offspring. This proposition provokes many thoughtful questions. It may help us to understand contemporary patterns and predict how they will change.

What are males like? What is their human nature as seen from evolutionary biology? Men typically produce billions of tiny sperm from early adolescence to the end of their lives. They never get pregnant, give birth, or have a period, not even once. A male may go from female to female contributing sperm and thus may have a great many offspring, some of whom he may not know about or who are in various stages of gestation and growth simultaneously. A male must theoretically be worried about the competition, about the availability of females, and about how much mating will cost him. This is called mating effort.

For a male there is no physical connection between fertilization and childbirth. Under many circumstances, however, there are deep economic, psychological, or social bonds between men and their offspring. So a **male parental investment** centers on the contributions a man makes to the growth or fitness of his offspring. Males are also affected by the degree of confidence they have in their own paternity. Unlike females, they can never really be certain. On the other hand, males may assist in rearing children who are not biologically theirs.

Given these two styles of reproduction, we can see strikingly different tactics that females and males use in what we can call reproductive and sexual careers. For example, females may be very careful in choosing a mate; we will ask the question, Is he a good provider? I have heard women say, "So he's not a perfect husband, at least he's good to the kids."

Men of the human species, however, may well emphasize physical qualities in women that highlight sexuality and maternity. This includes breasts, fat storage on buttocks, and youthfulness. This theory explains men who are old, ugly, and smelly but rich or powerful. They can compete successfully with other males for young females. By the same token, the theory explains how and why women promote or acquiesce to alliances with such men.

The theories about differential strategies are sometimes used to explain marriage systems that emphasize brides' virginity, dowries, chaperones, modesty, chastity, or punishments for women who commit adultery. A woman has access to a resource base and child-rearing assistance in exchange for a guarantee that all the children she bears belong genetically to her husband. All kinds of customs can be explained in this framework. This theory also makes sense in understanding soap operas!

Poor dead Charles Darwin. He and his theories of evolution have been dragged out for almost 150 years to justify whatever is politically current in fashions for the treatment of women. It is clear that complicated genetic, biological, or hormonal processes are in operation in our animal lives. But it is not at all clear why or how. It seems clear there are evolutionary advantages for survival of species. But scholars don't agree about the mechanisms. These theories do not provide us with models for marriage, monogamy, sexual adventures, or other social practices humans engage in. We are different from chimpanzees or baboons.

Human courtship customs are complex and full of emotions. They cannot be summarized easily. In fact, we can and regularly do have sex when we could not possibly conceive or when our motivations and feelings have little or nothing to do with "a sex drive." Human females conceal our ovulations; it is unclear if we are fertile, infertile, or even interested in trying. We place value judgments on copulation; we call it making love, promiscuity, adultery, safe sex, marital hygiene, screwing, rape, or many other terms. Humans, generally speaking, don't have intercourse in public. But we have sex without intercourse and with a variety of people; we have intercourse without pregnancy. We make connections between intercourse, pregnancy, birth, and social paternity. We think of males as husbands and fathers. We attribute immense moral and social characteristics to having and feeding an infant. We call this "motherhood."

One place in which evolutionary biology has been seriously confused with contemporary gender politics is what we should call the "cultural construction of motherhood." Examples are rife. Yes, some women have babies. Does that mean that all women's place is "naturally" in "the Kitchen, the Church, and the Nursery" as one German proverb states? Some women don't want to have children. Some who have them are not great mothers. Some women feel sensual pleasures in activities like nursing. Others have babies without sex. These women are not "unnatural."

Studying the Social Life of Primatologists

Why are there so many women studying primates? There are more women in primatology than in general biology, and women study primates more than they study snakes, birds, fish, or other animals. There are the same proportion of women as in the parent fields of anthropology, psychology, and animal behaviors. Why have women been so attracted to this field? Because, some argue, female primates are a "success story" in their own societies. We can also compare species as we compare human cultures; so we have cross-species analysis as well as cross-cultural analysis. Men may share the same views, but women seem to do so in larger amounts. Women, says primatologist Linda Marie Fedigan,

> are likely to seek subjects that touch experiences vital to the human experience of the world rather than subjects that deal in hard abstractions or other worldly subjects, such as mathematics, chemistry, physics, or engineering. They find meaningful subjects through which interior change is possible—enlargement of individual scope, shaping of identity, interior liberation. (Fedigan 1994:537)

A generation of female primatologists have changed the way we see the world. Many think that these professional women engender an uncommon grace in their disciplines, primarily anthropology, psychology, and animal behavior. Here is a list of four qualities female primatologists are said to bring to their work (Fedigan and Fedigan 1989:53). I issue the usual warning: Not all women in primatology are like this; many men in primatology are like this; many professionals in other fields share these qualities. But the following qualities are a measure of central tendency or a model and value system for other women.

1. *They pay attention to individuals and unusual cases, not ideal types or stereotypes. They use statistics as methodology but do not treat animals as numbers.*

2. *They acknowledge humility in the face of complexity and avoid reductionist arguments.*

3. *They use seeing as "listening" and intuition as a "feel" for the organism.*

4. *They persist under difficult conditions. These may include years spent in uncomfortable places, fund-raising duties, juggling families and work, or thriving despite academic politics.*

I add the following characteristics to the list:

5. *They have built deep currents and connections of friendships which link both women and men, inside and outside of anthropology.*

6. *They integrate the personal with the professional in creative ways. Many who talk about nursing infants, seducing males, or earning a living have done it.*

7. *They translate research and scientific achievements into practical, ethical, or moral initiatives that in some way demonstrate a deep caring for people, the planet, animal welfare, or their discipline.*

From primate studies we learn that: Primate societies are less "natural" and more intricate and fascinating than Charles Darwin ever imagined. Matrifocal units and stable females are the basic building block of primate society. Mothers are critical and mothering is hard work. But there are many styles of mothering and no instincts and no blueprints for such complicated work. Mating and sex serve the purpose of making offspring; they are not the only building blocks of collective existence. Power, authority, status, or domination occur in complex and negotiable situations. Friendship and Friends are fundamental.

Kinship groups like the matrifocal units discussed in this chapter appear in many forms in this book. We talked about our early ancestors and matrifocal families in chapter 1; they are one style of partnering in chapter 5 and part of "modernization" and the feminization of poverty in chapter 9. Single-parent and female-headed households are the fastest-growing lifestyles on the planet.

In the next chapter, we will look at different forms for families and a number of ways to find partners in human societies. We will see romance, resistance, more alpha males, and matrifocal units, as well as another view of the social life of the human female.

Some Evolutionary or Revolutionary Books to Read

Dian Fossey was the second of Louis Leakey's protegés. She studied mountain gorillas in Rwanda. For Fossey, who was a physical therapist, this quest was as much for private fulfillment as for scientific knowledge. Before she was murdered by poachers, she had established organizations to help save the habitat of the mountain gorillas as well as the species themselves. Her only book, *Gorillas in the Mist* (1983), is partly autobiographical and contains most of what she ever published about the mountain gorillas. Read it and follow it up with a biography about her. I recommend Farley Mowat's *Woman in the Mists: The Story of Dian Fossey and the Mountain Gorillas of Africa.*

Donna Haraway's *Primate Visions: Gender, Race, and Nature in the World of Modern Science* (1989) is a brilliant, original, and groundbreaking history of primate research. Framed in the postmodernist ethic, it tells about love, power, prejudice, and science in the last half of a mad century.

Large and long, Jane Goodall's *The Chimpanzees of Gombe: Patterns of Behavior* (1986) is still the major work in primatology. Many of the questions you have will be answered in her beautifully clear chapters on such topics as friendship, object manipulation, territoriality, aggression, sex, relationships, communication, and emotional lives. *Through a Window: My Thirty Years with the Chimpanzees of Gombe,* (1990) is Goodall's most recent and readable of her books. It carries on where her first best-seller, *In the Shadow of Man,* left off.

Other primate books that depict the personal and intellectual growth of the researcher as well as the complexity of primate societies include Barbara Smuts, *Sex and Friendship in Baboons* (1985), and Shirley Strum, *Almost Human: A Journey into the World of Baboons* (1987).

Sarah Blaffer Hrdy, *The Woman That Never Evolved* (1981), writes with a unique and provocative combination of feminism and evolutionary biology. She rebuts the myth of the passive, kind, always nurturant female–mother as a model for women's behavior. In its place, she offers female primates as activists to make and protect babies and have sex under their own control.

There are a number of excellent books about biological or cultural constructions of motherhood and the consequences for human females. Here are a few I recommend. Ellen Lewin's *Lesbian Mothers: Accounts of Gender in American Culture* (1993), is a very important ethnography of yet another kind of matrifocal family. Diana Eyer wrote *Mother–Infant Bonding: A Scientific Fiction* (1992), about some of the current confusions around biology, "nature" and cultural systems of motherhood. Bonding is not what you thought it was!

Issues about parenting and early child-bearing are particularly important in the contemporary political climate. I suggest Judith Musick *Young, Poor and Pregnant:*

The Psychology of Teenage Motherhood (1993); or two edited volumes: Jane Lancaster, Jeanne Altmann, Alice Rossi, and Lonnie Sherrod, *Parenting Across the Life Span: Biosocial Dimensions* (1987); and Jane Lancaster and Beatrice Hamburg, *School-Age Pregnancy and Parenthood* (1986). Nancy Chodorow's, *The Reproduction of Mothering* (1978) is one of best psychological–anthropological, post-Freudian, theoretical books in the literature.

Chapter Five

Patterns of Partnering from Romance to Resistance

"And so they lived happily ever after." Or did they?

No other topic in *A World Full of Women* is as pervasive and personal as partnering. "Marriage and family" are the well-worn traditional terms. But for most people, these words call up images, memories, and value judgments that are difficult to sort out. Furthermore, women's experiences in partnering do not fit neatly in these boxes.

In all human cultures, most women typically marry and bear children. Regardless of what women personally want to do or actually succeed in doing, we live our lives against the backdrop of the social structures, rules, and expectations for a particular point in history and within those cultural frameworks. There is no right way or wrong way. But there are strategies. Anthropologist Louise Lamphere said it well:

> *I have taken a female perspective, treating women as political actors who employ strategies to achieve ends. Women's strategies are directly related to the structure of power and authority in the domestic group and to a woman's position with relation to the developmental cycle. . . . Women quarrel with or dominate other women when it is in their interest to do so; they share and exchange with other women when it suits their own goals. Cooperation and conflict among women in family or kin groups cannot be understood without reference to domestic power structure, to women's place within it, and to the factors that shape the relationship between the family and the larger society. (Lamphere 1972:111)*

Marriage is one of the major strategies on the planet. The practice is universal, all human groups recognize and establish rules and values surrounding marriage. Within the institution, some individuals find salvation, romance, or eternal validation; others find slavery, violence, or psychic death. Marriage as an option in one's life is different from marriage as inevitable or marriage as a career. It is difficult to talk about something so fundamental, yet so diverse. One thing is clear: It's still work.

In some societies, virtually everyone gets married; many people do it often. Even when getting married or staying married is difficult for us, it is still held up as the ideal thing to do. Even when there are no ceremonies or registration procedures, we still say people are married. In many places and in many times, emotional qualities in marriage are absent or incidental. In effect, exchanges between wives and husbands are "numbed down." A woman's relationships with her children may be more intense and long-lasting and partnering may be only a convenient way to have children. In some cases, the quality of interactions between husband and wife are prescribed by gender ideologies, not by individual personalities. Often, as we shall see in this chapter, friendships, kinfolk, and other women are as important as husbands.

The most common reasons for getting married are (1) to have someone to share work, resources and status with; and (2) to raise children with. This makes sense: Men need the services and bodies of females to make babies. Women need help from someone committed to them and to their babies. Kinship systems will not work without marriage.

Varieties of Arrangements

The chapter is inspired in part by the many different experiences my friends, students, colleagues, and I have had with the marriage systems in the United States. Studying anthropology has taught me that the world offers many alternatives and that all women everywhere have to deal somehow with patterns of partnering. So I have picked some key examples of partnering across the globe. They are:

- *the matrilineal Iroquois of Native North America*

- *matrifocal or "mother-centered" households*

- *marriage patterns in Catholic Latin America*

- *traditional patriarchal and patrilineal families of China*

- *African systems of kinship, marriage, and multiple mates*

- *romance as relationship in the contemporary United States*

Each of these cases has a woman-centered point of view. Several themes are woven loosely throughout this chapter. Marriage is mostly about economics, or how people earn a living, and about structures or rules. Women use many strategies to deal with these facts of life. Friendships and feelings matter, but they may have little to do with a spouse.

It matters where we live with our partners. "Your house or mine?" is more than an idle question. Predictably, a bride's life has different meanings if she lives with her kinfolk or his after the wedding. Anthropologists call this **postmarital residence patterns**. There are three kinds in this chapter: matrilocal residence patterns, such as the Iroquois; patrilocal residence patterns, such as the Chinese; or neolocal residence patterns, such as Americans know in our own experience. In primate species, females are rarely required to move from their natal group. As we saw in chapter 4, males are generally more mobile and females stay as anchors. Humans, however, regularly practice living patterns that send daughters away to become wives. This has consequences for women. Residence patterns are deeply connected to gender ideologies and the treatment of women.

Another theme is how women turn people into relatives. We give birth; this creates **consanguineal kin,** or relatives connected to us through blood. When we marry we have **affinal kin,** or relatives connected to us through marriage. Human beings also create **fictive kin,** informal and formal kinship connections based on the parallels of relationships through birth; adoption is a good example. We also define partners in many different ways.

The Five Fires of the Longhouse

Across the southern region of the Great Lakes, in what is now the United States, lived a group of five tribes called the Iroquois. The Iroquois practiced **matrilineal kinship**. That is, they traced their kinship to each other through women and used this principle to structure their entire social life. They also lived in **matrilocal residences**. This means that a group of women and men related to each other by blood lived together in the same house; when they married, their husbands joined them there as guests. The matrilocal dwellings were called **longhouses**. In effect, Iroquois women owned the houses, the fields, the crops they produced, and a number of very interesting political rights and responsibilities. For these reasons, they are often thought of as a **matriarchy**, a society controlled by women (or mothers) instead of men. As one anthropologist remarked,

> Indeed of all the people of the earth, the Iroquois approach most
> closely to that hypothetical form of society known as a matriarchate.
> (Murdock 1934:302)

The longhouse of the Iroquois is a critical example of women-centered architecture. The longhouse was not just a dwelling; it was the metaphor for their political and spiritual lives. As one man noted, "We constitute but one house, we five Iroquois nations, we build but one fire and we have through all time dwelt under the same roof" (Morgan 1851: II, 301). Figure 5.1 shows the floor plan of a longhouse. There were two entrances, one at each end. Berths, benches, or partitioned rooms along the sides accommodated individuals, couples, children, sleeping, and storage. The winter supplies of corn, fur rugs, equipment, or tools and other prepared foodstuffs were stored in the rafters. The middle aisle, with cooking fires, was the indoor social center. Kids played there and adults worked there. A typical longhouse was perhaps 20 feet wide and 150 feet long. They were grouped in permanent villages.

The members of a matriline—that is, the senior women, their daughters, the daughter's children, their brothers, and their unmarried sons—built and owned the longhouse. In other words, those who lived in the longhouse were linked through the females of the clan. Husbands lived there too, but as outsiders; their homes were with their own matriline.

The women of the longhouse held garden plots and tools in common. They planted, weeded, and harvested corn, beans, and squash, and gathered abundant wild plants. They did all the processing, storage, and distribution of food. It is said that Iroquois women provisioned men's war parties. If the women did not approve and give food, the men could not go to war.

A nineteenth-century lawyer in New York state named Lewis Henry Morgan wrote some extremely significant documents on the Iroquois. We will hear more about Morgan later, but first listen to his interpretation of Iroquois's patterns of partnering:

> From the very nature of the marriage institution among the Iroquois,
> it follows that the passion of love was entirely unknown among

Figure 5.1

Iroquois longhouse

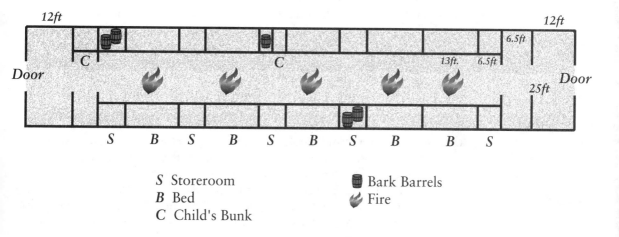

S Storeroom   🛢 Bark Barrels
B Bed   🔥 Fire
C Child's Bunk

Source: Lewis Henry Morgan, *League of the Ho-De-No Sau-Nee or Iroquois* (1851), volume II, 295

> *them. Affection after marriage would naturally spring up between*
> *the parties from association, from habit, and from mutual depen-*
> *dence; but of that marvellous passion which originates in a higher*
> *development of the powers of the human heart, and is founded upon*
> *a cultivation of the affections between the sexes, they were entirely*
> *ignorant. (Morgan I:313)*

Morgan's assumption that humans "naturally" feel passion in marriage was one of his Victorian conceits. No one really knows how people felt, certainly in private, in other cultures or in the past. But this particular form of matrilineal kinship and matrilocal residence allows us to discuss how husbands and wives acted in public.

For starters, having a husband or a wife in Iroquois society (and other matrilineal groups like them) was not crucial for regular meals and a roof over one's head. Kinfolk, not spouses, provided those. Iroquois did not have nuclear families as we know them nor the expectation of romance or romantic love as the basis of marriage. Iroquois wives and husbands did not share domestic economies with each other. Iroquois children belonged to their mother's lineage and clan. So there was no such thing as custody arguments, illegitimacy, or abandonment. You can see that the kinship system and the architecture made divorce easy. The first Catholic missionaries to this region were horrified to see Iroquois women who placed their husbands' belongings outside the longhouse and declared themselves divorced. Women also took temporary "husbands" (or lovers) when their own were absent.

Children called their mother's sisters "mom" and their grandmother's sisters, "granny," or the Iroquois equivalent. They knew who their biological kin were, but the terms were broader than those in English. So were the circles of responsibility. Anthropologists think that mother's brothers or grandmother's brothers, "uncles" who were clan members, took "fatherly" interests in the lives of their sisters' children. In other words, neither biological fathers nor mothers carried the task of child rearing alone. Women worked in cooperative work groups, lived together, and raised their children in concert.

Iroquois women appear to have power or status in striking ways. A council of fifty elders, each of whom held the title of **sachem,** governed the five tribes or fires of the Iroquois Confederacy. Only men could hold this position. But only senior women, Iroquois **matrons,** could nominate and, in effect, select new members for the council. They selected from within their matrilineal kin. Sometimes the matrons picked a young relative and acted as regents in his place until he grew up.

After contact with Europeans and the changes that resulted, Iroquois households began to form on the European model of patrilineal, nuclear families. They lived in single-room log cabins. Today, in some areas, worship services and community gatherings are held in longhouses. No one lives in them.

Anthropologists and feminists have discussed the status of Iroquois women for decades. They are a major sources of evidence in the debates about the power of women in the world. If we believe that women are inevitably subordinate to men, then we have to explain away people like the Iroquois. If we think the Iroquois had a matriarchy, then we want to know how it worked and what insights it offers us. Generations of scholars have projected their own lives on this group in ways that have influenced world history. In chapter 8, we will return to issues of matriarchies and spirituality. In chapter 9, we will see how the writings of Lewis Henry Morgan on the Iroquois influenced Karl Marx and Frederick Engels, their critiques of capitalism, and their problems with women.

"Mother-Centered" Models in the Caribbean

Once we get past the idea of nuclear families as normal, natural, or standard, we often find female-focused kinship units or **matrifocal** households. Like primates, humans have kinship systems in which primary links are between mothers and children. Anthropologists have documented many varieties of cultural settings around the world in which women are mothers, heads of households, key decision makers, and financial support for their families.

There are systems of matrifocal kinship in West Africa, the Caribbean, and among other groups of people descended from Africans in the diaspora to the New World. There are rural villages and poor urban neighborhoods around the world where men cannot find work or have migrated to find work; in any event, they are unavailable as husbands. In Europe and North America, professional and working women often head our own households. There are divorced women, lesbian mothers, single mothers, and the hundreds of thousands of other women who do not fall into the stereotyped nuclear family. Matrifocal households are not limited to lower-class, economically distressed groups or just to societies that are changing rapidly. They seem to occur where women live—by choice or by necessity—economically separate from husbands. Matrifocal patterns of partnering are fluid. Please note that a society may have matrilineal or patrilineal descent, monogamy or polygyny, and still have matrifocal units at its core.

Some social scientists think of matrifocal households and, by extension, the women who head them, as deviate or pathological. They say we are "at risk." Others have viewed the phenomenon of female-headed households as an adaptive strategy to poverty, unemployment, or male work patterns. Others are surprised to find so many social systems in which women as mothers are central.

In the Caribbean, where matrifocal families are customary, couples frequently do not live together in the same household. Nonetheless, they regard themselves as partners. This style of marriage or conjugal bonds is often called **visiting relations** or **consensual unions.** A woman and a man may be in a meaningful, often long-term and committed relationship. They may be parents as well as partners, but they do not share the same household. Women may share affection, love, and mutual respect with their partners. But getting married, if or when it occurs, is likely to be for older people in their thirties or forties, after the children are grown.

In matrifocal, or "mother-centered," households, kinship is not defined by marriage but by blood or consanguineal ties. There is a saying that "blood is thicker than water." In matrifocal families, mothers, children, and siblings are blood; husbands and fathers are water. Matrifocal families are, like all marriage and kinship systems, a way of channeling resources and a way of raising kids.

Male and female relationships are characteristically unstable in matrifocal households. Anthropologist Marsha Prior reports on her research in Jamaica and she applied her analysis to the Caribbean, as a whole as do other authors (see Momsen 1993 and Steady 1981):

> *Male and female informants readily acknowledged the shifting allegiances between men and women. Men were known to keep several girlfriends at one time, and marriage, common-law or legal, was no guarantee that monogamy will follow. Women also admitted to keeping an eye out for a better partner and said they would initiate a change if they so desired. (Prior 1993:314)*

The key feature of matrifocal households is women as mothers. Motherhood, not marriage, turns women into adults. Men are not marginal. First of all, they reside somewhere as brothers and sons. Second, they have a claim on a woman through children and money. Men have a kind of power in that they may have more than one woman; women cannot eliminate men from their lives. Women must work in local economic systems that offer them only low pay and frequent unemployment. As workers, women have low status.

> *These women are members of a culture that may value women as mothers, but women in general do not necessarily enjoy a high status.*

> *In other words the* mother *role is valued, but women are overall sub-ordinate to men. Male informants felt it was their right to physically coerce or punish women as they saw fit, but a man would almost never physically abuse his own mother. (Prior 1993:316)*

Working-class women in the West Indies told anthropologist Yolanda Moses that getting married restricts their alternatives. They would be financially dependent on one man. He would have to hold a steady job and agree to support them and their children. As wife, a woman would have to give up a great deal of support from kin group and female relatives.

> *Working class women know they cannot always depend on males in the role of husband–father for economic and emotional support, so they take what they can get from their conflicted situation. They may form a series of "friending" relationships with men for sex, presents, and status. While a man may not be able to provide for a woman economically, her status in her circle of friends is enhanced if she can "hold a man" and keep him satisfied sexually. (Moses 1981:509)*

Neither men nor women believe this is the ideal pattern. To the contrary, women may say that men should take care of them and make the decisions. Men say that they should be providers and protectors. But men migrate or cannot find work, and women have to take over.

Getting children seems to be more crucial to a woman's life than getting a husband. A woman's aunts, grandmothers, other female relatives, or close friends may adopt or foster her children; these are called "borrowed children." Children born to a woman before she marries are called "outside children." "Inside children" are those born to a current spouse or mate. Mothers and daughters, more than mothers and sons or wives and husbands, are the domestic foundation through time.

If having a husband is not one's primary job, then how do women earn a living? Anthropologist Sidney Mintz separates the cultural patterns brought from Africa from those brought from Western countries like Spain, France, or England. There are long-established and documented African traditions of women controlling internal markets, of economic independence of wives and husbands from each other, and of a sexual division of labor quite different from Western ideas.

> *The fact is that West African and Afro-Caribbean societies have been able, in some contexts, to achieve sexual equality still quite unheard-of in Western societies, for all of their vaunting of individual freedom. The independence and authority exercised by a West African or Haitian market woman in regard to her uses of her own capital, or in regard to the economic influence of her husband, has few parallels in the Western world, where individual prerogatives are commonly seen as flowing from individual* male *wealth, embedded in a nuclear family organization. (Mintz 1981:531)*

The Afro-Caribbean patterns contrast sharply with the European-derived patterns of the same geographical area, where a wife customarily takes her husband's name, his social standing, and perhaps his orders.

A particular type of house is characteristic of matrifocal families in the West Indies or Caribbean. The **houseyard** is a West Indian residential unit and a female social space, a cluster or compound of buildings unified by a matrifocal head. Figure 5.2 is an example of Miss Joy's Yard.

Here is an explanation.

> *The houses are surrounded by other structures: sheds, animal pens, detached kitchens, ovens, work benches, laundry facilities, showers and privies. Scattered over the entire yard is an array of plants: food plants cultivated for consumption by people or animals in the yard*

Figure 5.2

Miss Joy's Yard

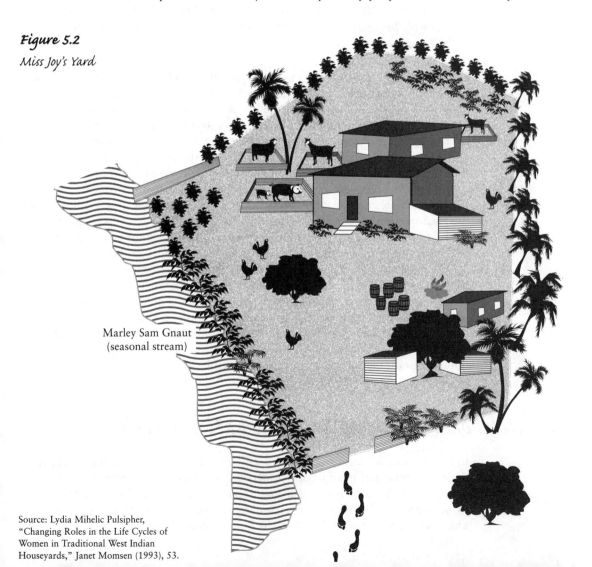

Marley Sam Gnaut
(seasonal stream)

Source: Lydia Mihelic Pulsipher, "Changing Roles in the Life Cycles of Women in Traditional West Indian Houseyards," Janet Momsen (1993), 53.

and other plants tended because they are useful as ornamentals or medicinals or for performing some practical chore like fending off mosquitos or scrubbing cooking pots. The entire yard is marked off from adjoining property by a fence, a hedge of useful plants like bamboo, aloe, or agave, or some other perceivable boundary . . . The relationships of those who occupy a particular house in a yard are varied and include the following possibilities: a mother and her young children (occasionally visited at night by one of their fathers), an older woman and several of her adult children (sometimes male, but more often female) and their children, adult (uterine) siblings and their children, a single adult with "borrowed children," a lone single adult, a sexually cohabiting couple with only their common children, or with their common as well as "outside" children, or a couple living alone (usually elderly) who have no common children. (Pulsipher 1993:50)

This description of a houseyard by geographer Lydia Pulsipher illustrates both contemporary living situations and evidence of how people lived in the past. The houseyard is site or sanctuary for the stages in individual lives and the continuity of the mother-centered kin unit through time. Residents of the houseyard care for the children born there. Adult women can emigrate or take jobs elsewhere, knowing their children are cared for. Older people, male and female, have cash-producing activities that allow them autonomy and authority.

A great deal of research points to a growing number of matrifocal families in the United States and around the world. For decades scholars have talked about the phenomenon in African American families; some have seen this as adjustment to the conditions of slavery; others as pathology or an unfortunate matriarchy. Still others see it as necessary adjustments to class, gender, and race.

We must not either romanticize or dismiss this pattern of partnering. Matrifocal lifestyles do not mean that women live separate lives from men or have control over their lives. It does not mean that women are free from racism, sexism, or the hidden injuries of class. Women may still be abused, mistreated, poor, or oppressed in matrifocal families. Women in matrifocal situations do not automatically acquire status and power. It does mean, however, that women are not trained, nor do they expect to be dependent on husbands for their intimate or economic lives.

Variations on the Virgin Mary in Latin America

In this section, we want to examine ideologies of gender and the realities of marriage in several settings in Latin American societies. The literature on women's lives in Latin America is full of stories about, analyses of, and reasons for unhappy marriages, male irresponsibility, and female suffering. As anthropologist Tracy Ehlers says about her fieldwork in the highlands of Guatemala:

Rich or poor, in towns and villages across the highlands, rarely a day passes without another woeful tale of offenses, abuses, and bad habits of men. . . . Marcela's common-law husband gambles every night and refuses to marry her because he has another wife—and five children—in the next town. Dona Violeta is called a widow, but everyone knows she was abandoned by her husband after the birth of her third child. Carmen had to send her children to live with her mother since their father left her and her new husband refuses to raise another man's offspring. Dona Magdelena's husband drank up her wages, beat her when she complained about it, then spent the next two weeks with his lover, leaving Magdelena penniless. (1991:1)

What is the problem with these men? Why are these women putting up with it? One of the most common models suggested for understanding the marriages typical of Latin America is a dual complex called **machismo** and **marianismo**. These are belief systems about female–male relationships in Latin America and other Spanish-speaking or Catholic countries. The term marianismo refers to the Virgin Mary in Christian theology and usually denotes an attitude of saintliness, passivity, and suffering in silence. Women are believed to be morally superior and spiritually pure. This gender ideology promotes a sacred rationale for female subordination.

Machismo is the name for a belief system about men's relationship to women. The word, derived from **macho**, or animal, refers to the qualities of a "real man." This male superiority complex promotes men as virile, husbands as kings, and homes as their castles. Sexual aggressiveness, excessive drinking, violent behavior, and other types of risk-taking are part of the ideology. In the face of macho men, women must maximize their lot in life by using feminine power within their households. They benefit from their status as wife and mother and accept stoically what they cannot change.

What's wrong with this theory? Human beings, female or male, are not just a collection of ideal roles; we are not just the victims of gender ideologies. The core issue is work and earning a living. As Tracy Ehlers argues,

I maintain that in Guatemala's patriarchal society, the sexual division of labor excludes women from valuable income-producing activities, thus giving them no choice but to accept irresponsible male behavior. Among Mayas and ladinos, the prevailing ideology of male domination in the economy minimizes the contribution women make to family survival and their ability to manage without a resident man. In this system, men are valuable scarce resources who can misbehave with impunity, assured that their wives and mistresses need them for economic reasons. (1991:2)

In this view, women compete with each other for a limited amount of a good thing: husbands who earn money. They put up with men because they have few other choices. As we shall see in chapter 9, processes we call modernization and economic development may mean that men make more money as women make less.

Many anthropologists think that economics and how women organize resources for survival, not the role assignment of martyred suffering, are the determining factors. Anthropologists Carole Browner and Ellen Lewin examined the Virgin Mary complex and strategies for survival in two groups of working-class Latin American women. What is a strategy?

> *We define a strategy as a pattern formed by the many separate, specific behaviors people devise to attain and use resources and to solve the immediate problems confronting them. (Browner and Lewin 1982:63)*

The first group Browner and Lewin looked at was women in Cali, Colombia; they are called Caleñas. The other women live in San Francisco; they are called Latinas. Whether they live in Cali or San Francisco, women have little access to good-paying jobs. So they need either husbands or other economic resources.

> *In Cali, mothers have few alternatives other than to rely on men for subsistence, and Caleñas use their femininity and sexuality in efforts to establish what they wish to be permanent conjugal unions. Latina mothers also generally rely on husbands to meet subsistence needs, but in contrast to the Caleñas, Latinas can and do seek public assistance in the event their conjugal relationships prove unreliable or unstable. Freed of the worry of satisfying immediate needs, Latinas on welfare devote themselves to building intense ties with their offspring, whom they hope will care for them later in life. Unlike Caleñas, Latinas place little emphasis on conjugal affiliation but instead adopt a stance of self-abnegating martyrdom in efforts to cement bonds with their children. (Browner and Lewin 1982:61)*

The women of Cali, Columbia, reported to the interviewers: "It's a rare husband who doesn't beat his wife, who doesn't have mistresses, who is loving." The interviewer asked them: "If he's so bad, why do you stay with him? Why is it important that you be with someone?"

One women responded: "Well, in the first place, there's the respect that the children get coming from a family in which the parents are married . . . Say I left my husband for another. I could end up with someone who didn't want to support my children. They wouldn't be his children you know. My husband is very poor, but he's more or less responsible toward the children."

Others said, "For the sake of the children." "It's better to be with someone you know, at least you know how you're going to suffer, than to be with someone you don't know."

And another said, "Certainly it's good to live with a husband. Not only are the children more respected, but you are more respected in the barrio besides. You can hold your head up and not feel ashamed of your life."

Latina women in San Francisco say: Love is "only an illusion, nothing more." "If your children know what you've given up on their account, they are bound to do what you want them to for the rest of their lives." "Some women don't mind if their husbands do X [drink excessively, sleep with other women, stay out all night, hit them, or other offenses to domestic stability]. But if my husband ever did X, I would take my children and leave him for good." "Everyone always says, 'for the children, for the children.' But you know what you end up with when you stay for the children? More children!"

Here is a husband's point of view: "When men pay for everything, they can have things the way they want them. But once a woman has her own job and her own money, she begins to feel like more than just a woman, and she starts to make demands and want things too."

In both cities, the anthropologists asked this question: "What do you like best about your husband?" In both cities, the most common answer was: "He brings his paycheck right home." "He gives me what I need to live on." For women in both cities, marriage was a lottery. Everyone played but no one knew who would win.

Marriage may be the only viable economic strategy under the circumstances. Having a husband is the best way to have children. Husbands provide money for the children. He is her job, even when the pay is not good nor the benefits all that great.

A women's faith in romantic love and monogamy, her need for resources to raise children, and her conformity to a life as True Woman and Ideal Mother conflict with physical abuse, abandonment and "the other woman." In this picture, partnering may be unavoidable, but it is also unhealthy. Marriage may make women sick.

Duties and Obediences in China

For thousands of years, the people of China have organized family life around the principles of **patrilineal descent,** or tracing inheritance and identity through lines of males. No one argues with the assessment that traditional Chinese life was **patriarchal,** or officially under the control of men. For thousands of years, Chinese girls left their parents' homes and went to live with the family of a husband they had typically never met. This type of postmarital residence is called **patrilocal.**

Traditional China means the People's Republic of China before the Communist Revolution. But the core patriarchal values and practices did not end by governmental decree or so-called modernizations. So they continue in the lives of people of the countries and subcultures who share this historic worldview.

The box, "Ideals for Chinese Women," illustrates the duties of a proper Chinese woman. It is adapted from the teachings of the great patriarchal philosopher, Confucius. In sharp contrast, Confucius enjoined Chinese men to display filial piety or respect for their fathers, to have male children, to make their parents happy and bury them respectfully.

The lowest moment of a woman's life in traditional China was her wedding day. Cut off from her first or natal family, the young bride was an outsider and the object of deep suspicion in her new husband's household. She could not expect her husband to side with her against his family. The only way to earn a place for

Ideals for Chinese Women

The Three Obediences

In Childhood, Before Marriage, Obey Your Father

In Adulthood, During Marriage, Obey Your Husband

In Widowhood, After Marriage, Obey Your Son

The Four Virtues

—*Your conversation is always gentle and polite. You never raise your voice or talk against your father or your husband.*

—*You respect your mother-in-law. You obey your husband and are faithful to him (regardless of whether he is faithful to you or not).*

—*You will keep yourself beautiful for your husband. This includes your face and your body. You are always nicely dressed for him.*

—*You will know many skills, particularly how to cook and do hand-crafts such as sewing and knitting.*

Source: Adapted from Confucius by Tina Soong

herself was to have sons. She would have to placate her mother-in-law and sisters-in-law, ally herself carefully with other young brides, and make deferential friendships with older women. She would learn to use discretion in gossiping about her household or listening to the gossip of others while, at the same time, establishing herself in the invisible but influential women's community. Treated well, other wives offered advice, comfort, peacemaking, and gradually some protection. Eventually, the accumulation of age and common residence started to pay off. As the young bride matured, her husband started to seek advice from her. Her sons honored her. By menopause she could expect to wield considerable power and to be protected in her old age.

In a system as structured as traditional Chinese life, the effect of personalities was especially strong. Imagine what happened to a bride with few social skills who antagonized her mother-in-law. Imagine a rebellious bride who ignored the informal women's community; who would help her then? Imagine a bride who carefully and quietly did her work, banking courtesies and obedience against the day she was no longer a bride but a mother and mother-in-law. We would not be surprised to find that some women became tyrants and domestic despots; others remembered their pain and provided support to younger women in their turn.

There are many Chinese stories about wicked mothers-in-law. In one tale, the mother-in-law placed her foot-binding cloths in the bridal chamber; in another she required the new bride to launder them by hand. From their own experiences, older women knew the tricks to keep a husband and wife apart, even in the privacy of a couple's bedroom. When women can gain power or even minimal comfort only through men as husbands and sons, they predictably use gossip, guile, and circuitous tactics.

It is difficult to find examples of strategies or resistance to this very controlling system of marriage. There are legends about women who found power in some clever manner. There are many fewer stories about women who found romance, love, autonomy, or independence. Anthropologist Andrea Sankar researched a fascinating set of stories about a movement of Chinese women who chose not to marry and who supported themselves. This option was not open to very many women; so the stories show how the marriage system worked and could be manipulated.

From approximately 1865 to the 1930s in the Pearl River delta of China, there was a sisterhood of women called "self-combers." They took a vow to dress their own hair in a style different from the fashion of married women. They were able to find jobs in the silk industries of the region. Small, deft hands could reach into boiling water, pick up, and unwind the delicate silk thread from the cocoon or perform the other tasks of making silk. These jobs, however difficult or painful, gave them economic alternatives to the arranged marriages and submission to Confucian authority that most Chinese women faced. Note the association of single women with spinning.

These working women banded together in sisterhoods or unions to manipulate the marriage customs for their own benefits. Here are some examples: Some women lived with their brother's families, contributing wages and helping to care for their nieces and nephews. Other women went through a marriage ceremony but did not reside with their husbands after marriage. In some cases, the "bride" sent money to the husband's family, in effect buying her freedom. Married women used the hair-combing vow as a type of divorce. They pledged to remain with the sisterhoods and sent their wages back to their husbands as the price of autonomy. Some sisterhoods pooled their earnings and bought other women to substitute as concubines, to replace their members as wives and mothers. Some families encouraged a daughter's hair-combing vow because they could profit from her earnings. Other women moved out of their parents' house and built a spinster house, usually with other women like themselves; this gave them independence, a retirement home, and a way around the ideology that unmarried women brought spiritual damage to their families. However threatening the presence of unmarried women was, their wages apparently compensated and quieted the elders.

Family members nagged the woman about violations of sexual morality. Unmarried women caused Chinese men to worry. They were, by definition, forward, assertive, or lewd; they were probably having affairs with married men; in short, they were out of control sexually. Accusations and belief systems about women as sexually wild and out of control are common when women operate independently outside the legal and religion-sanctioned marriage systems.

Sometimes the emotional bonds forged in the sisterhoods were sexual. Chinese writers tended to ignore females who made love to each other, although they fiercely condemned men who had sex with other men: Such acts did not perpetuate "the Chinese family."

> *In traditional Chinese culture marriage was for production, reproduction, and the maintenance of ancestor worship. Parents or relatives arranged marriages because they understood that it was important for marriage partners to have a successful life. They believed such business was too serious to be left only to sexual attraction. Folk wisdom warned against the instability of love matches. (Sankar 1985:80)*

In fact, the existence of the sisterhoods was a way to avoid marriage and still provide oneself with secure work and retirement; it was not about finding a fulfilling sexual or romantic life. As a result, the lesbian relationships among the women of the sisterhood were typically volatile or temporary. Lives based on romance and abiding passion are problematic in such a system, no matter who does it.

Women who managed to resist marriage often found security, companionship, and affection in the sisterhoods. These were like labor unions or social clubs and ranged in size from small groups of three to seven members to larger associations of up to forty members. These ties of sisterhood were often the major relationships for women; this is particularly true as the chaos of war and violence swept women, families and local communities asunder. Today sisterhoods still exist in cities of Southeast Asia, Hong Kong, and the People's Republic of China.

A Circle of Wives: African Experiences

The marriage system in which a man has more than one wife is called **polygyny** or polygynous. The word translates as "many women." Anthropologists note that it is fairly common around the world. We fail to note, however, that our analyses are done from a male point of view. Women involved in patterns of polygyny have, by definition, only one husband but one or more co-wives. From a woman's point of view, this system is called **monandry,** or having one husband.

> *Because women in 99.5 percent of cultures around the world marry only one man at once, it is fair to conclude that monandry, one spouse, is the overwhelmingly predominant marriage pattern for the human female. (Fisher 1992:69)*

From a statistical point of view, monandry is the most common form of marriage on the planet. Moreover, women who live in polygynous systems share the status and work of wife with other women. But there are no terms for this pattern.

Polygyny as a marriage system has one of its most vivid expressions on the continent of Africa. This practice is often thought to oppress women. Many contemporary scholars of African life point out, however, that polygyny fostered an ethic of independent action for African women. Filomena Chioma Steady is a scholar from Sierra Leone. She notes that the function of marriage in Africa, as elsewhere, is economic and points to the advantages of polygyny for women.

> *In fact the double standard of morality characteristic of monogamous marriages was not the rule. It was quite acceptable in many societies for women in polygynous households to have lovers. Social organization being communal, rather than composed of nuclear family units, ensured a certain amount of socioeconomic security and cooperation among members of the polygynous household. Polygyny also guaranteed the social and economic responsibility of males for their children. As a result women did not have to struggle for their survival or bear the sole responsibility for their children's care, but could at the same time have a certain amount of independence from absolute male dominance. (Steady 1981:16)*

At this point, most people ask, How do people involved in polygyny feel about it? How does it work on a personal level? Here Mabel Segun, a journalist, novelist and writer from Nigeria, talks about the customs of plural marriages. Note that she uses the term **polygamy.** This term means "having more than one mate." Theoretically, the term can apply to a woman having two or more husbands, a man having two or more wives, or anyone having one spouse and one or more lovers simultaneously. In this way, we note the formal as well as the informal arrangements common in the world. She also uses the term polygamy to refer to **serial monogamy,** or being married to a number of people—one at a time.

> *In the days when I was a schoolgirl, everybody understood what was meant by polygamy. It did not have to be defined. It simply meant having more than one wife. But nowadays when you talk about polygamy people ask, "Which kind?" For it seems there are now three kinds of polygamy. One is the traditional form practiced by our forefathers and a number of unprogressive contemporaries. Under this system a man has two or more wives all of whom are officially recognized under customary law. This form is considered by educated people as "bush" and "out-of-date." The more enlightened form of polygamy and one that benefits the educated man of the twentieth century is the one in which ostensibly monogamous husbands have what some people refer to as "external affairs." The third form of polygamy is the "one-by-one" type popularized by Hollywood. (Segun quoted in Busby 1992:373)*

According to Segun, the actions resulting from feelings of jealousy are a major problem. A husband in a polygynous situation has to act fair and use good managerial skills. Yes, a man may enjoy having a wife kneeling to him as she presents him with a drink. Yes, he may enjoy women vying for his favors, available to him at night, every night. But this may be at the price of quarrelling among his wives. Wife 2 parades her children in front of Wife 1 who has none; Wife 3 decides to sweep while Wife 2 is eating a meal. Wife 1 sings songs that seem to insult her other co-wives. What if two or three wives are pregnant at once? Can he separate them into different households? Yes, but this is expensive. Can he act as judge, listen to each case, and beat them on occasion? Yes, but they will find means to retaliate.

There were, contrary to appearances, some advantages to plural marriages. Sometimes senior wives provided the bride price so husbands could acquire another and junior wife. If a husband were going to have a new sweetheart, the first wife could keep a firm eye on her and keep the family income under one roof. This is one way women could exercise some control.

A compelling reason for women to cooperate in plural marriages was to have a "helpmate" or a co-wife to assist in the household work. Traditional housework involved tedious preparations like grinding or carrying foods from market. In fact, female companionship was a major appeal of polygyny. If the marriages worked out and the co-wives liked each other, they would have someone to gossip with. Co-wives as allies and friends meant control over their joint husband, household, budget, and children. They might even find other wives to wait on them!

Polygyny is as much about women's relations to each other as it is their relations to men. Her husband's other wives may well be the most hostile, controlling, cooperative, or loving relationships a wife ever experiences outside her natal family. Polygyny worked best when women liked and conspired with each other. The box, "Chorus Sung by Co-Wives to One Another," is a song about a co-wife. It suggests the frustration and unhappiness of sharing a husband and a yearning for something like exclusivity or romance.

Generally, the senior wife set the tone. Like a mother-in-law in other settings, she could use her power as friendship and cooperation or as dominance and meanness. She had power but a later wife may have been her husband's love match. There are many stories about married woman who left husbands because of co-wives. The stories conclude, "The man was all right, but those other women were impossible!" By contrast, wives may get along splendidly. In one West African story, a man wakes up to find his three wives vanished with all their children. They have decided they like each other best and can support themselves in a joint business venture. He whines, "Who's going to fix my breakfast now?"

Many authors talk about the central values and practices in African kinship. These include the centrality of children, multiple mothering, fostering, and the primacy of kinship ties over marital ties. Children in ancestor-worshiping cultures mark the connections between the dead, the living, and as yet unborn; they promise continuity of generations in a more articulated fashion than we normally understand it. **Consanguineal kin,** or those related by blood, are closer and more dependable than spouses are.

If we examine the perceptions of contemporary African women, it is evident that they see themselves as working for their own and their

Chorus Sung by Co-Wives to One Another

Woman, your soul is misshapen,

In haste was it made;

So fleshless a face speaks,

Saying your soul was formed without care.

The ancestral clay for your making

Was moulded in haste.

A thing of no beauty are you,

Your face unsuited for a face,

Your feet unsuited for feet.

from Dahomey–Benin

Source: Melville J. Herskovits (1938) Volume 1, 343. Translated by Frances Herskovits.

children's benefit, not for their husbands. It seems probable that earlier generations of African women held similar views. Although a woman may have contributed to her husband's accumulation of wealth and status, in practice men seldom exercised direct control over wives' productive activities and could not appropriate their produce in many places, even where there were ideologies of male ownership. (Potash 1989:193)

Mothers in so-called polygynous households are usually the central figure in family life and households whether they reckon kinship through the mother's line or through the father's line. This means matrifocal units are still the core of emotional life. It also means that women have, at least before colonialism, significant economic independence. Men as husbands have limited authority in their wives' households. A man as brother is extremely important to his sisters and his sisters' children, all of whom share the same matrilineage, property, and ritual responsibilities.

Moreover, the polygynous kinship systems of Africa allowed women to have wives. How is this possible? Taking a wife was a mark of wealth and success. So women who had the means and resources took wives too. Women, that is, biological females who worked as wives to female husbands, did the same things all wives do. They worked at status enhancement and were a major asset in helping their female husbands accumulate wealth. They freed their husbands from domestic work. The female husbands could have the status and power that men had by becoming like men.

This was not necessarily about having sex (although men worried about and commented on that possibility). This is about kinship and using the rules of marriage to advance oneself. Nigerian sociologist Ifi Amadiume grew up in and did research in the Igbo area with a group called Nnobi. She explains:

> *In indigenous Nnobi society, there was a direct link between accumulation of wives, the acquisition of wealth and the exercise of power and authority. The ultimate indication of wealth and power, the title system, was open to men and women, as was the means of becoming rich through control over the labour of others by way of polygamy, whether man-to-woman marriage or woman-to-woman marriage. The Nnobi flexible gender system made either possible. (Amadiume 1987:42)*

The strategic uses of kinship went beyond female husbands. For the Igbo, land was the basis of how people earned a living and men needed heirs in patrilineal societies. So men without sons converted a daughter into a kind of man—the kind who could inherit land. So a woman became a male daughter and landowner.

In many areas of Africa, women grew and sold their own crops, manufactured products for sale in the local markets, and managed their own money. Women who became successful traders took "wives" for themselves. Adult women could become "husbands" that is, pay bride-price to gain rights in the labor of women.

> *If women are expected either to exercise power or to symbolize power, they must be conceptualized as male, or at least not take on the subordinate status of wife. . . . What more effective symbol than a reversal from the expected roles of wife and mother to those of husband and father. (O'Brien 1977:122)*

Among the highly stratified states of West Africa, women as wives in polygynous households often had formal relationships with each other. Girls were often betrothed and married soon after puberty to men much older than themselves. The groom's kinfolk paid a bride-price to the bride's kin. This bride-price gave the new husband and his family the right to claim her children for their lineage (the only way to have children in a patrilineage is to buy or otherwise acquire the services from a woman who is not a relative). Wealthy men had several wives; typically, each wife had her own house in the compound and a plot of land to cultivate. She could sell the products in the market and keep the proceeds, generally to assist her children with their education.

The longer a wife was married, the more benefits and freedom she was likely to enjoy. This included intimacies, both sexual and economic, with other women. Taking co-wives as lovers was safer and easier than meeting men outside the compounds. Women did not inform their husbands about these arrangements. Husbands tended to hear gossip and to feel threatened about them but did not have the power to order them stopped. In some groups, women staged a ritual to create a formal and permanent bond between them. By doing this, women probably extended and confirmed their economic networks, enhanced their position in the community, and improved their emotional life (Blackwood 1985a, b).

African polygyny reminds me very forcefully of the contemporary blended family and multiple marriages in the United States. Divorced people often have assorted relationships with an ex-husband's new wife, their new children, her ex-husband, their children, as well as the new mate's former spouses, lovers, and children. Everyone has strong feelings about these arrangements. Sometimes we act strategically, creatively, or romantically. Sometimes we are mean and resistant.

Questioning Romance

Suppose you went to a wedding shower in the United States and the bride said, "I'm getting married because he has money and he can afford to support me and my children well. Keeping house for him will be the best job I could hope for." Sounds unromantic, doesn't it? Alternatively, imagine that your sixteen-year-old daughter has just brought home her new "boyfriend." She sighs, "We are totally in love. We want to get married. We are old enough to know what we are doing. I never felt this way before. You just don't understand."

The notion of romantic love has always been around. The attachment of this idea to marriage is probably recent. Marriage as a universal institution is not the same as the set of feelings called romance or romantic love. Typically, "falling in love" has not been the primary reason for getting married. Economic realities, the desire for children, and the duties of kinship are.

The ideas of romance and romantic encounters are most often associated with affairs or rebellion against authority. They offer adventure, excitement, or defiance. Falling in love is rebellious and subversive; it may be a powerful form of resistance. Romance is a kind of shorthand for the emotional qualities attached to a cultural institution like marriage or to specialized interpersonal relationships. The so-called "traditional" pattern for marriage across the planet is for the families to help young people in finding a mate; sometimes these are outright arranged marriages, others are a little contrived, just short of a business deal. Other times, there are expectations so subtle and pervasive that everyone just goes along with them. Traditional patterns of marriage offer some surprising benefits. A shy or noncompetitive person can still end up with a good partner. Those who arranged the marriage owe the couple; this may range from lifetime economic support to the equivalent of room and board. Many people in arranged marriages expect to fall in love later.

In the United States, ideas of romance, love, of falling in love, and of being in love are central to formal and informal relationships between females and males. Americans express these beliefs in books, movies, music, and every other media. We export this gender or partnering ideology. Our representations of romance in partnering are one of the most powerful and influential forces in the world.

One of the best examples about partnering in this familiar context are romance novels. In fact, many people think that romances are the quintessential myths of partnering in this culture. They are profoundly woman-centered and reveal a great deal about marriage in America. Romance, whether in books or in lives, is the primary ideology about why people get married and live in the same place together. Romances are a major piece of women's folklore and women's culture. They are also a primary example of the social production of stories by women and for women. Writing them is one example of career development for women.

Romance novels are about 45 percent of all mass market paperback book sales in the United States and 30 to 40 percent worldwide. Harlequin alone sells almost 200 million books in some twenty languages to loyal readers around the globe.

In some social circles, romance novels are stigmatized as escapism, soft-core pornography, and antifeminist. It is said (in criticism of the genre) that anonymous writers crank out only one single monolithic story for their brainless readers. But women keep reading them. Why? What do they say to us?

Below are some quotes from some women who write romances. They believe that they speak for themselves, for their characters, and for their readers. Here are the major themes they identify about the subculture of romance novels, romantics and readers.

First: Romance novels are about privacy, fantasy, and interior lives, about experiences out of time and space. Of course, they are an escape from bickering children, needy husbands or bosses, and boring chores. Between books, however, real life is real life. No one actually confuses them.

Laura Kinsale got a graduate degree and worked as a uranium and petroleum geologist before she began to write prize-winning historical romances. She says:

> *In the reading of a romance, the conflict and resolution of a romantic relationship are entirely within the reader and have nothing directly to do with the reader's husband, boyfriend, male boss, male co-workers, except as they may interfere with the reading process itself. (Krentz 1992:39)*

Second: Romance novels are about female empowerment. Women are heroes, independent, subversive, and powerful. They speak a special code in the language of sexual politics. Romance writing and reading romances are forms of resistance to male-centered cultures. Jayne Ann Krentz, a former college and corporate librarian, is also known as Amanda Quick, Jayne Castle, and Stephanie James. She says of the heroine in romance novels:

> *With courage, intelligence, and gentleness she brings the most dangerous creature on earth, the human male, to his knees. More than that, she forces him to acknowledge her power as a woman. (Krentz 1992:5)*

The hero, or alpha male, as romance writers call him, may be older, stronger, and more worldly than the heroine. The heroine has limited resources; she must confront him with intelligence and courage. She always wins.

Third and most important: Each romance is a journey, a retelling of the mythical and classical tales of partnerships between women and men. Linda Barlow, who put aside her dissertation in English literature to write romances, says:

> *What we are dealing with in romance novels is the inner material of feminine consciousness, passionately and defiantly expressed by women who have been oppressed and repressed by the forms and strictures of the patriarchy. Because of the deep-seated nature of this material, the romantic myth will continue to be dreamed and explored by women, and hard-eyed heroes will continue to rage against the plucky heroines who defy them until they are forever united by the reconciling power of love. (Krentz 1992:52)*

To these women, romance stories are modern examples of the basic myths and legends of thousands of years and thousands of cultures. Women tame dangerous men; in effect, women domesticate wild creatures through love.

These modern mythologies are a powerful feature of American marriage systems. The entire system of kinship and marriage is based on emotion and feelings. As one of my friends said, "Being in love is the only thing that makes the institution of marriage bearable." Here are some questions: Are the ideologies of romance a form of resistance to, escape from, or conformity to monogamous and neolocal marriage patterns? Are women oppressed or liberated by the romantic ideologies of partnering? Are the ideas of love and romance universal? Was Morgan wrong when he said that the Iroquois felt no such emotions? Is romantic love a gender ideology? If so, whom does it serve? Is romance another form of women's work?

You may have noticed that I omitted discussion of a prominent feature of partnering: wife-beating and wife-battering. We will cover this important topic in chapter 10, in the context of violence against women around the world. This discussion of "marriage and family" leads us into the next chapter, to systems that segregate the lives of females and males in highly structured ways and buttress their segregation with elaborate ideologies and myths. Following that, in chapter 7, we will look beyond these cultural constructions about partners, gender, and kinship to the third sex and the range of alternatives and options available in human societies.

Reading from Romance to Resistance

Here are some suggestions for books that follow the topics in this chapter. Filomina Chioma Steady edited a very readable collection of articles called *The Black Woman Cross-Culturally*. She gathered a significant but scattered body of cross-cultural literature on Black women in Africa, North America, South

America, and the Caribbean. The book centers on the creative survival strategies of women in the African Diaspora.

All good ethnographies cover topics like "marriage and family." However, not all of them cover women's lives with sensitivity and insight. Here are a number of suggestions. Sally Price has a second edition of *Co-wives and Calabashes,* a readable ethnography about the Saramaka Maroons, descendants of Africans brought as slaves to the Dutch colony of Surinam. Gender is complex and fascinating in this matrilineal and polygynous society.

After having two kids, Diane Bell finished high school, went to college, and got a doctorate. She has published widely in anthropology, history, law, and women's studies. Her book, *Daughters of the Dreaming* (1993, 2d ed.) is a tale both of her fieldwork in the central Australian desert and of women's lives in an absolutely fascinating setting, rich in ritualism and spiritualism against all odds.

Sumiko Iwao, a social psychologist, wrote *The Japanese Woman: Traditional Image and Changing Realities;* here is an excellent way to get into the literature on women in Japan. She confronts the stereotypes of passive, obedient wives and geisha girls and shows Japanese women as ambitious and strategic. This approach has important implications for gender ideologies in the United States.

Virginia Kerns wrote *Women and the Ancestors: Black Carib Kinship and Ritual* (1989). In this black Caribbean society, older women occupy central positions as mothers of the living and daughters of the dead, valued and self-respecting leaders in religious life. This book is also a major contribution to a sparse literature on the "anthropology of aging."

Do not discount sisters as "partners" or as key players in partnering. You can see how this works in Lynn Bennett, *Dangerous Wives, Sacred Sisters: Social and Symbolic Roles of High Caste Women in Nepal* (1983); and Karen Sachs, *Sisters and Wives: The Past and Future of Sexual Equality* (1982).

If you want to see wives' strategies for economic advancement and survival, read Garcia Clark, *Onions Are My Husband: Survival and Accumulation by West African Market Women* (1994). The status of widows (former wives) is crucial in a number of kinship systems in the world. Betty Potash edited an excellent collection of articles that emphasizes marriage as women's work, and marriage as an economic institution in the political economy: *Widows in African Society: Choices and Constraints* (1986).

The Communist Revolution was supposed to free Chinese women from the virtual gender slavery of the traditional marriage system. So what happened? Read Margery Wolf's *Revolution Postponed: Women in Contemporary China* (1985). Here an experienced anthropologist who has written about Chinese women for many years describes the conflicts and contradictions of equalizing relations between the sexes. The book has been described as chilling, sensitive, and astute.

Living arrangements, postmarital residence patterns, physical spaces, and a "room of her own" are very important considerations for the lives of women. Although this book edited by Hemalata Dandekar anticipates the material in chapter 9, the topic of housing is intimately a part of partnering. *Shelter, Women and Development: First and Third World Perspectives* (1993) is a collection of articles with a very grounded and practical sensitivity to women's needs around shelter.

The powerful own the rights to name and define. Language really does encode culture. Words really do matter. Jane Mills's collection, *Womanwords: A Dictionary of Words About Women* (1993), contains examples taken mostly from classical and Western sources. Trace the term **housewife,** meaning respected domestic administrator in the Middle Ages, as it becomes hussy or loose woman in later times. The term **maid** first meant a girl, then a young unmarried woman, then a female virgin. Eventually, the term means a domestic servant in which virginity and marital status are both related to employment. Other words about women are equally fun to follow.

Another dictionary to consult is Barbara Walker's *The Woman's Dictionary of Symbols and Sacred Objects* (1988). Or you might read Casey Miller and Kate Swift, *Words and Women: New Language in New Times* (1991), for examples and discussions about nonsexist language usage.

For an anthropological viewpoint quite different from this chapter, you might try Helen Fisher, *Anatomy of Love: The Mysteries of Mating, Marriage, and Why We Stray* (1992). Reviewers called this book provocative, enlightening, and controversial. Fisher, anthropologist at the American Museum of Natural History, has some evolutionary theories about infatuation, female orgasm, and human pair-bonding.

Chapter Six

A Two-Bodied World

Cultural Systems for Separating Females and Males

*J was born in a harem in 1940 in Fez, a ninth-century Moroccan city some five thousand kilometers west of Mecca, and one thousand kilometers south of Madrid, one of the dangerous capitals of the Christians. The problems with the Christians start, said Father, as with women, when the **hudud**, or sacred frontier, is not respected. I was born in the midst of chaos, since neither Christians nor women accepted the frontiers. . . . When Allah created the earth, said Father, he separated men from women, and put a sea between Muslims and Christians for a reason. Harmony exists when each group respects the prescribed limits of the other; trespassing leads only to sorrow and unhappiness. But women dreamed of trespassing all the time. The world beyond the gate was their obsession. They fantasized all day long about parading in unfamiliar streets, while the Christians kept crossing the sea, bringing death and chaos. (Mernissi 1994:1)*

In many human cultures, women and men live apart from each other in fascinating and complex ways. These **sexual or gender separation systems** are historically based styles of living and social organizations in which the lives of women and the lives of men are substantially segregated. In these groups, people manipulate the biological facts of sex and reproduction and the social necessities of kinship. They invent or embroider whole arenas of social life around the notion of gender.

This chapter contains three examples. The first takes place in the rain forests of the Amazon in a group called the Mundurucú. The second example concerns selected groups in the culture area of Melanesia. The third example comes from some of the nation states of the Muslim Middle East. We will conclude with Moroccan sociologist Fatima Mernissi, who grew up in one of these systems of separation. The opening paragraph of her autobiography, quoted above, sets the themes of this chapter.

Why do such segregated systems exist? There are as many theories as there are anthropologists, ethnographers, historians, or other commentators. As you will see, mythologies, ideologies, or sacred scriptures justify but do not explain the segregation of sexes. Insiders and outsiders or participants and observers usually have strong opinions and deep emotions about such gender-differentiated lives. No one is safely objective. There are no agreements about what these systems ultimately mean or how they came to exist. Sometimes, but not always, these systems appear to be cases of male control or dominance. Much of the time, however, they look like an elaborate game of creativity wrapped in the symbols and perceptions of a two-bodied world. Each example in the chapter contains these multiple perspectives.

On one level, these dramatic systems are still about partnering, kinship, family and marriage; the same work still gets done. So this chapter is an extension of chapters 4 and 5. We have merely turned up the volume on one characteristic, gender separation.

The following themes appear in each. First, significant items of material culture symbolize the sexual segregation systems. This includes such objects as trumpets, flutes, veils, masks, banana fiber skirts, string bags, and many others. Body decorations, costumes, and clothing are often pronounced between genders. Living quarters are physically separated: men's houses, women's houses, or men's sides, women's sides.

Second, each example centers on assertions that there are only two genders and men and women are not equal or interchangeable. Our human "natures" are different. People in these kinds of cultures have elaborate mythologies which establish sacred justifications for how relationships between the sexes are supposed to be. They apply the myths to conception as well as life after death. They have to work out the practical considerations in separating genders. What happens to young boys, born to women, who must grow up to be men? What if women question the system or have their own system? Who does the work and who gets the credit? What about having sex? What about personal feelings, emotions, or sentiments, such as love?

Third, women are powerful in unexpected ways.

Amazon: Women of the Forest and the Flutes

In 1952 two young graduate students at Columbia University, Yolanda Murphy and Robert Murphy, married and went to South America to do fieldwork in anthropology. The research they did together in the rain forests of Amazonian Brazil led to one of the first ethnographies that actually looked at and saw women's lives.

> *Because women are placed below men in the order of things, we assume that they are submissive. Because they are excluded from so much of what is reported by anthropologists as "the culture," we assume that they do not have one of their own. Because they have a traditional position within the society, we assume that the women accept it without question. And in reporting on what is conceived by men to be the proper domain of women, we all too easily believe, with them, that this is indeed the reality of everyday life. (Murphy and Murphy 1974:52)*

The Murphys did not listen just to what men said about women. Nor did they have the kind of marriage in which she wrote about women and he wrote about the "real" culture. This is why their book, *Women of the Forest*, has become an icon in women's studies.

There are three points in time for Mundurucú gender relations. First is the mythic past, when women owned and played sacred musical instruments. Second is the ethnographic present, the moment the Murphys witnessed, of uneasy truces, fear, and anger between women and men. The third moment is the future. The Murphys arrived as traditional Mundurucú life was changing to resemble other poor people within the nation state of Brazil.

In the past, the Mundurucú, like other groups deep in the forests of the Amazon, made gardens, collected wild fruits and nuts, hunted, or fished for a living. The heavy task of clearing the land for gardening was men's work; they helped in planting the manioc shoots. But all the rest of the planting, harvesting, and food processing was done by women. Manioc, the bitter staple of their diet, was inedible without the time-consuming, physically laborious, and exhausting work of women in processing the tubers.

The Mythic Past of the Mundurucú

The Mundurucú tell a tale, a myth about sex, sacred objects, men's groups, and women's work. The story in a shortened version in the box, "The Myth of the Mundurucú," is the basis for their view of the social lives of the sexes. There are many such mythologies in the world.

This story outlines the mythic past of Mundurucú males and females and justifies the separations of the present. Women once owned and played with the sacred trumpets. Men wrested them away. Men hunt; meat is the only proper food for honoring the ancestors. Women make manioc cakes; everyone eats them every day, but they are unfit for offering to the ancestors. The men live in men's houses with each other and the trumpets. Women live in dwelling houses where men enter at will. So women cannot refuse the sexual needs of men.

Such stories of power and gender reversals laced with sexual and phallic symbols are common, although not universal, in the world. They act as spiritual permission or as a supernatural charter for how separate sexes are supposed to, or allowed to, treat each other. They justify but do not explain.

The Ethnographic Present

In the ordinary times of the 1950s, Mundurucú men were uneasy and fearful in their control. The male creed said that women were inferior and ungovernable. But women also threatened men. After all, they once owned the trumpets and found private pleasure in them. Men were insecure: They could deny formal authority to women, but they knew the oppressed had potential power. According to the Murphys, the two genders were not just ranked higher or lower than each other. These were not individuals in role conflict. They were opposing armies.

Men wanted women to be passive and retiring, to close off their eyes and mouths. Women were not supposed to participate in political or religious affairs nor question the ways of men. A woman who violated these rules was said to be wanton and promiscuous, a Mundurucú nymphomaniac. Men used gang rape to punish any woman who violated their taboos. These ranged from acting seductive to spying on the sacred flutes. So women had to work and travel in groups of two or more. If a woman walked alone outside the village, she was assumed to be heading for a rendezvous. Just being alone made her available and gave men the right to stop her and demand intercourse. The Murphys called this a classic example of phallic sadism.

The Myth of the Mundurucú

Once, three women collecting firewood heard the sound of music in the distance. They went in the direction of the music. Deep in the forest they found a beautiful, clear lake and some fish swimming in the shallows. They rubbed the mouths of their nets with a nut that made the fish drowsy, and each woman caught a fish. Each fish turned into a hollow flute-like trumpet.

The women hid their trumpets in the forest. They abandoned their husbands and their housework to go there and play with their sacred instruments. But their husbands and brothers grew suspicious, followed them, and discovered the secret. The men said, "You can play your instruments; just bring them out of the forest and into the houses."

On the day arranged for the entry of the trumpets to the village, the women ordered the men to shut themselves inside the dwelling houses. The men refused and insisted on staying in the men's house. Finally, a compromise was reached. The brother of one of the women who discovered the trumpets said, "We will go into the dwellings for one night only. Then tomorrow we will take the trumpets. After all we are the only ones who can go hunting to catch meat for ceremonials and offerings to the trumpets."

That night, the women marched around the village playing the trumpets. After dark, the women entered the dwellings one by one and forced the men to have sex with them. The men were not allowed to refuse, and the women returned to the men's house all sticky and slippery. The following day, the men seized the trumpets and the men's house. The women returned to the dwelling houses and cried for what they had lost.

Source: Adapted from Yolanda Murphy and Robert Murphy, *Women of the Forest* (1974), 88.

Mundurucú men asserted that they possessed the crucial ingredients for siring offspring. But women actually bore and nursed the children. This fundamental contradiction was partially resolved by a kind of folk-science about reproduction. The Mundurucú believed that seminal fluid coagulated and formed the fetus. So a woman needed to have a number of sexual contacts with a man before she could become pregnant. In this reasoning, men provide all the raw material to make a child; women merely did the work of carrying them. One consequence of this belief was that women's frequent extramarital affairs were not counted toward conception or pregnancy building; only her husband's efforts mattered. Folk beliefs like this reduce women's work in reproduction to something resembling an incubator. Most societies (ours included) have folk embryology or folk genetics—conception ideologies that reveal relationships around gender and sex.

In their dirt-floored communal dwellings, there was no "housework" as we know it. The major work of Mundurucú women was making manioc. The tubers from the manioc plant grew year round in the poor soils of the forests. But manioc is bitter and nauseating unless carefully processed. So groups of women worked long and hard to peel, chop, and grate the tubers. They hauled water by hand and poured it over the pieces to leach out acids. They toasted the lumpy manioc flour over a fire until dry. In addition, they gathered, gardened, and cared for children. All the work was competently supervised by experienced older women. These women served as midwives, advised on matters such as hammock-making, and exercised a mild but undisputed authority.

As women processed the manioc, they gossiped. This activity must not be overlooked or trivialized. Gossip is the primary form of social control in face-to-face groups such as villages, companies, neighborhoods, or sororities. Most of it is the exchange of valuable information about other people's activities and behaviors. Gossip may be thought of in this context as personal strategies, apprenticeship learning, or social control.

Everyone ate manioc everyday, but they preferred to eat meat. Men hunted only irregularly and with unpredictable results, but they garnered attention and recognition for it.

> *The men think of themselves as hunters, not as gardeners or fisher-*
> *men, the religion is oriented toward hunting, and the spirit world is*
> *closely associated with the species of game. It is the skillful hunter who*
> *is honored, not the industrious tiller of the soil. Hunting is central in*
> *Mundurucú culture because it is men's work, and not vice versa. In*
> *actuality, gardening provides a larger proportion of the sheer bulk of*
> *Mundurucú food intake and the subject of greatest labor investment,*
> *albeit mostly female labor. (Murphy and Murphy 1974:62)*

Women's work went on steadily each day. Whether a hunt was successful or not, there would always be manioc and gathered food to eat.

The architecture of their domestic life was one of the most telling features of how women and men related to each other. A traditional Mundurucú village had a number of dwellings and one men's house. The dwellings were open; they had no compartments and no privacy. Females regardless of age and boys below the age of puberty lived there. Household members hung their sleeping hammocks at the quieter ends of the dwelling and used the busy center for cooking, nursing babies, and visiting back and forth. Children and dogs wandered in and out. Men dropped by for food, sex, or visiting their babies, but they were marginal to life within the dwellings. Men took the young boys away from the communal dwellings at some point before puberty. Both women and men agreed that the only enduring bond was between mothers and daughters. Sisters and the residential bonds of shared work and shared children came next. Despite patrilineal descent and the male myth of control, the reality was matrilocal and matrifocal, mother-centered living arrangements.

The women of Mundurucú lived in deep solidarity with each other. They shared farming, manioc flour-making, common dwellings, and caring for each other's children. Women traveled in bands for protection. When men asserted authority and the power of the myth, they only increased women's cohesion with each other and their hostility toward males. Women dropped their eyes or averted their heads around men.

> *In one sense, this behavior can be interpreted as submissive, although at another level it is a primary form of defense. Women guard their emotions before men, communicate as little as possible of their subjective states, set themselves off with reserve. The woman who casts down her eyes when near men is not really saying that she is inferior, but that she is apart and distant, that she is not to be interfered with. She becomes symbolically impenetrable. (Murphy and Murphy 1974:137)*

The Murphys described the women as "secular" and "pragmatic." Women knew about the trumpets and ritual equipment hidden in the men's house, but seemed indifferent both to the objects and men's anxieties about them. Women said that men were lazy. In fact, women were more loyal to housemates than to husbands.

Under these circumstances, why would women bother with marriage? They fed children with their own labor and shared domestic quarters with other women. Marriage, however, as the Murphys noted, was simply the normal state for adults and the smallest building block in a functioning society. For women, marriage appeared to be an investment, a status, a presumed or usual activity. It was not compelled by feelings. A woman understood that intercourse was the way to get and keep a husband and that male sexual satisfaction was the goal. So adultery was a form of revenge on an erring husband, not a means of enjoyment for a woman.

Most of the women complained to the Murphys about frequent childbearing. They blamed men for the pregnancies, miscarriages, and stillbirths they experienced through adulthood. They told the anthropologists about several birth control remedies made from roots. The same concoctions could also be used to induce abortions. They kept all these matters secret from men; it was simply none of their business.

The Future Arrived

Everyone has heard about the deforestation of the Amazon basin, the development policies of nation states like Brazil, and the profound and irreversible changes of modernization. The village traditions of the Mundurucú were already under pressure when the Murphys arrived. Brazilians were clearing the forest for plantations, agriculture, and ranching. Some villages were already involved with the cash and consumer economy, missionary stations, and wage labor. What happens to women, men, and systems of separation when the entire economic and social base shifts?

The Murphys profiled the processes already underway in some villages. Mundurucú, like former traditional peoples anywhere in the world, have smaller households and nuclear families. There are no longer dwellings arranged by gender, no more sacred instruments to support the oppression of women, and no more groups of men making demands. What we call a nuclear family becomes the unit of work and common meals.

Women still do most of the work, simply because in smaller couple-centered households, there is no one else. Husbands will "help," but at the expense of women's vital connections with each other. Preparing manioc flour is easier with new equipment but bereft of cooperation, amiability, and female socializing. Men will take care of babies more often, simply because there is no one else to do it. In contrast to the old forest dwellings, small households have few back-up baby tenders.

Mundurucú women want husbands to live with them and provide for them. They want Western consumer goods: metal pots, pans, knives, axes, clothing, ornaments, canned foods, and the things they know women in big cities have. They want hand-turned, mechanical grinders for manioc. This simple tool speeds the processing a hundredfold and alters the sexual division of labor in manifold ways. So Mundurucú women urge their husbands to take wage labor jobs to earn cash. They nag and sweet-talk them into harder work or debt. Husbands work for hourly wages when they can and use the money to buy Western consumer goods. Religious and festive gatherings will be at the mission station and in the bars of small towns. Men will be able to buy alcohol.

Are women better off with all these changes? Cohesive women's work groups and female-centered living arrangements are gone. The source of solidarity in the forest dwellings came from shared, kinship, space, and workloads. One does not retrieve profound connections in shared visits between houses. Senior women no longer provide leadership. Men, as husbands, are the heads of households.

> *Instead of asking ourselves who has it best, perhaps we should be asking the Mundurucú woman. The answer here is quite unequivocal: with few exceptions they prefer the nuclear family arrangements of the new communities. They do so because trade goods are more readily available, and they prefer their men to help them. On one level, this is exactly what the women want—they seek aid and relief in the drudge work of manioc growing and processing . . . . And though there may have been little absolute improvement in their situation, the gap between them and the men is perceived by them to have narrowed. The women may not have been elevated, but the men surely have been reduced. (Murphy and Murphy 1974:202)*

Yolanda Murphy and Robert Murphy had gone to Brazil as two individuals and left as "time-tested veterans of the connubial state" (1985:75). Yolanda Murphy had been absorbed into village sisterhoods as a friend and advocate. The women "looked upon her as a person with the same basic problem as theirs: men" (1985:70). Robert had been an outsider even to Mundurucú males. He slept, quite literally, with his wife, and didn't know how to hunt. The couple may have lived in the same quarters, but they hadn't lived in the same world.

Something profound happened within their marriage. Many anthropologists leave their field site and head for divorce court. Others never agree on what they saw or what it means. But in the two decades between fieldwork and joint publication, the Murphys used their marital and professional collaboration to forge a fascinating picture of gender. The publication of *Women of the Forest* in 1974 came during the period when anthropologists had begun to notice women in a new light. The fieldwork that changed their partnership changed our view of gender.

Melanesia: Birth and Semen

The gender separation systems of Melanesia are probably the most dramatic in the world. Accounts and analyses of aggression and antagonism between men and women pervade anthropological research. Some of this was evident in the discussions of Sepik River cultures. Here are some additional examples of sexual segregation, drawn mostly from the highland or intermontane region of New Guinea.

The social order in most (although not all) of Melanesia seems to be divided by gender. Here anthropologist Roger Keesing talks about these systems of segregation.

> *A first pervasive theme is that males and females are radically different in their physical and psychological being and that the fluids, essences, and powers of women are dangerous and inimical to those of men. This premise renders cosmic and natural the terms of men's domination of religion and ritual, and the limited coparticipation of men and women in domestic life. (Keesing 1982:7)*

In ordinary life, men and women are separate. They work apart and spend leisure hours apart. Their tasks and family responsibilities are different; so are their authority and powers. In many cultures of New Guinea, rules of residence separate husbands and wives into different houses. In many places, women go to menstrual huts or birth huts. Young boys are often removed from the company of all women, including their mothers, and taken into the men's houses. There, initiation rituals for the boys dramatize the dangers of pollution or injury caused by women and teach the boys ways to purify themselves. Males have strong anxieties about sex and the polluting powers and dangerous "natures" of women. Many rituals and myths reflect an ideology of mutual danger. Each gender would be safer if they could only avoid the other. But such a life is impossible. Baby boys would die without their mothers, husbands and wives must share work and food, and everyone is at the mercy of their sex drives.

Here are some characteristic statements from the highlands of New Guinea that give the flavor of gender relationships there:

> *Women: "No wonder that log defies your efforts—you cannot even raise your own tiny penes [penises]!"*

Men: "Stand aside or close your legs lest our huge logs burst your dragging vulvas."

Men: "Women are rubbish."

Women: "Men are no good." (Meggitt 1964)

Blood Fears and Womb Envy

Many Melanesian men believe, often fervently, that contact with women and their generative powers, particularly menstrual blood, is dangerous. Females free themselves of contamination at regular intervals because they menstruate. So men have rituals of bloodletting that imitate females. They start in puberty and may continue throughout their lives or until the dangers they imagine are gone. The following example of what men must do to protect themselves from the dangers they perceive comes from the Wogeo. Ethnographer Ian Hogbin called this place in lowland New Guinea "the island of menstruating men." Similar accounts exist for other parts of New Guinea.

> *The technique of male menstruation is as follows. First the man catches a crayfish or crab and removes one of the claws, which he keeps wrapped up with ginger until it is required. He also collects various soothing leaves, including some from a plant whose fruit has a smooth skin of deep purple color. From dawn onwards on the day he has fixed he eats nothing. Then late in the afternoon he goes to a lonely beach, covers his head with a palm spathe, removes his clothing, and wades out till the water is up to his knees. He stands there with legs apart and induces an erection either by thinking about desirable women or by masturbation. When ready he pushes back the foreskin and hacks at the glans, first on the left side, then on the right. Above all, he must not allow the blood to fall on his fingers or his legs. He waits till the cut has begun to dry and the sea is no longer pink. (Hogbin 1970:88)*

This fellow, temporarily saved from the dangers of female pollution, wrapped his penis in leaves and returned to the men's house. There he rested for three days while the soreness wore off.

Accounts from other areas of New Guinea report that men inserted sharp-edged reeds in penises, noses, or other body orifices to induce bleeding. Sometimes groups of men went off together to have their purifying periods. Sometimes they lacerated their genitals, pierced the septum of their noses, raised ridged scars across their bodies, or otherwise permanently marked their bodies.

But having regular periods is not enough. Women create babies in their own bodies, they give birth and nurse infants. So in some groups, men have created initiation ceremonies and other rituals that mimic or mirror female powers of reproduction. These male cults are ripe with pseudo-procreative symbolism. They emphasize the passage of male children safely through puberty and the growing of boys into men through the agency of other males. Some groups sponsor initiation ceremonies in which older men ceremonially give birth to the younger ones.

In many of the male ideologies, semen is the equivalent of breast milk. So men nourish or feed boys with semen, or male milk, through fellatio or anal intercourse. This is what anthropologist Gilbert Herdt calls "ritualized homosexuality" (1982, 1984, 1987a, b).   Men insist that the elaborate ceremonialism and symbolic structures help prepare young boys for adulthood, the dangers of sexuality, marriage, fatherhood, hunting, and the endemic warfare that characterized many areas before contact. We should not be surprised that in some groups men keep sacred flutes in their men's houses and recount stories of having wrested them from the women. The sounds of the flutes are said to be the voices and visitations from the spirit world. The threat of gang rape or death hangs over the head of any woman who witnesses the ceremonies, discusses the flutes, or challenges the deception. From all accounts, rape appears to be a common and predictable feature of women's lives. There are few models of companionable, shared lovemaking.

These cults of manhood show us how a culture constructs men and the principles of maleness. Boys become men, not through an ordinary process of maturation, but through elaborate rituals of isolation, ordeal, instruction, revelation, fear, and suffering. Females may make babies, but only males can make men.

> *The rites celebrate, not the unity and power of* society, *but the unity and power of* men. *They celebrate and reinforce male dominance in the face of women's visible power to create and sustain life, and in the face of the bonds between boys and their mothers which must be broken to sustain male solidarity and dominance. Women's physical control over reproductive processes and emotional control over their sons must be overcome by politics, secrecy, ideology, and dramatized male power. (Keesing 1982:22, 23)*

This kind of analysis opens the door for female-centered viewpoints. It is reasonable to note that Freud's penis envy, which women are said to have, is matched here by cases of womb envy. It is possible to read the ethnographic accounts and see groups of men who want the privileges and powers of reproduction which only females have. This means that the men do not just want to control women, but (dare we think it) to become women. One can "read" the ceremonies as men's attempts to appropriate women's bodies, emotions, feelings and, above all, the monopoly on creativity.

On the other hand, it is possible to read these accounts and dismiss symbolism and the intricacies of the human mind in favor of an argument about power. The ideologies of danger and the cults of manhood can be interpreted as instruments of subordination and systematic deception. As anthropologist Lew Langness says:

There are four areas in which males are not otherwise assured of power and control. These all have to do generally with female resources—fertility, childcare, labor, and periodicity . . . . The social solidarity rests upon a power structure entirely in the hands of males, a power structure supported where necessary by a variety of acts that are magical, pure and simple, and designed to keep power in the hands of males. (Langness 1974:19)

Whatever the psychology of envy, the net social effect is one of control and confiscation. The dilemmas of this system of gender separation are exceptionally poignant and instructive. While separation from women is cosmically ordained, men must still depend on them. They eat the food women grow and harvest. Even the sons and nephews of the next generation are courtesy of excluded and demeaned females. Men have painfully tried and failed to produce and reproduce themselves without women. Even with the best protections and regular periods, men are still in danger.

Looped String Bags

It is difficult to detect the substance of women's lives in places like Melanesia. Men lead such dramatic lives. In addition to the vivid ceremonialism discussed above, men typically wear striking costumes, decorate themselves in theatrical styles, and are more conspicuous. The ideologies of gender give them top billing. Sometimes even anthropologists defined women by what men say women do or by complicated analysis of kinship or social organization.

The most defining feature of women's lives is, quite simply, the looped string bag or **bilum** they carry everywhere. The contrast of this piece of equipment with the drama of men's lives is striking and illustrates the scale of gender separation. Figure 6.1 shows the techniques and hours of work that women put into a bilum.

Both men and women carry looped string bags everywhere, everyday, throughout the Highlands of New Guinea. Women always wear the large bilums with the strap suspended from their foreheads. The bags hang down their backs and their necks or shoulders carry the weight. Men wear smaller bilums slung from their shoulders or across their chests. All are constructed from a single strand of spun plant fibers. Artist, anthropologist, and photographer Maureen MacKenzie did research on the role of string bags in Highland New Guinea. Here she comments on the central place of this item of material culture to women's lives.

Throughout most of the interior highland region, from the remotest rural village to expanding town suburbs, the ubiquitous string bag is used to transport, shelter, store and contain a wide variety of objects including foodstuffs, firewood, utensils, personal belongings, babies, piglets, puppies, spirits and material representations of cultural knowledge. Being one of the few forms of indigenous fabric, the bilum is also used as a garment, ornament and ritual adornment. (MacKenzie 1991:2)

Figure 6.1

The Making of a Bilum Bag

8–10 lengths of
string in the handle
40–50 metres
4–7 hours work

5–6 lengths of string each
side of the mouthband
55–60 metres
6–9 hours work

2–3 lengths of string in
the joining stitches
10–15 metres
2–3 hours work

65–70 lengths of string in
the body of the bilum
325–350 metres
68–80 hours work

Source: Maureen MacKenzie, *Androgynous Objects: String Bags and Gender in Central New Guinea* (1991), (Permissions from Harwood Academic Publishers).

Bilums make women beautiful. The bags themselves are aesthetically pleasing and display meticulous attention to detail and design. Bilums have hundreds of purposes. They serve as

> *container, baby carrier and cradle, pocket, quiver, attire, dancing regalia, ornament, amulet, toy, trade commodity, wealth item, marker of identity, spirit catcher, shrine and source of all cultural resources.* (MacKenzie 1991:6)

Women and men say, bilums are our mothers. The box, "The Bilum Is Our Mother," quotes two women of highland New Guinea about their bilums. The analogy between the bellies of pregnant women and the expanding open-looped bilum filled with babies and garden produce is unavoidable. Bilums are external wombs, cradles in which babies sleep, nurse, and live for most of their first year of life. In some cultures of Melanesia, placentas are called bilums; they too nourish babies.

Women are not fully dressed without bilums. Social events, ritual transactions or stages in the female life cycle are not complete without an exchange of bilums. The string bags are "widow's weeds" for formally mourning a dead husband. Young girls show readiness for adult responsibility by looping a bag; old women wrap themselves in many bags down to their knees. Women loop in menstrual huts and in birth huts—where such customs exist. In particular, they loop with each other as they gossip and talk.

> *Women carry around with them an unfinished bilum, looping as they walk to and from their gardens and market; as they attend local village meetings; or closer to home, as they cook food sitting around the hearth side. In fact, no matter where a Telefolmin woman might*

Women wear the bilums suspended from their heads.

be, whether sitting or walking, her hands are rarely idle, her fingers
are perpetually working in the continuous tasks of spinning fibers
and looping bilums. (MacKenzie 1991:61)

A very strong case can be made for the curative, even spiritual qualities, of repetitive hand tasks such as weaving, looping, knitting, cross-stitching, quilting, and other crafts women typically do around the world. Such self-soothing activities are not just productivity or work in the raw economic sense. There is a profound attraction that only those who do it know.

Sometimes men make bilums or decorate the large ones made by kinswomen. In some places, young male initiates receive a string bag from maternal uncles. The bag contains what they will need to protect themselves from the power of women. These and other customs only enhance the association of women with string bags.

In chapter 1, we discussed women's work in carrying and constructing containers. This was probably an unsung but fundamental contribution in becoming human beings. The women of Melanesia who loop, make baskets, pottery, and other containers are one of the best examples of the carrying complex anywhere

---

The Bilum Is Our Mother

Quotes from women in the New Guinea Highlands:

Meta: *Men sometimes tell us to put our bilums away and cook*
         food, or they talk cross because we are sitting making
         bilums, not working in the garden. But we talk back. We
         tell them, "Making bilums is number one work. We can't
         go to the garden if we haven't got a bilum to fill up. You
         keep on like that and we women will just make bilums
         for ourselves and not give them to you men to use"
         (MacKenzie 1991:64).

Tona: *"If there wasn't such a thing as a bilum,*

         then, my word, there wouldn't be anything.

         The bilum is the bones of our people.

         We need to know how to make one thing, the bilum,

         because it is such a good and useful thing.

Source: From Maureen MacKenzie, *Androgynous Objects: String Bags and Gender in Central New Guinea.* (1991).

in the world. In fact, the bilum bag is an official symbol of the nation of Papua–New Guinea in the post-independence period. Making them is a means of personal expression and artistic innovation.

Wok Meri: "Mothers of Money"

The traditional ways in which women and men in Melanesia are separated extends into the present. Men monopolize business enterprises in the new money economy just as they controlled ceremonial transactions like initiations and bride wealth in the old traditional systems. But beginning in the 1960s, women in some groups in the Highlands of New Guinea developed a savings and exchange system called **Wok Meri,** or "the work of women." Both males and females agree that Wok Meri groups started because women were angry about males who squandered money on gambling and alcohol. So women formed networks of autonomous groups ranging in size from two to thirty-five. They recruited each other from the traditional kinship units. These lineages and clans staged important traditional rituals to mark the life passages and routinely borrowed shells, pigs, and produce from each other.

The prime mover in each Wok Meri is a "big woman," a senior female who establishes and maintains ties with other "big women." Big women organize and lead meetings or ceremonies. They help young women save money and hire young men as bookkeepers, truck drivers, or advisers. Wok Meri groups invest their money in such businesses as trucking, running small stores, wholesale trading, or coffee-bean production. Wok Meri is not a movement to maintain or create new systems of separation for men and women. Instead, Wok Meri emphasizes the collective actions of established kinship networks with females as the link. It allows women property rights relative to men. But the importance of Wok Meri extends beyond economic relations into the entire fabric of social and cultural life. Through Wok Meri, women have established their presence in ceremonial and commercial arenas of Highland New Guinea life. As anthropologist Lorraine Sexton points out:

> *Wok Meri ideology, rituals, and symbols reveal women's analysis of their own importance and capabilities, the stereotype of the male personality, and their evaluation of men's social responsibilities and the manner in which they fulfill them. These data are noteworthy because we know little about Highland women's perceptions of themselves and of men, although there is a large body of literature about Highland men's perceptions of women as polluting, danger-ous, disruptive, and in need of control. In Wok Meri women express in words, actions, rituals, and symbols their own interpretation of gender roles. (Sexton 1986:141)*

In Wok Meri ceremonies, women claim to be the "mother of money." They are declaring both ownership and their role in producing income. Their rituals reen-act both childbirth and betrothal ceremonies. They give birth to "daughters" symbolized by bags of coins. Women say, "We are like coffee trees that bear fruit that we can trade and sell. So too, women bear children, the daughters of coffee, who marry and link men, women, children, and clans in reciprocity and exchange."

In the midst of so many symbolic interpretations about women's dangers and men's painful rituals in New Guinea is a practical instance of banks, capital development, credit, and lending institutions organized for and by women. Women keep men out of financial transactions because, they say, only women linked through birth and blood can be trusted with money.

Islamic Middle East: Veiled Separations

The Islamic world is gendered. A variety of systems, concrete and symbolic, separate the lives of women from men. Anthropologist Lila Abu-Lughod uses the phrase **mutual avoidance** to describe the rules or principles that dominate the separate social lives of women and men in the Islamic Middle East (Abu-Lughod 1985:638).

The literature on women in the Middle East is particularly problematic. First is the obstacle of Orientalism, a Euro-centric and ethnocentric view of the Middle East as a monolithic "Other," the object of cliches and colonial ownership. Outsiders often attribute strange sexual moralities or judge the men in these countries harshly for the treatment of "their" women.

> *Moreover, the Middle East is staggeringly diverse in modes of economy, culture, ethnicity, race, language, class, ideology, and religions. The intersection of class, ethnicity, and religion, for example, is a dynamic that confounds our scholarship a great deal. The ways in which indigenous religions, economies, and cultures have interacted with British (and many other) imperialisms further compound analyses. (Hale 1989:246)*

Second, within the limited frameworks Westerners bring to this topic, women are seen as objects and cardboard cutouts. Everyone knows the stereotypes of belly-dancers, mysterious, sexy, veiled women out of the *Arabian Nights*. We have seen pictures of women so shrouded that they are only shadows with eyes. Many Westerners believe that Islam is a monolithic, omnipresent force whose purpose is to lock up women. Scholarship in the West often assumes that women are only fixtures of households, domestic domains, tribes, or ethnic groups. Men who worked in the area often left collecting data about women up to their wives. In short, we have observed women in the Middle East through our own veils.

Fatima Mernissi, whose autobiographical quote opened this chapter, directs Western women not to compare themselves with Middle Eastern women. She says that all of us live under systems of domination and separation, that both the Muslim East and the Christian West are based on systems of sexual inequality. If a woman like Mernissi is to be liberated or a feminist in the modern Arab–Islamic world, she must be anticolonial and anti-Western. So the assumptions developed in Western women's movements are not applicable at best. At worst, they are patronizing and intrusive.

This said, we must still find a way to discuss this widespread and important system. The symbol most people associate with gender separation in the Islamic Middle East is "the veil." This is a generic term for coverings of the female form that range from a dress with long skirt and sleeves to a total body covering (sometimes including eyes and hands). Sometimes a "veil" is only a filmy scarf draped across a woman's lower face.

> *There are few, if any, other regions of the world where one element in the culture still symbolizes so much to scholars and observers as does the veil in the Muslim Middle East. It is used a symbol by nationalist apologists and by Middle Eastern and Western feminists alike. It conjures up the exotic, erotic, the process of seclusion, the **harem**, marginalization, modesty, honor and shame, social distance, gender segregation, and, of course, the subordination of women. (Hale 1989:247)*

Why do women "veil" themselves? What does it mean? There are immense individual differences. Some women say that veils, in whatever form, are practical. In olden times, veils kept blowing sand away. Others say veils are progressive or modern. They keep strangers from staring. The custom of wearing veils is in accordance with religious beliefs; it promotes self-respect and modesty. A veil is voluntary. It's because men cannot handle the uncovered power of women.

Whatever interpretations one may have heard, it is widely assumed that veiling is related to the commands of the Prophet Muhammad and the religion of Islam. A widely quoted verse from the Qur'an, the sacred scriptures of Islam, commands:

> *And tell the believing women to lower their gaze and be modest, and to display of their adornment only that which is apparent and to draw their veils over their bosoms, and not to reveal their adornment save to their own husbands or fathers or husband's fathers, or their*

There are immense individual differences in why women veil themselves.

sons or their husband's sons, or their women, or their slaves, or male
attendants who lack vigor or children who know naught of women's
nakedness. And let them not stamp their feet so as to reveal what
they hide of their adornment. (Qur'an, Surah 24)

This quote would seem to give scriptural authority to the practices of wearing veils and other prescriptions for modesty. However, veiling or other forms of seclusion are not necessarily symbols of female subordination. Women have many different interpretations of what they mean and how an individual fits into these customs. A good way to approach this topic is to let women who have lived these features of sexual separation speak for themselves.

Bedouin Veils

Anthropologist Lila Abu-Lughod lived for two years with the Awlad Àli Bedouin in Egypt. Semi-nomadic pastoralists in the process of settling down, they combined sheep and camel herding with trade. Abu-Lughod herself came from an Arabic and Muslim background; her father introduced her in an appropriate manner to the Bedouin group. Since young women never live alone and kinship always defines identity in such groups, she embraced and immersed herself in the small, intimate community of women as an adopted daughter.

The Bedouin women she knew lived neither in harems nor in seclusion. In truth, they could not afford such luxuries. But the principles of sexual segregation, distinct from the systems of seclusion in urban areas, were nonetheless real. Bedouin social world was divided into two parts. Women and children were in the first part and men in the other. In the past, separate lives were marked by nothing more substantial than a woven blanket through the middle of their tents. Or women wore veils and men averted their gazes. Controlling one's eyes or mouth is an effective form of separation.

Women in Bedouin society are secluded and, by American definitions, subordinated. But women do not hold these images as their own. They speak of female communities that give them strength and personal feelings of power. They speak of passion in their relationships to men. There is love, anger, yearning, sensuality, and occasionally, something we might call romance. Above all, there are secrets women share with each other, not with men.

Abu-Lughod makes two compelling points about the consequences of the Bedouin separation systems for women. First, the community of women created under these circumstances is almost a feminist fantasy come true. Women's lives with each other are intense and close. Within that intimacy is freedom for personal expression.

Individual development among women does not occur in opposition
to male development; indeed cultural ideals of the feminine "personali-
ty" resemble the masculine and include enterprise, boldness, pride, and
independence. Because of the denial of sexuality among Awlad Àli,
women do not orient themselves toward men or try to please them.

> *Instead they value competence, self-sufficiency, and respectful distance.*
> *They orient themselves toward other women. (Abu-Lughod 1985:657)*

Cut off from men is not cut off from life. Women can be informal, relaxed, and honest with each other. Moreover, they share common and inevitable suffering: babies who die, husbands who take a second wife or abandon them, or arranged marriages that please others but not themselves.

Her second point is more subtle. She calls this "veiled sentiments." Bedouin women do not ask for autonomy or social and economic independence. Instead they write poetry to speak their yearning for bonds of affection with men, men as lovers, husbands, and kinsmen.

> *More often than not, the poems voice sentiments of sadness, unful-*
> *filled longing, or suffering caused by painful losses or sense of aban-*
> *donment. What is striking is that most often, the poems seem to con-*
> *cern love relationships with men—the very relationships whose*
> *importance is continually minimized in ordinary social interaction.*
> *Women—who otherwise vehemently denied attachment to their*
> *spouses, seemed unconcerned with their marriages, and admitted no*
> *interest in sexual matters or in members of the opposite sex—recited*
> *poems that expressed their vulnerability to and emotional depen-*
> *dence on men. (Abu-Lughod 1985:654)*

Her interpretation of Bedouin women's poetry is ironic and compelling because marriage is a set of crises for them. Men and women spend very little time with each other. Married couples don't "live together." Moreover, their private lives seem to be intimately public. For example, Abu-Lughod writes about the key moment in a young bride's life, her wedding night and the blood of honor (1993:90). In this story, the entire camp has been riveted by the approaching nuptials. Young girls and female relatives sing and recite their poetry to the bride:

> *May she be good*
> *And bless us with children and wealth*
>
> *May she be a real Arab*
> *To enter the community and not make trouble*
>
> *Make her dear mother happy, Lord*
> *Hanging her cloth upon the tent ropes*
>
> *I'm confident in the loved one*
> *you'll find it there intact . . .*

Reread the last two stanzas again. They refer to the "blood of honor," which brides must manifest at their wedding. The verses express the hopes that her virginity is "intact." A bloodstained handkerchief or cloth would be proof. The groom is supposed to use his finger to acquire the evidence of honor.

Amidst noise, singing, and high-energy expectations, the groom was ushered into a room alone for the first time with his bride, Selima.

> *It seemed like forever (though later they said two minutes, stopwatch timed). My heart was beating and my camera trained on the door when it was finally flung open. I jumped as the guns went off and the men rushed away. The women streamed in to surround Selima, dazed and limp in the arms of a relative, singing and dancing with relief. The cloth with its red spot of blood, a faint mark, was waved above our heads. Selima's maternal aunt exclaimed, "Praise God! Blessings on the Prophet! How beautiful!" (Abu-Lughod 1993:191)*

Here we see that women are in control of other women's morality. Succeeding at the standards of virginity and other women's work of modesty brings honor and dignity to everyone.

Female Faces and Female Spaces

Anthropologist Unni Wikan accompanied her husband to the town of Sohar in Oman, Arabia. Because she spoke Arabic, she was able to talk to women about the customs of seclusion and separation. In this region, some women wear a dark mask or **burqa** across their faces. Most women wear a length of fabric as shawl or scarf over their hair, and loose clothing that covers them modestly.

The facial mask was the most striking aspect of their attire and their separation from men. To a Westerner, such customs are irresistible, and Wikan wanted to understand why and how the masks were situated in women's lives. The women she came to know told her in dozens of different ways: "It is not that we wear burqa because it is shameful to go without it, but because it is beautiful to go with it!"

There are elaborate rules of wearing the facial mask. Married women remove it only before Allah and their husband. At home, when the chances of encountering a stranger are slim, they wear it perched on top of their heads for convenience, like others wear sunglasses. But women often wear the facial mask when it is not required; older women apparently feel it is part of their personality. The colors and styles of women's clothing are strictly conventional. But a woman controls her burqa, and with it she makes a fashion statement and exploits her freedom to the fullest.

> *First, the burqa beautifies in a spiritual sense. Donning her burqa, the woman signals her moral excellence in a tangible way. She communicates a beautiful aspect of her person and, in the act, she herself becomes beautiful. But furthermore, the burqa itself—as a symbol of all things beautiful, female modesty and grace, decency, and poise—is intrinsically beautiful. Like a jewel, it adds to what is already there. No matter how beautiful the woman, it cannot fail to make her even more so. Because she and it are both beautiful. (Wikan 1982:101)*

The Sohari women did not question the canons or premises of sexual modesty and segregation. Those were facts of life, like the sun rising or regular meals. Not everyone might agree, but Wikan's field research left her with a sense of powerful women in constricted situations.

> *There must be few contemporary societies where law and customary rules combine to define so powerless a position for women as in Oman. They have little say in the choice of spouse, cannot leave their house without the husband's permission, are debarred from going to the market to make a single purchase, often may not choose their own clothes, must wear masks before all males who are marriageable, and so forth. And yet I have never met women who seem so in control of themselves and their situation. Omani women impress with their self-assurance and poise. (Wikan 1982:185)*

Husbands and wives do not spend much time in each other's company. Where several women share a husband, it may be only a few times a week. Where men migrate to work, a wife may see a husband only a few scattered weeks per year. Yet every account speaks of the rich communal lives women share with each other and their successes at wringing meaning from cloistered worlds. Each man, on the other hand, must worry continually about how the conduct of wives, daughters, and female relatives reflects on him and his honor in the face of other men. Men believe that female relatives, mothers, sisters, daughters, and wives may stray sexually; they are potential sources of dishonor and humiliation. No action of his can erase this stain. So a man must be ever vigilant of women's chastity.

In her ethnography about women in the country of Yemen, Carla Makhlouf interprets veils and the customs of veiling as allowing symbolic statements and subtle manipulations of social situations. Elaborate veiling, she says, does not reduce all women to anonymous shadows. Yes, the full body veiling allows modesty, but it is also provocative.

> *What is seen after being concealed is all the more attractive, for the veil clothes women in an aura of mystery and contributes to the imagery of the ideal woman. By making all women look alike, the veil provides a certain freedom of movement: a veiled woman could go with men and have affairs without being caught. (Makhlouf 1979:33)*

Makhlouf questioned women in Yemen again and again about customs of veiling and seclusion. And still they denied that their veils caused or reflected their subordinate status. Women objected to their veil on the grounds they were cumbersome or meaningless. Most of all, women saw veils as both the symbols and the objects that prevented them from open, sincere interactions or associations with men. Veiling prevented friendship.

Harems and Other Female Worlds

In the harem in which Fatima Mernissi grew up, men and women lived separate existences in marked social spaces. At the courtyard level, life was formal, proper, and strict; men made the rules. Upstairs, however, life was dominated by an emotional quality she identifies as tenderness, freely and unconditionally given. Widowed aunts, assorted relatives, and their children all resided there.

> *The number of relatives living with us at any one time varied according to the amount of conflict in their lives. Distant female relatives would sometimes come to seek refuge on our top floors for a few weeks when they got into fights with their husbands. Some would come to stay, with their children, for a short time only, just to show their husbands that they had another place to stay, that they could survive on their own and were not desperately dependent. (This strategy often was successful, and they would return home in a stronger bargaining position.) But other relatives came to stay for good, after a divorce or some other serious problem, and this was one of the traditions Father always worried about whenever someone attacked the institution of harem life. "Where will the troubled women go?" he would say. (Mernissi 1994:16)*

The kind of harem Mernissi grew up in was certainly not the imperial Turkish harems or those of the *Arabian Nights,* which have obsessed Westerners with polygamy, slave women, eunuchs, and the romanticized trappings of empire. Those were gone. She grew up in a domestic harem, which she characterizes as rather dull and strongly bourgeois.

> *In these domestic harems, a man, his sons, and their wives lived in the same house, pooled their resources, and requested that the women refrain from stepping outside. The men need not have many wives, as is the case in the harem which inspired the tales in this book. What defines it as a harem is not polygamy, but the men's desire to seclude their wives, and their wish to maintain an extended household rather than break into nuclear units. (Mernissi 1994:35)*

So young Fatima asked her maternal grandmother about the sacred frontiers that women and foreigners were forbidden to cross. Her grandmother replied that any space you entered, a courtyard, a room, a balcony, even a street, had invisible rules. The rules were like the foundations of a building, the laws of mathematics, or the legal codes of Islam and the nation. Stick to the invisible rules and nothing bad can happen, she explained. But then her grandmother added, "It's too bad. The rules were not made to help women."

As an adult and a professional, Fatima Mernissi kept asking, why do these systems of segregation for males and females exist? Her own answer comes from personal experiences, scholarly research, and a singular concentration on the question. She concluded that men somehow come to believe that the presence of women and their uncontrollable essence or "nature" are too dangerous. Passive men cannot control themselves sexually (or believe they cannot); women are lusty creatures who tempt them and lead them astray. That is why the Qur'an allows elderly women to go about unveiled.

Mernissi points out that Islam does not say that women are "naturally" inferior. Quite the contrary, Islam says: Women are dangerous and powerful and must be restrained with customs about modesty, with separated social and material spaces, and with legal and mythical sanctions. Why? Because men need these protections; they fear they will lose control over their minds and fall prey to disorder and chaos. Chaos, she says, is represented by an unveiled woman.

Mernissi presents a strongly researched and reasoned analysis of male and female relations in Islamic society. She finds historic reasons to believe that before the Prophet Mohammed's time, women had considerably more self-determination than they do now. Marital unions were less subject to family control. After the prophet's death, the systems of seclusion grew. The key, she says, was keeping a husband and wife from falling in love with each other.

> *Does love between man and wife threaten something vital in the Muslim order? We have seen that sexual satisfaction is considered necessary to the moral health of the believer. There is no tension between Islam and sexuality as long as that sexuality is expressed harmoniously and is not frustrated. . . . Heterosexual involvement, real love, is the danger which must be overcome. (Mernissi 1975:62)*

These accounts by women who grew up in, speak the languages of, or participated in the practices of seclusion are full of comments about the positive and paradoxically freeing nature of veils and seclusion, symbolic or real. Muslim women often see the patterns of seclusion as a source of pride and prestige, not as a source of oppression. Indeed, harems, the ultimate form of seclusion, required huge economic assets and large staffs. Only a rich husband can afford such conspicuous consumption. Many women interpret concealing cloaks, veils, or masks as a liberating invention. It is a safe way out of enclosed living spaces, a kind of portable safety. Many Muslim feminists want to find ways to interpret the Qur'an and still remain within the fold. So in the Muslim Middle East, men and women endlessly debate the sayings of the Prophet. Both sides take comfort in holy words.

Conclusions:

What Do Systems of Separation Mean?

Where do these sexual tensions and gender divisions come from? Why are there human cultures with a gender civil war in their midst? For some observers, the answers to the questions asked above is that men need these systems. Here is what the Murphys wrote.

> *If the men's house symbolism has any function at all in Mundurucú*
> *society, it is to conceal from the men the fragility of their own supe-*
> *riority; it perpetuates an illusion. Their position is a vulnerable one.*
> *They are transients in their houses and their communities, their own*
> *sense of unity is uneasily maintained, and the collegiality has begot-*
> *ten an even stronger unity among the women. Perhaps Margaret*
> *Mead [1972] summed it up best when she said, in a passing remark:*
> *"If men really were all that powerful, they wouldn't need such rig-*
> *marole." (Murphy and Murphy 1974:226)*

Egyptian feminist writer and physician Nawaal El Saadawi argues the same points. She says that veils actually protect men from women who are more powerful. It is male honor and morals that have to be shielded. The last word goes to Fatima Mernissi. She notes that the English word "sexist" carries the connotation that males are favored over females. On the contrary, she says, we should look at what men are losing in systems of segregation. "It is my belief that, in spite of appearances, the Muslim system does not favor men; the self-fulfillment of men is just as impaired and limited as that of women" (Mernissi 1975:105).

Many skilled observers have noted, sometimes ruefully, that nothing in human social life is so potentially explosive as sex or as universal as gender. It is little wonder that in some places and in some times women and men want to claim the ultimate credit for giving life or want to control the awesome power of sexuality.

So we might conclude that gender is the most fundamental organizing principle on the planet, the one most capable of elaboration and codification. We might conclude that systems of separation only intensify the connections between women and men, and that any system which oppresses women will correspondingly oppress men. We might conclude that these elaborate systems are another form of control over women's sexuality and reproduction, for whatever motives men might have. We might offer symbolic or psychological explanations for these phenomenon. Or we might conclude that things are not always as they seem.

The systems of separation described here lead us into the next chapter. There we shall see females and males who have crossed these boundaries. Just as arbitrary political borders change or shift from time to time, so do the boundaries between the genders or the sexes. While the accounts in this chapter appear to draw strict lines between females and males, between men and women, the borders do not always hold.

Check Out These Books

The books quoted in the chapter are well worth reading. Here are others equally helpful on some of the same topics.

Maria Lepowsky's engaging study, *Fruit of the Motherland: Gender in an Equalitarian Society* (1993), counters the belief that women are universally subordinated. Here, on an island in New Guinea, Lepowsky makes a case that gender does not always pull men and women apart. Maria has been widely quoted in the national and international press for this careful and readable study. It is a valuable antidote for this chapter.

Marilyn Strathern did field work in highland New Guinea and wrote *Women in Between: Female Roles in a Male World* (1992). This book first came out in 1972, an auspicious time for women-centered ethnographies. The development and sophistication of her theories stemming from her research in Melanesia can be further traced in *The Problem of the Gift: Problems with Women and Problems with Society in Melanesia* (1988). Another important contribution to gender studies is her edited volume, *Dealing with Inequality: Analyzing Gender Relations in Melanesia and Beyond* (1987). Paula Brown and Georgeda Buchbinder edited a classic collection of articles: *Man and Woman in the New Guinea Highlands* (1976). It is important to point out in this context that good ethnography endures for us to learn from after those who lived it and those who produced are gone.

It is also important to find the widest possible viewpoints and to listen to women's voices. I recommend another book by Fatima Mernissi, *Doing Daily Battle: Interviews with Moroccan Women* (1989). This book is an intense expression of the rapid changes in women's lives in recent decades and an excellent view of the contemporary problems Moroccan women have with men! Bouthaina Shaaban also has collected women's stories in *Both Right and Left-Handed: Arab Women Talk About Their Lives* (1991). She interviewed women in Algeria, Lebanon, Syria, and among Palestinian exiles and refugees.

A favorite writer in anthropology is Elizabeth Fernea. Her book, *A Street in Marrakech* (1988), is the personal story of an American anthropologist living in Morocco with her husband and three kids. It has the texture of a good novel and complements other related books on women in the Middle East. I also recommend a book by Erika Freidl, *Women of Deh Koh: Lives in an Iranian Village* (1989). This is a delicate, finely tuned record of the cloistered lives of women in Iran, one of the strictest Muslim societies. It is a rare, intimate, and confident portrait of women's lives in systems of segregation.

There was no opportunity in this chapter to discuss systems of separation or purdah for women in India. So I recommend two excellent books for comparative purposes: Leigh Minturn, *Sita's Daughters: Coming Out of Purdah* (1993); and Sara Mitter, *Dharma's Daughters* (1991).

The classic studies about women in Melanesia start with Malinowski's *The Sexual Life of Savages,* first published in 1929. Despite the lurid title, the book is about the Trobriand Island's matrilineal kinship system and their "virgin births." More than a half century later, Annette Weiner went to the Trobriands. Her book, *Women of Value, Men of Renown* (1976), moves the lives of women to center stage as she shows how women give birth but also give death. Bundles of banana leaves are the key.

Chapter Seven

A Third Sex?
Gender As
Alternative or
Continuum

ost of us have grown up with what anthropologists call a **natural attitude** about gender. This means we believe that:

1. There are two sexes: male and female, girl or boy. People are born this way and they remain in one of these two categories all their lives. We assume that half of the world have penises and the other half have vaginas. So, in essence, genitals are gender.
2. This is a "natural" dichotomy because god, science, doctors, mothers, or other authority figures said so. There are no exceptions. No one is allowed to pick a sex, convert to the opposite gender, invent a new sex or gender, or mix them up together in daily life.
3. "Naturally," the objects of one's sexual desires are from the "opposite" sex or gender. "Normal" people wear the clothing and exhibit the personal habits of the gender into which they were born. Only during well-defined ceremonial occasions with symbolic and elaborate rules is it permissible to dress up as a person from the "opposite sex."

The core concept in this chapter is that sex and gender are not necessarily, essentially, or "naturally" limited to two forms or two styles. The **third sex** is a convenient way to describe human alternatives to the "natural attitude" and to illustrate how gender, sex, or sexuality can be constructed. Some of the studies presented here show structured, culturally patterned systems in which males adopt female clothing or other attributes and do women's work. Similar comparative examples illustrate cases in which women elect to take on male responsibilities and qualities. The examples invite questions about same-sex friendships and cross-sex or cross-gender activities.

Alas, we cannot cover all the research in the depth it deserves, but we can ask a few questions. Why would men want to be women or be like women? Or vice-versa, what advantages does a female have in being or acting like a man? Can a person convert to another gender? Can a culture invent a third or even a fourth gender? How do they do it? Why? What does this mean for the study of women, of gender, of sex?

Western social scientists have typically believed that all human groups perceive sex and gender as dichotomous or binary. But this may be only a projection of our own cultural orientations, hopes, or fantasies. When we look at other groups around the world, we see many potentials and possibilities. Yes, social scientists generally agree that two sexes are needed for reproduction. But we also understand that life has meaning beyond reproduction, and there are more forms of sexuality than the kind needed for egg and sperm to connect.

This chapter is confusing because we are crossing a lot of borders you may have taken for granted or assumed were fixed. We will skirt the edges of an exciting and rapidly growing literature on homosexuality. Moreover, there are not-yet-fully explored connections between gender alternatives, homosexual lifestyles, and spiritual power. You will notice how often the topic comes up.

One purpose for this chapter is to move beyond dualism, beyond the two-bodied world, beyond masculine and feminine, and to explore how sex and gender may be fabricated in other settings. Dualism is limited whether it is nature or nurture, public or private, body or mind, good or evil, or boy and girl. None of these arbitrary divisions explains what anthropologists see in many human cultures around the world.

Making Out and Making Up Sexes and Genders

My students usually have a thousand questions at this point. They want to know why some people seem different. What are the causes, they ask, for men acting like women or for women who love each other. They hint that people in this or other cultures may be immoral, wrong, or sick. They want to apply television talk shows, new research in genetics, and personal experiences to confusing but fascinating situations. I would like to clear the air and as much as possible present a sensible outlook on these questions. Please understand that this is a new field and scholars are still working on the concepts and definitions we need.

Let's begin with three broad clusters of potential for human beings around the world. The circles in Figure 7.1 summarize these points. The first circle shows biological sex; the second circle is about cultural definitions; and the third circle is about the individual psychology of desire, eroticism, or identity. This drawing does not reflect all the possible permutations or complexities of human existence. It merely introduces some alternatives beyond the two-bodied world.

Biological Sex and Intersexes

Sexual and gender identities are composed of many steps and stages. Some of them happen even before the midwife announces, "It's a girl" or "It's a boy." First, each of us acquires a set of chromosomes that establish a baseline for classification by sex. The X chromosome is female. The Y chromosome is male. This means that a person with XX is female and a person with XY is male. But chromosomes may combine in other ways. Here are some known possibilities: XXX, YYY, XYY, XXY, and XO. Individuals conceived with such genetic patterns may be difficult to classify in binary systems.

After the chromosomes are set, there are various stages of fetal development in which reproductive structures form. Some of these, like penises and vaginas, are outside the body and will be visible. The rest of the reproductive structures, like ovaries and uteruses, are inside the body. Most of the time, the reproductive structures match each other and the chromosomes; sometimes chromosomes, internal structures, and external structures simply do not match.

During a number of points in fetal development, the endocrine and hormonal systems must mature and correlate with each other in complex ways. They must kick in at the right time and in the right way because these are the coordinating

Figure 7.1

The potentials for sex, gender, and desire.

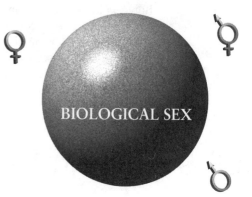

KEY

   Female

   Male

   Intersex

   Man, boy, husband, father, brother, son

●   Woman, girl, wife, mother, sister, daughter

   Androgynous

   Homosexual

   Transsexual or Transgendered

   Heterosexual

   Cross-dresser

systems for aspects of psycho-sexual development in later life. Sometimes, for various reasons, a fetus is exposed to masculinizing or feminizing hormones; these may influence development in a number of ways.

An estimated 5 percent of human births result in anomalous or unusual features. Sometimes babies are born with genitals that appear to be both male and female, or depending on how these matters are interpreted, with genitals of neither sex. Generally scholars say that such individuals are **intersexed.** Intersex is another category of phenotypic or biological sex in addition to the dichotomous categories of male and female. This means that humans are born in every society whose biological sex does not neatly fall into one of two categories (Katchadourian 1979). These possibilities are marked in Figure 7.1.

So we have reasons to doubt conventional wisdom or the natural attitude about two and only two genders. But the incidence of babies with unusual chromosomal combinations or atypical sex organs is too random and too small to account for the patterned social customs of crossing the boundaries of gender described in this chapter. So biology is only one basis for a third sex. If biological sex is malleable, then gender as a social construction must be even more so.

Social and Cultural Genders

Biology is just the beginning. At birth, midwives or their local equivalent say to a laboring woman, "Congratulations, you have a beautiful baby (fill in the blank)." This diagnosis opens the cultural processes of **gender attribution.** People in every social group expect certain behaviors from infants and children according to the category they are assigned at birth. So from this point on, it's pink or blue, guns or dolls, skirts or pants. Then, in early childhood, around the ages of two to four, little kids somehow decide or come to have the knowledge of which gender they are, boy or girl or other. This is called **gender identity.** Generally, most people come to the same conclusion as their chromosomes and the midwife did. In other words, their biological sex accords with their personal identity and the social category or gender to which they were assigned.

However, some people in many different human cultures remain convinced their bodies are one gender but their souls, spirits, or personalities are a different one. Anatomically correct males may be certain that a more authentic female lives inside them and wants to come out. The reverse is true for some people born as females; they believe themselves to be true or real males trapped in an alien body. In each case, these individuals feel very strongly that their body is the mistake, not their personality. Generally, we call such individuals **transsexuals.** Sometimes they respond by adopting the dress and work of the opposite sex. Sometimes they become a third sex or make other creative adjustments.

In recent years in Euro-American cultures, such individuals have often sought surgical and hormonal interventions which would give them the body that most closely approaches their personal identity. Males take female hormones, grow breasts, and ask to have their penises removed. Females take male hormones, grow beards, and ask for hysterectomies. They generally change their names, clothes, and hobbies to those resembling the desired gender. Their friends and relatives switch personal pronouns. I need to note that such surgeries seem to be based on the notion that there are two genders, and that problems can be solved by moving into the other one.

Objects of Our Desires

There is still more. A human being takes its chromosomes, hormones, a gender assigned at birth, and a gender assumed in childhood, and goes out into the world to engage in a lifelong process of noticing, defining, and finding its objects of desire. Sometime before or during adolescence, people focus on sex, how and with whom to do it. If biology is plastic and cultures offer a number of options, then sexual desire, preference, orientation or identity are even more elastic. The last circle in Figure 7.1 shows some possibilities for linking our sexual identities with what we desire or to whom we are attracted.

Margaret Mead and Ruth Benedict, of course, pondered the problem of how an individual picks up cultural cues; they noted that sex roles often crossed traditional boundaries. They opened the doors for fuller analysis of the cultural contexts of same-sex behaviors and cross-gender roles and meanings. As they taught us, "womanhood" and "manhood," or "masculine" and "feminine," are inconstant and unstable.

In Western culture, we are supposed to experience ourselves as female or as male and to display the clothing, mannerisms, or habits of those two ends of the continuum of gender. The popular and professional literature contains a variety of terms to describe people who transform, transcend, or challenge gender rules: sexual deviation, sexual aberrancy, female incongruity, hermaphrodites, men-women, inverts, homosexuals, transvestites, transsexuals, made-women, made-men, prostitutes, transgenders, and eunuchs. Many negative social judgments surround the practices described in this chapter. They include concepts like abnormal, deviant, perverted, sinners; they also include verdicts based on the natural attitudes, such as freaks of "nature" doing "unnatural" acts.

Having sex with another person is not always what it seems. Some groups with which we are familiar tend to define people in categories centered on who is having sex together: heterosexual, homosexual, or bisexual. The Western criteria for gender basically revolves around who to have sex with and who to marry. Other societies define sex as the act itself, insertive, receptive, or reciprocal, for example. Others seem to define forms of sexuality as age-appropriate rather than gender-appropriate. Others prescribe certain actions for marriage; the rest of your life is your own. Others say that only marriage between an anatomically correct male and female who have sex in the missionary position is "natural." Some cultures exhibit features, beliefs, or customs that researchers in this field call "sex-positive"; they can tolerate variety. Other have such punitive restrictions on gender and sexuality that we label them, "sex-negative." Others have elaborate categories that label and place people in boxes.

The feminist and gay movements of the last quarter-century have taught us that the personal is political. We have learned that what goes on in bedrooms or kitchens or boardrooms is structured by larger social relations of power, by history, and by the unseen hand of culture. The French anthropologist Claude Levi-Strauss contributed the idea of raw versus cooked. Biology is the raw material and culture cooks us until we're done. The recipes in different cultures translate our biology into social experiences.

Crossing Over and Cross-Dressing

The most accessible examples of sexual alternatives and gender constructions are probably the universal practices of **cross-dressing.** Dressing up in the clothes, hairstyles, or makeup of the "opposite sex" has a longer and more vivid history than most of us credit. The older term, no longer in vogue, is transvestism, which means "clothing across." In a fascinating study of this phenomenon in Western cultures, literature, media, and popular culture, scholar Marjorie Garber notes American obsessions with dressing up and the power of clothes. Her book, appropriately called *Vested Interests,* shows that popular culture is filled and overflows with cross-dressing and cross-dressers. Traditions of drag queens, female impersonators, and similar forms of gender bending are alive and well in the vast entertainment industries.

Garber argues that gender-bending is the cutting edge of artistic consciousness. As do other scholars, she notes that gender is overdetermined and that all binary thinking has problems, whether it is yes-no, self-other, Democrat-Republican, or black-white. She sees cross-dressing in Western history as a "category crisis." Arbitrary definitions and distinctions like male and female cannot hold in cultural transformations. So the borders become permeable and those who cross the lines challenge and change the categories. Once people push at the boundaries of any border, others are vulnerable. In talking about a concept like the third sex, we can no longer keep the rigidities of we/they or us/them.

Other times and places in the world reveal a similar fluidity of gender. When people cross the borders of gender, they first adopt clothing from the other category. Then they add work patterns, and spiritual, sexual, erotic, or artistic activities.

The kind of traditional healers anthropologists call shamans often dress in clothes of the opposite sex, or become what the pre-Buddhist folk religions of southeast Asia named halfman-halfwoman. Shamans journey to the spirit world through altered states of consciousness or trances. This means that they are crossing more boundaries than merely gender. Their strength in healing and the quality of their spiritual life, in fact, depends on transcending or crossing ordinary borders of consciousness, sex, and gender.

Military Maids

Private Lyons Wakeman of the Union army wrote home in 1863. "I don't believe there are any rebel bullets made for me yet. Nor do I care if there is." But Confederate germs, not bullets, killed him, and he was laid to rest in the Chalmette National Cemetery downriver from New Orleans. One hundred and thirty years later, Private Wakeman's letters reveal another part of the story.

Citizen Sarah Wakeman of upstate New York, the oldest of nine children, was working as a maid. So in 1862, at the age of nineteen, she ran away and joined the 153rd Regiment, New York State Volunteers, for a $152 enlistment fee and $13 dollars a month in pay. She listed her occupation as "boatman." Sarah was one of an estimated 400 such women who served in the Civil War; they dressed like and were treated as male soldiers (Burgess 1994).

It is difficult to document how many women have joined the military or worked successfully in men's jobs. In July 1777, courts in England began prosecuting "female husbands": women acting as men in military ranks who were married to women. Dozens of ballads and songs were sung about soldiers and sailors who followed their husbands into battle in the name of love or money. Historian Julie Wheelwright has found court cases, journals, newspaper reports, and many other accounts of women who abandoned dresses for trousers to escape unhappy marriages, to live with other women, to follow male lovers into battle, or to enter male occupations for economic reasons.

Frances Clalin served as a trooper in the Missouri militia.

The thread that pulls these stories together is women's desire for male privilege and a longing for escape from domestic confines and powerlessness. Many vividly describe a lifelong yearning for liberation from the constraints they chafed against as women. They were unconventional women who spent their lives rebelling against their assigned role before they pursued a male career. Most could only conceive of themselves as active and powerful in male disguise. Some were lesbians who bravely risked ostracism and punishment by symbolically claiming the right to women's erotic love through their assumption of male clothing. Many, when the initial purpose for their masquerade had been served, continued to pass as men or deeply longed for a return to their male role. Happy endings are all too rare in their stories. (Wheelwright 1989:19)

Some women lived as men all their adult lives; the military was the only life they knew. Others had a temporary adventure. Working-class women were probably used to hard physical labor, and upper-class women were often seeking an escape. The point is this: Women have long disguised themselves for safety when traveling, for access to male privileges or jobs, and for convenience or comfort. Given the sheer number of folktales, legends, stories, and examples, there is every reason to believe that women have lived male lives in many times and places where female lives were restricted.

In Western history, women who cross-dress, act like men, or claim male privileges have evoked severe displeasure and serious legal or religious sanctions. Joan of Arc's persecutors worried more over her male attire than her victories in battle. In pre-Christian Iceland, cross-dressing was grounds for divorce. In the nineteenth century in France, many legal codes prohibited women from dressing like men or entering the military in disguise. However, when women in these situations record their feelings, they say that living as a male was the most exhilarating and liberating experience of their lives.

When Boys Will Be Girls

In a variety of human societies, individuals who were not born female decide nonetheless to live as women do. These biological males dress and act in the manner their own culture prescribes for biological females. One term for this phenomenon is **gynemimesis,** derived from Greek words *gyne* or woman, plus *mimos,* mime or mimicking.

Dressing like women is the first and most obvious way to express a new gender identity. Then men do women's work, form communities with each other, or alter their bodies in some way to match their idea of women's bodies. Sometimes there is shared sexuality, either in ritual or lifestyle, as prostitution or as preference. Sometimes there is body mutilation; transforming the male body ranges from systematic removal of body hair to removal of penis and testicles or surgical construction of a vagina.

Why do men do this? What is so meaningful or attractive about being female? In situations where women's status is high and the social rewards seem to be great, then becoming a female makes some sense. Sometimes, however, becoming or imitating a woman is moving against the grain. What is the purpose of taking on the devalued and seemingly constrained roles of women? No one is certain why this phenomenon appears so regularly; we do know, however, that crosscultural settings give us the best opportunity to observe. In the following section, we will see a specific example of gynemimesis and gender alternatives from India. This example offers another way to understand how the continuum of gender constructs the choices people make in their lives. It is also a way to view women's lives.

Neither Woman nor Man: Hijras of India

The **hijras** of India are men who adopt female dress and other features of female behavior. They form a kind of intersex or third sex. Ordinarily they live together in groups and earn a living by performing at and blessing certain key rituals like weddings, births, and other festivals. They collect alms or offerings as well as payments for these performances. They worship Bahuchara Mata, one of many mother goddesses venerated in India. In devotion to this goddess, some men submit to castration or emasculation, removal of the penis and testicles. In their traditions, this act gives them the power to curse or to bless male infants. For hijras, surgery and worship of the goddess buttress their claims of special power and a place in Indian society.

Anthropologist Serena Nanda had done fieldwork in India for many years. Between field trips, she had also studied gender, sexual variations, and homosexual couples in the United States. She knew about hijras as one thread in the complexity of Indian cultures and subcultures. But on sabbatical in 1981, she had the unusual opportunity to contact a community of hijras in south central India; through them she met other communities of hijras throughout India.

No one knows how many hijras live in India; estimates range from 50,000 to 500,000. When Nanda asked them about their social identities, some replied, "We are neither man nor woman." Others said, "We hijras are like women." All of them explained that sometime in childhood or adolescence, they realized they would not be able to fit into the typical continuum of gender definitions in India; nor were they going to be able to act as a husband and consummate the heterosexual marriages arranged by their families. Many said, "We were born this way."

Hijras wear women's clothing and take on other defining aspects of female identity. Not all hijras undergo the surgery or even perform publicly. And some earn their living as prostitutes, although their claim to spiritual power rests on their renunciation of male sexuality and the embrace of "otherworldly" religious practices. But all have renounced the conventional Indian version of "real men."

The surgery is a rite of passage, moving a person from one status to another through rituals. The symbolism is painfully clear: The person who performs the surgery is called a midwife. The operation is conceived of as both birth and rebirth. The soon-to-be woman or hijra has the ritual status of a pregnant and

Hijras often earn a living by performing and blessing certain key rituals.

postpartum woman. When the forty-day recovery period after the surgery is over, the hijra community dresses her as a bride and presents her to the goddess, Mata.

The new initiate into the community will find established relationships and the possibilities for others. The teacher-pupil relationship between a guru and her disciple is a mutual obligation of aid and loyalty. In addition, hijras form networks of **fictive kinship.** They use biological relations as a metaphor or symbol for creating new formal and informal connections.

> *Rituals exist for "taking a daughter" and the "daughters" of one "mother" consider themselves "sisters" and relate on a reciprocal, affectionate basis. Other fictive kinship relations, such as "grandmother" or "mother's sister" (aunt) are the basis of warm and reciprocal regard. Fictive kin exchange small amounts of money, clothing,*

jewelry and sweets to formalize their relationship. Such relationships connect hijras all over India, and there is a constant movement of individuals who visit their gurus and fictive kin in different cities. (Nanda 1985:36)

We might also think of the surgery and the status of hijra as a form of career development. It is difficult to earn a living in India. But the hijras offer a niche for survival and an occupation with exclusive privileges and rights. The surgery offers physical and religious validation, a new family, and an economic monopoly over certain ritual occasions.

Hijras think of themselves as females; therefore they want what every good Indian woman is supposed to want: a husband and children. They also want to choose their own mates and enjoy the kind of romance and love they see in movies.

Serena Nanda explores this desire in the story of Sushila, who has lived as a woman since late childhood. Her family insists that she has always been a male. Within the hijra community, which she calls "people like me," Sushila does prostitution and other work. She has had several husbands. At the first interview, Sushila remarked that she wanted to give her current husband a child so he could live a normal life. Three years later she reported gleefully to Serena that she had achieved her goals as a woman.

Sushila had adopted a former husband as a son and arranged for his marriage with a friend's sister; that made her a mother-in-law. Their new baby son made her a grandmother! Proud statuses for an Indian woman. She remarks about the duties and advantages of being a woman and a proper housewife.

She should look clean, wear good clothes, comb her hair neatly, put flowers in her hair, wear bindi [the colored dot which indicates married women] on her forehead. I have my husband's lunch ready by the time he comes home. I tend to his house and am at home instead of going in the streets. . . . My daughter-in-law comes and I am queen of the house. I only fetch vegetables for her to cook for our meals. The rest of the work is done by her and I relax. I don't even wash the dishes. . . . Now I have my husband and he's the only man for me, instead of all the men visiting me from all walks of life and entering my home at all odd hours. Therefore, I am respected. Now I'm leading the life of a respectful woman with a husband, an adopted son, a daughter-in-law, and a grandson—running a house. For this we get some respect outside. (Nanda 1990:96)

Hijras dress as women, style their long hair, pluck out facial hairs, and use female pronouns and kinship terms. They sit in "ladies only" seats and count themselves as women in the census. But most make no real attempt to pass as women. They would have to follow standards of demure modesty and public restraint required of women. Instead, hijras offer caricatures or burlesques of standard females with heavy sexual overtones.

> It is not at all uncommon to see hijras in female clothing sporting
> several days growth of beard, or exposing hairy, muscular arms. The
> ultimate sanction of hijras to an abusive or unresponsive public is to
> lift their skirts and expose the mutilated genitals. The implicit threat
> of this shameless, and thoroughly unfeminine, behavior is enough to
> make most people give them a few cents so they will go away.
> (Nanda 1985:38)

Hijras are sexually ambivalent figures in Indian society. They are teased or mocked; they are valued and they are reviled. Indian mythology and traditional cultures contain many such androgynous figures. Hinduism teaches that everyone contains both female and male principles or characteristics. Some supreme beings in Hindu traditions have both male and female sex organs. Ambiguous figures can be powerful, and transcending one's sex or gender may be the road to enlightenment and salvation.

Although Indian men may dress in women's clothes or find religious justifications for a third sex, women in India do not cross that line easily, if at all. There are no comparable groups for females wearing men's clothes and performing men's work.

Two-Spirits in Native North America

By sharp contrast, in the traditional and preconquest societies of the New World, both females and males had opportunities to negotiate alternative identities or roles. In the following sections, we will look at individuals whom contemporary Native Americans call **two-spirits.** This is a generic term in English for people who are lesbian, gay, transgendered, cross-dressers, transvestites, transsexuals, or otherwise have "marked" lives in the bands, tribes, or nations where concepts of multiple genders occur.

Although many languages in Native North America had words for two-spirits, two terms have been used historically in English. They are **berdache** for men who voluntarily adopted female dress, mannerisms, speech, and social roles, and **amazon** for females in Native North American cultures who adopted men's dress and occupational status. It is important for us to note that these words are outdated labels that originated in Western thought, languages, and colonial practices. Europeans who brought very different and bifurcated systems of politics and religions to this continent had trouble understanding these ancient roles. In addition, Western observers projected their own negative judgments about women onto those they called Indians. Although the terms berdache and amazon appear in a number of publications, including this book, they do not accurately reflect patterns or values of gender variance in the contemporary communities of Native North Americans. The term two-spirits better integrates the sexual, gendered, political, artistic, and spiritual meanings of crossing the borders.

Anthropologists have documented over 130 societies in which two-spirited customs flourished. These range from small hunting and gathering groups to intensive agriculturalists of the Southwest, including tribes in the Midwest and western

Great Lakes, the northern and central Great Plains, the lower Mississippi Valley, Florida, the Southwest, the Great Basin, California, and scattered tribes of the Pacific Northwest, western Canada, and Alaska (Callender and Kochems 1983).

Many Native North American societies were as gender-equal as we are likely to find. Women's and men's tasks were complimentary and each gender was respected for the contributions they made. In many Native American tribes, female status was often high; therefore males who moved in that direction assumed that status.

Anthropologist Walter Williams traveled widely among contemporary Native American groups. He identified himself as a gay anthropologist who wanted to learn how other cultures accommodate the gender and sexual variations that create so many anxieties in Euro-American societies. His book, *The Spirit and the Flesh,* explores the implications of cross-gender and same-sex activities in the cultures of Native North America.

Williams used the term berdache for a morphological male who does not live out the standard male role. He may be stereotyped as feminine but is more accurately thought of as androgynous. Such a man does some women's work and mixes clothing, behaviors, and social expectations for women and men simultaneously. In the past, elaborate myths and folk traditions supported men in these choices. They were frequently renowned for spiritual, intellectual, or artistic achievements. They used their special powers to bless ceremonies, predict the future, assign personal names, or assume spiritual responsibilities. Many of these men had reputations for hard work and loving generosity, especially to children.

Parents and other family members recognized the unique characteristics and personalities of the two-spirits. Here Lame Deer, a Lakota shaman, speaks about his experiences:

> *They were not like other men, but the Great Spirit made them **winktes** and we accepted them as such. . . . We think that if a woman has two little ones growing inside her, if she is going to have twins, sometimes instead of giving birth to two babies they have formed up in her womb into just one, into a half-man/half-woman kind of being. . . . To us a man is what nature, or his dreams, make him. We accept him for what he wants to be. That's up to him. (Quoted in Williams 1986:25)*

Lame Deer suggests a number of causes or reasons for becoming a two-spirit: election by the spirits, prenatal or biological influences, or individual psychology as expressed in dreams. Above all, he notes: this lifestyle was acceptable.

In North America, such men helped women in their work, provided good company, and assumed many heavy tasks. They took no time off for menstruating, birthing, carrying a baby, or nursing. Since these men did women's work, they typically married men. Getting married means expanding one's kinship base, having someone to share work with and bringing other's experiences to survival tasks. If we start with this assumption, instead of genital-based roles, then we understand how two-spirited men got married and with whom.

> *Within a marriage in a gender-divided economy, there can be only*
> *two roles: husband and wife. The sex of the person who takes these*
> *roles may vary, but the roles generally do not. This is an additional*
> *reasons why two berdaches would not marry, and two masculine*
> *men would not marry. Masculine men might have sex, which is their*
> *private business, but marriage is a public matter and an economic*
> *concern. (Williams 1986: 111)*

Females, a Man-Woman, and Zuni Pueblo

The research on two-spirits in Native North America is strongly associated with the first generation of female anthropologists. These women are a veritable *Who's Who* of the early years of the discipline: Margaret Mead, Matilda Coxe Stevenson, Elsie Clews Parsons, Ruth Underhill, Ruth Landes, Ruth Bunzel, and Ruth Benedict. These women received some of the first doctorates, held some of the first full-time jobs, did groundbreaking fieldwork, wrote classic books, and left an indelible mark.

A number of these women worked at Zuni Pueblo in New Mexico, a magical place that appears to have changed their lives. Elsie Clews Parsons first visited Zuni in 1915 and became converted to feminism; she characterized Zuni religion as "social responsibility combined with individual tolerance" (Parsons 1939). Ruth Benedict used her fieldwork among the Zuni as an example of expanding our levels of consciousness and tolerance. For women like her,

> *the Southwest offered psychological as well as geographical space, an*
> *otherness that intrigued and renewed. It is to them that we owe nearly*
> *all of our knowledge of Zuni and Pueblo berdaches. (Roscoe 1991:xi)*

Anthropologists often regard Zuni Pueblo as a nearly perfect social order, democratic, pluralistic, and holistic. No groups dominated other groups. Moreover, Zuni Pueblo was classically matrilineal; the household or family group centered on a mother and her daughters. These women, with their sons and brothers, traced a common descent back to a mythical female ancestress.

Zuni is commonly referred to as a theocracy, where authority was vested in priests and religious concerns dominated private and public life. Religious societies maintained their own kivas, or round underground ritual chambers, and sponsored regular services that featured dramatic and colorful masked dancers. The people of Zuni are also known for extraordinary artistic productivity, such as pottery, murals, jewelry, and weaving. These products are created in a process that Zunis compare to giving birth.

In Zuni life, the sexual division of labor was as complementary as human beings are capable of. It is obvious that Zuni women enjoyed high status and economic independence. As examples, women plastered the outside walls of the houses men built. Men grew corn; women stored and distributed it. Men did not enter the granaries, because corn was sacred at a large number of symbolic levels.

Even art was divided by gender: Women made pottery and ceramics and used the small belt loom to make long objects like scarves and belts. Men made tools for their personal use, jewelry, and wove larger items like blankets and their wives' woolen leggings! Men carried a special responsibility for "things of the universe" that is, the welfare of the earth and all living creatures.

Women produced life; women then fed those lives. But life was not just babies. Life was corn and the spirit world. So women sprinkled ground cornmeal on the masked gods and joined the medicine societies to learn techniques for curing serious injuries and illnesses. Ruth Benedict said of the Zunis:

> *The Zuni are a ceremonious people, a people who value sobriety and inoffensiveness above all other virtues. . . . Pleasant relations between the sexes are merely one aspect of pleasant relations with human beings. . . . They do not picture the universe, as we do, as a conflict of good and evil. They are not dualistic. (Benedict 1934:116)*

Zunis did not have a "natural attitude." A two-spirited Zuni man did woman's work and wore women's clothes. He negotiated his status with his own character and personality. Ruth Benedict remarks of such people:

> *The men-women of Zuni are not all strong, self-reliant personages. Some of them take this refuge to protect themselves against their inability to take part in men's activities. One is almost a simpleton, and one, hardly more than a little boy, has delicate features like a girl's. There are obviously several reasons why a person becomes a berdache in Zuni, but whatever the reason, men who have chosen openly to assume women's dress have the same chance as any other persons to establish themselves as functioning members of the society. Their response is socially recognized. If they have native ability, they can give it scope; if they are weak creatures, they fail in terms of their weakness of character, not in terms of their inversion. (Benedict 1934:228)*

Typically, a young boy might demonstrate qualities that were known to lead into this status; he liked playing with girls and doing their domestic activities. His female relatives remarked on this. Sometimes he had experienced unusual dreams or a strange illness. The transition became final at adolescence, when he adopted the outward markers of women's dress.

Anthropologist Will Roscoe began his research with a group called Gay American Indians, who were sponsoring a history project. This led him to the archives of major museums in the United States. Like Walter Williams, he tapped into collections of oral traditions. He wrote, in effect, an ethnographic biography of a well-known Zuni two-spirit named We'wha. Here he describes We'wha's work.

> *Assisting the women of his household, We'wha daily set out piles of hewe' and steaming bowls of mutton stew for an appreciative family. He learned to keep the house neat, according to fastidious Zuni standards, by spraying water on the dirt floor and sweeping it several*

times a day. In certain chores performed by women—fetching wood,
carrying water from the well in jugs balanced on the head, plastering
the walls of houses, threshing wheat, winnowing grain and beans,
and tending the waffle gardens along the banks of the river—
We'wha's strength and endurance was especially advantageous.
(Roscoe 1991:39)

As Will Roscoe discovered, the life of We'wha had intersected with an unusual woman, anthropologist Matilda Coxe Stevenson. In 1879 she accompanied her
husband to the Southwest to study at Zuni Pueblo. He was the official leader of
an expedition from the U.S. government's new Bureau of American Ethnology
(BAE). Tilly, like many academic wives, was an unpaid and unsung assistant who
outlived and outperformed her husband. When her husband died in 1888, the
Bureau hired her (the first and only woman hired at the BAE for three-quarters of
a century). Ultimately, she wrote major cultural descriptions of Zuni life and
befriended We'wha.

Gender categories at that time may not have been as firm as we believe. Tilly
reported that her anthropological colleague, Frank Cushing, had not only gone
native and wore Zuni ceremonial outfits with lots of jewelry, but he put his hair
into curl papers at night. She herself was childless, widowed at age thirty-eight.
Her closest friendships were with other woman. In fact, the Zunis treated her as
a man and allowed her to make offerings to their ancestors with male prayer
sticks. She worked like a man, they said, with a head and a heart to match.

A well-known Zuni two-spirit: We'wha.

Indeed, until his death in 1896, Mrs. Stevenson treated We'wha as a close female friend. In writing of We'wha, she used the English pronouns she, her, and hers.

> *She was perhaps the tallest person in Zuni; certainly the strongest, both mentally and physically. . . . She had a good memory, not only for the lore of her people, but for all that she heard of the outside world. . . . She possessed an indomitable will and an insatiable thirst for knowledge. Her likes and dislikes were intense. She would risk anything to serve those she loved, but toward those who crossed her path she was vindictive. (Quoted in Roscoe 1991:47)*

Matilda Stevenson either believed that We'wha was a woman, or she knew and didn't care. She apparently thought he was the same kind of person she was, intelligent, independent, and self-confident. In fact, Tilly introduced We'wha to her own social circles in Washington, D. C. There they circulated freely at the White House and in the dressing rooms of elite ladies in the nation's capital. The newspaper accounts of their visit are instructive. Note what they say of We'wha.

> *The princess is an eccentric child of nature. Although she is moving at present in the highest circles of Washington and is the pet guest of Mrs. Stevenson, she yet has lapses from the conventionalities of life and goes back to the freer notion of life on the plains.*
>
> *The general style of the princess is massive. Her broad face, her worn features and the peculiar parting of her hair give her a masculine look among the pale-faced society ladies. (Washington Chronicle, April 18, 1886)*

In the style of that time, We'wha was called a priestess, a princess, a maiden, and a girl. He knitted continuously while in Washington; this was unremarkable in that setting; after all, he was a woman. But at Zuni Pueblo knitting would have attracted confused attention, since only men knitted!

So, was We'wha a male or a female? The Zunis said a not-man but also a not-woman. Here's where it may be helpful to think of two-spirited people in Native North America or people who adopt similar customs around the world as a third sex or an alternative gender. Zunis did. They had many powerful initiations and ceremonies for validating these statuses; they could distinguish between biological sex and gender identity.

Zuni men-women often formed long-term emotional and sexual relationships with regular men, sometimes in contexts which must be described as marriage. By the same token, females could choose to do Zuni men's work and wear their clothes. They were spoken of as "manly" or "like a man-woman." Unfortunately, we know much less about these women than we do about the men.

A Fourth Sex? Cross-Gendered Females

Two-spirits are a category in Native North America which included men, women, not-men and not-women. It may be helpful to think of such categories as a third sex or even a fourth sex. Unfortunately, there is little ethnographic evidence about two-spirited women. Most authors agree that men in transgendered statuses were more common than females were. The two-spirited world appeared to be more articulated and institutionalized for males than for females. However, anthropologist Harriet Whitehead notes:

> For someone whose anatomic starting point was female, the infusion of an official opposite-sex component into her identity was by no means so easily effected. Throughout most of North America, there was no recognized female counterpart to the male berdache. Yet women willing and able to traverse the sex boundary do not seem to have been in short supply. Wherever ethnographic attention has been turned to this subject, the impression is given that for every boy who dreamed of the burden strap, there was a woman who actually picked up the bow. (Whitehead 1981:90)

Walter Williams proposes reframing the ancient term **amazon** to refer to women in Native North America and elsewhere who go to war, hunt, wear men's clothing, and assume other attributes of men's lives. In using the term, he draws on the worldwide legends of women warriors and women who live as men or without men, which have earned an enduring place in human mythology. In Greek legends, Amazons were a group of warrior women who took part in the Trojan wars and founded a number of cities in ancient Greece that were leading centers for goddess worship. Other Greek myths mention Islands of Women where Amazons lived without men. They are said to have found males when they wanted to conceive children. It is said that women of the island of Lesbos loved each other, hence the term lesbian. Although the term amazon comes from deep in Euro-American mythic traditions, it does give some definition to the often hidden lives of females.

Many Native American groups had alternative gender categories for women as two-spirits; there were special names for "women who passed for men, dressed like men, and married women." In some groups, there were words that translated as **"manly hearted women."** The Yuman Indians said, "She wished only to become a man."

Gone-to-the-spirits

One of the most intriguing accounts of a woman who dreamed of a bow and arrows comes from the historical and anthropological literature for the Kutenai. Ethnohistorian Claude Schaeffer found a number of references to her.

> This singular woman, if we are to credit fur trader and native sources of information, carried on at maturity activities customarily

pursued only by men among her people. In 1811 she is described in historical narratives as assuming the roles of courier, guide, prophetess, and warrior. Again in 1825 she is seen momentarily as a person of prominence among the Kutenai; and finally in 1837, she appears as a peace mediator between the Flathead and the Blackfoot, before meeting her death at the hands of the latter. During these years she dressed in masculine garb and lived as "husband" of a succession of individuals of her own sex. (Schaeffer 1965:193)

Her sexual or gender career began when she married a French-Canadian man and accompanied him through the Rocky Mountains on several trading or exploring expeditions. According to journals and letters of that period, the couple parted, and when the former wife returned to the Kutenai, she announced,

I'm a man now. We Indians did not believe the white people possessed such power from the supernaturals. I can tell you that they do, greater power than we have. They changed my sex while I was with them. (Quoted in Schaeffer 1965:196)

In honor of her sexual metamorphosis, she changed her name to Gone-to-the-Spirits. Then she dressed in men's shirts, leggings, and loincloths; she carried a bow and arrows as well as a gun. Gone-to-the-Spirits went on raiding parties. Her hunting skills provided fish and game for her family. She proposed marriage to several young women; they declined. Many of her peers thought she had lost her mind.

Soon, however, Gone-to-the-Spirits attracted her first wife. The journal entries of trader David Thompson provide the earliest written report.

A fine morning; to my surprise, very early, apparently a young man, well dressed in leather, carrying a Bow and Quiver of Arrows, with his Wife, a young woman in good clothing, came to my tent door and requested me to give them my protection; somewhat at a loss what answer to give, on looking at them, in the Man I recognized the Woman [he had known her previously as Madame Boisverd]. . . . She had become a prophetess, declared her sex changed, that she was now a Man, dressed and armed herself as such, and also took a young woman to Wife, of whom she pretended to be very jealous. (Quoted in Schaeffer 1965:203)

Alexander Ross, another trader and journal-keeper in the region, called the pair "bold and adventurous amazons" whom he mistook at first for man and wife.

Some sources describe Gone-to-the-Spirits as quite large and heavy-boned; others say she had a delicate frame. Perhaps size is relative to perceived gender. All accounts note her determination to live as the men of her time did. They also discuss her abilities as a "prophetess." She practiced healing and divinations of a shaman. Some tribes called her "Manlike Woman" and spread her reputation for prophesy and other supernatural powers.

It is difficult to sort through the historical accounts and anthropological interpretations to find the people underneath. Note the culture-bound categories the writer employs here to explain a person such as Gone-to-the-Spirits.

> *In conclusion, the Kutenai "man-woman" appears to have been a female transvestite, with homosexualism as an erotic object, who adopted the role and status of the opposite sex. She was not an intersexed individual, as such a condition would have been known to her family and could scarcely have been concealed from her tribe. If our information is correct, her psychosexual transformation took place at maturity and followed up her marriage to a French-Canadian voyageur. Thereafter, she adopted men's clothing, assumed male activities, and lived as "husband" to a succession of women. (Schaeffer 1965:230)*

Many other accounts from Native North America tell about women taking on male roles such as hunting, leading war parties, seeking revenge, and marrying women. Woman Chief of the Crows was captured in childhood by the Crow Indians and raised by a warrior. She lived and died as a brave and a chief. She hunted successfully, took three wives, served in the tribal council, acquired fame, honor, standing, and a reputation for daring and extraordinary luck or power. Clearly, she was judged by her accomplishments.

Ironically, the women who went as wives to these female chiefs and manly hearted women are totally invisible in the literature. The men who wrote these accounts uniformly assumed that anyone who is a man or pretending to be a man automatically needs a woman. In fact, they had no firm boundaries between wives and servants. Therefore, once they accepted a women who acted like a man, it was easy to assume that "he" needed a wife.

Women hunted for the same reasons men did: They had children to feed. Other times women went to war for revenge, defense, necessity, or in response to a vision. Living as a man was, under many circumstances, a practical and socially responsible course of action. Here is an example.

The Kaska Indians of the Canadian Subarctic depended on hunting large game for their livelihood. If a couple had no sons to help them hunt, they performed a ceremony of transformation for their youngest daughter. They tied the dried ovaries of a slain bear to a special belt so she could not menstruate or become pregnant. In this group and others in the Subarctic, such women were known for their exceptional hunting skills. They participated as men in the male-only sweat baths; the men accepted them on the basis of their activities and behavior, not their bodies (Honigman 1954). Apparently, these ceremonially created men did not have sex with regular men. Intercourse with males would have compromised her skills in the hunt. But she could and did have sex with other women.

Anthropologist Harriet Whitehead describes Native Americans as amazingly dispassionate about females who hunted, warred, led like a man, and courted women.

> *A woman who could succeed at doing the things men did was honored as a man would be. Few, if any, tortured rationalizations were*

brought to bear upon her achievement. What seems to have been more disturbing to the culture—which means, for all intents and purposes, to the men—was the possibility that women, within their own department, might be onto a good thing. (Whitehead 1981:108)

In other words, Native American men seem to have had more trouble with their peers becoming or acting like women than with women becoming or acting like men.

The Cultures of Women-with-Women

The examples from Native North America challenge the concepts of owning a woman in marriage, being married as the central role in a woman's life, the idea of "two shall be as one," or other romantic fantasies. A woman's social status and affiliations were not dependent on a husband.

The important consideration in the Indian view is that they were still fulfilling the standard role of "mother and wife" within their culture. The traditional gender role for women did not restrict their choice of sexual partners. Gender identity (woman or amazon) was important, but sexual identity (heterosexual or homosexual) was not. (Williams 1986:247)

Paula Gunn Allen, a scholar and writer on Native American women, identifies herself as a lesbian and an American Indian of Laguna Pueblo and Sioux heritage. To her, heterosexual and lesbian are not reasonable categories to describe women in Native North America. In her book, *The Sacred Hoop,* she notes that tribal consciousness and social structures were worlds apart from anything with which Europeans at that time or we in the contemporary world are familiar.

Traditionally, proper behavior falls along gender lines, as did expectations, but gender is understood in a psychological or psychospiritual sense much more than in a physiological one. . . . It is no wonder that Indian people in general insist that among them women are considered sacred. Nor, as perhaps you can see, is this an empty compliment in a society that depends for its life upon the sacred. (Allen 1986:207)

Europeans called the indigenous inhabitants of this continent "the Red Man." They were not what researchers today call sex-positive. So we can not expect to find reasoned and sympathetic accounts of women or women-oriented-women under these circumstances.

Information on women's same-sex relationships among Native Americans is difficult to tease out of the sources that condemned women's same-sex lives as much if not more than men's. Women were expected to marry; but they also had bonds, some of them sexual, outside marriage. In the sexual division of labor and kinship, females were goddesses, spirits, mothers, healers, sisters, prophets, grandmothers, shamans, wives, and daughters. Men were gods, spirits, fathers, diviners, warriors, uncles, shamans, brothers, and husbands. So women spent a lot of time in each other's company. They grew up in a woman's culture and practiced a wide range of women's rituals and activities.

According to Paula Allen, women-identified-women fit into the ecumenical pattern in Native North America where sex was private, not sinful or dirty. Sex was for making babies, and women made their most definitive contributions in having babies. It is said that the Arapaho thought that dying in war and in childbirth were equal honors.

The core elements of women's identities came from a community of those moved by the same spirit. Those related through the spirit world were closer than those related by blood. In fact, relationships to the world of gods, goddesses, spirits, and metaphysical or occult forces, grew out of and transcended sex, sexual identity, or eroticism.

> *Within such systems, individual action was believed to be directed by Spirits (through dreams, visions, direct encounter, or possession of power objects such as stones, shells, masks, or fetishes). In this context it is quite possible that lesbianism was practiced rather commonly, as long as the individuals cooperated with the larger social customs. Women were generally constrained to have children, but in many tribes, childbearing meant empowerment. It was the passport to maturity and inclusion in woman-culture. An important point is that women who did not have children because of constitutional, personal, or Spirit-directed disinclination had other ways to experience Spirit instruction and stabilization, to exercise power, and to be mothers. (Allen 1989:109)*

For Native Americans, power did not mean control or the ability to coerce others to get one's own way. Power was supernatural; it was wisdom, awareness, mindfulness. Power often came from females or the female qualities in everyone. Power came through the vision quest, trance states, objects, and abilities to see, hear, heal, or hunt. Power was in the myths, dances, ceremonies, and art. People called "medicine women" or "manly hearted women" had exceptional powers. Like men who learned this kind of power, women probably became **androgynous.** They shared features of both male and female.

The Friendships of Women

The anthropological study of women is recent. And seeing women outside of traditional female roles is even more so. This is one reason why we have more information on men in alternative gender roles than we do about women. Anthropologists who saw women only in domestic roles such as food processing, child-rearing, or kinship obligations, probably could not see nonheterosexual activities.

The universal customs of marriage presume and privilege heterosexual lives. Women are "naturally" expected to marry and have children. The natural attitude puts serious legal and social constraints on female expressions of sexuality and power. More to the point, if women act in secret or in concert with others to break taboos or reject conventional and ascribed marriage patterns, they hope to go unnoticed.

Anthropologist Evelyn Blackwood notes that we often do not see women living out parts of their lives with other women. We are not prepared emotionally or intellectually to notice adolescent girls' structured sexual experimentation or adult women's lifelong friendships with each other. The social construction of being a lesbian (our current socio-political term) or being a woman-loving-woman (Ruth Benedict's phrase) varies enormously from time to time and place to place. As Blackwood notes:

> *The range of lesbian behavior that appears crossculturally varies from formal to informal relations. . . . Examples of such would be adolescent sex play and affairs among women in harems or polygynous households. Formal lesbian relations are part of a network or social structure extending beyond the pair or immediate love relationship, and occur within such social relationships as bond friendship, sisterhoods, initiation schools, the cross-gender role, or woman-marriage. An examination of social stratification suggests that, in societies where women have control over their productive activities and status, both formal and informal relations may occur. Where women lack power, particularly in class societies, they maintain only informal lesbian ties or build institutions outside the dominant culture. (Blackwood 1985:10)*

In a number of tribal settings, lesbian or women-centered friendships were an ordinary part and parcel of kinship, economics, and religion. In some groups, young girls typically play with each other's bodies before marriage. Among Australian aborigines, equalitarian gatherer–hunter societies, adolescent sex play for girls was structured within kinship categories for determining proper marriage partners. Thus a youngster could have mutually stimulating play with another girl as long as they were cross-cousins—that means linked to each other by parents who were siblings of the opposite sex, her mother's brother's daughter or father's sister's daughter. In fact, female cross-cousins would marry each other's brothers; these girls were destined to be sisters-in-law. These early sexual friendships set up bonds that may have translated into shared mothering, gathering, or other extensions of friendship.

In a number of societies in West Africa, teenage girls engaged in sexual play with each other as an ordinary part of adolescence. Later, as married women, they kept these activities secret from their husbands. Many opportunities were available for women in polygynous households. In many parts of Africa, female initiation societies included sexual play and erotic exchanges. This research points to a broad view of female sexuality and puts sensuality, touching, caressing, and verbal expressions of love before intercourse. In these African examples, women experience warm, nurturant, early mothering, genital sensuality in childhood, and institutionalized female friendships in adolescence.

Crosscultural research on women's friendships, the meaning and structuring of them, and their replacement of or coexistence with relationships of men and marriage, is just beginning. It is important to break free of ethnocentric polarizations and the rigid categories of homosexual and heterosexual to which we assign people. These categories do not explain what women's lives are often about and they ignore our creative responses to conditions we cannot control or did not produce.

Conclusions Beyond the Categories of Sex, Gender, and Desire

So how do we account for the third sex, the fourth sex, or the border crossings we have seen in this chapter? A person's morphological sex or her or his sex as assigned at birth can function independently of gender status, behavior and erotic attractions. Gender and sexuality appear to be immensely flexible. Why?

Many writers, anthropologists and others, say that third sexes are varieties of institutionalized homosexuality. But as we have seen in India and Native North America, adopting women's work and social habits seem to be more defining characteristics than the choice of a sexual partner. Much of what is important about the institutions of gender variance has been obscured by the problems or prurient curiosity about homosexuality.

> We can question whether a separated gay subculture, a minority lifestyle built around sexual preferences, is more preferable to integration of gender variance and same-sex eroticism into the general family structure and the mainstream society. We can use the American Indian concept of spirituality to break out of the deviancy model, to reunite families, and to offer special benefits to society as a whole. At the least, our awareness of alternative attitudes and roles can allow us to appreciate the diversity of the human population, and the similarities that we share across the boundaries of culture. (Williams 1986:275)

Another theory for the third sex involves the limitations of the gender roles available in any given culture at any time. Unusual or peculiarly talented individuals may want to be less or more aggressive, nurturant, artistic, athletic, or dressed-up than their cultural milieu generally allows. The best way or the only way to achieve these personal goals may be to borrow or adopt the desired behaviors from the other gender, to mimic, or to form new or autonomous genders. If work is assigned by gender (and it is), then careers and subsistence may only be possible by taking on the marks and status of another gender. Hence women as warriors.

There are elaborate and publicly-supported ceremonies and displays for people who want to cross-dress in New Orleans.

But this idea has problems. It suggests individuals are fleeing conventional or inadequate categories and static social roles, or that individuals themselves cannot cope. Anthropologist Beatrice Medicine says that

> *It seems unlikely that women could not meet the demands required of females in most Plains Indians societies. But then, the whole idea that sex role reversals, for either women or men, constituted deviant forms of escapism from "normal" behavior is open to question. Instead of looking at sex role reversals as a form of "deviance" derived from "incompetence" in the roles associated with a person's gender, it might be more productive to examine them as normative statuses which permitted individuals to strive for self-actualization, excellence, and social recognition in areas outside their customary sex role assignments. In this light, changing sex roles identity becomes an achieved act which individuals pursue as a means for the healthy expression of alternative behaviors. (Medicine 1983:269)*

By contrast, some anthropologists lean toward a theory that cross-dressing and gender-bending may be religious matters. In this approach, spiritual power is available to individuals who unite or transcend the oppositions of female and male. There is wholeness or oneness in androgyny, in creating new gender categories, or in eroticism apart from reproduction. The two-spirits of Native North America were not threats to rigid gender ideologies. Indeed, they transcend the division of human beings into female and male. Like the deities or spirits, they also cross the lines.

The idea of a third sex is an striking counterpoint to the Western ideologies of women and men as polar opposites, sexuality as reproduction, or sensuality as sinful. It offers a vision of reconciliation for our masculine selves and our feminine selves that goes beyond sexual politics. This possibility leads us directly into the next chapter, in which we will discuss women and spirituality at other levels.

Important Books Beyond the Natural Attitude

The literature on the third sex is large but still in the creative processes of defining terms and interpreting diverse human experiences. The most definitive collection of articles to date is Gilbert Herdt's *Third Sex, Third Gender: Beyond Sexual Dimorphism in Gender and History* (1993). Or you could start with his books on men and ritualized homosexuality in Melanesia listed in the Bibliography. Cross-dressing appears to be a very important institution in human societies, with far greater antiquity and spread than any of us may have imagined. Vern and Bonnie Bullough's landmark book, *Cross-Dressing, Sex and Gender,* (1993) is particularly valuable for looking at the questions cross-dressing raises about sex or gender.

Gay and lesbian studies is an exciting new field and the literature is growing rapidly. Kath Weston's book, *Families We Choose: Lesbians, Gays, Kinship Between Men, Between Women* (1991), is a major ethnographic contribution to gay and lesbian studies as well as to the conventional literature on "marriage and family." Her 1993 review article establishes definitions, creates a scholarly place for gay and lesbian studies, and offers an extensive bibliography.

Kate Bornstein was born a male named Albert Herman. His/her experiences as a gender outlaw are outrageous, funny, clever, and dramatically summarize everything you need to know about other genders, sexes, intersexes, or diversely interesting groupings. Her book, *Gender Outlaw: On Men, Women and the Rest of Us* (1994), also includes the text of a stage play called *Hidden: A Gender.*

There are a number of excellent studies of the social construction of gender in specific communities or situations. Anne Bolin's *In Search of Eve: Transsexual Rites of Passage* (1988) is fascinating ethnographic fieldwork in a transgendered or transsexual community. Bolin places the emotional, social, and physical transition from male to female into the context of ritual and life passage. Annie Woodhouse, *Fantastic Women: Sex, Gender and Transvestism* (1989), did fieldwork in Britain on the TV/TS Support Group, an organization for transvestite and transsexual men at various stages of border crossings. Their wives and other women in the Partner's Support Group also gave her interviews. Their case histories and personal experiences make this a valuable book in understanding the flexibility and potentials of gender and sex in the world. Or you might read Holly Devor's *Gender Bending: Confronting the Limits of Duality* (1989). She interviewed a number of women who, in varying degrees, challenged, rejected, or reformulated traditional "femininity."

Most people these days who take sex seriously read Michel Foucault's three-volume *The History of Sexuality*. Foucault's widely discussed and provocative theories about desire, identity, power, and sex are considered the most challenging viewpoints proposed in this century. He offers a dazzling and iconoclastic exploration of why we have sex, why we talk about it so much, and of the mechanisms of power that come into our bodies, our heads, and our beds. Follow these volumes with a dynamic, provocative, and sophisticated ethnography about sexuality and gender in Brazil by Richard Parker, *Bodies, Pleasures and Passion: Sexual Culture in Contemporary Brazil* (1991).

Chapter Eight

Women in the
Life of the
Spirit and the
Growth of the
Mind

or the last quarter-century, groups of women friends and I have been eating potluck dinners with each other. None of us wants to cook an entire meal, but some of us can shop creatively (a new form of gathering). A few of us have home gardens (an old form of horticulture). Most of us like to cook a special dish. We eat and we talk. We always mention our lives as mothers, our pregnancies, babies, teenagers, or grown children. We acknowledge each other's lovers, spouses, and partners. We discuss divorce, cancer, depression, suicide, hysterectomies, infertility, and not having any money. Sometimes we talk about abuse, rape, incest, molestation, beatings, or battering. We celebrate recovery and surviving. We mourn our dead. Sometimes we create little ceremonies to acknowledge a miscarriage, a splitting-up, a fiftieth birthday, a promotion or new job. We always laugh and talk; sometimes we cry and get angry. Is this religion? Probably not. But it comes close to spirituality, as we shall discuss in this chapter.

The major questions in this chapter will be: Do women have their own religions? Is there something we can call female spirituality? Do women act differently from men in these matters? For our purposes here, the answers will be yes, yes, and yes.

This being the case, we will investigate a few characteristics of women's religions and female spirituality with a series of examples. Some major themes will emerge:

- *Rituals, sharing and sisterhood in domestic settings*

- *Healing: the acknowledgment of sickness, suffering and death*

- *Healers: Midwives, shamans, witches, and others*

- *The supernatural world: Goddesses and visiting spirits*

- *Myths, motherhood and matriarchies*

- *Dangerous, sexy, frustrated, grieving, possessed, or caring women*

Women, Spirits, and Religions

The backdrop to women's religions are the **world religions,** which cover large geographical areas and are associated with contemporary nation-states and international politics. These belief systems expanded through military, economic, migratory, colonial, evangelical, or other means. They include Christianity (Catholicism, Protestantism, and Pentecostalism), Islam, Judaism, Hinduism, Confucianism, Buddhism, and Taoism. Within the world religions and the countries associated with them are a number of smaller and less visible traditions, religions that predated and exist apart from colonial, national, or world religions.

It can be safely said that none of the world religions supports women's religious enterprises apart from male-defined contexts. Within the establishment religions, women are often decorative, supportive, auxiliary, or compliant. Sometimes women "tame" or "domesticate" the systems of male control and ideology so they can live within them and find meanings for their lives. And sometimes women find or create alternative religions for themselves. We will call these **women's religions.**

It is clear that affairs of the sacred are gendered. Women seem to have a different set of experiences than do men. Men and male researchers often understudy and undervalue women's religious experiences. In fact, women's spiritual lives are often secret, muted, or marginal when we view them through the lenses of state governments and world religions. So women are just beginning to understand the characteristics and qualities of our religious and spiritual experiences in other times and places.

Human religions have their own sexual division of labor. Men generally get to do the thinking and women generally get to do the feeling. Thinking includes scholarship, scriptures, theology, philosophy, doctrines, and dogma. Feeling involves mourning the dead and celebrating the stages and transformations of giving life. In another typical division of labor, when religion is a job, men get it. Where religion is defined as public ritual, career tracks, bureaucracies, and is allied to government or the establishment in some way, men are paid to do it. Women are usually incorporated in the same symbolic manner that we see in marriage. We are auxiliaries and supporters; we cook and take care of children, status enhancement, and emotional needs.

However, women in many cultures act as religious specialists: midwives, fortunetellers, diviners, seers, mediums, shamans, and herbalists. Many forms of spirituality grow out of women's work in healing, mediating and nurturing. These activities often allow women to achieve status, prestige, and financial awards outside our domestic units or apart from mainstream religions and dominant cultures. Religious activities may offer women space for achievement and self-expression or serve as a locus of resistance and separation. Women may create a sense of female community, sometimes deep in the heart of separatist or patriarchal ideologies. Women typically assert the primacy of direct experience with the ordinary and spirit world over established religious bureaucracies or doctrines built on reason or other canons of what constitutes truth.

Twelve Women's Religions

Anthropologist Susan Sered works in Israel at the crossroads of three world religions, Judaism, Christianity, and Islam. She began to question how women defined and organized their religion and spirituality in societies dominated by such patriarchies. So she interviewed women and investigated women's rituals at shrines, maternity hospitals, and in situations in which sexual segregation was firmly established. Then she began to look for examples of women's religions around the world to compare.

Sered found ethnographic and historic materials from twelve groups in which women dominated both in leadership and membership. Each of these groups was independent from the patriarchal or male-dominated world religions entrenched within their nation states. Although men participate in most of these religions, the consciousness and awareness is female-centered. Her book, *Priestess, Mother, Sacred Sister,* is a careful study of twelve religions dominated by women. Here are short summaries of the groups Sered picked. This will give you an idea of the variety and patterning.

Many religions grew creatively from the terrible experiences of slavery, colonialism, and the Black Diaspora in the New World. Women are the majority of participants and leaders in these groups. In Brazil, many religions combine parts of African and Native American tribal traditions with folk Catholicism and spirit-centered practices. These Afro-Brazilian religions center on public rituals for curing illness and misfortune. Spirits enter and possess women's bodies in dramatic ceremonies. You might be familiar with names such as Candomblé, Umbanda, or Macumba. Throughout Central America, old women organize mourning and other rituals around their ancestors. The Black Caribs in contemporary Belize are the best documented of these groups.

In the many nations of Africa, women are taking elements of local traditions in art, music, trance, or dance and combining them with pieces of the world religions to create lively cults. The **zar** cult of northern Africa and the Middle East, one of many examples, involves curing or healing through possession states and trances. Zar are impulsive spirits who enter women, particularly married women. Other women in the cult help the newly possessed tame the zar spirits with dancing, food, and woman-centered rituals. The most notable feature of these groups is women as **adepts.** The term means "uniquely skilled" and is applied to the leadership styles of women, which contrast dramatically with leadership in "organized" religious bureaucracies (see Jules-Rosette 1979). In Sierra Leone and most of West Africa, groups of women control their own organization, called Sande Secret Societies. Older women of Sande initiate teenage girls into this all-female society and teach them about childbirth and other aspects of being adult women. Sande groups protect their members from men and nonmember females.

In four examples Sered found in Asia, it is clear that localized and female-centered spiritual traditions predate the arrival of any world religions and today exist apart from them. These women's religions are strongly tied to kinship and healing. In northern Thailand, where households are matrilocal and matrilineal, spirits are relatives too; they belong to the kin group. Members of the cults are all matrilineal descendants of the founding ancestress. In the indigenous religion of the Ryukyu Islands (of which Okinawa is the largest), women dominate the official and mainstream religion. Priestesses conduct rituals for households, villages and families and female shamans deal with personal healing and divination. In Burma the indigenous or pre-Buddhist religions involved careful handling of **nats,** spirits, gods, or ghosts, at rituals for curing sicknesses, at harvests, planting, births, initiations, deaths, or weddings. The nats entered and possessed the bodies of women. In Korea women conduct household rituals for the gods and seek out female shamans to help them with misfortunes and sicknesses within their families.

Sered reports on four women's religions from the United States. Christian Science, a religious movement that believes in the power of faith to cure sickness, was organized by Mary Baker Eddy in Boston in 1879. She taught that matter, and therefore illness, is only an illusion. The Shakers were an eighteenth-century migration of believers from England to rural America. Their leader, Ann Lee, was believed to be a completion or complement of Jesus. They emphasized agriculture, handmade crafts, celibacy, and ecstatic worship or "shaking."

Kate and Margaret Fox were sisters living in New York state. In 1848 they made contact with the spirit of a murdered salesman. This event is said to have been the beginning of the popular movement called Spiritualism. Nineteenth-century Spiritualism was a loosely organized religious movement based on the belief in the survival of human personalities or souls after death and in their ability to communicate with those left behind, usually through a medium or channeler. Spiritualism, or beliefs and practices that involve communications with dead people, is a very common phenomena around the world. Women are said to be more adept or receptive than men are. Today Spiritualist groups emphasize healing.

A contemporary religious movement in the United States called the Feminist Spirituality Movement is linked to feminism and the secular women's movement. Women borrow from the rituals, symbols, and mythologies of many cultures, particularly those of the ancient Middle East, Mediterranean, and western European traditions. They emphasize goddesses, matriarchies, and female energies within women's bodies. Parallel to feminist spirituality is **womanism** or **the Womanist Movement,** a contemporary spiritual movement of African American feminists. Womanism draws on such sources as literature, African American folklore, Christianity, and feminism. Womanists want to create new styles of partnerships with men.

There are other examples of female-centered spirituality from many times and places, for example: celibate Christian women's communities, women's healing cults, the Black Spiritualist churches in New Orleans, Haitian Vodou in urban America, and many others. It is important to know that groups like this exist and that they validate women's life experiences in many ways.

Qualities and Characteristics of Women's Religions

What are women's religions like? Women's religions are more likely to occur in societies in which women already have relative autonomy, for example, in matrilineal, matrilocal, or matrifocal groups. Or, like the societies of the Americas and Asia, they are so complex, new, or rapidly changing that women can find openings for themselves within the establishments.

Susan Sered sees two outstanding patterns in women's religious life. The first is experiences around motherhood or mothering, and the second is responses to patriarchy, male-dominations, or world religions. Women's religions must coexist with structured antifemale gender ideologies. So there are always conflicts or gender dissonance.

Within women's religions, the reality of motherhood, achieved, desired, or lost, shapes the lives of adult women. Motherhood is the pivotal motif or metaphor, the quintessential experience. Being a mother is more ingrained than being a sexual partner. This does not seem to mean that these religions have earth mother goddesses, elaborate birth rituals, or images of giant breasts everywhere. It does not follow that women's religions create good mothers, better mothers, or a universal standard for being mothers.

But we must note (once again) that women give birth and have intimate physical and psychological connections with children. This inevitably means that women are connected to each other, to children, to food and feeding, to ancestors, and to death. Beyond giving birth, the most common experience women as mothers share is loss or the death of children.

> My argument is not that child death leads women to "escape" into religion. My argument is that child death encourages women to ponder existential and theological questions. As part of that process, some women change their religious beliefs and affiliations. In sum, although Western-style mother-love is not universal, child death is something with which women in all cultures must grapple, albeit in different ways. Encouraging motherhood, rejecting motherhood, and the loss of motherhood are important to women, and all of these themes surface in women's religions. (Sered 1994:90)

The world religions do not provide practical or impressive relief for suffering and sickness. So women's religions emphasize the daily experiences of nurturing others with the corresponding dangers of losing them. They do not focus on the symbolic meanings of childbirth (as in reborn theologies) nor on all-powerful mother goddesses. Women's religions are centered in earthy, practical, or everyday realities. Women's religions tend to make ordinary experiences sacred, to find the supernatural in familiar happenings, and to invite the magical or the mystical into their bodies.

Everyday Acts and Ordinary Rituals

The most common patterns of women's spiritual lives are the ordinary rites and ceremonies that women celebrate on our own. These are rarely publicized or studied. At the absolute heart is shared food: preparing food, serving food, and thinking about food. Babies need to be fed; husbands ask, What's for dinner? The ancestors or other spirits are honored with offerings of various delicacies. In women's religions, a morning meal or an evening dinner may be an occasion to put an offering on the hearth to honor the spirits, to sit in silence, to offer a prayer in memory of beloved dead ones or to acknowledge the labor of women in providing food. Holidays and annual observances are occasions for intense preparation and lavish displays of food.

In women's religions, the work that women do anyway, everyday, is made sacred. Women share the food they prepare directly with the gods and spirits. In women's religions, food is never served in small symbolic portions or burnt up and sent away in smoke. Instead, religious occasions are public, communal, and overflow with food. All the people and all the spirits eat and drink well. Deities are invited to descend and join in human social life. Spirits are guests at the parties, as it were. Then women take home the leftovers and eat them later.

The richest descriptions of women's ceremonialism comes from traditional societies anthropologists study. These are the kind of celebrations, rituals, or spiritual occasions that contemporary women's movements have mourned as lost, updated as needed, or retrieved from women's history. Women have often invented rituals and religions because necessity is the mother of invention.

Intuition or Authority, Magic or Science

Anthropologists may have neglected or trivialized very crucial areas of women's religious or spiritual activity. For starters, there is magic, or techniques for making good things happen for us. The box, "Love Magic," shows examples from Santeria. Getting a mate to notice us, love us, or marry us and getting the children we want or don't want are everyday acts. These practices are universal where women gather, and they have an enviable reputation for success! I have often been asked for help of this kind or needed it myself. Unfortunately, I wasn't raised in a coherent tradition of women's magic.

Women everywhere practice **divination,** or knowing about the unknowable, imaginative techniques for acquiring information or knowledge where empirical facts are not available. Women regularly foretell or foresee the sex of an unborn child, a person's future happiness, the outcome of a journey or business decision, the location of lost articles, or the source of illness. To learn about the future, to understand the past, and to seek advice or wisdom, is akin to therapy at its deepest levels.

Some sources of knowledge or wisdom that humans have include intuition, revelation, common sense, books, teachers, doctors, theologians, dreams, trances, angels, therapists, or mothers. But the official source is what we call **authoritative knowledge.** These are systems of knowledge, explanation, or power that become ascendant. The American medical systems of the twentieth century or the theological elaborations of the Middle Ages in Europe are good examples of systems of authoritative knowledge. Systems of authoritative knowledge are constructed in a kind of group consensus-building. There are known penalties for going against these systems; one may be gossiped about, banished, or excluded. Authoritative knowledge seems reasonable, and people routinely participate in these systems. As Brigitte Jordan says, "The power of authoritative knowledge is not that it is correct but that it counts" (1993:153).

People or groups involved in the reward systems of authoritative knowledge are called **gatekeepers** or **stake-holders.** Those of us who ignore standards of authoritative knowledge are said to be ignorant, naive, or dangerous to ourselves and to others. We need to be controlled for our good or punished for deviance from the "natural" order. Women, natives, pagans, children, or those in any category of "other," often violate or fail to subscribe to authoritative systems of knowledge. When any one system of thinking, knowing, or believing becomes the legitimate authority, then other systems are seen as backward, ignorant, primitive, illogical, or troublemaking. A good example are midwives and home births versus the medicalization of childbirth in hospitals; another example is "home

Love Magic

Santeria is an African religious tradition that uses some Roman Catholic rituals and symbols. Yoruba people brought to Cuba as slaves on sugarcane plantations originated these practices. Santeria calls on the Yoruba spirits, **orishas,** and selected Catholic saints. Santeria was the religion of oppressed peoples who had every reason to hide their elaborate ceremonies and belief systems. Here are a few of the many spells available to the women of Santeria.

To Get Married

Gather some of his semen on a piece of cotton. He must not know what you intend. Form the cotton into a wick. Make an oil lamp from a hollowed-out lily bulb. Write his name on a little piece of paper in the form of a cross. Place it in the bottom of the bulb. Add quicksilver and a series of oils [recipes vary] and float the cotton in it while invoking Oshún to intercede and convince him to marry you. Light the lamp at nine o'clock for five nights and call forth the blessings of Oshún. This spell is said to be infallible.

To Get Pregnant

Enlist the aid of the beautiful moon goddess, Yemayá, patroness of motherhood. Bring her a pomegranate cut in half and smeared with honey. Write your name on a piece of paper and place it between the two halves of the pomegranate and reunite them. Invoke Yemayá and ask her to bless you with health and fruitfulness, as the pomegranate is rich in seeds. On the first day of your new menstrual cycle, burn a blue candle in her honor. Do this every day for a month. It is common to become pregnant during this month.

Source: Adapted from Migene Gonzáles-Wippler, *Santeria: African Magic in Latin America* (1981).

remedies" or holistic, alternative, or woman-centered health care practices, which abound informally in contemporary society.

Women's religions are uniformly set apart from systems of authoritative knowledge. Women typically learn and pass knowledge on through apprenticeships with each other. Women typically practice what anthropologists call **embodied knowledge.** In response to the question, "How do you know?" the answer is "I feel it in my gut." Or, "What's wrong with her?" "She has a broken heart." It is the equivalent of telling your mechanic that the car is making a funny noise, or intuiting a problem in your body before a medical diagnosis. Embodied knowledge is also the ability to do something practical. Women often experience and practice knowledge as narrative, stories, and first-person accounts. Women embrace knowledge as experience, revelation, and intuition. But these qualities or abilities do not often "count" in world religions.

Healers and Healing

In anthropological studies of religion from around the world, women routinely act as curers, healers, nurturers, and mediators. Once again, as a warning against generalizing, it is not exclusively women who perform healing roles across human cultures. Men do them too—but not as often, as predictably, or with the same qualities that mark women as healers. Men as healers simply do not treat women as women do. Western biomedical practices are part of systems of authoritative knowledge, but they exist side by side with woman-centered systems of healing.

> *As nurturers, healers protect, comfort, and guide patients to restored health in the same way that mothers care for their children. And like dependent children, patients look to healers to meet their physical and emotional needs. . . . As mediators, healers cross symbolic boundaries, particularly those separating the human world from that of spirits and ancestors, and intervene with the latter on behalf of their patients or clients. In yet another sense, healers mediate between forces that cause illness when the body experiences imbalance: hot or cold, excess emotion like fright or anger, harmful natural qualities like the wind or magnetism associated with eclipses, and so forth. (McClain 1989:73)*

The most common aspect of women's religions are explaining, acknowledging, and alleviating suffering. Women around the world are not simply resigned to pain, bad luck, or an evil fate. Suffering is not inevitable. Something can be done about it. Healing in women's religions is eclectic; women pay little attention to authorities or explanations which preach the one and only true way. As Sered notes:

> *Let me say from the outset that I have not found any particular healing technique to be unique to women's religions. What is striking about women's religions is the accent on healing and, in most cases, the multiplicity of healing procedures. In addition, the healing approaches of women's religions tend to be characterized by a holistic mind-body-spirit approach. (Sered 1994:103)*

Two aspects of healing seem to be particularly striking in women's religions. First, women's healing rituals acknowledge that suffering is real. When the dominant mode of reality or the authoritative systems of knowledge are modeled on men's perceptions and experiences, then women may feel "crazy" about themselves. We ask, Am I hysterical, neurotic, a malingerer, or a hypochondriac? Women's religions offer communal, even public, affirmations that there is genuine suffering and the need for healing even for conditions that have no names in conventional religion or science.

Second, the healer herself has suffered; she knows about pain and loss and fear in her own gut. She is not an authority and has probably received her training through observation, participation, and apprenticeships. Only experience and the willingness to enter these feelings in order to help others makes her an expert. This brings suffering and healing into the context of community and interpersonal relationships.

Most women as healers work, out of necessity, in informal and domestic settings. They treat relatives, neighbors, and each other for illnesses that are not life-threatening. They make the decisions to consult specialists, either indigenous or biomedical.

The quintessential healers in human societies are midwives. Pregnancy, birth, and babies have been women's work in the majority of times and periods on the planet. In many groups around the world, women as mothers are not trivialized or isolated and pregnancy is not an illness. Long before authoritative systems of knowledge about pregnancy and childbirth existed, women placed their experiences and skills in the service of others.

> *Descriptions of traditional midwives from India, Pakistan, Bangladesh, Nigeria, Tanzania, Brazil, Mexico, Guatemala and Jamaica describe them as mature women who have themselves born children. All descriptions indicate that they achieve their status rather than having it ascribed by birth. The successful ones command great respect, have more clients and are very close to the families under their care. In the Sudan they are regarded by the children they deliver as a second mother, or the "mother of all people" in Iraq. In Guatemala midwives are regarded with deference and respect. They are addressed with an honorific title, asked to godmother and given gifts. All the children a midwife has delivered greet her with bowed head and kiss her hand. (MacCormack 1982:11)*

In many places, spirits call women into the service of midwifery. In Sierra Leone, the ancestors direct certain women personally to perform these valuable tasks for other women. In some African spirit possession cults, birth is compared to baptism. That means that a midwife makes new members of the church as well as ritually purifying pregnant women through confession and exorcism so they can safely give birth. Afro-Caribbean women in Jamaica and other places may experience birth as a state of altered consciousness. In fact, giving birth can be a spiritual or religious experience. Midwives are spiritual experts for whom there are no male equivalents. This may explain the fears projected onto midwives or for official jealousies and appropriation of women's reproduction powers.

Traditional midwives give a variety of services far beyond what those in the Western biomedical culture have ever imagined. They commonly diagnose the pregnancy by touch, estimate the date of delivery, and teach the woman about each stage of pregnancy. They give full-body massages during pregnancy, birth, and for periods afterward. They may cook, care for a woman's other children, offer rich companionship and reassurance. They prepare herbal remedies, call on supernatural powers, and cure stretch marks or nausea. They give advice on sex, birth control, abortion, baby care, and breast-feeding; they may stage appropriate or comforting ceremonies. Women who are prepared for giving birth and are supported by friends and relatives generally have an easier time. In these cases, embodied knowledge is power.

Visiting Spirits

Anyone who wants to understand women's religious experiences on the planet will need to start with **spirit possession.** This is the idea that supernatural personalities can enter, own, and use people while we are in an **altered state of consciousness** or a trance state. Possession cults grow out of these shared experiences with spirits. These experiences are typically part of women's religions, spirituality, and resistance to organized religions. As Susan Sered says, "I am struck by the uses to which possession trance is put in women's religions: to build and strengthen interpersonal relationships, to deconstruct gender, and to heal" (1994:191).

Women regularly journey into or accept ecstasy, altered states of reality, trance, or possession. Typically, those who can go into these states of nonordinary reality or altered consciousness can come out and use their experiences to help others. Many scholars think that women are particularly adept at accommodating possession states. The association of women with intense feelings and ecstasy in contexts of self-knowledge and helping is universal. The specific patterns vary tremendously.

> *Religious movements valuing possession experiences and ecstasy*
> *seem more open to women than are the formal, structured traditions*
> *often described in textbooks on religion. Religious laws and bureau-*
> *cracies can dictate that only men shall be priests, but the gods choose*
> *whom they will. (Falk and Gross 1980:39)*

Those who help others through spirit visitations are called various names depending on the context: mediums, channelers, shamans, seers, or diviners. So frequent is the association of women with spirit possession that it begs for an explanation. One prominent theory talks of women trapped by the double standards of male-female relationships or by the socioeconomic conditions of colonialism.

People afflicted by the spirit receive extra attention and sympathy. After all, someone entered by a capricious spirit cannot be held to blame for her actions. The spirits themselves cannot be controlled; they may return at any time. The cults are ways in which powerless people (predominantly women) work out their anger of and fears about more powerful people. I. M. Lewis calls them "cults of affliction" because they grow out of deprivation and circumstances in which women's aspirations or intelligence outstrip their opportunities for expressing them. He says that in these cults of affliction, women find release from and alternatives to male-dominated societies and husband-dominated marriages.

> For all their concern with disease and its treatment, such women's possession cults are also, I argue, thinly disguised protest movements directed against the dominant sex. They thus play a significant part in the sex-war in traditional societies and cultures where women lack more obvious and direct means for forwarding their aims. To a considerable extent they protect women from the exactions of men, and offer an effective vehicle for manipulating husbands and male relatives. (Lewis 1971:31)

Lewis notes that the possessing spirits typically visit marginal or peripheral people, lower-class or otherwise socially powerless women and men. Typically, those possessed are women in male-dominated societies. But poor women living in male-dominated contexts are probably the plurality if not the outright majority of the world's population. There's nothing marginal about sheer numbers or obvious needs.

The affliction argument does not go far enough. There are other reasons to seek out these groups, particularly for help in coping with illness and grieving. For example, many women of Luvale in Zambia have experienced terrible losses such as barrenness, miscarriages, and babies dead at birth or in infancy. Others have illnesses that are difficult to understand, refuse to go away, cause pain, depression, or weakness (Spring 1978). Women become adept in trances or possession states to call on their female ancestors to help them conceive or carry a living baby to term. Women form bonds with each other, with living descendants and their deceased ones, to become mothers and to heal from the losses of motherhood.

Theories that suppose that women are somehow deficient are a problem. So let's ask again: Why are women so strongly associated with possession states? Perhaps we might ask why men can't seem to have extraordinary experiences, reenter ordinary reality, and assist others with the knowledge as easily or as routinely as women do. In fact, we could consider this ability one of the gifts of gender for women. After all, if men and babies enter or inhabit our bodies, then spirits can too. Susan Sered says:

> Could it be that possession trance is a normal and healthy part of human experience, but men have trouble with it because they have a problem with relationships? (Sered 1994:281)

From Housewife to Shaman

Here is a concrete example of how spirit possession works. It comes from Korean housewives whose domestic or traditional roles are suffocating them. Many women can identify with this problem. The Korean women suffer what Americans call a "nervous breakdown." Koreans say that such women are "harshly fated." The resolution to the crisis is prescribed in Korean folk therapies or ethno-psychiatry.

Youngsook Kim Harvey traced the spiraling development of this breakdown and its resolution in the lives of six Korean women. She reports the following stages: (1) The victim experiences severe conflicts within herself, with being a housewife, and with important members of the family, such as her husband, mother-in-law, and/or sisters-in-law. (2) The victim feels overwhelmed and helplessly trapped by these struggles. (3) The victim falls ill with vague symptoms and is granted some released time from household responsibilities. (4) The illness persists, and the family reduces or completely eliminates its normal demands on the victim while mobilizing its resources to rescue her from her sickness. (5) Under these circumstances, the victim recovers and resumes her usual functions. (6) Now reassured by her recovery, her family reassumes their old patterns of interacting. (7) The cumulative strain of living with the conflicts again becomes unbearable, and the victim again becomes sick. This cycle will be repeated several times until the victim and the family reach an impasse.

So the illness builds. At first, the symptoms are vague: tiredness, faintness, dizziness, headaches, aches in her limbs, insomnia, or heaviness in the heart or tightness of her chest. These do not respond to Chinese herbal treatments or Western medications. In time, the woman begins to have strange dreams or visions. She is socially disruptive. Her family and neighbors regard her as immoral or crazy. They think she talks too much.

> *Worst of all, as far as the community is concerned, victims may speak too frankly and accurately about things going on in the community that would normally not be openly discussed. They may, for example, say that the chronic illness of a young housewife is due to bottled-up resentment toward her abusive mother-in-law or toward her husband, who will not curtail his gambling or extramarital affairs. Or they may refer to the well-known, but never publicly discussed, history of a man who repeatedly fails in his business ventures and puts the blame for his failures on the disturbance created in his household by his nagging wife. They sometimes reveal adulterous affairs among neighbors that, in all likelihood, everyone has known about but no one has openly acknowledged. (Harvey 1980:44)*

At this crucial moment, a shaman diagnoses the afflictions as possession sickness. As the shaman says, the victim has been "caught by the descending spirits." Although the families are embarrassed and defensive, they believe that the spirits are particularly attracted to those whose suffer in this fashion. Eventually, family members prevail on the victim to accept her calling as a shaman, a psychic healer.

In this quote, a Korean woman who went through this personal transformation talks about a spirit visit she received.

> *I went looking for my spirits one day about two months after my mother called me out of death. . . . No, I wasn't hallucinating, but I was, I think, in a state of possession. I had my eyes closed and was muttering something when, vaguely at first and then more clearly, an old woman appeared before me. She said, "Oh, I'm so-and-so, I'm*

> *seventy-four years old and my birthday is August 2. I became a mudang [female visionary and shaman] when I was nineteen. I've three sons. Come see me." I told her I didn't know where she lived, but she would not answer me. She just left. But I saw the very spot where she lived very clearly in my mind and the way to the place. (Harvey 1979:153)*

As a shaman and not a victim, this Korean woman grew into spiritual authority, earning power and full health. She struck a firm bargain with family members. Because the spirits have called these women to be shamans and healers, the situations that provoked the breakdown (such as an abusive husband or cruel mother-in-law) are neutralized. Better still, the women are paid for their healing and counseling services. Income, independence, and a new status help cure the breakdown and offer the chance to aid others as well (see Kendall 1985).

Ritualized Rebellions and Extraordinary Emotions

It is striking to compare "a nervous breakdown" with the crosscultural patternings of women's ecstatic rebellions. These spiritual transformations, however, have their own difficulties; the transition is particularly traumatic and some women do not make it through. They may kill themselves or not reenter ordinary realities. Women who assume these specialist roles as diviner, shaman, medium, or trance adept typically have had a serious illness as child or teenager or have had unusual dreams and other psychic experiences.

Spirit possession has a quality of **immanence,** which means an immediate indwelling presence in the here-and-now. This contrasts sharply with male-dominated religions that emphasize the quality of **transcendence,** something that is supreme or superior, above the ordinary, transcending time or the universe, abstract or idealistic. So people in possession trances actually become spirits. This fact is important. It means that members of the audience witness an individual woman who becomes the spirit being.

> *Deities are seen to be physically present on earth, and seen to look like—to wear the bodies of—women. (Sered 1994:192)*

The gender of the visiting spirit is immaterial. Spirits appear in many forms and change shapes regularly. What matters is that women and men see, hear, and feel the spirits as they possess the earthly bodies of other women.

But possession experiences and spiritualist cults are not just about manipulating the limited social world many women face. Possession cults, far from being different or exotic, are another form of women's adjustment and health-seeking. They are also about direct experience with the nonordinary or spirit world, with ecstasy, sensuality, or sexuality. There is a major difference between knowledge based on prophesy, vision, revelation, or other forms of direct personal experience and religions based on male authority, sacred scriptures, creeds, or received wisdom. The link of women with direct personal experience is the golden thread that runs through all of women's religious lives.

Matriarchies and Patriarchies

In the last half of this chapter, I wish to take on one of the toughest topics in women's studies and religious studies: the meanings of matriarchies and the origins of patriarchies. I will only be able to summarize a few key points, but the reading guide at the end of the chapter suggests other directions for you.

Let's begin with a very powerful set of stories about goddesses, gods, women, men, human society, and the spirit world. These stories date from the period after 5000 B.C., when large-scale civilizations and the world religions came into being in the Middle East, the Mediterranean, and Europe.

New ways of relating to the environment and earning a living, which we call the **Neolithic** Revolution, meant significant social and economic changes in the status of women. Plow agriculture and the domestication of animals supplanted horticulture and gathering. Kinship, marriage and household arrangements changed. Through time, villages turned into cities and traditional cultures into civilizations. The world religions evolved along with ideas like governments, legal systems, and writing. Scholars have amassed magnificent and voluminous evidence from art, archaeology, history, anthropology, theology, literature, and the comparative study of languages. In these disciplines for centuries, researchers have observed the shift from the veneration and ceremonials for spirits and powerful goddesses to the worship of a single male god. Monotheism appears to have replaced polytheism as priests took over from priestesses. These historic shifts happened at various times and in complex ways in the Middle East and Europe. That they happened is well-documented. Why they happened and what this may mean for women yesterday and today are still open questions.

In the stories and myths from these periods, human society was originally **matristic.** Neither males nor females dominated, but all lived in a kind of partnership. The kinship systems were matrilineal and religions centered on the principles of spirituality, generativity, fertility, and death we associate with females. Sometimes these early societies were called **matriarchal,** or under the political control of women. Actually, the term translates as the rule of mothers; the word could refer to nurturing as the leading quality for government or management.

A number of key authors took the stories, the archaeology, and the history and proposed that human societies went through universal stages like primitive to barbarian to civilized, or from matriarchy to patriarchy. A classic example is a Swiss lawyer named Johann Jacob Bachofen, who examined Greek and Roman mythology, ancient laws, and religions. In his influential book, *The Mother-Right,* published in 1861, Bachofen proposed that matrilineal kinship combined with matriarchy was the first stage of human development. Since no man could be certain about the paternity of a child, he said, kinship and inheritance could only be reckoned through mothers. Therefore women held positions of high status, respect, and honor. In effect, women regularly ruled over early groups in what he called a **gynocracy.**

> *Matriarchy becomes a sign of cultural progress, a source and guaran-*
> *tee of its benefits, a necessary period in the education of mankind,*
> *and hence the fulfillment of a natural law which governs peoples as*
> *well as individuals. (Bachofen 1967:91)*

The myths of classical literature, said Bachofen and his small circle of contemporaries, point to a historic struggle. "Father-right" and monogamy won and deposed "mother-right" and women-centered lifestyles. Women, once powerful, lost to men. The Victorians (from whom we have taken many of our contemporary myths about women) loved this theory. It romanticized a primitive, hence inferior, period of history. For them the myth actually buttressed the idea of the patriarchy, clearly a later and superior period.

As we know from chapter 5, the upstate New York lawyer Lewis Henry Morgan wrote about the matrilineal, matrilocal, and horticultural Iroquois. Morgan went further than Bachofen. He believed that patriarchal rule replaced matriarchal social life as agriculture evolved. He argued that the concept of private property and ownership of previously communal farmlands allowed men the power to overthrow the matriarchy. Men instituted the idea of permanent monogamy and exclusive pairing. Only in this way could men control women and be certain of their paternity so they could pass on property to their male heirs.

Stories about an early stage of matriarchy in human cultures also show up in the doctrines of socialism and communism. Karl Marx and Frederick Engels loved Lewis Henry Morgan, Iroquois women, and the idea of an early, deposed matriarchy. Following Morgan closely, they proposed the revolutionary change in economic patterns and how people earned a living as the turning point in the collective lives of women. Marx said, as men controlled the herd animals and the farmlands that marked the Neolithic and early civilizations, they come to control women too. Men set up the ideas of private property and monogamy. Monogamy was defined as the lifetime fidelity of a woman to a man, and women became property. Engels called this "the world historical defeat of the female sex." In the next chapter, we will return to Marx, Engels, and the condition of women in the world.

Other important theorists, like Sigmund Freud, Carl Jung, and the psychoanalysts who follow them, talked about the restoration of male dominance when the patriarchy became the reigning social order. In recent times, many feminists have borrowed these myths of early matriarchies to argue for female competence in the wider world. Today therapists of many kinds access the stories of the goddesses and their personalities to help women adjust to the demands of the patriarchy. These images of women in ritual, myths, dreams, and art are often used to affirm the golden age of matriarchy when mothers controlled the world in the name of nurturing and peace. The mother-goddess and matriarchy complex with its reversed imagery of our Euro-American world has retained or regained its popularity in this century.

Coming up are three brief examples from history and anthropology that illustrate matriarchies and patriarchies, gendered religions in world history, or the spiritual conflicts between men and women. The examples are the sacred prostitutes of Mesopotamia, the goddesses of Old Europe, and the hunted witches of western Europe. There are many other possible illustrations, but these three have a deep resonance in women's studies and in the contemporary reworking of the myths of matriarchy.

Whores and Other Sacred Women

Today a prostitute is defined as a person, usually a woman, who exchanges goods or money for providing the service of sex. Synonyms include call girl, streetwalker, whore, or hooker. Terms for women who sell sex are judgmental and pejorative. But many of these words appear to stem from practices in the past in which women controlled their bodies and sexuality in ways we can only begin to imagine.

For historian Gerda Lerner, there were two forms of organized prostitution in the emerging civilizations of the ancient Middle East. The first was religious or sacred sex work as priestesses associated with the goddesses of that time. Some historians call these fertility cults; she calls this "cultic sexual service." Then there was prostitution as secular sex work, a commercial endeavor. Women themselves controlled both forms before the establishment of patriarchal economics and government. Ancient Mesopotamia was the heartland of the Neolithic and the homeland of three world religions (Judaism, Islam, and Christianity), so the records of women's lives bear on contemporary sensitivities.

Scholars like Gerda Lerner talk about single, probably upper-class women, who lived and worked within the large temple complexes of urban areas. They participated in the annual rituals she translates as "Sacred Marriage." In those days, people believed that the fertility of the land and its citizens depended on the sexual blessings of the goddess. During these ceremonies, women as priestesses impersonated or became the goddess. Then they had sex with various gods. These were probably spirit or possession trances.

> The annual symbolic reenactment of this mythical union was a public celebration considered essential to the well-being of the community. It was the occasion of a joyous celebration, which may have involved sexual activity on the part of the worshipers in and around the temple grounds. It is important for us to understand that contemporaries regarded this occasion as sacred, as mythically significant for the well-being of the community, and that they regarded the king and the priestess with reverence and honored them for performing this "sacred" service. The Sacred Marriage was performed in the temples of various fertility-goddesses for nearly two thousand years. (Lerner 1986:127)

These women had titles best translated as sacred prostitutes or sacred whores. There are records of priestesses who offered a combination of mother love, tenderness, comfort, mystical enlightenment, and good sex. It is quite apparent that groups of women in many ancient times and places controlled and marketed their own sexuality. They used it in the service of healing or other religious activities, such as predicting the future, counseling others, or keeping track of time.

Such women often commanded high status and respect for their learning. On occasion, they married well and became empresses or queens in the ancient world. They served as sorcerers, seers, diviners, or mediums. These ancient accounts indicate that priestesses or sacred women practiced some kind of matrilineal or matrifocal lifestyle. They apparently chose their lovers or husbands as they willed, and passed on their occupations to their daughters.

At the same time, other classes and conditions of sexual service came into being. Scholars believe that the concept of private property as well as the notion of buying and selling sex were developed at the same point in these historic cultures. Armies captured women in battle, women became symbols of power and ownership. Lerner says that the concept of women as private property was the hinge on which the newly emerging patriarchy swung. Slavery was invented and first practiced on women.

At the same time, ideologies about conception or the question of who gives life also began to change. Images of goddesses who bestowed fertility and nourished the earth with their bodies were replaced with references to "male seed" and customs such as circumcision, cutting off the foreskin of the penis, to establish a covenant with a male god. Men plowed, furrowed, and deposited their "seeds" in the waiting ground. Females were fields to be sown and harvested. Like the earth, they were only there to be used. With the growth of the patriarchy and the patriarchal religions of the ancient Middle East, men owned sex and gave life.

The Goddesses of Old Europe

A fascinating source of evidence for what goddess-worshiping and matristic societies might have looked like comes from European archaeologist Marija Gimbutas and her decades of work. She paints a compelling picture of a long-ago culture she calls **Old Europe.**

What was Old Europe like? The people who inhabited Europe from the seventh to the fourth millennia B.C. (between 6500 and 3500 B.C.) were Neolithic farmers. Gimbutas says that the cultures of Old Europe were "peaceful, sedentary, matrifocal, matrilineal, and sex equalitarian" (1991:352). They were matristic rather than matriarchal. Rather than controlling, women practiced a type of partnership with men.

People of Old Europe lived in populated towns, in houses with four or five rooms, and built temples several stories high. They honored some features of female spirituality in the person of a Great Mother Goddess and other goddesses; they developed what looks like a writing system or sacred script and made images in pottery, wood, bone, and other materials, which still have the power to move us. They were artists, artisans, and traders in pottery, weaving, copper, and gold metallurgy. They participated in flourishing trade networks that reached across Europe and into the adjoining regions. According to Gimbutas, the cultures of Old Europe challenge the assumption that warfare is endemic to the human condition. Weapons are absent in the archaeological excavations. The art they produced does not depict arms, that is, weapons used against other people. Their unfortified villages were located in places with good soils, convenient pastures, and running water.

But by 4300 B.C., Old Europe began to change irrevocably. Waves of people from the east started to move in. They brought new customs, new ways of earning a living, and new ways of worship. This transition did not happen suddenly. But over the 1,500 years that followed, the cultures of Europe changed dramatically. Gimbutas calls these invaders or migrants **Kurgans.** The Kurgan cultures brought the earliest Indo-European languages into Europe; so they are also called Indo-Europeans. Seminomadic pastoralists who depended on herding and breeding animals, they were a stark contrast to the people of Old Europe.

Based on comparative linguistics, mythology, and archaeology, Gimbutas offers reasons to think that the Kurgans were patrilocal, patriarchal, patrilineal, pastoral, mobile, and warring, with a pantheon of male gods. The newcomers carried long daggers or knives, spears, halberds, or broadaxes, and bows and arrows. According to Gimbutas, they gradually overwhelmed the social structure, economy, and religion of Old Europe from 4300 B.C. to 2800 B.C., when the transition was complete.

The Kurgans rode horses. In breeding their steeds, they developed ideas about male "seed" and paternity. The people of Old Europe did not domesticate or ride horses. Fertility was a quality of being female and generativity came from the goddesses. So riding and breeding horses allowed an elaboration and celebration of male power in ways early Neolithic settled life did not. After all, one does not go into battle with cows, pigs, or chickens. The main gods of the Indo-Europeans were usually depicted as warriors with weapons, horses, and chariots. The Kurgans built no temples or structured altars. They erected stone pillars on which they carved solar symbols and masculine equipment like daggers and axes. This is consistent with a seminomadic life, but a remarkable change from the early religious architecture and artifacts of Old Europe, the altars, sculptures, vases, and models of temples.

The new people on the block were responsible for something else: plows. This simple tool is credited with altering the balance between men and women, perhaps forever. In gathering and horticulture societies, as we have seen, women use hoes and digging sticks; women produce food directly, often working together in processing and distribution. But after about 3000 B.C., various groups in the Middle East and Mediterranean developed styles of agriculture that used domesticated animals to pull plows. For a variety of reasons, this kind of farming became men's work and spread widely. Men with plows and draft animals replaced women as primary producers. This is, of course, a source for the notion of "male seed" as the dominant image of fertility.

Even their graves reflected the differences between the worldviews of Old Europe and the new Indo-Europeans. Graves and the goods buried in them speak for relative equality in Old Europe. No classes, no chiefs, no warriors, no slaves.

> *In spite of the revered status of women in religious life, the cemetery*
> *evidence throughout the 5th and most of the 4th millennia B.C. does*
> *not suggest any imbalance between the sexes or a subservience of*
> *one sex to the other. It suggests, instead, a condition of mutual*

> respect. The primary grave goods for both sexes are symbolic of the
> sacred cycles of regeneration, although burial goods also honor per-
> sonal achievements in the arts, crafts, trade, and other professions.
> (Gimbutas 1991:x)

By contrast, the later-arriving Indo-Europeans seemed to believe in life as a
straight line. When they died, they entered the world of the dead. So they took
their belongings with them—tools, weapons, clothes, and jewelry they would
need on the other side. They apparently took their social status with them, and
high-ranking men even took wives, servants, children, dogs, oxen, and horses
with them! Once in the world of the dead, a dreary underworld ruled by an all-
powerful male god, there was no return.

Is this story of Old Europe true? Is this archaeological proof for an ancient conflict between men and women? Gimbutas suggests a framework in which to place
these questions.

> The collapse of Old Europe coincides with the process of Indo-
> Europeanization of Europe, a complicated transformative process
> leading to a drastic cultural change reminiscent of the conquest of the
> American continent. Archeological evidence, supported by compara-
> tive Indo-European linguistics and mythology, suggests a clash of two
> ideologies, social structures and economies. (Gimbutas 1991:352)

If we compare the changes of the late Neolithic in Europe to the changes wrought
on Native Americans after the conquest of the New World, we see similar patterns.
We know something about the lives of women and men in the Iroquois's League of
the Six Fires before Indo-European speakers brought horses, new weapons, and ideologies of war to this continent. We have records of matrilineal, matrilocal, and horticultural peoples like the Iroquois or the Zuni. We know that the invaders practiced
monogamy and patrilineal descent; they worshiped a creator male sky god, their
Great White Father. In both of these historic cases, we have reasons to think that
women's lives and spirituality were forever altered.

Midwives and Other Witches

The third example of the conflicts of men's religions with women's religions are
the infamous witch hunts of western Europe. From the fourteenth to the seventeenth centuries, from England to Germany, a campaign of terror was directed
against largely female and largely peasant populations. No one knows how many
people perished in this crusade. Some scholars say as many as 4 million; others
lower the figure to hundreds of thousands. They agree that 85 percent of those
killed were women, some very young and others very old. Many were widows, or
women with belligerent personalities or sharp tongues. The focal targets, however, were midwives.

Why did this happen? In the surviving accounts, women are depicted in the
typical activities of women's religions. They cured sick people, delivered babies,

and addressed human suffering. They apparently engaged in spirit possession or trance states. They knew about and employed a sophisticated and effective herbal pharmacopeia. It seems clear that many traditions from earlier tribal cultures, similar to those of Old Europe, were alive and well into the periods when Christians were fighting to establish religious hegemony. Christians called people like this "pagans." Pagans left few records about their lives in their own words.

In medieval Europe, those in authority apparently feared midwives for their connections to pagan times, to goddess worship, spirit contacts, and mother-centered kinship systems. As the Catholic Church increasingly gained power, they declared war on women, particularly "wise ones." They cloaked their fears in magical silliness, like the belief that midwives offered newborn children to the service of the devil with illegal baptisms under full moons.

In 1486 two Dominican priests published an authoritative handbook on how to recognize and punish witches. This document was called the *Hammer of Witches*. In the box, "The Hammer of Witches," the authors pose this question: "What Sort of Women Are Found to Be Above All Others Superstitious and Witches?" Note their answer.

Bear in mind our discussions in chapter 3 about women's knowledge and experience in matters of birth control, abortion, infanticide, and sexual practices. Then compare women such as these to the accusers, a celibate male clergy most charitably characterized as sexually naive, confused, inexperienced, or anxious. The authors of this tirade strike me as hysterical. Others say they are sadistic or misogynist.

What were witches guilty of? The tract condemns midwives and other women who commit four horrible crimes with the assistance of assorted devils. Women failed to complete intercourse. This is probably a reference to coitus interruptus or other ways to avoid pregnancy while still having sex. Women were accused of preventing conceptions. They could cause a miscarriage with magical potions. They disposed of unwanted infants. The clergy imagined that women devoured children or gave them over to the devil.

> *Undoubtedly, over the centuries of witch hunting, the charge of "witchcraft" came to cover a multitude of sins ranging from political subversion and religious heresy to lewdness and blasphemy. But three central accusations emerge repeatedly in the history of witch-craft throughout northern Europe: First, witches are accused of every sexual crime against men. Quite simply, they are "accused" of female sexuality. Second, they are accused of being organized. Third, they are accused of having magical powers affecting health—of harming, but also of healing. They were often charged specifically with possessing medical and obstetrical skills. (Ehrenreich and English 1973:10)*

As the witnesses noted, "No one does more harm to the Catholic Faith than midwives" (Kramer and Sprenger: 1928, 66). It is quite obvious that women were guilty, midwives more than most. The work of midwives, some of which happened at night or in remote places, was evidence of witchcraft, given the definitions. It is

The Hammer of Witches

What Sort of Women Are Found to Be Above All Others Superstitious and Witches?

Three general vices appear to have special domination over wicked women, namely infidelity, ambition, and lust. Therefore they are more than others inclined towards witchcraft, who more than others are given to these vices. Again, since of these three vices the last chiefly predominates, women being insatiable, etc., it follows that those among ambitious women are more deeply infected who are more hot to satisfy their filthy lusts; and such are adulteresses, fornicatresses, and the concubines of the Great [Devil].

Now there are, as it is said in the Papal Bull, seven methods by which they infect with witchcraft the venereal [sexual] act and the conception of the womb: First, by inclining the minds of men to inordinate passion; second, by obstructing their generative force; third, by removing the members accommodated to that act; fourth, by changing men into beasts by their magic art; fifth, by destroying the generative force in women; sixth, by procuring abortion; seventh, by offering children to devils, besides other animals and fruits of the earth with which they work much harm.

To conclude: All witchcraft comes from carnal lust, which is in women insatiable. Wherefore for the sake of fulfilling their lust they consort even with devils. More such reasons could be brought forward, but to the understanding it is sufficiently clear that it is no matter for wonder that there are more women than men found infected with the heresy of witchcraft. And blessed by the Highest Who has so far preserved the male sex from so great a crime: for since He was willing to be born and suffer for us, therefore He has granted to men this privilege.

Source: Heinrich Kramer and James Sprenger, *The Hammer of Witches: The Malleus Maleficarum,* 47.

difficult to control such women, and the thought of knowledgeable women in charge of their bodies and sexuality probably was scary.

Remember that during this time, men believed that their semen contained very tiny, fully formed babies called **homunculi**. The learned medical authorities in the fifteenth, sixteenth, and seventeenth centuries taught that men deposited a homunculus with their semen into women at intercourse. The homunculus merely grew larger; it acquired no attributes or qualities from its female hostess during the nine months it took to grow to newborn size. Women were only temporary, albeit necessary, dwellings for men's babies. Women had nothing to do with the physical or spiritual formation of infants. In fact, the homunculus was in mortal danger from women like midwives and mothers until men could baptize it after birth.

The historic events surrounding hunting and punishing witches has contributed to a contemporary paranoia in the feminist movements and a revitalization of interest in women's ceremonialism and curing. As Barbara Ehrenreich and Deidre English note:

> *This early and devastating exclusion of women from independent healing roles was a violent precedent and a warning: It was to become a theme of our history. The women's health movement of today has ancient roots in the medieval covens, and its opponents have as their ancestors those who ruthlessly forced the elimination of witches. (Ehrenreich and English 1973:6)*

The Myths of Matriarchies: What Does All This Mean?

Ironically, anthropologists and archaeologists generally do not subscribe to the view that matriarchies preceded the current patriarchal stage of human history. Few anthropologists today argue for the nineteenth-century view of an early or universal stage of matriarchy. In fact, not everybody is agreed that a patriarchy ever existed or even exists now. My colleagues point to a number of problems with these concepts.

Yes, there are matrilineal societies. But they are not remnants or survivals from an earlier age; they exist in their own contemporary right. Matrilineal does not equal matriarchal, and matrilineal societies may also include male dominance or low social status for women. Yes, there are thousands of magnificent and moving female figurines found in archaeology sites. These include the **Venus figurines** from 20,000 to 30,000 years ago, to the statues of goddesses from early Mesopotamia to Old Europe. But there are also male figures, animal figures, and other objects, which may have been used as ornaments, toys, teaching devices, or for purposes we can only guess at. Dynamic representations of females in myths or art do not necessarily translate into or equate with high female status in everyday life. There is no necessary parallel between the gender of sacred images or mythic figures and the social roles of ordinary women.

Yes, there are societies that worship female gods or have myths about the domination of women in the distant past. But there is no evidence that female political supremacy went along with this. The status of ordinary women in the goddess-honoring societies can be very low, even dreadful. Furthermore, men are involved in matrilineal or matrifocal situations, just as women figure in the myths and art of patrilineal societies. A major contribution of anthropologists to this debate is the fact that myths are not history, and all of us project onto the archaeological and ethnographic records what we want to see.

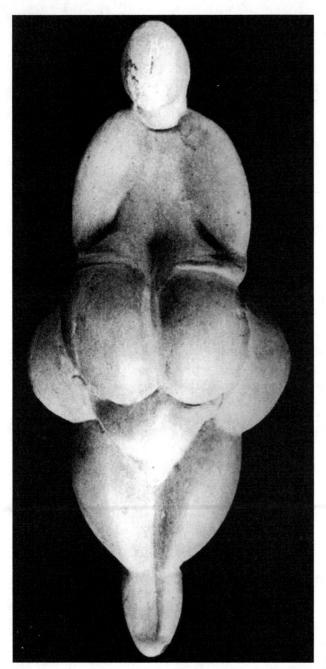

The Venus of Lespugne.

These myths about matriarchies and goddesses are important, however, for two reasons. First, they are the core mythologies of contemporary women-centered religions, ritual practices, and healing groups. Anthropologists are not in the business of ratifying one religious system over another, but we do take very seriously how people assign meanings to their lives, either individually or collectively. And

The Venus of Willandorf.

second, the myths, the research, and the theories reveal something very important when they talk about times and places when women were more powerful or more deeply honored than we ourselves have ever experienced.

The most sensible and sensitive resolution to the differences of opinions about matriarchies comes from anthropologist Paula Webster, who says,

> *We do not agree with some of our sisters within anthropology that any attention paid to the matriarchy question is a waste of time at best, or a destructive diversion at worst. The more we read, the clearer it became that matriarchy is the only vision we have of a society in which women have power, or at least one in which men do not. As such it forced us to imagine a form of social organization that we had never experienced, and to pose critical questions about the relationship between power, gender, and social structure. . . .*
>
> *Though the matriarchy debate revolves around the past, its real value lies in the future: It pushes women (and men) to imagine a society that is not patriarchal, one in which women might for the first time have power over their lives. . . . Because the matriarchy*

> *discussion uncovers the inadequacies of old paradigms, it encourages*
> *women to create new ones. (Webster 1975:145,155)*

The myths of matriarchies are also important because they make patriarchies into just another cultural system. In their light, male dominance is only another form of cultural relativism. This means that male dominance does not result inevitably from biology and sexual differences, nor has it been ordained by the cosmos. It is not the last word in authoritative knowledge. Like other cultural phenomenon, systems of patriarchies are limited to certain times and places. This opens a path to the future.

Women and the New Spirits

The 150-year-old debate about matriarchies and patriarchies has provoked and promoted a paradoxical and fascinating religious movement for women in America that is loosely called feminist spirituality. It seems to include the Goddess Path, the pagan path, neo-paganism, eco-feminism, Wicca, and other labels. As a movement, feminist spirituality is unorganized and decentralized to the point of anarchy; there are no official gurus. The closest thing to leaders are the authors of best-selling books, both novels and nonfiction. No one even knows how many people are involved; there are certainly enough to sustain conferences, retreats, covens, congregations, bookstores, mail-order houses, support groups, discussion groups, and many other manifestations of a growing movement.

In her book *Living in the Lap of the Goddess,* theologian Cynthia Eller lists five features at the heart of feminist spirituality. These are (1) magic and ritual in the service of being female; (2) respect and veneration for the environment (Mother Nature); (3) working for women's empowerment; (4) women as the focus of religious inquiry; and (5) a recognition of the movement's sacred history. However, given the movement's commitment to diversity, no one is required to believe all of the above nor to give up prior religious practices or affiliations with normative religious groups.

> *The feminist spirituality movement is interesting primarily in terms*
> *of its religious syncretism and its gender politics. Most new religions*
> *show an interest early on in consolidating their belief systems and*
> *establishing authority structures. Spiritual feminists, however, remain*
> *determinedly eclectic, borrowing deities, meditation techniques, and*
> *magical recipes from whatever culture appeal to them. . . . Though*
> *feminist spirituality is syncretistic, it has a definite selection criterion*
> *in mind: namely, that all beliefs and practices, whether individual or*
> *communal, must be conducive to the feminist struggle against a*
> *patriarchal social order. (Eller 1991:281)*

Susan Sered notes that the feminist spirituality movement has developed in a social and political climate in which women marry late, divorce often, and become single parents through choice or necessity. American women are, in effect, creating matrifocal families and acting as heads of households. This is certainly true for many lesbians, divorced, and professional women. The women in the movement tend to be white, middle-class, and literate. There are probably more lesbians and victims of traumas at the hands of men (incest, molestation, battering, beating and so forth) than the population figures alone would predict.

Practitioners and followers of feminist spirituality say that women were not treated well in the image of the divine or the sense of the sacred in world religions. So they have turned to a variety of charismatic sisterhoods, goddess-centered rituals, circles of healing, and matrifocal households. Furthermore, women and feminists in the movement have become social and political activists who seek alternatives to hierarchical, rule-based, and vertical models of the patriarchal religions. Although men are included, female principles of sacredness and women-centered experiences are paramount.

This new women's movement has resurrected and recreated a sacred history. The roots of this sacred history are in female-friendly and relatively equalitarian societies, in the goddesses and life-affirming rituals that empowered women in the past. They look to prehistoric matriarchies. In anthropology they find cultures that are matrilineal, matristic, matrifocal, or gynocentric in some enviable fashion. They invoke the witch hunts as evidence of malice, violence, and even conspiracy from male-centered religious and economic systems. Many in the feminist spirituality movement call themselves witches. They form covens and stage rituals similar to those of pagan times; Wicca is a good example. They take the terms "pagan" and "witch" as a positive heritage of women-centered spirituality. Many turn to herbal remedies, alternative healing, midwives, and trance work.

As women in the movement say, the ground of the sacred is here and now. In other words, human beings are not just passing through this life, and women do not have to wait until death to alleviate suffering or find justice or mercy. Spirits and deities are immanent, that is, they are in and of everything. They are not transcendent, above all or on top of a hierarchy. There are multiple paths to the spirit world. There is not one way, one truth, one god, one government, or one husband. The feminist spirituality movement shares these characteristics with other women's religions around the world and with manifestations deep into the human past. As Susan Sered says:

> Comfortable with other people, women are willing to meet their gods and goddesses face to face and even share their bodies with divinities (in spirit possession). Transcendent, monotheistic male deities have little meaning for mothers who daily confront existential issues of birth, suffering, and death. (Sered 1994:285)

As the final characteristic of women's religions, Susan Sered reports that none of the groups she studied go to war. None have militaristic inclinations or justify aggression. None convert others with force, reason, or guns. Moreover, none of these women-centered religions worships a single, powerful male god. These observations lead us directly into the next chapter, which is about the ultimate consequences for women of the patriarchal trinity: Christianity, colonialism, and capitalism. It is also about women's response, resiliency, and resistance.

A Field Full of Books to Read

Writers within the new feminist spiritualities are prolific. They use anthropology, history, theology, therapy, myths, rituals, and healing in dynamic and innovative ways. Start with the novel by Marion Zimmer Bradley, *The Mists of Avalon.* Then try Margot Adler's *Drawing Down the Moon: Witches, Druids, Goddess-Worshippers, and Other Neo-Pagans in America Today* (1986); or read Charlene Spretnak's collection of articles, *The Politics of Women's Spirituality: Essays on the Rise of Spiritual Power Within the Feminist Movement* (1982). Another excellent collection is edited by Carol Christ and Judith Plaskow, *Weaving the Visions: New Patterns in Feminist Spirituality* (1989).

The following ethnographies or ethnographic collections add significantly to our knowledge about women's religions in the world: Bennetta Jules-Rosette, editor, *The New Religions of Africa* (1979) is a strong original collection of firsthand field reports and analyses about contemporary African cults and churches. She emphasizes the importance of religion as both agent and symbol of change, and more to the point, the central roles of women in African religions. Religious fundamentalism is a worldwide phenomenon and one of the predictable issues is controlling women's sexuality, reproduction and work. John Stratton Hawley has edited a collection of articles, *Fundamentalism and Gender* (1994), which brings fresh and challenging perspectives to this pressing and gendered debate.

Laurel Kendall, *Shamans, Housewives, and Other Restless Spirits: Women in Korean Ritual Life* (1985), is a thoughtful complement to Youngsook Kim Harvey's research as well as this chapter. Kendall's research convinces readers that the spiritual lives of Korean women have much to teach us. Loudell Snow did twenty years of fieldwork in many settings in the United States. In *Walking Over Medicine* (1993), she presents the voices of those who seek healing with extraordinary clarity. Her wonderful book concerns the living, breathing folk medicines African Americans invented and use. Ruth Landes studied the **candomblé** religious society in Brazil immediately before World War II and wrote *The City of Women.* Then she was cited as of the pioneering practitioners of what we now call postmodern anthropology, and now a 1994 edition has been reissued with an introduction by Sally Cole.

Judith Gleason wrote *Oya: In Praise of the Goddess* in 1987. This study of the goddess Oya in Yoruba religion and Santeria movements is one of many such works that come directly from personal experiences and informed scholarship. Another such book from Paula Gunn Allen, *Grandmothers of the Light: A Medicine Woman's Sourcebook* (1991), is a collection of Native American myths with plenty of goddesses and female shamans. Karen McCarthy Brown wrote *Mama Lola: A Vodou Priestess in Brooklyn* (1991). This is an ethnographic and intimate spiritual biography of a Haitian woman in New York, a priestess of vodou, an engaging storyteller, a healer, and a teacher. Brown's fieldwork research was an apprenticeship to Mama Lola, and the narrative is unusually rich, personal, and feminine. Jeanette Rodriguez interviewed Mexican-American women who told her about the most powerful icon in Mexican culture. The resulting book, *Our Lady of Guadalupe: Faith and Empowerment Among Mexican-American Women* (1994), shows the liberating and empowering forces

Guadalupe modeled for them. This is also the story of theologian Jeanette Rodriquez's personal journey and search for spiritual authenticity.

Two books by Kaya Finkler are must-reads: *Women in Pain: Gender and Morbidity in Mexico* (1994), and *Spiritualist Healers in Mexico* (reissued in 1994). Her research on spiritualist healing in Mexico shows that women are the majority of the healers and the majority of the patients. She examines a paradox: Women worldwide report experiences of pain and sickness more than men do, but women live longer. Women's suffering is real but not life-threatening. So it is no wonder that in so many places in the world women seek help from women's religions and spiritualism for a disease we call "nerves." Oppression requires healing too.

Barbara Ehrenreich and Deidre English wrote a slim little volume, more pamphlet than book, in 1973. Feminist Press continues to publish it. *Witches, Midwives and Nurses: A History of Women Healers* is still the most accessible introduction to the subject of women as healers in western European history. By contrast, Brian Levack edited a collection of the absolutely classic articles and the best authoritative knowledge on witches. There are twelve volumes, one just on women: *Witchcraft, Women and Society,* volume 10 in *Witchcraft, Magic and Demonology: A Twelve Volume Anthology of Scholarly Articles* (1992). The best contemporary study of the culture of witches is by Loretta Orion: *Never Again the Burning Times: Paganism Revived* (1994). This is a fascinating ethnography about the complex belief systems and characteristics of the witchcraft movement and the singular subculture of witch communities in the United States.

Chapter Nine

Invisible Workers

Women As the Earth's Last Colony

J magine a woman who works with poor people in India and who won an international peace prize for helping them.

Did you guess Mother Teresa? She is a Roman Catholic nun who works with poor and dying people of Calcutta. She won the European Nobel Peace Prize in 1979.

Or did you guess Ela Bhatt? She founded the Self-Employed Women's Association of Ahmedabad in 1972. SEWA is a trade union for women who work in the informal sector outside the regular wage economy. Many people think that SEWA is the most successful women's grassroots organization in the world. A Hindu by birth and a lawyer by profession, Ela Bhatt received Asia's top award, the Ramon Magsaysay Foundation Prize, in 1977 for her work with poor women.

Women's work is often invisible within the Eurocentric view of the world, within agencies for international development, and to those who profit from women's work. So the purpose of this chapter is, literally, to make women's work visible. The work of women discussed in this chapter still looks like the four kinds we saw in chapter 1: production, reproduction, status-enhancement, and emotional work.

First, we will look at some somber statistics on the working and living conditions for women worldwide. Then we turn to the processes of "modernization" and "development" in international agencies like the United Nations. We examine the consequences of colonialism and capitalism on some arenas of women's lives and consider the critique of capitalism in the works of Frederick Engels, Karl Marx, and Eleanor Leacock. Last, we will take up two examples of women's resistance and grassroots movements.

Some questions about women's lives that will come up in this chapter deserve fuller treatment. This includes the climate of violence against women and sex work, sexual slavery, or prostitution. You will find these topics treated in chapter 10.

The stage setting for this chapter is **colonialism**: the processes and policies in which a nation-state acquires, extends, or retains its political, social, cultural, and economic dominance over other peoples or territories. World history in the last 500 years has been shaped by European nations that established hegemony over "their" colonies, immense groups of people unrelated to them by geography, history, language or culture.

The European colonizers believed they were doing the "natives" a favor by bringing them the benefits of civilization. The people whom they subjected were said to be "primitives," "savages," pagan, underdeveloped, natural, or romantic. Mostly they were of a different color. Since colonized people did not belong to the culture of empire with its superiority complexes, they became "the Other." The culture of empire exported and projected its own assumptions about the world and what was "natural" onto those they controlled.

By the turn of this century, European countries had taken over more than 85 percent of the globe. This is why people used to say that the sun never set on the British Empire. After 1945, colonies began to achieve independence from colonial rulers, some through formal political processes, others through bitter wars and revolutions. After World War II, newly independent nations in Asia, Africa, and Latin America adopted the term **Third World** to distinguish themselves from the "First World," the Western democracies, and the "Second World," the Soviet-bloc nations.

The term Third World contains some contradictions. For example, it is often viewed as a synonym for poverty or used to belittle and judge other people. Many Third World countries, however, have higher standards of living than do entire segments of First World countries. Capitalist and democratic nations like the United States have huge populations of very poor people. In rural areas and urban centers alike, the poorest are inevitably female. Meanwhile, the Second World, the Soviet-bloc nations, no longer exists; but there are women and men living in the new countries created out of upheaval. Moreover, the Fourth World are groups descended from the empires and tribal peoples that existed before world colonialism. Sometimes Native Americans refer to themselves as the **First Nations,** the cultures of this hemisphere who inhabited North and South America before Europeans arrived and who observe tribal traditions and ethnic identities in contemporary multicultural settings. There are women in all these groups.

A dominant ideology of European colonizers was a belief in an economic system called **capitalism.** In this system, private individuals and corporations invest in and own the means of production. They distribute and exchange wealth. So a capitalist is a person who has capital—money, assets, land, factories, investments, and other means of production. Capitalism contrasts with socialism (in which governments own and distribute wealth) and the economic systems of communal or tribal societies that existed prior to capitalism.

Whatever the benefits or advantages of capitalism, it is not a system that has been uniformly kind to women. Long after subjected groups gained independence from their colonial masters, women's lives did not change for the better. Indeed, there is considerable evidence that they only got worse. In 1970 Ester Boserup published an eye-opening book in which she asserted that there were no good explanations for the existence and increase in poverty for women in the Third World. She said that modernization and development initiatives that claimed to improve the lot of people in underdeveloped countries had, paradoxically, deeply negative effects on women. Expensive and highly touted projects failed either to address women's issues or failed to see women as workers. By any calculation, women were working harder for less return. Females were poorer, sicker, and more exhausted than they were before help arrived.

So, for purposes of this chapter, women are the last and the largest colony on earth. We are "the Other." Our labor or work is appropriated, devalued, or ignored. Women are treated as part of nature, a resource like air, water, and land that exists to be used up. And most important, women around the planet share characteristics with each other that are not shared with men, regardless of the countries any of us live in.

Characteristics of Women's Lives in the Last Colony

What do we mean by invisible workers? The United Nations summarized the principal trends in women's lives on the planet for the decades 1970 to 1990. Here is what they concluded.

Table 9.1 *Water is work.*

> ## Woman-hours per week drawing and carrying water, by country
>
> Villages in Mozambique
> 15.3 hours per week in the dry season
> 2.9 hours per week in the wet season
> Farming villages in Senegal
> 17.5 hours per week
> Rural areas of Botswana
> 5.5 hours per week
> Baroda region of India
> 7.0 hours per week
> Villages in Nepal
> 1.5 hours per week for girls age 5-9.
> 4.9 hours per week for girls age 10-14.
> 4.7 hours per week for females 15 and older.
> United States and Canada
> 0.0001 hours per week
>
> Source: United Nations, *The World's Women: Trends and Statistics 1970–1990*, (1991), 75.

More than three-quarters of the world's women live in so-called developing regions. The absolute majority of them are poor. Everywhere in the world, workplaces are segregated by sex.

Women do domestic tasks such as fetching water and firewood. Women process and prepare food. In developing countries, particularly in rural areas, there is often no safe water to drink, much less water to cook and wash with. People don't have basic sanitation or electricity. Table 9.1 shows woman-hours per week spent in carrying water in selected countries.

Women care for children. There is no country in the world, regardless of its ideologies, in which men as leaders, men as husbands, or men as fathers provide more than a fraction of the care children require. This principle holds true regardless of how much any citizen, mother or wife, son or daughter, might need.

Parenting is a female task, and males have proved highly resistant to doing women's work anywhere on the globe. When food is in short supply, crops fail, or parents lose their jobs, children go hungry. But their mothers usually go hungry before that. Women and children may not get the right kinds of food to nourish their brain, their growth, or the sheer physical labor exerted to get that food.

Forever Working

Through the decades 1970 to 1990, women's opportunities in wage employment in agriculture, industry, and the service sectors did not increase. Occupational segregation, unemployment, and underemployment also failed to improve. So women have increasingly turned to work in the informal sector. In some countries, informal sector earnings showed dramatic increases. Self-employment may be considered the major form of work for women in the world. This kind of work is not secure and pays far less than the formal sector, generally less than the minimal wage. Although women bear the costs of setting up their informal activities, they often do not control the benefits; fathers, husbands, and sons may take the profits as their own.

The major occupations available for women in the world are street-selling, factory assembly lines, piecework, cash-cropping and commercial agriculture, prostitution or sex work, and service in domestic settings, like maids who change the sheets on hotel beds. Many jobs are physically demanding and the working conditions are dangerous. Women are predictably and consistently paid less than men for any job.

Women produce 75 percent or 85 percent or 90 percent of the food crops in the world; estimates vary but they are always high. Women usually have no title to the land they work and depend on. They cannot get credit, cash, or build equity by owning property. Women contribute most of the labor to raise cash crops that increasingly encroach on land needed for food. Cash crops such as cotton, tea, sugar, cocaine, jute, or rubber cannot be eaten. Husbands or male relatives often sell these crops, keep the money, or distribute it at will. In this way, women are treated as skilled and necessary workers, but still dependent and invisible.

The statistics-keepers at the United Nations say that work in the informal sector is extremely difficult to measure. This is another way in which women are invisible. When the second shift or the double days are calculated (and this is not consistent or easy), then women work harder and for more hours than men do.

The United Nations' statistics include a chart called "Value of Unpaid Housework to the Gross National Product." The statistics-keepers at the UN calculate the contribution of women's unpaid housework to the formal economic sector. To use the United States as an example, they estimate that if domestic labor and housework (including the most common kinds, child care, house care, husband care, and elder care) were acknowledged, the economic productivity of the United States would increase by about 25 percent. This is another view of invisible work (United Nations 1991:95).

According to the United Nations, not a single country in the world, no matter how the statistics are gathered or reported, contains men who come anywhere close to women in the amount of time spent in housework. Housework is cross-culturally and universally defined as food processing and meal preparation, child care, shopping, household cleaning, and management (1991:102).

Meanwhile, fewer women are getting married. Cohabitation is increasing. The average household size is decreasing in most regions. Women-headed households are a growing worldwide phenomenon. People living in female-headed households are poorer in general than people living in other kinds. Collectively, the birth rate seems to be falling, yet more single women are giving birth to children than ever before.

Men often migrate; they leave to find work elsewhere. This means a high divorce rate or informal divorces; some husbands do not return or send money back. A significant proportion of the world's households have no adult male worker; the estimates vary from 40 percent of households to 80 percent. Something has happened to men as husbands. These are major changes since 1970.

Poor women do not and probably never did live in the style middle-class people in the United States call "staying at home." Poor women's work is underreported and underestimated, especially when they do it to support their families.

These statistics and the quality of life they represent are often summed up in the phrase, the **feminization of poverty.** This is a term for the social and economic conditions characterized by women-headed households with few or no legal protections, double-day housework, and caring for children, combined with low wages in the formal or informal economic sectors. Such female-headed households are regarded as the largest definable group of poor people worldwide. This may also be called the pauperization of women.

Death and Poor Health

Women worldwide make the same observation about their health: "I feel very, very tired, most of the time." Women also get beaten and hurt a lot of the time. As the United Nations reports: "Many countries are now recognizing that there is significant violence against women both in and out of the family" (1991:19).

The most revealing statistic about women's health is probably **maternal mortality.** This is a figure calculated on the basis of how many women die during pregnancy and giving birth within a year; it is expressed as the number of female deaths per 100,000 births. All countries keep these records. Combined with figures on infant deaths, the deaths of women in pregnancy-related events are the single best indicators for a nation's health status and commitment to women and babies. Rates of maternal mortality show a greater disparity between the developed and developing regions than any other health indicator. Table 9.2 shows some of the death rates for women in a selection of countries.

Pregnant women in developing regions face a risk of death in pregnancy that is 80 to 600 times higher than women in developed regions. Why? Women die when they give birth without knowledgeable helpers or where there are few backup services for emergencies or difficult pregnancies. Pregnant women die from anemia and endemic malnutrition. Women who have already had many children die.

According to the World Health Organization, AIDS is now the leading cause of death for women twenty to forty years old in some major cities of Europe, South America, and the United States, as well as in significant areas of sub-Saharan Africa (United Nations 1991:62). **Sexually transmitted diseases** (STDs) like syphilis, gonorrhea, or HIV are the most contagious conditions on the planet. STDs affect women more harshly from men, but treatment programs are few and far between.

In the developmental literature, women are often put in an appendix as "special considerations." Or women qualify for assistance in economic development projects, "where applicable." In national and international programs, the term "family" is a euphemism for women. There are no programs anywhere in the

Table 9.2 *Death by motherhood.*

Maternal mortality in selected countries

These figures represent the number of women who died in some pregnancy-associated event per 100,000 live births through the decade 1980–1990.

Sweden	3	Zambia	151
Canada	4	Zimbabwe	480
Denmark	4	Bolivia	480
Romania	149	Costa Rica	24
United States	8	Cuba	47
Ghana	1,000	Haiti	230
Congo	1,000	Puerto Rico	13
Central African		Paraguay	365
Republic	600	Afghanistan	690
Egypt	319	Bhutan	1,710
Algeria	140	China	44
Kenya	170	North Korea	41
Nigeria	800	South Korea	14
Somalia	1,100	Nepal	830

Source: United Nations. *The World's Women: Trends and Statistics 1970–1990* (1991), 67–70.

world with the word family in the title that target men. Any situation that affects women negatively affects children even more so.

Depressing statistics like these are available from a number of sources besides the United Nations; I have not made them up. Figure 9.1 is entitled, "According to Statistics, She's Not Working." Pictures like this may be worth a thousand statistics.

International Strategies for Solving the Problem(s) of Women

Students offer various suggestions. Why not give poor women charity? Why not help their husbands get jobs? Why not send women to school for job training? Why not pass a law saying that banks have to give out loans to poor people? Why not encourage landowners to treat women better? Why not motivate poor women to work harder? Why not reason with the governments and tell them how much the work of women contributes to national economies? Why not provide birth control services? Why ask for a grant from a private international foundation? Why not elect better officials? Why not lobby governments to provide better services? Why not do a research study, conduct a national survey, or appoint a task force to study these serious problems? Here is a long answer.

Figure 9.1

According to statistics, she's not working

Carrying firewood for the daily cooking in Katmandu, Nepal. UN PHOTO/John Isaac.

Improving statistics and indicators on women
INSTRAW

INTERNATIONAL RESEARCH AND TRAINING INSTITUTE
FOR THE ADVANCEMENT OF WOMEN (INSTRAW)
César N. Penson 102-A, P.O. Box 21747, Santo Domingo, Dominican Republic
Tel. (809) 685-2111, Telex 326-4280 WRA SD.

In 1975 the United Nations declared an International Women's Year; the response was enthusiastic. But the problems were larger than the UN had imagined, so the year lengthened into a decade. Demands came from many sources for more integration of women into development projects. Many countries started women's bureaus, agencies, departments, commissions, and organizations.

The founders of this decade acknowledged that myths about women and work make the situation worse. The primary myth was: Men produce the world's food; women prepare it for the table; women work to supplement the family's income. Women contribute a minor share to the world's economic growth. In short, women don't work; they stay at home and take care of children. But myths are not facts. So the informal slogan of the Decade of Women became:

> *Women do two-thirds of the world's work, receive 10 percent of the world's income and own 1 percent of the means of production.*

High Fashions for Low Incomes

Here is a capsule appraisal of how officials in various development endeavors have constructed women's work. Caroline Moser, who devised this list, is an experienced planner. She understands agencies like the World Bank, the United States Agency for International Development, the World Health Organization, and the legion of nongovernmental agencies that establish projects in underdeveloped countries.

From about 1950 and into the 1970s, women in the Third World were treated as passive and needy; they were thought of as incompetent mothers. So most international development schemes attempted to change women's child-care and reproductive activities. This meant food handouts, nutritional counseling, and family planning. Moser calls this the **welfare approach.** It challenges no one and blames mothers, so it remains popular (1993:231).

Then the United Nations' Decade of Women, from 1976 to 1985, selected **equity for women** as its goal. Women were supposed to be active participants in development goals. The UN acknowledged the difficulties for women who lack the political and economic autonomy men have, so this viewpoint challenged women's subordinate positions. As a result, it is unpopular with national governments who think that Western feminists are behind the idea. The equity viewpoint is often known by its initials: WID or Women in Development.

The second wave of WID toned down the notion of equity in favor of **antipoverty.** The problem for women, developers said, is not inequality and oppression. Women are just poor. This approach appeals most to nongovernmental and private organizations who like to sponsor small-scale projects in which women earn some money.

The third wave of WID has been about **efficiency.** This centers on the belief that when women participate in economic systems in a more businesslike manner, their income will improve. Efficiency will automatically insure equity as well. This approach relies on an elastic concept of women's time and workloads. This competency model assumes that women will extend their workday to compensate for a decline in social services. Hence it is a very popular approach in development circles.

The latest fashion in development for women is called **empowerment.** The most articulate versions come from Third World women themselves. They state that male oppression is no different or no worse than colonial, postcolonial, or neocolonial oppression. They say that gender ideologies or sexism are not as dreadful as class prejudices and racism. This viewpoint seriously challenges Western feminism as well as national governments, international development agencies, and private organizations. Some watered-down versions of empowerment see power as something that can be handed to cooperative women as a gift rather than a quality of self-reliance, if not resistance.

In the box on page 226, two women from Africa comment on these high fashions for low incomes. The issues of development and modernization reminds me of a definition of marriage I once heard: "Marriage is having someone to help you with the problems being married to him has created for you." Could one say this about international development? The former colonial powers (read, the developed nations) try to clean up the problems the ideologies of capitalism, male domination, and racial superiority have created. As nations gained independence and autonomy, women did not. The analogy with marriage is not as far-fetched as it may sound.

Two African Women Speak Out

"The problems that beset Black women are manifold. Whether she is from the West Indies, America or Africa, the plight of the Black woman is very different from that of her White or Yellow sisters, although in the long run the problems faced by all women tend to overlap. Their common condition is one of exploitation and oppression by the same phallocratic system, whether it be Black, White or Yellow. . . . Where Black women have to combat colonialism and neo-colonialism, capitalism and the patriarchal system, European women only have to fight against capitalism and patriarchy."

Source: Awa Thiam, *Black Women Speak Out* (1986).

"For the majority of black women, liberation from sexual oppression has always been fused with liberation from other forms of oppression, namely slavery, colonialism, neocolonialism, racism, poverty, illiteracy, and disease. Consequently, her feminism has relevance in human terms rather than narrow sexist terms. The manifold nature of her oppression not only heightens her consciousness about the economic basis of oppression but also indicates its roots. For the black woman, the enemy is not black men but history . . . For the black woman, the issue is not increasing participation in the labor force, for she is already overburdened with participation. Unlike the typical white middle-class 'housewife', the black woman has had to work outside the home for the survival of herself and her family."

Source: Filomina Chioma Steady, *The Black Woman Cross-culturally* (1981).

Work and Housewifization

One of the toughest barriers to solving problems and improving the lives of women is what some scholars call **housewifization**. This awkward term comes from "the housewife," who is the primary model for female labor in the postcolonial and capitalist world. In fact, some feminists say that the relationship between capitalist systems in the First World and the Third World mirrors the relations between husband and wife in the West.

The operative principle is this: Women are defined primarily in terms of familial roles. Our work is only an extension of our domestic life. Hence we are invisible "outside the home." The idea of "the housewife" emerged in the First World during the nineteenth century in the same cultures that invented the family wage laws and colonialism. It was the reigning paradigm for women's lives in the United States during the 1950s when doctrines of "modernization" and international development were implemented.

What matters is not the actual work a woman does; it is the conditions, in particular, the relations of power, under which she does the work. In the international sexual division of labor, women are housewives and men do paid work.

> *To be defined as a housewife does not mean that women de facto work only in the home—in any case, what would "home" mean? A wind screen, a hut, a pavement? It means that they have to do any work at any time and at any place, not paid or poorly paid, and that this low pay is justified by the fact that they are considered to be materially dependent on a male "breadwinner", irrespective of whether or not there is such a man, or whether or not he is capable of providing "bread" for the family. (Mies 1988:9)*

Many programs for development, particularly those in agriculture, education, and occupational training, see women in nurturing and homemaking roles. So they emphasize "home economics" as a remedy to world poverty. The housewifization of international development projects reinforces the primary Western middle-class ideology that mothering is a full-time job and the only work women have. The worst part is that these ideologies ignore the resources mothers require for children as well as the competencies and skills they may have.

> *The care of children is of course a major concern of women everywhere; however, the need is not for lessons in "mothercraft" from self-appointed outside experts, but for the means of feeding and maintaining the children. This means generating food and income by their own work in agriculture or other activities. A major finding of a study of poor women in Tamil Nadu, India, was that most of them defined their role "as a woman" not in the expected Western terms of being a wife and mother, but "to earn and support the family." (Rogers 1986:91)*

Women may work harder and even make more money. But that matters little if they cannot control the products of their labor. Many male workers benefit from systems of low or unequal pay for women's work. For most women in the world, life as just a "housewife" is inconceivable. They have never had a choice to "stay at home." The men they know are poor too.

Global Perspectives on Women's Work

Women's status and freedom everywhere is linked to whatever local accommodations are made to the global economy. In this, the last decade of the twentieth century, women's jobs are factory work, housework, sex work, growing or serving food, child-care work, and jobs in the service sectors. Here are two examples of the most common jobs women are likely to have around the world.

Housework Revisited

A common and commonly invisible form of work for women around the world is working in other people's homes; the term for this is **household worker.** Household workers are people recruited from outside the employing household to perform some portion of its reproductive work. The tasks may be done indoors or outdoors; they involve equipment and machinery as well as emotional and psychological work. Such employees are also called servants, domestics, nannies, maids, housekeepers, menials, or retainers. As my dictionary reports, the opposite is master.

In a world of refugees, migrants, emigrants, landless, dispossessed, and outright poor people of so many kinds, recruiting household labor is easy. Housework includes home care of frail elders, children, or sick people, as well as cooking, cleaning, yardwork, shopping, driving, and the myriad tasks of running a household. It bears an uncanny resemblance to work many of us do as mothers, wives, or daughters. The difference is the economic relationship.

> *At root in all cases is an employer-worker relationship. Household worker labor is put to the tasks of reproduction rather than production. While housework does not produce capital directly, workers perform socially necessary household maintenance, food preparation, child care and socialization, and other reproductive tasks for a wage. The value of household workers' labor is transferred to members of the employing household, permitting them to allocate their time and energies in other ways—to more remunerative or prestigious productive work, leisure, or investment in social relations. The essential point is that the workers' labor is utilized to maintain and advance the position of members of the employer household. The labor for which employers pay frees them for other, generally preferred, activities. (Sanjek and Cohen 1990:3)*

Somebody must do this work. If we don't do it ourselves out of duty, love, habit, or similar motivations, then we must compel or hire others to do the work. Household work is not only largely invisible to men; it is also invisible to the women who use it.

The relationship of household worker to employer is characterized by its solid inequality. Household workers can lose their jobs at any moment; they must follow orders. There is always a power differential between employer and employee; it may be gender, age, class, ethnicity, race, or citizenship and migration status. So the customs of hiring household workers also ratify power relations and reinforce inequality in each local society where it is found. In societies with social ranks and classes, household work carries a stigma. Somehow, it is associated with dirt, with uncleanliness. Like other women's work, it is necessary but devalued.

Caring for, cleaning up after, or feeding others, especially infants and children, is also emotional work. That is why employers often pretend to have fictive kin relationships with employees. Despite all rhetoric to the contrary, such workers are not kinfolk. They are not "one of the family," "a daughter," or most telling of all, a maid. Calling a household worker by her first name, the way Americans address children, only hides the employee-employer relationship. We might call this maternalism or patronizing.

Housework is status enhancement for someone else, women's work we discussed in chapter 1. People who can afford to transfer jobs in their households to someone else have more resources to invest in other activities like play or social relationships. They may do volunteer work, give elaborate parties, or take up exotic hobbies. The household worker does not enhance her own status; her work enhances someone else's status. A household worker still has to do her own household work after her paid household workday.

Working Daughters: The Feminization of Factories

A large portion of what we call modernization and economic development in international settings depends on women's work in factories. In contemporary jargon, the factories are called "export processing zones," "Free Trade Zones," "flexible labor systems," or "offshore manufacturing." The early women's movement called such worksites "sweat shops." By whatever name, the factories of transnational companies depend entirely on sources of cheap labor. Workers make computer parts, electronic equipment, textiles, apparel, footwear, toys, and other consumer goods sold all over the world. Anthropologist Aihwa Ong did ethnographic research in some of these factories in Malaysia. Here she comments on the labor practices of the multinational corporations that own the factories.

> To achieve global dominance, Japanese and Western companies
> bypassed high production costs, labor militancy, and environmental
> concerns at home by moving to Southeast Asia or Mexico. Such rapid
> shifts with respect to labor markets and their attendant maneuvers in
> new financial markets enhance the flexibility and mobility that allows
> corporations to exert greater labor control worldwide. . . . The most
> important recent experiment in corporate production is its flexible
> combination of mass assembly and subcontracting systems, of mod-
> ern firms and home work as linked units dominated by transnational
> capital. (Ong 1991:282)

How does this translate into the lives of women? Eighty percent of the workers on the floor are young Malaysian women from rural villages. They assemble computer parts. All the managers and executives are male, usually from Japan, India, or other "developed" countries. Female workers in relative isolation from each other work under male eyes, pressured to produce in work speedups and penalized for trips to the locker rooms. Dress codes, moral instructions, and policies about menstruation, pregnancy, and privacy are based on management's ideologies about "women's nature." The managers of the transnational companies say that their female workers "naturally" have nimble fingers and docile personalities.

Women who work in the factory zones are generally between sixteen and twenty-four years old. If they have a child, they will be dismissed. The jobs are full-time, the shifts are long. The work is so stressful that few expect to survive, physically and psychologically, beyond a few years. Managers assume, correctly, that young women have to accept these conditions and that factory work is only an interlude until they can do better.

These young women are called **factory daughters;** they constitute the lowest-paid and the lower half of the total industrial work force in developing countries. Policy makers and businessmen consider them a secondary labor force; they say women only work until they can get married. So young women are daughters at home and "daughters" at work. Ong concluded: Yes, women are free to work, but subject to male authority. Yes, women's work is necessary, but civil treatment is not.

Many countries look like Malaysia. Families in China, Taiwan, and other areas of Asia still regard daughters as poor long-term investments who should pay back their natal families for the gift of life and childhood care. Proper, respectful daughters go to work in factories and give the money to their parents. A daughter's income may help her brother through his education. The families claim their daughters' labor; the daughter receives some affection and security.

In the Special Economic Zones of China, women and children return from job or school to work on electronic parts, toys, clothes, or artificial flowers. In Hong Kong, extended families contract with large transnational companies for piece-work. Businessmen say that "family production units" ensure a disciplined and docile workforce and "peaceful industrial relations." The building blocks of this entire economic system are daughters. In the Philippines, where wages are among the lowest in Asia, the garment industry is built largely on the base of women who sew at home in their villages. Corporate executives speak in glowing terms about "the Asian family" in which children (factory workers) obey their parents (managers).

Along the United States–Mexican border, housewives do their "homework" for international corporations that pay them little or only by the piece. When there are not enough young women, their biggest labor pool, companies hire children.

Factory workplaces are typically sexualized. Managers promote Western images of sex appeal and sexual availability. Women can get jobs and keep or lose them on the basis of using sex as a strategy. Simultaneously, sexual harassment, rape, and other forms of control over women make factories look much like harems.

On the other hand, industrial employment for some young girls may be a glimpse of freedom. They can live away from home, have boyfriends, save for marriage, help out parents, escape a poor village, and have some discretionary income. In a few cases, they can get some education. Women in these situations rarely think of themselves in terms of global sisterhood or even a collective force. Their work is like marriage and family; factory daughters may be aware of their condition but unable to negotiate or escape.

Contrary to Western feminist expectations, most working daughters did not seek more equal relations at home and would gladly trade

> *their "bitter" independence for the security of a college student who*
> *has a family to look after her needs. (Ong 1991:298)*

Factory daughters do not challenge the industrial system; factories are only a stepping-stone. These young working women hope to graduate from the assembly line altogether; many consider prostitution as a step up and marriage as a wonderful dream.

The new international division of labor and the feminization of industrial work looks like older-style patriarchal families. Women in factories speak about their immense tiredness, injuries, dangers, poor sleep, and missed periods. Factory daughters say that they don't mind hard work. "But we would like to have justice, recognition, and respect from our bosses."

A Marxist–Feminist Thinks About Women and Work

Since the landmark research of the 1970s, anthropologists and scholars in other disciplines have discussed, debated, and argued at length about women's status. Many assumed that male dominance was simply a fact of life, the painful part of "it's only natural." Some anthropologists pointed to cultures that seemed reasonably good compared to the United States; other scholars offered studies of groups in which women's position was worse.

Sometimes anthropologists picked one dimension as the comparative key to women's lives. We analyzed rituals, symbols, availability of birth control or health care, matrilocal households, and how much husbands helped. Sometimes we defined the key to women's status as elections, promotions, equal opportunity, equal employment, or other state-controlled arenas of our lives. We argued whether women had ever been equal to or superior to men; this is the substance of the debates about matriarchy, for example. Then we argued about equality in our own countries, within our own homes, with fathers, husbands, or bosses.

To answer these personal and professional questions, many anthropologists, sociologists, historians, and other social scientists (many of them feminists) have followed a path that leads from the Iroquois women in Native North America to the factories of the industrial and postindustrial revolutions.

Let's turn once again to Lewis Henry Morgan, who wrote about the Iroquois, men and women who lived in matrilineal groups and matrilocal longhouses. His book, *League of the Iroquois,* published in 1851, is thought to be the first complete ethnography ever written. As he described the Iroquois, women owned the fields not as private property, but as the necessary means to produce food for their matrilines and villages. Whatever land women needed and could effectively put under cultivation they "owned." They didn't "own" the land in the sense of buying and selling or in the sense of alienating the land from its productive, food-growing purposes. Nor did any one woman "own" land as an individual. If a person or a group did not use the land for food production, then someone else could use the land. In other words, no one could "buy" or "sell" land and build a shopping mall on it. No one can miss the comparison to capitalism here.

Meanwhile, in Europe, groups of men were making revolutions; these began with the French Revolution in the 1790s and continued throughout the nineteenth century. These groups of men protested the class and economic structures of their time. They asked: Why did a few men have most of the money while the majority of other men literally starved on the streets or worked for wages that did not begin to feed their families? The two most powerful theorists to come out of that period are Frederick Engels and Karl Marx, from whose name are derived the theories called Marxism.

To Marx and Engels, the best examples of how humans should relate to each other came from the women of the Iroquois Confederacy. Their worst examples came from English factories, their exploited workers and capitalist owners. When Engels read Morgan's book, he realized that Iroquois women were not the property of their husbands. He saw the institution of monogamous marriage as the basis for treating women as private property. For him, this was the beginning of the patriarchy and repression of women. Engels proposed a more elegant version of housewifization.

> *With the patriarchal family and still more with the single monogamous family, a change came. Household management lost its public character. It no longer concerned society. It became a* private service; *the wife became the head servant, excluded from all participation in social production. . . .*
>
> *The modern individual family is founded on the open or concealed domestic slavery of the wife, and modern society is a mass composed of these individual families as its molecules. . . .*
>
> *In the great majority of cases today, at least in the possessing classes, the husband is obliged to earn a living and support his family, and that in itself gives him a position of supremacy without any need for special legal titles or privileges. Within the family he is the bourgeois, and the wife represents the proletariat. (Engels 1972:137)*

Both Marx and Engels believed that the transformation of matrilineal and matrilocal cultures such as the Iroquois into patriarchal and capitalist societies was a great tragedy. Here is Frederick Engels's most famous declaration of his position.

> *The overthrow of mother right was the **world historical defeat of the female sex**. The man took command in the home also; the woman was degraded and reduced to servitude; she became the slave of his lust and a mere instrument for the production of children. (Engels 1972:120)*

Engels believed that the custom of monogamous marriages put control of sex in the hands of men as husbands so they could be assured of their own paternity. In the past, during the stages of history Engels characterized as mother-right, women controlled their own sexuality, including the right to sell it or give it away as they chose. But monogamy made women property and their work invisible and unpaid.

Eleanor Leacock

The theories of Karl Marx and Frederick Engels have had an enormous impact on the development of feminist thinking about women's work in all the social sciences during the last quarter-century. Their theories, however, would have made much less sense were it not for anthropologist Eleanor Leacock, who retold these grand narratives and put women into the foreground.

Eleanor "Happy" Leacock was attending Columbia University when World War II ended. She audited Ruth Benedict's course on personality and culture.

> *I still quote her phrase, "You can't beat your culture." Cross-cultural knowledge certainly enables one to gain a useful perspective on one's culture, but it is folly to think one can transcend it. I tied Benedict's point in with a dictum of Engels that was oft-quoted in my undergraduate days: freedom lies in the understanding of necessity. As I saw it (and see it), one aims as best one can to understand the constraints within which one lives, and to define realistically the actual alternatives one has to choose among. I was pregnant when taking Benedict's class, and soon to be plunged into the agonizing dilemma faced by young couples who challenge the structure of gender but are trapped in the structures of child rearing: Which of the attendant problems are caused by the structure itself and which by personal limitations in commitment and understanding? (Leacock 1993:14)*

Leacock had married while still in college, and had two children by the time she went to Labrador for fieldwork with the Montagnais–Naskapi. This group is sometimes called Algonkins or Algonquins after the language they speak. Earlier ethnographers believed that the group owned private or family hunting territories and generally practiced patrilineal ownership and kinship.

But Leacock reconstructed the movements and relationships among bands for the two generations back in time. Instead of hunting territories, she found equalitarian communities where individuals and groups of cooperative relatives used trap lines. She showed that the male-centered hunting territories and patrilocal living patterns came into being after European colonies, laws, and customs came to Canada. In earlier, precolonial, times women lived in matrilocal households. They also held considerable power and autonomy. The situation she described mirrored the neighboring Iroquois. For Leacock, this meant that Engels and Marx had read Morgan and the Iroquois wives correctly. There was no prehistoric, universal or essential pattern of male dominance.

Women's Autonomy Through Time

In 1972 Leacock wrote an introduction to a new edition of Engels's classic work, *The Origin of the Family, Private Property and the State.* In this highly influential piece and research that followed, she made three points that bear directly on this chapter.

First, she used her own fieldwork to show that in hunting–gathering and horticultural societies women and men, husbands and wives, were **relatively equal.** Such groups had diffused or consensual decision making, and both women and men did work of comparable worth. In what Marx called "primitive communism," people had **relatively equalitarian** social lives compared to societies formed irrevocably on class differences. Leacock noted that cultures who trace descent through the female line or have matrilocal residence tend to give women more status.

> *The significant point for women's status is that the household was communal, and the division of labor between the sexes reciprocal; the economy did not involve the dependence of the wife and children on the husband. (1972:33)*

Leacock's second point was that oppression is not somehow "natural," nor is it just in our heads. The origins of oppression for women in contemporary life are not in "nature" or biology, sex or gender differences, nor the results of symbolic and cognitive processes. Anthropologist Christine Gailey comments.

> *In all of her work, the underlying theme is clear, and clearly supported: human nature, flexible to a fault, is not inherently hierarchical. Women's oppression, thus, is not due to some universal will to power or innate quality of maleness, but due to concrete trajectories—locally variable, always reversible or open to transformation—of political, social, and economic change. (Gailey 1993:74)*

So Leacock argued against any theory of universal female subordination. Capitalism, market conditions, missionaries, colonial governors, development agencies, and national or state governments determine gender relations, she said; they are not the solution to the problems they have created. Monogamy, private property, and social classes are all part of capitalism and the patriarchy, she insisted; they are all political. The objections of Leacock, Marx, or Engels to monogamous marriages are not criticisms of men or husbands, individually or in groups, but in the powers assigned to them in such customs as the family wage laws.

In other words, the statistics cited at the beginning of this chapter have not always been true. Most pointedly, Leacock said, women are not automatically relegated to second-class status because of childbearing and childrearing.

The third major point Leacock made is this: At key moments in human history, women lost autonomy and equalitarian status as economic systems changed. This occurred when the concept of private property, monogamous marriage, and class or ranked societies come together. For Leacock, the oppression of women comes with the "transformation of their socially necessary labor into private ser-vice through the separation of the family from the clan" (Leacock 1972:41). So here is a summary of her major points:

> *Whatever the status of women in any given society at any given time,*
> *it just got worse with the introduction of colonialism, capitalism,*
> *and Christianity or other patriarchal institutions.*

Eleanor Leacock ended her career with a research field trip to Samoa. She wanted to understand the problems of adolescents and young people, indeed, to revisit Margaret Mead's original questions. Some people said that Mead had it wrong: that delinquency, suicide, depression, school failure, unemployment, and other traumas of the teenage years were only signs of problems within Samoan culture itself, problems that had always been there. But Leacock agreed with Mead and other ethnographers in the Pacific that being a teenager in Samoa had indeed changed dramatically. From relatively little stress, Samoan adolescent life had changed to one marked by suicide, acting out, and severe dislocations between the lives their parents led and the limited opportunities open to them under colonialism. In 1987, on her way home from the second field trip to Samoa, Eleanor Leacock died suddenly.

Leacock threw light and energy on key words: female autonomy, authority, and decision making. She used the concepts of production and reproduction in pow-erful new ways. She is widely credited as the first anthropologist to put women's loss of control and autonomy into historical terms. As anthropologist Rayna Rapp explains:

> *Leacock urged feminist anthropologists to write for three concrete*
> *reasons: (1) to provide "material to counter widely held assumptions*
> *that male dominance and female subservience are inevitable as out-*
> *comes of a natural division of labor by gender . . . to effectively chal-*
> *lenge ideologies of nature"; (2) to further the analysis of women's*
> *work and family life during the period of modernization and indus-*
> *trialization of Europe; (3) to analyze the sexual division of labor and*
> *the effects of that division on women's position in Third World*
> *nations. That list represents her gift from anthropology to the field*
> *of women's studies. (Rapp 1993:91)*

Women's Powers As the Roots of Grass

Faced with the awesome difficulties outlined above, what do women do? Women resist, organize, and invent new forms of social cooperation. **Grassroots movements** are a prime example. The name poignantly suggests their origin. Grassroots organizations spring up where national governments have been unwill-ing or unable to provide basic services like accessible water, electricity, schools, health clinics, transportation services, or access to banks or land ownership. These communal or cooperative women's movements are often concerned with immediate survival issues like food, fuel, credit, physical safety, child care, and health. Ordinary people, mostly women, and always distinct from the elites who hold power, have formed literally thousands of these small-scale organizations around the world. Many are spontaneous, addressing an immediate problem. Others become significant bureaucracies and agencies. All provide apprenticeships and allow women to assert personal power.

Considerations of space allow us only two examples of the thousands of women's grassroots movements and collective actions. We will begin with an example about the meanings of motherhood and military dictatorship, and finish with Ela Bhatt and the Self-Employed Workers Association.

Mothers, Family Values, and the Military

In Argentina in 1976, a military coup brought a change of leadership. Young people who objected to the new military regime started to disappear. A young man was seized from the doorstep of his mother's house. A couple was kidnapped from their car. A young teacher never returned from her school. Several medical students were taken from hospitals late at night. One woman lost four daughters, two of them pregnant, and two sons-in-law. Their relatives could not locate them or find any word of their safety.

Maimed bodies turned up. Tales of torture in military prisons began to circulate. Gradually, Argentine citizens began to realize that the kidnappings took place with the knowledge and cooperation of other countries, businessmen, those in the legal system, and indeed, virtually with the blessings of the Catholic Church. In futile rounds, families went to the military headquarters, to courts, and to prisons. But government officials lied or refused to respond. Slowly, the despairing families began to see a pattern of kidnapping by military authorities, of a state-organized system of oppression and terrorism. Finally, women turned to each other.

But what kind of power do women have against the entire establishment of a country, against a military dictatorship? As Maria del Rosario remembers:

> In April 1977, after a year of going in groups from one place to another, one of the mothers, Azucena Villaflor de Vicenti, said, "Let's go to Plaza de Mayo and when there's enough of us"—a thousand she said—"we'll go together to Government House and demand an answer." (Quoted in Fisher 1989:28)

But how could they recognize each other in the large crowds? Again Azucena had an idea. She asked the women to wear one of their children's old diapers as a head scarf. She said mothers always keep little things their babies wore. So women wore baby diapers or other white head scarfs to identify themselves.

The mothers began to walk together in the Plaza de Mayo. The military responded swiftly. As another mother, Aida de Suárez, remembers:

They started to call us las locas *[the madwomen]. . . Of course they called us mad. How could the armed forces admit they were worried by a group of middle-aged women? And anyway we were mad. When everyone was terrorized we didn't stay at home crying—we went to the streets to confront them directly. We were mad but it was the only way to stay sane. (Quoted in Fisher 1989:60)*

In December of 1977, the military kidnapped fourteen of the mothers, including Azucena and two nuns. The women never saw them again.

The mothers appealed to every international forum. The pope granted an audience but never replied to their questions. The bishops and many of the priests in the Argentine church hierarchies preached resignation and passivity. Most refused to say masses for the disappeared children. Only foreign journalists seemed to understand the meaning of a mothers' march every Thursday afternoon. Women in white head scarves became the only visible evidence to the world that the government of Argentina was lying.

In 1978 the military government stepped up harassment, arrests, and threats. Unable to attack the mothers in the face of the world press, the junta closed off the Plaza de Mayo at the end of 1978. Through 1979 the women made lightning strikes on the plaza; they hurried in and made their statement as best they could. Sometimes they sang the national anthem because soldiers had to lower their weapons.

On the first Thursday of the New Year of 1980, the mothers returned to the Plaza de Mayo to stay. If they were taken prisoner or killed, they decided, nothing mattered but to march for their children. As Maria del Rosario said,

The beatings and threats continued, but that year we returned to the square and they were never able to stop us again. (Quoted in Fisher 1989:108)

As Aida de Suárez said,

In some ways we were always there. If there were twenty of us, there were twenty. If there were fifty, there were fifty. From 30 April 1977 we've always been there because this square is ours. On Thursdays at half past three this square belongs to us. (Quoted in Fisher 1989:108)

Among the Thursday marchers were grandmothers searching for grandchildren, the babies of their disappeared ones. A number of young women had been kidnapped while pregnant. Their captors waited to torture and kill them until after they gave birth. Stories began to circulate of babies sold or adopted into the families of the military. Many women had grandchildren they had never known. So the grandmothers of the Plaza de Mayo came into being.

Without intending to, these women had also developed an organization, a grassroots collective. The Mothers might accept that their children were dead, even that their bodies might never be returned or identified. But they would never accept official denials of their very existence and the meaning of their deaths. In August of 1979, the women registered themselves as the Mothers of Plaza de Mayo. Soon the organization acquired a meeting house. Forensic archaeologists and geneticists helped them establish formal programs to locate missing relatives through gene tracing, and to identify bodies, the causes of death, and the guilty parties, where possible. Today the Mother's organization provides counseling, financial assistance, and programs to work for the quality of social justice they feel their children died for.

These women challenged a regime who talked about family values and the duties of motherhood. The Mothers wanted the murderers named, acknowledged, and brought to justice. They wanted men held accountable for their actions. They wanted justice and mercy from the Catholic Church, which they believe acted as an accomplice. They wanted the unions to speak out. By 1982 thousands of people had joined the Mothers at the Thursday marches. In 1983, the military rule fell. By that time, 30,000 people, all of them someone's children, had disappeared.

The women say, we're only mothers; all the disappeared are our children. As a result of the Mothers of the Plaza de Mayo, women in white scarves are marching in other Latin American countries. Argentina is not the only place with dictators and disappeared children. Writer Jo Fisher asked the Mothers how their lives had changed. The box, "Two Mothers Speak Out," contains their answers.

Self-Employed, Organized, and Cooperative

In Ahmedabad, the state of Gujarat, western India, in the early 1970s, some women carrying freight on their heads noticed that men who were members of textile unions had advantages they did not have. So they approached the Textile Labour Association, India's largest union of textile workers, and there found Ela Bhatt, heading the women's wing of the union. She had an answer for their questions: "You need to organize."

Fully half of the workforce of India's cities are what international development reports call informal, marginal, unorganized, or peripheral workers. Ela Bhatt calls them **self-employed workers.**

> *Self-employed is a broad term covering all the workers who are not in a formal employer-employee relationship. It means women who work at home—weavers, potters, garment and quilt stitchers, patchworkers, embroiderers, bidi [cigarette] rollers, incense stick makers, milk producers, spinners, basket and broom weavers, metalworkers, carpenters, shoemakers, painters, sculptors, and toymakers. It includes women who sell or trade their services or labor—agricultural workers, headloaders, hand-cart pullers, waste paper collectors, acrobats, cleaners, and construction workers. And it includes the multitude of hawkers and vendors who carry out trade in the streets and markets from their baskets or cartloads of wares. Both traditional and modern occupations come under SEWA's definition*

Two Mothers Speak Out

Maria del Rosario

It only now that I think—I used to be different. I used to be able to spend the whole afternoon shopping for a pair of shoes. . . . For us there is only one future, to continue the struggle until the day we die, so that justice will be the guarantee of life in the Republic of Argentina. . . . I always say that our struggle is like a branch that always has new leaves because after we're gone the young people who work with us will continue the battle.

Beatriz de Rubenstein

In the beginning we were just like everyone else. Maybe we could see what was happening was wrong, but we still believed in Argentine justice, in the church, in the institutions. We weren't conscious. It was our children who fought injustice then. We didn't become conscious until it affected our own families. . . . I don't believe we're feminists. I believe that women in Argentina are oppressed, by the church and by our laws, and I consider that women are equal to men but I believe that this country has a lot of problems that affect men and women. You have to learn a lot of things before you can understand feminism. Many of us have had problems with our husbands. The men have given up. They've resigned themselves to the fact that the children aren't going to come back. There are many women who have been left widows. Many husbands died of grief. It seems that men have less capacity to deal with something like this. Many believe it's all finished and some of them don't want us to go to the square anymore. We go anyway. In that sense we're feminists.

Source: Jo Fisher, *Mothers of the Disappeared* (1989), 149,150.

of self-employed, from the bartering of goods to capitalistic piece-rate work. (Rose 1992:17)

Why are these women self-employed? Because they have no education, skills, jobs, or access to resources such as a bank account or because they had migrated into cities from the even more desperate countryside. Under these circumstances, women exercise extraordinary ingenuity. They do not remain "unemployed" when no appropriate "job" can be found. Women combine many kinds of work to bring in small amounts of cash. They trade and barter for food or clothing. They exchange services, sell consumer goods, collect wood or produce, and recycle materials for money.

Besides piecing together family income from hard work and cleverness, they spend most of their earnings on their family, on food, clothing, and meager shelter. The women of SEWA say that about one-third of poor families are supported solely by self-employed females. If a woman has a husband and if he has a job (big ifs), he typically contributes only a portion to household expenses.

The first problem the women attacked in their organizing drive was fair credit. Understand that self-employed women typically earn only enough money for day-to-day maintenance. They must spend part of that as working capital, for example, to buy raw materials, rent stalls or pay bribes, fines, or fees. When they borrow money on a daily basis, they must pay exorbitant interest rates; as much as 10 percent per day is not unusual. Beyond the expenses of daily business, families have emergencies and social obligations. A baby needs medical treatment or a family member dies and must be buried. The national banks of India wanted nothing to do with female customers who could not sign their names, wanted only small loans or practiced a different set of manners. Borrowing money from landowners, traders or businessmen only left a self-employed person deeper in debt. Wages dropped even as women added hours of work.

The solution was obvious: women needed their own bank. So they formed one, ignoring all the professionals who said it could not be done. As women carried heavy loads on their heads through the city, they talked to other women. They pooled small amounts of cash from many women. They put their pictures on their bank books and left them at the bank rather than risk taking them home. From the earliest days the atmosphere in the lobby of the bank was informal. Women laughed, cried, smoked, and talked with their banking sisters. One woman gave birth at the bank. Ela Bhatt tells these stories about the woman-centered services:

> *One of our members was married to a policeman. They had not been speaking to each other several years, but lived together in a sort of quiet hostility. She cooked for him, and he gave her money to run the family. She wanted to buy a used sewing machine, and earn her own money. Her husband used to be a tailor and had a machine in the house, but how could she negotiate with him? So the bank went to his office and negotiated the price for him to sell it to her. What other bank would do this? (Rose 1992:173)*

> *In 1975 when the bank was not taking many risks, a vegetable vendor came who was under such economic pressure that she was absolutely desperate. Her husband was an unemployed textile worker, and he would somehow roam about and fill his belly each day, but it was a very difficult situation for her and her children. The bank decided to extend her a loan of 50 Rupees, and someone went with her to buy green masalas like coriander, mint, ginger, garlic, and chillies. That day SEWA cared for her children, who were sick and hungry. The woman earned 6 Rupees profit that day and her children had dinner. Each day she parlayed the loan into more profits and within a week returned 51 Rupees to the bank. It was hardly*

> *any risk for the bank, and it literally meant life or death for that*
> *woman. After that we started extending those 50 Rupee loans to*
> *many women. (Rose 1992:173)*

Now women say, "SEWA is our mother and the bank is like our mother's place." The doors are always open for her daughters. Women can tell secrets, find help, learn new skills, or borrow some money. The bank is their only door to the formal, bureaucratized, and institutionalized world of money. A poor woman can borrow working capital at low interest rates and make loans to buy tools and raw materials she needs. Since most of their depositors could not travel long distances to make regular deposits, the bank went to them. When women escaped the high-interest debts that were never paid off, they began to save and invest their money. The SEWA bank is the best model for women worldwide.

Ask Ela Bhatt why women should have assets in their own names, why every district should have a woman's bank, or why loans to women nurture life and leadership. She will reply:

> *Because women's income is used mostly for "bread, clothes, and*
> *house," the more cash income which goes into her hands, the faster*
> *the family's quality of life goes up. And secondly there is an increasing*
> *number of women headed households, and in times of crises, assets are*
> *the only things which help them. (Quoted in Rose 1992:198)*

> *Women are poorer than men amongst the poor. They are the worst*
> *victims of all socio-economic decay, degradation, and distortions. Yet*
> *I envisage poor women as being in the vanguard of development*
> *processes and movements. (Quoted in Rose 1992:263)*

Building SEWA has not been easy. It has grown from a loan network and trade union to a women's movement. SEWA operates as a shadow government for women, providing services which the formal sector and the developmental agencies cannot or will not. It is the international model for women's banking and self-help financial services. Figure 9.2 shows all of the helping hands of SEWA.

As you can see from the diagram, SEWA has grown from banking to many other arenas. It includes cooperatives for vendors, artisans, and service workers. SEWA remains for women only; they say that men do not share or understand women's problems. The primary values of SEWA are nonviolence, arbitration, reconciliation, and a quiet, fiercely determined resistance to exploitation, whether from husbands, colonial powers, or the government of India. The women of SEWA say: "We not only want a piece of the pie, but we also want to choose the flavour and to know how to make it ourselves."

Conclusions in the Postmodern Manner

Sometimes, sitting at my computer in blue jeans and T-shirt, I am uncomfortably aware of the little tags in so many things I buy. They say: Made in China,

Figure 9.2

The SEWA tree: A women's support network

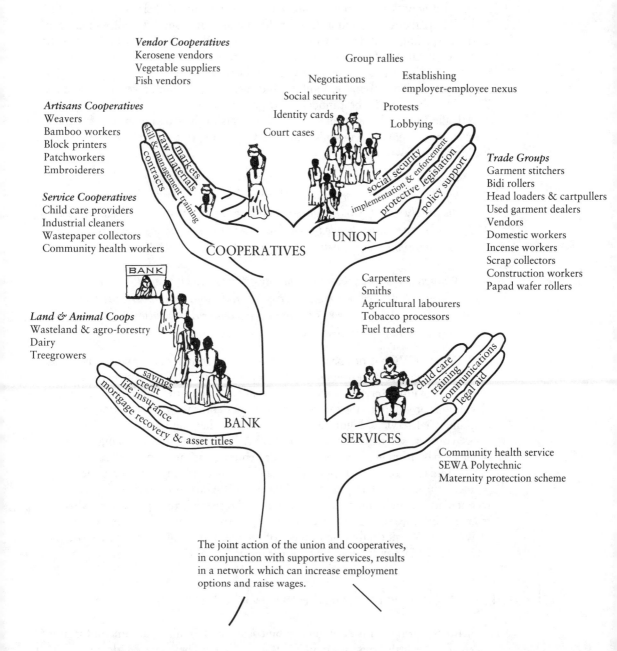

Vendor Cooperatives
Kerosene vendors
Vegetable suppliers
Fish vendors

Group rallies

Negotiations

Establishing
employer-employee nexus

Social security

Artisans Cooperatives
Weavers
Bamboo workers
Block printers
Patchworkers
Embroiderers

Identity cards

Court cases

Protests

Lobbying

Trade Groups
Garment stitchers
Bidi rollers
Head loaders & cartpullers
Used garment dealers
Vendors
Domestic workers
Incense workers
Scrap collectors
Construction workers
Papad wafer rollers

Service Cooperatives
Child care providers
Industrial cleaners
Wastepaper collectors
Community health workers

skill & management training
raw materials
markets
contracts

social security
implementation & enforcement
protective legislation
policy support

COOPERATIVES

UNION

Land & Animal Coops
Wasteland & agro-forestry
Dairy
Treegrowers

BANK

Carpenters
Smiths
Agricultural labourers
Tobacco processors
Fuel traders

savings
credit
life insurance
mortgage recovery & asset titles

child care
training
communications
legal aid

BANK

SERVICES

Community health service
SEWA Polytechnic
Maternity protection scheme

The joint action of the union and cooperatives,
in conjunction with supportive services, results
in a network which can increase employment
options and raise wages.

Malaysia, Philippines, Korea, or India. Then I read some of articles and books listed in the bibliography. My colleagues talk about capital accumulation, the politics of postmodernity, the ethnography of work and cultural struggles. I sit awed by the work of invisible women. As Eleanor Leacock said:

> *Third World women suffer manifold forms of oppression: as virtual slave labor in households, unpaid for their work as mothers who create new generations of workers, and as wives or sisters who succor the present ones; as workers, often in marginal jobs and more underpaid than men; and as members of racial minorities, or of semicolonial nations, subject to various economic, legal, and social disabilities. All the while, women bear the brunt, psychologically and sometimes physically, of the frustration and anger of their menfolk, who, in miserable complicity with an exploitative system, take advantage of the petty power they have been given over the women close to them. Perhaps the most bitter reality lies with the family, which is idealized as a retreat and sanctuary in a difficult world. Women fight hard to make it this, yet what could be a center of preparation for resistance by both sexes is so often instead a confused personal battleground, in which women have little recourse but to help recreate the conditions of their own oppression. (Leacock 1981:311)*

Marx, Engels, some feminists and many others believed that socialist societies would free women from private service to husbands and the unpaid drudgery of domestic labor. Like Lenin at the beginning of the Russian Revolution, they paid lip service to liberating women from household oppression. But socialist dogmas and communist rules have not achieved the reformation in women's lives they once proclaimed. The box on page 244, "The Personal Matters," is the best analysis of their failures in this respect I have ever read.

Now the scholars and theoreticians say the "modern" period is over and we live in a state called **postmodern** and in a condition of **postmodernism.** These are difficult concepts to define. Postmodern has come to mean the emotional, social, and intellectual currents that began in the 1950s and 1960s in capitalist Western countries and are characterized by such concepts as pluralism, multiplicity, differences, ambiguity, fragmentation, and discontinuity. These stand in sharp contrast to the simple constructs about culture Margaret Mead and other anthropologists proposed.

The ideologies that sustained colonialism and capitalism are unstable, dead or dying, the postmodernists say. From the idea of modernization as a straight line of progress from backward to progressive, the Enlightenment notions of reason and freedom, the Marxist stories of class conflict and the state in service of the people, to Freud's theories about drives and repression, the old narratives fail to explain the qualities of contemporary human existence. Postmodernist critiques of contemporary life highlight issues of power, desire, ethnicity, gender, sex, and race. The motto of postmodernism may well be, Everything is political. All theories about the

The Personal Matters

Writer and journalist Slavenka Drakulić grew up in the former Yugoslavia. She worked and traveled widely in the countries behind what we used to call the "Iron Curtain." On one occasion, Slavenka's mother returned from a journey and brought her something special:

> three dozen sanitary napkins made of terrycloth and a belt. The napkins had buttonholes at each end to fasten them to the belt, so they wouldn't slip. She would hand-wash them, then hang them on a clothesline in the bathroom to dry overnight. More than thirty years later, in Sofia, my friend Katarina saw my package of tampons in her bathroom and asked if I could leave it for her. I am going to Zagreb and she needs them when she has a performance in the theater. 'We don't have sanitary napkins and sometimes even cotton batting. I have to hoard it when I find it, or borrow it,' she said. For a moment, I didn't know whether I should laugh or cry. I sprinkled Eastern Europe with tampons on my travels: I had already left one package of tampons and some napkins, ironically called 'New Freedom', in Warsaw (plus Bayer aspirin and antibiotics), another package in Prague (plus Anaïs perfume), and now here in Sofia. . .
>
> After all these years, communism has not been able to produce a simple sanitary napkin, a bare necessity for women. So much for its economy and its so-called emancipation, too.

Source: Slavenka Drakulić, *How We Survived Communism and Even Laughed* (1933), 30.

world must account for systems of power, particularly those that fall so heavily on our physical bodies, sexuality, and unconscious minds.

Leaving the capitalist masters of the First World, the collapse of the communist Second World, the deprivations of the Third World, postmodernism and the invisible work of women in the world's last colony, we turn to the last chapter.

Reading, Writing, and Resistance

Autobiographies, biographies, oral histories, poetry, and other ways of telling our stories are important to women. Today women emerging from colonial empires are speaking out. Here are only a few of the many extraordinary tales that are told.

Rigoberta Menchú won a Nobel Peace Prize for her organizing work against dictatorships and domination. Her life story is told in *I, Rigoberta Menchú: An Indian Woman in Guatemala* (1984). Elizabeth Burgos-Debray edited the book and Ann Wright translated it into English. Maria Elena Lucas is a tireless activist for migrant workers in the United States. Fran Leeper Buss transcribed the interviews and edited the story of Lucas's emerging consciousness and resistance: *Forged Under the Sun: Forjada bajo el sol: The Life of Maria Elena Lucas* (1993). Daphne Patai's collection of first-person accounts is a book that is hard to put down: *Brazilian Women Speak: Contemporary Life Stories* (1993). And Awa Thiam's *Black Sisters, Speak Out: Feminism and Oppression in Black Africa* (1986) takes readers out of Western and colonial mindsets.

There are hundreds of theoretical works or collections of articles about women, work, development, and economics worldwide. Here are a few really good ones. Joan Mencher and Anne Okongwu (editors), *Where Did All the Men Go? Female-Headed Households in Cross-Cultural Perspective* (1993). Marilyn Waring, *If Women Counted: A New Feminist Economics* (1988). Maria Mies, *Patriarchy and Accumulation on a World Scale* (1986). Barbara Rogers, *The Domestication of Women: Discrimination in Developing Societies* (1986). Marge Koblinsky, Judith Timyan and Jill Gay (editors), *The Health of Women: A Global Perspective* (1993). Marion Fennelly Levy, *Each in Her Own Way: Five Women Leaders of the Developing World* (1988). Sue Ellen Charlton wrote the introduction.

If you are interested in a specific region of the world or a specific pattern about the work of invisible women, the following books will be particularly helpful: Helen Safa, *The Myth of the Male Breadwinner: Women and Industrialization in the Caribbean* (1994). Sally Yudelman, *Hopeful Openings: A Study of Five Women's Development Organizations in Latin America and the Caribbean* (1987). Lesley Gill, *Precarious Dependencies: Gender, Class, and Domestic Service in Bolivia* (1994). Lydia Kung, *Factory Women in Taiwan* (1994). Jocelyn Linnekin, *Sacred Queens and Women of Consequence: Rank Gender and Colonialism in the Hawaiian Islands* (1990). Mac and Leslie Marshall, *Silent Voices Speak: Women and Prohibition in Truk* (1990).

For more material on women's struggles in Latin America, see Marjorie Agostin's compelling collection of articles called *Surviving Beyond Fear: Women, Children and Human Rights in Latin America* (1993). Or read Marguerite Bouvard's account of the mother's movement in Argentina, *Revolutionizing Motherhood: The Mothers of the Plaza de Mayo* (1994).

Closer to home, the best oral history of American women as household workers and household employers is by Susan Tucker. It's called *Telling Memories Among Southern Women Domestics* (1988).

Chapter Ten

Who Owns Her Body?

Challenges to Cultural Relativism

*B*ut can we ultimately take a stance of cultural relativism to systems that systematically use pain, fear, and deception to dominate boys and subordinate, demean, and oppress women by threat of rape and murder? Anthropologists will not all share my views. I, for one, find the systems described here to be expressions of cruelty, inhumanity, oppression, and error, as well as of cultural creativity. (Keesing 1982:37)

This quote from anthropologist Roger Keesing refers to the vivid initiation cults for young boys and the elaborate systems for separating women and men in Melanesia discussed in chapter 6. These customs disturbed Keesing. He wondered how to reconcile his personal and his professional responses.

Anthropologists say that people in human cultures act out of sets of customs that are deeply twined with their history, environment, ways of making a living, and belief systems. But it is one thing to report "objectively" that a group in India is burning widows on their husbands' funeral pyres. It is quite another to explain the reasoning and rationale for such a practice and to acknowledge similar customs of sacrificing women as wives in our histories or cultures. When a widow ascends the pyre, she offers a blessing upon her family for generations to come and a curse to prevent anyone who would thwart her right to die. Would you stop her? Should someone stop her?

Here is the first challenge to cultural relativism. Are all cultures and ideologies equal? Are all customs neutral or justifiable because some culture or another does them? Can we be objective about these customs? Should we be objective? Are some things just wrong? What about individual choices and rights?

The core idea of cultural relativism in anthropology means that we do not judge others by our own standards. Anthropologists commit to describing and analyzing other cultures and cultural systems on their own terms, often in their own languages. Franz Boas, founder of the first anthropology department and teacher of Margaret Mead, Ruth Benedict, and many others, first articulated this principle for anthropologists. But when we apply the anthropological principles of cultural relativism to the study of women or to our hopes for better lives, tensions start to build.

Here is the second challenge to cultural relativism. Flatly stated, the treatment of women in human societies transcends cultural boundaries. Patterns of hurting women and girls or using them for sex and reproduction in what appear to be bitter and destructive ways take on striking similarities wherever we happen to be on the planet. What we call domestic violence, for example, looks roughly the same in any household regardless of its cultural contexts.

The phenomenon of **gendered violence** seems to go beyond cultural relativism and suggests a kind of gruesome universality about owning, using and hurting women. Anthropologists face an agonizing dilemma.

We respect the right of other peoples to hold values different from our own, and it is not our place to criticize them for behavior that is acceptable in their society but that is unacceptable and the subject of political agendas in our own. On the other hand, we are uncomfortable with analyses that are restricted to describing and explaining violence toward women and with explanations that seem almost to justify practices that we personally find abhorrent—practices that may result in the suffering, maiming, suicide, or murder of women who have befriended us and whom we care for and respect. We are caught between our own ethnocentrism on the one hand and the sterile aloofness of extreme relativism on the other. (Counts, Brown, and Campbell 1992:xii)

To illustrate the dimensions of these dilemmas, I have selected two very broad or worldwide conditions of gendered violence.

1. Wife-beating and wife-battering. This is the most common form of family violence across the planet, and is the obvious conclusion to chapter 5 on patterns of partnering.

2. Asymmetrical and gendered sexual services, including prostitution, sexual slavery, and rape or sexual violence around the world. Once again this category of treatment falls unequally and unevenly on females; in significant ways, it transcends cultural definitions, standards, or practices.

Then we will take up four short case studies that challenge our ideas of cultural relativism in other ways. These include gang rape on American campuses; the one-child policy in China; dowry deaths in India; and female genital surgeries in Africa. The goal for all the examples is to validate experiences that many women have with gendered violence.

Human Rights and Cultural Relativism

Unfortunately, neither feminists, anthropologists, or other thinking people have easy answers, good theories, or workable solutions to the problems presented here. What reasons can we offer? Who gets the blame? Capitalism, colonialism, Christianity, culture in the abstract, evolution and biology built into our bodies and brains, the "nature of mankind," or some specific men? More to the point, there is no such animal as "womankind," so we cannot speak as if women somehow had an answer. There are millions of women who live different social existences in a variety of social settings. For one woman, working as a prostitute and sending the money home is daughterly duty done; for another, it is liberation, a nest-egg, or tuition money. Yet a third woman finds only degradation and death. How do we understand their lives: by the codes we live by, by the codes they live by, or by universal codes of rights and responsibilities that transcend culture? Can we be pro-female and culturally relative at the same time?

The examples in this chapter reflect these tensions; they are uncomfortable and raise more questions than they answer. There are not two sides to these stories; there are dozens. No one, least of all me, is objective. Everyone lives in complex and shifting structures of histories and cultures. We all have feelings, opinions, beliefs, and experiences. These examples will elicit strong feelings and many personal, moral, or intellectual judgments, some of them conflicting. It is acceptable, although very uncomfortable, to feel this way.

The Western feminist in me says that all women have a right, even a responsibility, to control our sexuality, to have autonomy over and within our bodies. At the same time, I recognize that women in other places, in other times, have not believed in the same principles I do. The anthropologist in me thinks that reproduction and sex are always embedded in collective lives and community structures, regardless of how these are defined and regardless of how support and control are acted out in the lives of individual women. These parts of me are in conflict.

It is easy to talk about human rights, to discuss the rights of women, minorities, ethnic groups, or homosexuals, for example. But the very idea is a distinctly Western European cultural concept forged in particular histories and personalities. Do we have "the right" or the responsibility to make other groups on the planet adopt the principles of individualism or majority vote we espouse? Can we make other countries treat their citizens as individuals, in some way we understand as "equal"? Is this a kind of imperialism or another colonialism?

Are women's rights different from or the same as men's rights? Do human rights include women's rights or do "human rights" actually refer to men? If women have rights, what are they? Is this just another "women's issue"?

The "Nature" of Violence

Part of this chapter is about violence against women. Yes, women are capable of violent acts and do act violently on occasion. But violent acts on the planet are strongly gendered. Frequently, and in predictable and patterned ways, some men hurt some women and some children. Students beg to know why, to have answers. Many ask about the origins or meanings of culture-bound mistreatment of women. For some the question is, Why do men do it? Or why some men and not others? For others the question is, Why do humans do it? But "It's just the custom" is no longer the answer.

Here is a summary of major explanations that scholars offer. First, some point to genetics, neurology, chemistry, and physiology. They see violence coming out of the operations of human brains. Second, others believe that social conditions, such as poverty, unemployment, and substance use, generate frustration, stress, and family strains. Third, yet others point to the violence that occurs in the power relations between men and women, individually and in groups (Van Hasselt, Morrison, Bellack, and Hersen 1988). There is significant merit in each approach.

Here is the only answer that I personally have been able to work out for myself. If this answer is unsatisfactory to you, please search for another one and let me know.

First: People do violence **because they can.** This means there are chances, occasions, and structures of opportunity. Ideologies that justify and sustain violence create the openings. There is violence because there are differentials of size, strength, power, and access to the means of violence between men and women.

Second: People do violence **because it feels good to them.** Violence is connected to rushes of feelings, sensations of release, relief, and meeting needs. Sometimes we call this "acting out" or finding an outlet for anger. There may be chemicals and hormones associated with these feelings; adrenalin, serotonin, dopamine, or testosterone are examples.

A Worldwide Case:
Wife Beating and Wife Battering

Anthropologist Dorothy Counts conducted research in Melanesia on such topics as mythology, economics, death and dying, and female suicide. Anthropologist Judith Brown, whom we met in chapter 3, has written widely on initiation rites for girls, female economic roles, and middle-aged women. Jacquelyn Campbell teaches nursing and does research on battered women in the United States. These three scholars organized and published the first international, crosscultural, and ethnographic collection on the topic of domestic violence.

These scholars developed definitions that can apply in most cultures or settings around the world. They define **wife beating** as a man deliberately inflicting physical pain on a woman within a male–female relationship or partnership. This is "normal," that is, expected in the customs of the culture. The men who beat the women in their lives do so with cultural authorization and approval. Women do not like the beatings and would prefer to have husbands who did not beat them. But women are not always meek or passive; they often have strategies to defend themselves.

Wife battering, on the other hand, goes beyond the physical reprimands that characterize wife beating. It includes the possibilities of severe injuries, maiming, and death. Battering is usually not acceptable to members of social groups; there are few or no cultural approvals or authorizations. Sometimes bystanders may intervene in ways they would not consider for wife beating. In other groups, mistreatment of wives, up to and including murder, is not remarkable; that is, no one comments and there are no effective sanctions (Counts, Brown, and Campbell 1992:1).

The definitions exclude psychological abuse: insults, threats, blackmail, or verbal assaults. These are not easy to define in our personal experiences and impossible to identify with the current skills of field ethnography. So these anthropologists do not cover individual psychology and motivations. For Counts, Brown, and Campbell, it does not matter whether or not the partners are officially married; they are still involved with each other.

Their research on wife beating challenged both their relationships to colleagues as well as their own concepts of cultural relativism.

> *The reactions of some of our colleagues when we began to discuss wife-beating and battering as a cross-cultural problem gave us insight into why anthropologists have until very recently either ignored domestic violence or given it only summary treatment. Some*

> *argued that we should not exploit our host's hospitality by exposing a dark side of their culture; other said that they would talk about the problem but would not publish it because they feared such publication would result in their being denied permission to return to the field; some were concerned that their informants might be punished if it were known that they had discussed the subject with an outsider. . . . Others argued that if we raised the topic we would be imposing our political agenda on other societies with results that might be harmful to them. One colleague—an indigenous member of one of the societies being discussed—argued that the topic of domestic violence should not be examined. He feared that if women were encouraged to protest traditional gender roles in marriage—including the right of men to beat their wives—the institution of marriage would be destabilized and family life in his society would suffer. (Counts, Brown, and Campbell 1992:xi)*

Is mistreating women as partners universal? Basically, yes. The range is from mild physical rebukes to murder. In some societies, violence and mistreatment of women is extremely rare; in others it is a daily and predictable occurrence. The authors point out the variety of wifely transgressions that demand a reaction: A husband's meal is not on time or doesn't taste right. A wife has not paid appropriate attention to her in-laws. She has dressed immodestly or is believed to be unfaithful. The merest suspicion of adultery is enough. Worldwide, the worst crimes wives commit are disobedience and insubordination.

> *The latter two wifely offenses are widely viewed as egregious and are punished with the extreme severity typical of righteous indignation. Surprisingly disproportionate vehemence and violent rage are seen as justified, because of the firm belief that the entire social fabric would unravel if such wifely behavior were countenanced. A wife's assertiveness or her flirtations with autonomy are viewed as equivalent to insurrection and as a threat against the sacred social order. (Counts, Brown, and Campbell 1992:3)*

When women are economically independent or contribute substantially to subsistence and household economies, they are beaten less. After all, an injured woman cannot work as well or may require money for medical care. Younger women are more likely to be mistreated than older women. Older women who have extra-domestic support, adult children, particularly sons, and some degree of autonomy, are safer from abuse. Wife abuse and domestic violence are linked to specific kinship structures. For example, in some cultures, a man must be seen to be in control of his wife or his standing with male peers and family members suffers. In some cultures, older women as senior wives or mothers-in-law may promote and assist in mistreating junior brides or daughters-in-law.

The most crucial factor in wife abuse is probably **social isolation.** Rules for post-marital residence make good examples. A woman who must live in her husband's community and kin group, away from her natal kinfolks, is the most vulnerable. Marital privacy, that is, the social isolation of a couple with each other, is a critical factor in mobile societies like the United States. Women suffer when domestic life is separated from public life, as in nuclear family systems.

The dangers of violence are greater when they are veiled in privacy and secrecy. When women live as isolated individuals, they are far more vulnerable. Women need everyday, communal, and public connections to each other. Women are socially isolated when their communities offer few or no alternatives and institutions. As Dorothy Counts says, in Melanesia, where judges, lawyers, and policemen beat their wives regularly, women cannot expect legislative relief, justice, or help.

Do women somehow even the score? Yes. Women may leave their husbands or boyfriends. Others strike back with weapons or words; shame and gossip can be powerful instruments of social control. Some women attempt suicide, poison a man's food, or bring the wrath of supernatural entities down on him. Others take lovers or flaunt their autonomy. Yet others deprive him of that which he claims to have beaten her for: her respect and attention.

What about husband beating and husband battering? Aren't women guilty too? There are those who claim that women beat their husbands just as much as they themselves are beaten; in other words, domestic violence is symmetrical. This is a painful issue for feminists who prefer to see women as victims rather than as perpetrators; it is a controversial issue in popular American culture, with its fixation on male bashing and backlash. But the crosscultural evidence simply does not support a claim of gender equality in beatings and batterings (Dobash, Dobash, Wilson, and Daly 1992).

Researcher Daniel Levinson has done an extensive crosscultural study of family violence drawn from a world sample of ninety cultures or societies worldwide taken from the Human Area Relations File (1988, 1989). Husband beating was reported in 26.9 percent; by contrast, wife beating occurred in 84.5 percent of the same groups. When Levinson looked at the number of households within each group, he found that husband beating occurred in the majority of households in only 6.7 percent of those societies he sampled, and wife beating occurred in the majority of households in 48.7 percent of the groups.

So women beat their husbands on occasion, but not in the same frequencies as men beat their wives. In fact, there are no societies reported from anywhere in the world in which women beat husbands but husbands did not beat wives. There are, however, many societies in which men beat women unilaterally, in which couples typically have mutually violent partnerships, or in which women fight back or act in self-defense. So beating is not symmetrical. Battering is even less symmetrical. Men batter, kill, and maim women in domestic partnerships with far greater impunity and frequency than women do.

Are there any solutions? Counts, Brown, and Campbell conclude that two things really do matter in shifting the unequal equation: these are **sanctions** and **sanctuary**. A sanction is an authoritative response, ratification, validation, or support given to an action, in this case, wife beating. There is a bit of feminist folklore about the phrase "rule of thumb": It is said that in English custom, the stick used to beat one's wife could be no thicker than a man's thumb. So beating wives was not in dispute, only the appropriate size of the instrument. This is an example of a sanction, a tacit endorsement for customary activities. But sanctions against wife beating and battering will work in the opposite direction. Obviously, some cultural groups have strong sanctions against wife beating and battering. It stands to reason that approval and positive sanctions for treating wives well are humanly possible. A social work professional who conducts therapy groups for batterers told me that he requires the men to use the first name of their wives. They are not allowed to depersonalize or privatize the relationship by saying "my wife."

Sanctuary means a safe place and people committed to women's safety. Battered women's shelters are an example of sanctuaries. As Counts, Brown, and Campbell report: Systems of female solidarity and cultural patterns such as matrilocal residence reduce battering and beatings. Anything that enhances personal autonomy, economic opportunities, or links to other women contributes to women's safety. Many small-scale groups have ways to address beating and battering. People in these groups do not reward or excuse batterers. They will not keep secrets. They gossip and make public announcements about the men. Where there are places of refuge, systems of community solidarity and mediation, or intimate intercessions against men who batter, women are safer.

Another Worldwide Case: International Sexual Services

In chapter 1 we talked about sex as work and sex workers as women who want job benefits in their chosen profession. In chapter 8 we talked about sacred prostitutes in ancient Mesopotamia whose sexuality may have served spiritual purposes. In this chapter, I want to present a continuum of sexual services that range from kept women to female captivity. Once again, we note that men may be prostitutes, but it is not the mirror image, the same phenomena, or in the same frequencies as that which happens to women. The continuum from voluntary sex work to female sexual slavery and rape is quite specific to females. Sexual service is gendered work across the planet.

There is a long, slippery gradient between voluntary sex work and sexual slavery. Women work at prostitution to support themselves and their families in one of the most readily available jobs in the world. At the same time, illegal traffic in women and children as a cheap labor supply in international prostitution may be a form of slavery. What are the dimensions of the problem?

> There are no comprehensive studies of the problem of prostitution worldwide, its incidence and impact on different societies; nor are there any statistics on how many persons, including children, may be involved. Even less information is available about the men who benefit from the trade, as either clients or procurers. It is necessary to rely on the scant data provided by governments to various UN bodies, the limited material released by Interpol, and the information, although anecdotal, points nevertheless to a problem of staggering

dimensions. It is estimated, for example, that in the United States child prostitution earns up to two billion dollars a year. In Brazil, female prostitutes are said to number five million, many of them children. Sex tourism, or the organization of tours from industrialized countries for the specific purpose of buying sexual services of women and children in the third world, is reported to have become a multibillion dollar industry which figures prominently in the economies of Thailand, South Korea and the Philippines. Estimates of the total number of prostitutes in those countries run into the hundreds of thousands. It is widely believed that, because of the global economic crisis, prostitution follows only domestic work as women's major employment in many areas of the third world. (Reanda 1991:205)

Please note that no knowledgeable person seriously suggests that so many children and young women go into prostitution for personal fulfillment and sexual satisfaction. In chapter 9, I thought that women as housewives to world economic systems or as daughters to the factories of international industry were depressing themes. But here is a step further: Serving men sexually is one of the leading forms of employment and survival for women on the planet.

Sexual Tourism

Travel, tourism, and the international hospitality industry is either the second largest economic enterprise in the world or the first. The figures vary; either way, this is an impressive facet of capitalism, development, modernization, or colonialism. The international tourist industry has formed around leisure services and cultural experiences as consumer goods. Prostitution is a core element, and the sexual services of young females are increasingly valuable to the industry and to many countries in the world.

Since the 1970s, tourism has become one of the leading strategies for development or modernization everywhere in the world. Tourists bring in lots of money. Countries pressed for cash (and what country isn't) look to the infrastructures of international travel. Women and sex are prominent enticements of tourist destinations. That means that bosses and managers must ensure a continuous supply of labor.

In a remarkable study of sexual tourism in Southeast Asia, Thanh-dam Truong talks about her personal experiences and the questions that led to her research. Note the layers of her conflicts about cultural relativism in just one paragraph.

Being Vietnamese, I witnessed the spread of prostitution in my adolescence in South Vietnam during the Indochina conflict. Forced urbanization campaigns, carried out for military reasons in the 1960s, uprooted millions of peasants in an effort to destroy the rural bases of communist guerrillas. Many rural women were drawn into the cities and to areas surrounding US military bases, where a service economy instantly sprung up and revolved around personal services provided to US military personnel. Brothels and sex establishments mushroomed in these areas and enriched many of their owners. The profitability of prostitution made the entrenched Confucian ethics of the society and its codes of sexual conduct almost irrelevant for many. Where there was a certain awareness of the fragility of our social fabric during a period of major upheaval, the internal causes of prostitution were rarely discussed. It was far easier to blame American imperialism in order to defend one's own cultural integrity. From 1968 to 1973, as a student in the United States, I was exposed to the anti-war movement and the pertinent debates prevailing at the time, of which the controversy surrounding prostitution was one. At that time notions about prostitution were reversed. With some exceptions, the blame was placed on the loose sexual mores of Vietnamese women, or on the backwardness of Vietnamese men who found it legitimate to sell women, including their female kin. (Truong 1990:x)

For American servicemen, the sexual services of prostitutes were part of "R and R," rest and recreation. Many military bureaucracies, including the United States, organize and supervise brothels or support institutionalized prostitution. When the war in Vietnam ended, businessmen replaced military men in Thailand and other places in Asia. Today, hundreds of thousands of women serve men sexually. They are called "Comfort Women," "Hospitality Girls," or "Go-go girls." Planes land, busses stop, and cruise ships dock. Soldiers, businessmen, and other travelers debark for sex tours advertised and promoted internationally.

Although prostitution is illegal in many countries, governments sanction or overlook its presence. Escort services, sex holidays and resorts, sex therapy centers, telephone-sex calls, and dating services are only a few examples. Some observers say that legally sanctioned overseas employment agencies and international mail-order bride agencies are often fronts for traffic in women across international borders. There are many reports of violence, deception, blackmail, and contracts to sell daughters.

Thailand is often cited as a country in which women hold their families' purse-strings, work in their own businesses, or hold wage-labor jobs. The country is also credited with one of the most elaborate, repressive, and lucrative commercial sex operations in the world. The tourist industry, coupled with the longstanding sexual practices of Thai men and ideologies about women, provide the climate for sex as a growth industry.

The traditional duties of Thai females include the care of younger siblings or aging relatives. A daughter or sister who prostitutes herself can provide her family with otherwise unobtainable consumer goods, build them a house, or save the family land. Although such a daughter cannot earn merit within the Buddhism by giving food to monks or going to temples on holy days, a prostitute can earn merit through contributions of cash. Monks will not discuss how much of their living comes from the dutiful daughters of prostitution. There are accounts in Thailand of middle-class women, including university students, who are part or full-time prostitutes.

In the past, Thai men took many wives, major and minor. Although neither polygamy nor prostitution is legal, the practices and ideologies continue. In the reigning gender ideologies, men (particularly elite ones) are given the right to rule over women. In this quote, Chiang Mai, age fifteen, explains sexual tourism and her role as a prostitute in Thailand.

> *At first I was very scared, but after a while I got used to it. None of the girls thought about running away because they came for the money, every one of them was there out of necessity . . . . If there weren't any girls working at the country's border, would the foreigners bother coming in? Another point is that the girls make money, the men have a good time. It's a business. Even though I don't like working that way, just think, if the girls are caught, where else can they go to earn money? (Quoted in Muecke 1992:896)*

The stories of women who enter prostitution in Thailand sound similar to those in the Philippines, Korea, or many other countries. Rural families saddled with debts make a contract for their teenage daughter; someone promises her a good job and gives them a lot of money. In some places, these contracts look like traditional arranged marriages; they give similar rights to the labor contractors that husbands received. Or young girls flee homes where abuse, poverty, or alcohol make life on the streets seem safer or easier to them. The real prostitution may be in ideologies of family loyalty, religious obligations, business bottom-lines, and governmental denials. For example, the Thai government blames prostitutes for the spread of HIV-AIDS and other sexually transmitted diseases. Yet women in the sexual service industries are more vulnerable than the men who pay them, more at the mercy of asymmetries in relations of power.

Female Sexual Slavery

In the 1970s, sociologist and feminist Kathleen Barry became hooked on studying the international traffic in women. The subject was effectively buried under layers of silence. Very few people believed that women were coerced, trapped, kidnapped, or sold into a form of gender slavery. Until the women's movement, no one had looked at sexual violence against prostitutes (it was just part of the lifestyle), or against wives (there was no such thing as marital rape).

For Barry, a prostitute is a woman reduced to her sexual utility. Female sexual slavery, as she defines it, has three qualities: being trapped, having no freedom, and experiencing violence and exploitation.

> *Female sexual slavery is present in* all *situations where women or girls cannot change the immediate conditions of their existence; where regardless of how they got into those conditions they cannot*

> *get out; and where they are subject to sexual violence and exploitation. (Barry 1979:40)*

Who are these women? After the collapse of communism in eastern Europe, many women from these chaotic countries answered advertisements for jobs in prosperous western European countries. On arrival, they discovered various strategies to keep them in servitude; their passports were confiscated, they owed large debts for room, board, and travel. Some were bound, gagged, and drugged. In some countries, parents customarily accept payments like bride price or bride wealth for their daughters' work. Many parents accept much-needed cash from men who pose as potential husbands or employers. Young girls from rural areas of Third World countries have only a few job opportunities and even fewer skills. Poverty and the international tourist industry are situations that cross national boundaries and set up the conditions for commercial sex or buying and selling female bodies and labor.

> *Prostitution is also a means of escape for girls who try to avoid forced marriages and migrate to the cities. Where sex discrimination creates few employment opportunities for women and women are kept uneducated, prostitution is a likely alternative. . . . In such situations forced marriage, polygyny, prostitution, and economic discrimination form one highly interdependent system. (Barry 1979:166)*

For example, forced marriage for women is outlawed in many countries now. But there are many ways to engineer consent or buy submission. In some countries, there are also military brothels, rape camps, and rape as military policies. For Barry, prostitution and sexual tourism, mail order brides, date rape, or battered wives are subtle, but very real forms of sexual slavery.

In the light of prostitution as transnational business, the distinction between "voluntary" and "enforced" servitude is difficult to sustain. More and more scholars are growing into a painful awareness that domestic violence and child abuse are horribly and intricately linked to prostitution. Many, some say most, prostitutes in the world are victims of incest, violence, or rape (Reanda 1991). In this view, prostitution is a status of servitude in which women are coerced, blackmailed, threatened, and abused. Thus made vulnerable, they can be separated from familial and institutional assistance and blamed for their conditions. This gives credence to those who call international patterns of prostitution a form of female slavery.

Prostitutes, Whores, and Feminists

The questions about prostitution are thorny. At the heart of the debate is work and sex, two of the most vital issues of gender on the planet. Are prostitutes criminals or are they promiscuous? Is prostitution about vice or lasciviousness? Why does women's sexuality have to be a problem? Are men's sexual needs and women's availability somehow rooted in our human "nature" and biology? Or is the willingness and ability of men to pay for sex a part of ideological, institutional, and behavioral controls and exploitation of women? Is prostitution just another form of work and prostitutes another example of invisible workers? Is prostitution a form of social service or social welfare?

In a position paper from the Second World Whores' Congress in 1986, prostitutes or sex workers commented unfavorably on feminists and those in women's movements who oppose the institution of prostitution while trying to help, support or save individual prostitutes.

> *Due to feminist hesitation or refusal to accept prostitution as legitimate work and to accept prostitutes as working women, the majority of prostitutes have not identified as feminists; nonetheless, many prostitutes identify with feminist values such as independence, financial autonomy, sexual self-determination, personal strength, and female bonding. (Quoted in Delacoste and Alexander 1987:307)*

What sex workers point out, to the discomfort of most of us, is the disturbing similarity between marriage systems and sex work or prostitution. Many women who call themselves whores and hookers quote Frederick Engels, who believed that women are often coerced or impelled into marriages of economic advantage, convenience, or family duty. In such marriages, a wife "differs only from the ordinary courtesan in that she does not let out her body on piece-work as a wage worker, but sells it once and for all into slavery" (Engels 1972:134).

Philosopher Christine Overall asks this question: What's wrong with prostitution? How can females and feminists evaluate sex work? In a carefully wrought argument, Overall answers herself and argues that sex work is inherently asymmetrical. It encodes all the power relationships of contemporary society: class, race, gender. Although prostitution may be a commercial endeavor in which women are paid, it is different from working as a waitress, hotel maid, administrative assistant, or college professor.

> *In a culture where women's sexuality is used to sell, and women learn that sex is our primary asset, sex work is not and cannot be just a private business transaction, an exchange of benefits between equals, or an equalitarian trade. Like rape, sexual assault, sexual harassment, and incest, prostitution is inherently gendered, a component and manifestation of the patriarchal institution of heterosexuality. Prostitution is structured in terms of a power imbalance in which women, the less powerful, sell to men, the more powerful. (Overall 1992:721)*

What's wrong with prostitution, Overall says, is that women service men's sexual needs under capitalist and patriarchal conditions. According the gender ideologies, men "naturally" have these needs. What women need, sexual or otherwise, is not addressed. Sex sells; it sells products and people. Sex is money, profit, and development. So there is no reversibility, there is no sexual equality possible in such a social contract.

Sexual servitude and violence against women are global. They cut across cultural boundaries. The women quoted above argue that we cannot excuse sexual slavery or violence on the grounds of cultural relativism nor can we buy into arguments about protecting the privacy of household life or of men's rights.

For the remainder of the chapter, we will take up four culturally grounded examples that challenge how we think about the treatment of women in human society. Each of these case studies illustrates a different view of the central question in this chapter: Who owns her body? Each example challenges cultural relativism anew.

Case Study Number 1: Rape on a University Campus

The first case study hits close to home. Anthropologist Peggy Sanday has studied and written about violence and rape crossculturally (1981). She argues that men are not "naturally" programmed to rape any more than women are "naturally" programmed to be motherly. In extensive crosscultural research, she found societies that were largely free from rapes and others she characterized as "rape-prone." Sanday argues forcefully that rape is part of certain cultural complexes that include interpersonal violence, ideologies of male dominance, and systems of gender separation. Her most chilling ethnographic example of how rape is patterned comes from fraternity row on an American college campus (1990).

At the University of Pennsylvania, a female student reported a gang rape by a number of the brothers at a fraternity. When Sanday investigated the case with an anthropological eye and began to collect similar accounts from other campuses, she discovered customs, beliefs, and a subculture that condoned and created conditions for gang rape and other forms of sexual violence against women. Through testimonies, court transcripts, interviews, and comparative materials, Sanday reconstructed the "group-think" and gender ideologies that made gang rape normal and even commendable behavior for many men on fraternity row. Their activities served as powerful bonding mechanisms among fraternity brothers and were buttressed by elaborate rituals, social class privileges, and the systematic denials of college and university administrators.

Lois Forer presided as trial judge. Here she speaks about the fraternity males charged with gang rape.

> *I was amazed to learn that the attitudes, language, behavior, and literacy levels of these fraternity members are identical to those of young, under-privileged criminals. Both groups frequently engage in sexual behavior that others call gang rape. Both call it "playing train" or "pulling train" (one man follows another). Both groups consider it a form of male bonding for which the female is merely an available instrument. Both may prepare themselves for this test of manhood by ingesting quantities of alcohol and fortifying themselves with drugs. Both consider this acceptable, indeed, normal conduct. Both are amazed to learn that such actions could be crimes. These*

*fraternity brothers, like slum hoodlums, are often semiliterate and
unable to present coherent and intelligible statements in their own
defense even though they are high school graduates and students in
good academic standing at elite universities. The difference between
the two groups is that fraternity brothers are rarely, if ever, prosecuted for their conduct whereas slum youths are prosecuted, convicted,
and imprisoned. (Forer in Sanday 1990:xiii)*

Anthropologist Sanday and Judge Forer analyzed the reactions of the university administrators. Their responses can be summarized in the immortal words of
the women's movement, "They just don't get it." Most simply did not understand
how and why their policies penalized women and privileged acts that are crimes
in civil contexts. Women's responses to stories of fraternity gang rape ranged from
"cut it off" or "hang them high" to defense, understanding, and support of the
young men and the social institutions involved. Men talked about "situations that
got out of hand." They said, "Perhaps she asked for it." They asked, "What was
she doing there in the first place?" They customarily drank a great deal and took
turns having sex with an anonymous woman in the presence of each other. For
the men accused of gang rape, the identities of the women they assaulted were
irrelevant.

Case Study Number 2:
The One-Child Policy in China

At liberation in 1948, the new Communist government made women free citizens
of the People's Republic of China. The leaders abolished practices of the traditional patriarchy such as polygyny, arranged marriages, female infanticide, and
the sale of daughters. The new marriage laws, the availability of child care, medical care, access to contraception and abortion, as well as employment opportunities for women, impressed feminists in the West.

The People's Republic of China has the largest population on the earth, roughly 1.2 billion people. After 1976 and the end of the Cultural Revolution, leaders
in the Chinese government decided to limit the population of China. Apparently,
they believed that population control and limiting each couple to one child would
help to avoid chronic famines and raise the standards of living.

How did the Chinese leaders propose to reduce population growth and limit
family size? First, national bureaucracies set strict quotas on the number of births
for local areas and within the work units that organize the daily life of most people in the People's Republic. At first, no woman was allowed to bear a child within four years of her first one. Third children were strictly forbidden. All women
who had borne three or more children by the end of 1979 were ordered to submit to sterilization.

By the early 1980s, the government moved to a one-child policy. Young couples had to apply for marriage licenses as well as licenses for getting pregnant. If
a wife did not succeed in getting pregnant, she and her husband might be sent to

the back of the line to wait their turn to try again. At various times during the pregnancy and after the birth, a local population control worker visited the couple to obtain their signatures on a one-child agreement. In other words, couples would serve their work units and the socialist goals of China when they agreed to have only one child. The central government favored sterilization, voluntary or involuntary, as evidence of compliance.

If the woman became pregnant again, local committees and population control officials found various ways to enforce the strict sanctions against having a second child. Officials fined the couple, cut off government services or education for offending couples and their children, or brought enormous pressure to bear in a variety of ways. Medical technicians performed abortions through the last month of pregnancy. There are stories told about full-term second children killed at birth and of abortions performed without the mother's permission. Since local officials endured enormous pressure from their superiors to meet the quotas, they in turn found ways to ensure compliance of women in their work units.

Representatives from local population control committees check the contraception plan for every couple in the work units. The birth control pills manufactured in China are strong; there are side-effects but only a small chance for an accident. In some places, married women must register their periods every month, so they cannot claim an accidental pregnancy. Women who are not sterilized or taking pills under close supervision are fitted with IUDs, or intrauterine devices. The old-fashioned steel IUDs possess only one advantage: they can be seen on an X-ray. The IUDs have no cord to make removal easy, so women sometimes seek an illegal extraction of their IUDs under dangerous conditions: the Chinese version of back alleys and coat hangers. This is another example of the "do anything" principle we discussed in chapter 3.

The one-child policy appears to have worked better in the cities than in the countryside. In rural areas, where the majority of China's citizens live, the policies have had devastating effects on women. Informally, many stories circulate about the heroics of women in hiding out for the term of a second or third pregnancy or in tricking their work units. Their resistance has prompted some changes in policy. Some couples are now allowed to have second children when the first was a girl or under other circumstances. Ironically, most Chinese families say that the ideal size is two children (Conly and Camp 1992).

Households under the Communists hold many of the ideologies and practices of the traditional patriarchal, patrilocal ones. Girls are a liability because they will have to leave home when they marry; they can never repay their parent's investments in them. Sons are a parents' retirement and social welfare safety net. The desire for sons is so strong that families take desperate measures, many of which injure and traumatize women. Women who bear daughters may be punished severely by their husbands and mothers-in-law. Many women commit suicide. Wife battering and domestic violence increase dramatically when family hopes for a son fail. Despite propaganda campaigns and public education efforts, mothers, not fathers, are blamed when the newborn baby is a girl.

In some areas, there are more boys than girls or more firstborn sons than the randomness of conception would predict. Although female infanticide is illegal, unusual sex ratios and folklore suggest its prevalence.

Women undergo the sterilization procedure far more often than their husbands do. Chinese say that men should be spared surgeries because of their importance as workers. In the event of divorce, a man may remarry and have other children. When women resist and try to conceal their pregnancies, they are sometimes tracked down and forced to undergo surgical procedures like induced labor, late abortions, and subsequent sterilizations. Although such actions are technically against the law, the national government has not taken responsibility for the abuses of its policies. When women resist, often in public and dramatic ways, or when local work units exceed their quota of babies or fail to meet their quota of sterilizations, the Chinese government blames what they call the persistence of feudal-patriarchal ideologies.

China's one-child policy is the largest experiment in government control over reproduction ever conducted. (For fuller descriptions see Hardee-Cleaveland and Banister 1988; Whyte and Gu 1987; or Mosher 1993.) In this example, we see the government of China acting much like a traditional father or a mega-husband. State officials tell women how many children to have and when; the policies reinforce the value of sons and use women's bodies to transform national economic life. The burden of government policies about population control and economic development falls unevenly on Chinese women. Women are drafted into a form of compulsory heterosexual monogamy. They must work at assigned jobs whether they want to or not. Their decisions in family size, birth control, abortion, or sterilization are mandated. In fact, Chinese women appear to serve the People's Republic the way they once served their mothers-in-law.

The one-child policy of China challenges our own ethical dilemmas about production, reproduction, and the control of women's bodies. Anthropologist Anna Anagnost did research in the PRC on women's responses to the one-child policies. She comments on the challenges these policies present to women outside the PRC.

> *For pro-life advocates, it provides a horrific image of to what extremes the legality of abortion might lead. At the same time, it provides those who are pro-choice with an equally horrific image of the dangers of state intervention into reproductive decisions. The appropriation of the forced abortion issue by the pro-life movement has fueled the abortion controversy in this country. But the issue is just as potent a weapon for those who are pro-choice. The question is over who has the authority and the right to make choices: the state, the patriarchal family, or women as individuals. (Anagnost 1989:336)*

The example of the one-child policy of China crystallizes many feverish debates in the politics of reproduction. How far can or should governments go in regulating the reproductive lives of individual women? What about the justifications for a population policy for the world's largest country? Can China feed itself and avert crises without dramatically reducing its high population growth? Isn't the reduction of the population of China good for all of us? Doesn't an improved standard of living for most of the country justify this policy? Are there parallels in our own cultural experiences?

The United Nations has given the Chinese government prestigious awards to recognize their successes in reducing population growth. Many nations and other international agencies have praised the modernization of China, the progress and development of this previously backward giant. One Chinese writer, the mother of a thirteen-year-old daughter, commented to me, "This is what I can do to help my country. The one-child policy works for the good of everybody."

Case Study Number 3: Dowry Deaths in India

Statistics of the ratios of men to women in some areas of India show that there are 120 men for every 100 women (Von Willigen and Channa 1991). Figures like this or worse are reported from some regions of China too. When the number of females in any one place is low relative to the number of males, then observers suspect foul play. For India, this suspicion has a foundation.

For rich and poor alike, having sons amounts to a national obsession. Sons take care of parents, validate their existence in dozens of ways and, at last, light their funeral pyres. It is not surprising that women will do anything to have a son; it is a woman's ultimate triumph and a significant measure of personal safety.

Daughters are considered a liability on several fronts. Therefore, they must be married off as soon as possible. Unmarried daughters in their natal household are unthinkable. In Hindu belief systems, women cause pollution and harm unless they are married.

Many parents say that baby girls are a financial burden. Families cannot afford the clothes, the ceremonies for them, and above all, the dowries that permit them to marry and cease to be a financial drain on their natal families. Sometimes, it is said, killing baby girls at birth is kinder to them than a life of tears.

In fact, an entire industry and range of consumer choices are available to assist parents in their gender preference ideologies. In a country starved for medical care, the biggest health-care expenses many poor families make are amniocentesis or an ultrasound test to determine the sex of the fetus. Parents schedule abortions when they do not like the results. In a country where oxen wear yokes to pull plows and women wear yokes to carry water, high-technology ultrasound is more available than running water. Abortions for sex determination are big business. But the government sees amniocentesis, ultrasound, and abortion as much-needed forms of family planning and population control.

In time-honored customs, a bride's family makes substantial payments to a groom and his family. This dowry may amount to the equivalent of a year's salary or the price of a house. Weddings are actually commercial transactions, a transfer of capital. A bride's family may have trouble accumulating such a payment. This hardship alone prejudices families against female children.

The practice of dowries has fostered substantial violence toward women. Indian newspapers labeled this "bride-burnings" or **dowry deaths.** Suppose that a husband or his mother decide the dowry is inadequate or too slow in arriving. Suppose the young wife does not get pregnant or she gives birth to a series of daughters. Suppose the family wants sons and an infusion of cash. Mysteriously, the bride is found soaked with kerosene and burned to death in her kitchen.

Sometimes these are ruled suicides. Indeed, some daughters commit suicide to help their parents avoid the dowry payments, just as brides kill themselves when the pressures for continuing payments and the violence become too great. More often, however, the burned brides have simply been murdered.

India has a great many pro-male property laws, the heritage of thousands of years of religious and civil traditions. For example, the patrilineal and patrilocal families privilege the birthright of sons to inherit property. So a daughter's dowry represents a kind of inheritance given to her before the death of the parent. But a bride does not control the gifts or dowries given at her marriage. If she dies, it remains with her husband's family. She cannot expect to divorce and ask for her share. Widowers are allowed, even expected to remarry; they acquire a dowry with each marriage. Widows, however, are a social liability. They are rarely allowed, and certainly not expected, to remarry.

Although the Indian government outlawed the practice in the 1961 Dowry Prohibition Act, the law has failed. In many circles, bride burning is seen as "only" domestic violence. Even those who bemoan the deaths of young women, support the custom of dowry. And if women have no employment opportunities in an inflationary economy, then investing in a husband for one's daughter might be an act of love.

As we noted in chapter 1, the association of wives with fire is also expressed in the custom of **sati,** burning a widow on her husband's funeral pyre. Journalist Sakuntala Narasimhan compares this custom, which still goes on in the religious circles of some regions, with bride-burnings and the lust for sons.

> *We have a plethora of statutes for women's welfare; at the same time we have seen crimes against women increase over the years, with dowry deaths alone by the hundreds testifying to the increasing degradation of women in society. We boast of the latest in medical technology—and at the same time see the use of sex-determination tests for the selective destruction of female foetuses because girls are unwelcome and seen as a burden in our society. (1990:150)*

Feminists and other women's organizations in India are fighting these gendered practices in a number of ways. Some women's groups seek tougher laws. As in other nations where shelters for women have been established, the sanctuaries are not adequate to meet the need. Books, poems, plays, television programs, and many other media sources address the problem. They call into question how girls are raised and the conflicts between the ideals of womanhood and the actual dangers of being a woman. Sometimes they chide women for their treatment of their daughters and daughters-in-law. They also recognize the national unemployment rates and the rising tide of consumer demands.

Some women's groups feel that dowries are only the symptom of a larger social sickness, the worthlessness of women. The solution, activists say, is not in treating the symptoms but in reframing the terms of women's lives and increasing the economic independence of women. Women lack alternatives such as access to education, good paying jobs, and the right to inherit property from their natal families.

The patterned deaths of females in India present serious challenges to cultural relativity as well as to feminism or other woman-centered analyses. If we validate ancient and embedded cultural traditions, then valuing sons and giving dowries make a certain sense. If we validate the experiences of women, then dowries may be only a branch of a poisonous tree.

Case Study Number 4:
An Ancient Operation in Africa

In 1985, at the United Nations Decade for Women Conference in Nairobi, Kenya, the debate about female genital surgeries was fierce. Western feminists decried the practices of clitoridectomy and infibulation; they called this mutilation and cited horrible stories of young girls bleeding to death and older women in chronic pain. African women reacted angrily to a tone of voice they heard as colonial, post-colonial and neocolonial. "Stop groping about in our panties." they retorted.

Dr. Nawal El Saadawi, an Egyptian physician and novelist, known for her writings on women in Arab society, criticizes the "let's help those poor people" approach. She applies her brand of cultural relativism to foreigners such as development experts and feminists who want to save Africa.

> *That kind of help, which they think of as solidarity, is another type of colonialism in disguise. So we must deal with female circumcision ourselves. It is our culture, we understand it, when to fight against it and how, because this is the process of liberation. (El Saadawi 1980)*

In vehement contrast, American writer Alice Walker states, "Torture is not culture." Walker, whose novel *Possessing the Secret of Joy* explored the life of an African woman who underwent the surgery, calls them genital mutilation and the sexual blinding of women. She followed her novel with a film, *Warrior Marks*. In a book by the same title, she explores her passion about the topic and her hopes for ending the practices. Here Walker passionately denounces cultural relativism.

> *Clearly, female genital mutilation is a painful, complex, and difficult issue, which involves questions of cultural and national identities, sexuality, human rights, and the rights of women and girls to live safe and healthy lives. But this complexity is not an excuse to sit by and do nothing. Who cares if African women and children are subjected to violence?* **We should all care.** *If one hundred million white women and children were being mutilated as a matter of course in the name of tradition, the earth would by now be shaking with the tremors caused by voices of protest and righteous anger. (Walker and Parmar 1993:95)*

Alice Walker asked many women she met in Africa why they practiced these surgeries. Some women believed that Islamic scriptures and codes of conduct prescribed the practice. Others recounted stories or theories about dangers from the clitoris. "It's dirty and has to be destroyed." "The clitoris would grow like a penis and hang between the legs if it is not removed." "The clitoris is an evil, which makes men impotent and kills children at birth." Most talked about the social dangers. A woman will remain childless if she is not excised. A woman cannot marry; she will never find a husband and her social identity" (Walker and Parmar 1993:139). Although the custom may be as old as 6,000 years, there are no ultimate reasons why it is done. There are songs, myths, stories, and centuries of traditions that support this practice.

One of the reasons genital surgeries are difficult for many to accept is the complicity of women. Genital surgeries often take place in matrilineal societies, in matrifocal families, and under the supervision and support of women as grandmothers, mothers, midwives, sisters, and friends. In West African countries like Liberia, Sierra Leone, and the Ivory Coast of Guinea, women's secret religious associations, like the Sande Society, take young girls away for months to bush schools. There the girls learn about being a woman, household tasks, and adult forms of cooperation with other women. They do spinning, weaving, learn household management and local systems of medicine, herbs, and healing techniques. They join a Sande sisterhood and learn that their ancestors and the sisters within Sande will punish any man who hurts a member. Genital surgeries, usually clitoridectomy, are part of the initiation ceremonies (see Bledsoe 1980; MacCormack 1979; and Bellman 1979).

Here is a major dilemma. Religious sisterhood resonates with meaning for many inside and outside these cultures. But is sisterhood achieved at the price of mutilation? Are all the surgeries a form of mutilation or equally mutilating? Many women say this ritual is an important rite of passage and the only ritual over which they have control. Others say they plan to circumcise their daughters as they themselves were operated on. Many women from these countries living abroad go to elaborate lengths to perform or have performed the surgery on their daughters. Other African women have sought asylum in France and other Western countries to avoid the operation.

Feminist scholar and theologian Mary Daly treats these female genital surgeries as another pan-human and crosscultural example of atrocities committed against women. She criticizes outside observers who consider the deadly practices just another "custom." Daly rails against ideologies that claim women's bodies are polluting or that women are completed only through relationships with men. She points out that African women say the surgeries must be performed if young girls are ever to marry. This viewpoint, in Mary Daly's strong language, makes women into "token torturers" for men. Men are absent from the "sadistic rituals" but nonetheless benefit (or appear to) from ideologies and practices which subdue and control women (1978:163).

The country of Sudan is probably the epicenter of the most severe forms of female genital surgeries. Anthropologist Carolyn Sargent speaks about women in Sudan and what role, if any, anthropologists and other outsiders ought to play.

> *During the last fifty years, colonial legislation, current government policy prohibiting the practice, the efforts of international health agencies, and Sudanese and other women's organizations have not resulted in an effective movement against clitoridectomy and infibulation. While it is appealing to assume a universal feminist solidarity that unites in opposing female circumcision, it is not clear that Sudanese women welcome the interventions of outsiders, whether from women's groups or others critical of the operation. (Sargent 1991:24)*

Anthropologist Janice Boddy believes that we must understand the cultural and historical contexts for the operation as much as we do the medical, sexual, and physical consequences.

> *The latter disgust us because we can well imagine ourselves as suffering them; the former, because, perhaps, we cannot. It may be our hubris as anthropologists that we cannot—or dare not—imagine ourselves so immersed in any culture that we would buy its multiplex rationalizations—its meanings—however subtle and persuasive and coherent they may be. And yet we submit ourselves to cesarean sections and mechanized childbirth to produce the "perfect" baby; inculcate in our daughters, albeit implicitly, that they must diet, exercise, dye, and depilate to achieve the "perfect" body; we tweeze and pluck and color and conceal to attain the "perfect" face. We work hard at being women, spend considerable sums of money, suscept ourselves to bunions and bulimia and worse. (Boddy 1991:16)*

These anthropologists suggest that American women should ask ourselves about the beauty myth, the thin-fat agonies, and other body alterations in contemporary American culture before we pass judgment on other peoples' cultures. Writers like Gloria Steinem and Barbara Ehrenreich point out that nineteenth-century medical texts in Western Europe and America proclaimed genital operations as the best treatment for nymphomania, hysteria, masturbation, and what we still call "nervous breakdowns."

In fact, crusades of women from Africa against genital mutilation have grown dramatically. A number of prominent organizations hold conferences and work with the media and other women's organizations to stop the surgeries. The women who work for these organizations say that solutions lie in improving women's education, job opportunities, economic independence, and making key marriage reforms. But efforts ring hollow in the face of Africa's problems and the failures of international programs to address women's issues at structural levels. At the same time, the practice is remarkably persistent.

Conclusions: Can We Live Together?

So who owns a woman's body? Father, mother, government, religion, husband, boss? Can a woman own her own body, all by herself? Is there any hope for alleviating some of the gendered violence and damaging gender ideologies discussed in this chapter? Alas, I still have no answers. But in conclusion, I want to present a few ideas that various women have offered as relief if not remedy.

A Room of One's Own: The Politics of Separation

In 1982, in the central desert of Australia at a town called Alice Springs, a group of Aboriginal women proposed their solution to lawlessness, interpersonal violence, and public drunkenness. They wanted separate women's camps, taboo to men. They told the Australian Law Reform Commission they would be safe with other sober women; therefore there would be less need for police, jails, and law reforms.

In pre-contact Aboriginal society, men and women had complementary and interdependent relationships to each other. But colonialism and the introduction of male-oriented Australian rule in a frontier atmosphere changed this to sexual asymmetry, where women were defined only in domestic spheres. Forced to give up their roaming lifestyle and settle down in government or mission reserves and towns, Aboriginal women had copied precontact patterns of living. They had formed **jilimi** or single women's camps. At the core of these camps are widows who have not remarried or women who don't live with their husbands. Older women are leaders in the women's rituals and spiritualities. There are always young single women who are avoiding an arranged marriage, or women who need a place of safety from husbands. Women who are sick, in mourning, need the company of women. Children accompany their mothers and siblings. Married women visit during the day. The women's camps are a refuge, a power base for women's solidarity, home to women's rituals, and safe from men.

But this was not a perfect solution, as anthropologist Diane Bell reports (1987). In the contemporary colonial context, single women may live in their own camps, but they are locked out of national arenas in which decisions about them are made. There is no official recognition or help to establish women's communities for healing, ritual, safety, and friendship. Their requests were turned down.

Dual-Sex Political Systems

Nigerian sociologist Ifi Amadiume advocates another kind of separation or autonomy. You will remember her from chapter 5. She says the best strategies for women and for national politics would be based on the patterns of sharing power between men and women that characterized traditional cultures. Under Western colonial influence, however, "local men now manipulate a rigid gender ideology in contemporary sexual politics and thereby succeed in marginalizing women's political position, or in excluding them from power altogether" (1987:194).

Ifi Amadiume recommends building a true dual-sex political system modeled on many traditional and precolonial cultural practices. She advocates voting blocks based on a constitutional recognition of gender and a formal structure of legislative and executive rights over "female" domains and "female" affairs in a

Women's Council, Women's Cabinet, or similar places where men have titles and responsibilities. Women are to have clearly defined spheres of interest in households, markets and subsistence economies, and in all matters of women's health and safety.

Amadiume asks the question, "Whose culture is it, anyway?" Her answer is, "There are many cultures, women's culture and men's culture, African cultures, anthropological cultures, and the cultures of empire. Women can take back the cultures once we owned."

The Feminine Principle

Vandana Shiva is a physicist, philosopher, and feminist, a prominent Green or environmentalist who abandoned her career in India's nuclear energy programs to speak out loudly for what she calls the **feminine principle.** For her, this is gender-based embodied knowledge and a quality of life radically different from colonialism, ecological destruction, and the oppression of women.

> *Recovering the feminine principle as respect for life in nature and society appears to be the only way forward, for men as well as women, in the North as well as the South. The metaphors and concepts of minds deprived of the feminine principle have been based on seeing nature and women as worthless and passive, and finally as dispensable . . . . If production of life cannot be reckoned with in money terms, then it is economic models, and not women's work in producing sustenance and life, that must be sacrificed. (Shiva 1989:223)*

Vandana Shiva says there are paths to harmony, survival, and diversity for both men and women. There are nonviolent and inclusive alternatives to the dominant paradigms and contemporary ideologies in the west. The feminine principle is about sustaining and providing. It makes legitimate women's ways of knowing and being. The feminine principle allows for the diversity of experience across the planet. It creates spaces for women.

Chimpanzee mothers and baboon females showed us the first example of matrifocal units, generations, and connections that flow from mothers. Anthropologists provide models of women, men, and children living in a vast array of cultural alternatives for being human. Women of color testify to the ravages of racism, and in so doing, offer visions of women and men together in a world free of slavery and hatred. Spirits visit women and women's religions in the heart of patriarchies, and women take that healing to others. Radical separatists in lesbian communities point out that "women have no country of our own" and then work to establish autonomy and authenticity for themselves and others. Women's shelter movements around the world work to provide sanctuaries and safety in women-centered environments. The feminist spirituality movements speak eloquently of ancient myths, women's communities, and female rituals. Today many woman all over the world echo Virginia Woolfe's immortal call for "a room of one's own." We have models of deep and abiding friendships among men and women from primates to world assemblies for peace. And ordinary women everywhere form simple groups to meet their basic needs; they grow like roots of grass.

Women, Shiva says, know the path to take.

Some Powerful Books to Empower Us

There are many, many challenging books to read on the topics discussed above. Here is a short list of books that complement those discussed in this chapter.

Charlotte Bunch and Niamh Reilly's *Demanding Accountability: The Global Campaign and Vienna Tribunal for Women's Human Rights* (1994), is a book that begins to answer some of the questions raised in this chapter. This and other relevant materials are published by the Center for Women's Global Leadership at Rutgers University.

A group of women who publish together under the name of the Asian Women United Coalition of California have put together an excellent and imaginative collection, *Making Waves: An Anthology of Writings By and About Asian American Women* (1989). In many direct and indirect ways, they address racism, particularly against Asians and Asian-Americans, sexism, and other prejudices. This is a model of writing and publication for many groups of women.

Robin Warshaw's *I Never Called It Rape* (1988), is a classic in women's studies. The groundbreaking data come from American college campuses and *Ms. Magazine's* report on recognizing, fighting, and surviving date and acquaintance rape.

Victoria Burbank, *Fighting Women: Anger and Aggression in Aboriginal Australia* (1994), presents a picture of contemporary Aboriginal women and a powerful new perspective on anger and aggression within and between genders. She shows how violence and anger may be found in all human societies, but the expressions are culturally constructed. Here in this community women fight almost as much as do men, but they do so strategically. Victoria says there are no battered women in the sense we know them.

Sex workers and feminists met in a classic confrontation at a conference in 1985 to hash out their differences. The sex workers defended their dignity, their job choices, their right to work; the feminists listened and countered the arguments. The Women's Press of Toronto published a riveting transcript of their discussions. Laurie Bell edited the material; it's called *Good Girls/Bad Girls: Sex Trade Workers and Feminists Face to Face* (1987). To hear the stories of women in the sex trade from around the world, you must read Gail Pheterson's book, *A Vindication of the Rights of Whores* (1989). This is the first crosscultural anthology of the voices of prostitutes around the world. It is the result of fifteen years of activism on behalf of "whores" everywhere. The range and depth of this collection is sometimes depressing but always breathtaking. Shannon Bell has written a fascinating postmodern analysis, *Reading, Writing, and Rewriting the Prostitute Body* (1994).

A number of women have written accounts of female genital surgeries in Africa. The personal and professional involvements of their authors in the subject make these books worth reading: Olayinka Koso-Thomas, *The Circumcision of Women* (1987); and Hanny Lightfoot-Klein, *Prisoners of Ritual: An Odyssey into Female Genital Mutilation in Africa* (1989).

The most riveting account of China's one-child policy I have read is Steven Mosher's *A Mother's Ordeal: One Woman's Fight Against China's One-Child Policy* (1993). Chi An (not her real name) tells her extraordinary story to anthropologist Steven Mosher. Trained as a nurse, she performed abortions; she was forced to have an abortion when she became pregnant after the birth of her first child, a son. She was coerced into signing a one-child agreement, yet her work assignment was to manipulate other women into signing and complying. She wanted to be a loyal citizen of China; Chi An was the first woman to seek asylum in the United States because she refused to abort a pregnancy. What a story.

Elisabeth Bumiller, a reporter for the *Washington Post,* spent three and one-half years traveling around India and talking to women. If 400 million women living in another, very different, culture can be represented with some accuracy, clarity, and grace, then Bumiller did it: *May You Be the Mother of a Hundred Sons: A Journey Among the Women of India* (1990). John Stratton Hawley edited a collection of scholarly articles about sati, *Sati: The Blessing and the Curse* (1994). There are many meanings of sati in India and in the West, in literature, art, opera, religion, psychology, economics, and politics. Sati is one of those textbook test cases of cultural relativity and the treatment of women.

Faye Ginsberg and Rayna Rapp are the editors of *Conceiving the New World Order: The Global Politics of Reproduction* (1995). This collection of articles may well be the most extensive and challenging coverage on the politics of reproduction from around the world you will ever find. The authors have provided much inspiration for this chapter; they take up where I left off.

Tony Whitehead and Barbara Reid edited an important and very readable volume called *Gender Constructs and Social Issues* (1992). They take the theoretical work on gender developed during the 1980s and apply it to contemporary issues ranging from genital surgeries, marital rape, and mental retardation to spouse battering and pornography. What do these anthropologists conclude: Gender is a cultural construct that varies from culture to culture; and everything is gendered—whether we talk about health care, homelessness, guns, incest, or careers.

Peggy Sanday and Ruth Goodenough edited a provocative collection of articles that challenges the notion that women are the second sex: *Beyond the Second Sex: New Directions in the Anthropology of Gender* (1990). The authors and contributors ask many of the same questions this chapter does and conclude that what happens between men and women in daily life is full of conflicts, tensions, and paradoxes. There are no easy answers here. That's the best reason to read these books.

Glossary

The purpose of this glossary is to define technical terms as well as common words with distinct meanings in anthropology or related disciplines. Official, dictionary, common-sense definitions and woman-centered definitions are included. These helpful working explanations are distilled from many sources.

abortifacients: Drugs, potions, or other substances that cause or are believed to cause a pregnancy to end. See emmenagogue.

adept: A person skilled or proficient in a special area of knowledge, wisdom, or activity. In this context, the term refers to women with spirit, spiritual, or spiritualist contacts.

affinal kin: A kinship tie that involves marriage as the defining link; this contrasts with consanguineal or blood relatives. Affinal kinspeople include spouses and all their relatives; in-laws are examples of affinal kin.

African diaspora: The dispersal of people and cultures from Africa during the last 500 years, primarily through the practices of slavery and, primarily into the New World (the Caribbean, North America and South America).

alpha male: A term used to mark the highest-ranking male in a primate group. The term is also used for the hero in romance novels.

altered state of consciousness: A state of nonordinary reality such as sleep, dreaming, coma, intoxication, trance, psychosis, deep meditation, visionary episodes, or psychedelic experiences. Altered states are induced by a variety of factors, including hypnosis, fatigue, drugs, sensory deprivation, sensory overload, organic brain injury, fasting, biofeedback, psychological stress, or communal fervor. All cultures tend to define some of these altered states of consciousness as valuable and desirable and others as negative and undesirable.

amazons: The original term probably meant "moon-woman" but now is widely used for women as warriors. In Greek legends, the writer Homer tells of Amazons who aided Troy during the Trojan wars. Portuguese explorers named the Amazon river after they encountered women warriors in Brazil. Here the word refers to oral and written traditions about women who passed for men, dressed like men, and married women, primarily in the cultures of Native North and South America. See also **two-spirits**.

amenorrhoea: Having few or no regular periods.

androgyny, androgynous: Unisex, sexual neutrality or sharing features of both male and female.

authoritative knowledge: For any particular area of social life, there are systems of knowledge, explanation, or power that become ascendant and official. Examples of this are: traditional midwives versus the "science" and technology in hospital deliveries; Papal Decrees versus common sense, revelation, or intuition.

autonomy, autonomous: Independence or freedom. May also refer to a self-governing individual or community. In writings and theories about women and women's movements, autonomy is a key concept.

berdache: A Euro-American term for socially constructed patterns of gender alternatives among some Native American societies. It usually refers to males who assume female dress, mannerisms, speech, and social roles. The Native American name for these individuals (as translated into English) is **two-spirits**.

bicultural: The idea that women live in both male culture and female culture simultaneously. This does not preclude living in other cultures as well, hence multiculturalism.

bilum, bilums: Looped string bags that are the most visible and symbolic object in women's lives in most of Melanesia.

biocultural markers: The specific times in the female life cycle in which physiology and biology intersect with cultural programming. Human cultures may mark puberty, marriage, childbirth, or menopause.

biological anthropology: A discipline that focuses on the biological evolution of humans and human ancestors, the relationship of humans to other organisms, and patterns of biological variation within and among human populations; also called physical anthropology or evolutionary biology.

bride-price, bride-wealth: Cash or other goods paid to a bride's family by the groom's family around the time of the wedding. This is generally a transaction between the bride's father and the groom's father.

burqa, burka: Facial mask worn by women in the Muslim Middle East. Burqa is the spelling of the Arabic word in Oman.

capitalism: An economic system in which investment in and ownership of the means of production, distribution, and exchange of wealth is made and maintained chiefly by private individuals or corporations. This contrasts with state-owned wealth. Capitalists are people who have capital (money, assets, land, investment, and so on).

cash crops, cash cropping: Agricultural production that is not for subsistence, family consumption, or sharing, but is grown and marketed for money. Examples of cash crops include heroin, cocaine, spices, tobacco, rubber, and cotton or other fibers.

cervix: The large round muscle between uterus and vagina; the opening or passage between them is known popularly as the "eye."

child spacing: This refers to the practices, beliefs, or desires about appropriate intervals between births. May also refer to the elapsed time between births.

circumcision (sunna): Removal of the prepuce or hood of the clitoris, with the body of the clitoris remaining intact. See also **female genital surgeries**.

clitoridectomy (excision): Removal of the clitoris and all or part of the labia minora and/or all or part of the labia majora. See also **female genital surgeries** and **infibulation**.

coitus interruptus: The technical term for "pulling out" or ending intercourse before male ejaculation. Common form of birth control.

colonialism, colony: In the last 500 years, the history of the world has been characterized by European nations that had policies (colonialism) of extending or retaining their power or authority over other areas of the world (colonies) that were unrelated to them by geography, history, language, or culture.

complementarity, complementary gender roles: The idea that the sexual division of labor between genders completes or finishes off the other part. Some theorists use the term in the sense of equality, as in two sides of a coin; others for gender separation systems of ranking and hierarchy as forms of cooperation.

conception ideologies: Belief systems about the "real" or "true" religious, political, scientific, or cultural meanings of starting a pregnancy. Belief systems about conception are a part of gender ideologies worldwide.

concubine: A term widely used in the historic and anthropological literature. Usually defined as a woman who has a relationship with a man to whom she is not married or for whom she is not the first wife. In polygamous societies, a concubine may be a secondary wife with varying legal privileges. The term also has the connotation of mistress or girlfriend; in some contexts, it may also refer to sexual slaves. Concubinage is the state of doing this. There is no equivalent status for men.

consanguineal kin: Relatives connected to us by ties of blood; people related through parents, siblings, or both.

consensual unions: Female–male partnerships with children that resemble marriage but exist outside legal or religious ratification. These may also be called visiting relations or common-law marriages.

consort, consort pair, consortship: Terms from primate studies that indicate an exclusive although not permanent mating relationship between female and male adult primates. Sometimes such couples are called a pair bond, and the process of getting together is called a **courtship** or **pair-bonding**.

copulation: Another name for sexual intercourse.

courtship, courting: The time period during the life cycle and the social practices among animals (including humans) in which males present their case for mating and in which females solicit, reward, and establish appropriate responses.

couvade: Childbirth customs that involve fathers in the delivery or credit them with empathetic involvement.

crone: "Wise woman." A word recycled by the women's movement and feminist spirituality to indicate a status and position for older women where no term existed previously. Scholars have more reason to believe that the word comes from Greek, *chronios,* meaning long lasting, than from the seventeenth-century male slang word "crony."

cross-dressing: Widespread customs in human cultures of adopting the clothing, hairstyles, or other social attributes of other genders in daily, ceremonial, or ritual contexts.

cultural relativism: A viewpoint in anthropology that holds that the norms and values of each culture or subculture have their own validity and cannot be used as a standard for evaluating other cultures; that while human cultures are very different from each other, they are all equally valuable.

differential reproductive strategies, differential sexual strategies: The Darwinian notion that females and males act differently from each other in sex and reproduction, and that males and females have separate strategies for maximizing investments in and outcomes of mating.

distaff: A cleft stick used to hold wool or flax thread when spinning was done by hand.

The term came to stand for women's work and eventually for the female side of families.

diviner, divination: A diviner is a person who has nonordinary techniques for acquiring knowledge or information in circumstances for which empirical data does not exist.

double day: An entrenched division of labor by sex in which women are in charge of children, household, and domestic lifestyles, in addition to any full-time or part-time wage-labor jobs. See also **second shift,** the term popularized in the United States.

doula: A Greek word meaning "a woman who serves women" or a helper in doing women's work. A doula is an experienced woman, a friend, or a close female relative. Such women are also called childbirth companions or labor assistants, although they may provide service for other life stages and conditions.

dowry: A payment in money, land, or other goods to the groom or groom's family by the bride's family.

dowry death: A common term in parts of India that refers to husbands or family members killing or trying to kill a wife in connection with her dowry or another dowry they may hope for after her death.

embodied knowledge: Information, intuition, or knowledge that comes from direct personal experiences and is generally coded or perceived in parts of the body or mind.

emmenagogue: Drugs, potions, or other substances used to bring on a period or to establish regular menstrual cycles; this may also mean ending a pregnancy in its early stages.

empower, empowerment: Technically this means to authorize, enable, or permit, to give authority or power to. In contemporary women's groups, this concept carries the meaning of feeling and acknowledging personal power and acting out of that recognition.

estrus, estrous cycle: Estrus is a noun; estrous is an adjective. Technical terms for ovulation and the external markings in female primates. The skin of the genital area swells and turns pink, hence we say, "in the pink" or "pink ladies." Occurs normally midway in the thirty-five day menstrual cycle and signals ovulation and sexual interest for primate females. Corresponds to "in heat" or "horny."

ethnocentric, ethnocentrism: Means "group-centered." The tendency to use the norms, values, and beliefs of one's own culture or subculture as the basis to judge others. This concept is often contrasted with cultural relativism.

ethos: The ideas or qualities that hold a group together, that give congruency, consistency, and integration to cultural and social systems: as in the emotional color, texture, tone, or consciousness, the soul or genius of a culture or community.

Eurocentric, Eurocentrism: One of the ways to be ethnocentric; this one refers to the notion that Europe, a small geographic region and peninsula of Asia whose peoples and ideologies experienced rapid expansion during the last 500 years, is really the pinnacle of human evolution and world culture.

evolution: Systematic change through time, especially with reference to biological change for organisms and cultural change among social systems.

exchange value work: The production of commodities or services for sale, for the market; work as the exchange of goods or services for money or other financial considerations.

family wage, family wage laws, family wage ideology: Social, business, and legal customs formed around the belief that male workers are paid to support a wife and their children. Young, single women are not paid the same as men; they are not assumed to be supporting families. Married women are not assumed to work or to need other than a husband's income. This idea originated in industrial, capitalist societies in nineteenth-century Europe.

female genital surgeries: Practices in Africa and parts of the Middle East in which part or most of female external genitalia are removed. The extent and results vary. For specific kinds, see **circumcision, infibulation.** Also called female genital mutilation.

female mate selection: A concept proposed by Charles Darwin as one of the major mechanisms of natural selection and the evolution of species. Females of animal species exercise their personal choices among competing males.

feminist spirituality: This term refers to new or redefined patterns of women-centered spirituality and religious expressions in contemporary Euro-American societies that find roots in ancient practices and beliefs as alternatives to world religions. See also **Pagan path** or **Goddess path.**

feminization of poverty: A term for the social and economic conditions characterized by women-headed households with few or no legal protections, double-day housework, and child care, combined with low wages in the formal or informal economic sectors. Such female-headed households are regarded as the largest definable group of poor people worldwide. Also called the pauperization of women.

fictive kinship: Common customs in human societies for using biological relations as a metaphor for creating formal and informal connections. Includes adoption, fosterage, godparents, sisterhood or brotherhood, "families we choose," and other arrangements.

First Nations: The name Native Americans use to refer to the cultures of this hemisphere who inhabited North America and South America before Europeans arrived, and who observe tribal traditions and ethnic identities in contemporary multicultural settings.

food cycle: The activities of making food: field preparation, planting, weeding, harvesting, storing, transporting, delivering, preparing, processing, serving, consuming.

foraging: An economic system of gathering or collecting foods and processing them. Also called gathering–hunting or hunting–gathering.

formal work sector: The part of the economy included in official statistics such as the GNP (Gross National Product) and for which national records are kept and reported. Includes wages, investments, land transactions, and other economic activities regulated by national laws. Does not include housework, child care, barter, or work done in the informal sector.

fostering/fosterage: A form of adoption. Taking care of and raising the offspring of other biological parents. Called "borrowing" in the West Indies. See **fictive kinship.**

Fourth World: The people and groups descended from empires and tribal cultures that existed before world colonialism. Includes indigenous peoples. See also **Third World** and **First Nations.**

gatekeeper, gatekeepers: A term used to indicate any person within an institution who controls access to social, educational, economic, medical, or other kinds of resources or who controls the policies of access or exclusion.

gender attribution: A term that refers to the biological, social, or material criteria people of a social group use to identify each other as males, females, or any other culturally defined gender category. Usually assigned at birth.

gender identity: A term that refers to an individual's own feeling of whether he or she is a woman or man or other. This personal identity is believed to be formed during the first three or four years of life and exists regardless of genetic makeup or other social definitions of sex or gender.

gender ideology, gender ideologies: These are belief systems that encompass the meanings of male, female, masculine, feminine, sex, and reproduction in any given culture. These might include prescriptions and sanctions for appropriate male and female behavior or cultural rationalizations and explanations for social and political relationships between males and females.

gender role: This term describes what men and women actually do, their activity patterns, social relations and behaviors in specific cultural settings. Sometimes referred to as sex roles.

gender separation systems: Historically based styles of living and social organizations in which the lives of women and men are substantially segregated. This usually includes housing, economics, religion, and leisure activities. May also be called sexual segregation systems.

genital mutilation: See **female genital surgeries, clitoridectomy,** and **infibulation.**

Goddess Path, Goddess spirituality: These terms refer to new or redefined patterns of women-centered spirituality and religious expressions in contemporary Euro-American societies, which find roots in ancient practices and beliefs as alternatives to world religions. See also **Pagan Path** and **feminist spirituality.**

grassroots, grassroots organizations: The term refers to small-scale social movements formed by ordinary or common people, distinct from the leadership of elites of a country or region, often in rural areas away from metropolitan centers of power. In women's culture, grassroots organizations typically grow up where national and local governments cannot, do not, or will not provide basic social services for women and children.

grooming, social grooming: A term used in primate studies for cleaning, handling, or manipulating the skin, hair, or fur of another member of one's own species. Grooming serves functions of communication, sociability, and group cohesion.

gynemimesis: Derived from the Greek words *gyne,* woman, and *mimos,* mime or mimicking. Refers to men who act, dress, and live as females in the manner their culture prescribes.

gynocracy, gynocratic, gynocentric: Derived from the Greek words *gyne* or woman and *kracia* or government. Refers to societies in which women provide primary leadership or share in partnerships with men. The historic existence of such societies is an unresolved issue. See also **matriarchy** and **matristic.**

harem: Arabic for "forbidden." Refers to Muslim practices of identifying one part of a household as the residence of women. The term harem also refers to all women, mothers, sisters, wives, concubines, daughters, entertainers, slaves, and servants within a gender-segregated household. Often used in reference to animals in which the group consists of a number of females, their offspring, and one adult male. Sometimes defined in dictionaries as one male heading, leading, and mating a number of females.

head of household: A term for the adult who controls the distribution of family resources and the labor of family members. In patrilineal systems, the head of household is assumed to be any husband or the oldest male. Women as single heads of households are the fastest-growing family form worldwide.

hegemony: The term for the form of ideological domination based on the consent of the dominated, a consent gained by the diffusion of the worldview of the dominant class.

heterarchy: An idea of social formations characterized by multiple sources of status and power. The opposite of hierarchy.

hijras: Groups of men in India who form an institutionalized third gender usually marked by adoption of female dress, social roles, and work, as well as ritual responsibilities and male genital surgery.

hominid: Primates who walked upright (bipedal); this includes all modern human beings and our direct ancestors.

homunculi, homunculus: A conception ideology in Europe during the fifteenth, sixteenth, and seventeenth centuries. Medical, religious, and other male authorities believed that men's semen contained very tiny, fully formed babies called homunculi, (plural) which men deposited into women at intercourse. The homunculus (singular) merely grew larger; it acquired no attributes or qualities from its female hostess during the nine months it took to grow to newborn size.

household worker: A person who works in other people's homes; an employee recruited from outside the employing household to perform status enhancing and reproductive work. Also called servant, domestic, domestic worker, nanny, maid, housekeeper, menial, or retainer. The opposite is master.

housewife: In medieval times in Europe, the word denoted female coordinator or organizer of work activities in large estates. Only much later did it come to mean a married woman working without pay in small-scale domestic settings. See **hussy**.

housewifization: Using wives as the model for female work or labor in contemporary economic systems; used especially in Marxist and feminist analyses of colonialism and capitalism.

houseyard: A West Indian residential unit and female social space; a cluster or compound of buildings with a matrifocal head.

hussy: An abbreviation of housewife. Like many words in English relating to women, it lost the connotation of responsibility and status and acquired the connotation of "loose" sexual behavior.

infanticide: A term for killing infants after birth.

infibulation (or pharaonic circumcision): Removal of the clitoris, the labia minora, and parts of the labia majora, as in the clitoridectomy. In infibulation, the remaining sides of the vulva are stitched together to close up the vagina, except for a small opening for urine and menses.

informal work sector: Activities outside the formal economy not counted or listed in national statistics of productivity or regulated by national laws. Examples include street vending, subsistence farming, craft production, cottage industries, and selling sex.

intersexes: A category of phenotypic or biological sex in addition to the dichotomous categories of male and female. In some contexts, intersexed individuals may be called transsexuals or transgendered.

kinaaldá: Navaho puberty ceremony for girls at menarche.

Kurgans, Kurgan culture: A name given by Marija Gimbutas to the earliest group of Indo-European speaking cultures who spread into and overwhelmed the Neolithic cultures of Old Europe from 4300 to 2800 B.C. Based on comparative linguistics, mythology, and archaeology, this culture is thought to be patrilineal, pastoral, mobile, and warring, with a pantheon of male gods.

labia majora, labia minora: The inner folds of skin or "lips" in the vulva or external genitalia of females.

lactation: The major characteristic of mammals in suckling or nursing their infants and young, using special glands humans call breasts.

letdown reflex: A psychological and physical response in women during lactation and in nursing offspring; it is triggered by hormones and releases the richest portions of the milk. Women often report pleasurable sensations, a kind of mild trance state, sensuality, or heightened awareness.

lithotomy position: The physical position for giving birth to human infants in which the woman lies on her back with her legs in the air. This position is favored in the United States but rarely known or practiced elsewhere.

longhouse: The architectural structure occupied by the **matrifocal** and **matrilineal** household in Iroquois society.

macho, machismo: A Spanish word for the belief system about men's relationship to women in Latin America or other Spanish-speaking, Catholic countries. Derived from the word *macho* meaning "animal," macho refers to the qualities of a "real man." A male-superiority complex. See **gender ideology** and **marianismo.**

maid, maiden: Originally meant a girl in England in the tenth century A.D., then young unmarried women, then female virgins. By the fourteenth century, a maid was a domestic servant: young, female, and unmarried. Virginity was a condition of employment.

maidenhood: The culturally constructed period between menarche and marriage, motherhood or other adult statuses.

marianismo: A belief system about women's relationship to men in Latin America and other Spanish-speaking or Catholic countries. Derived from the Virgin Mary in Christian theology; promotes a sacred rationale for female subordination and suffering. See also **gender ideology and macho, machismo.**

maternal depletion: A term for the severe breakdown of health in women caused by chronic deprivation of food or other necessary resources, frequent childbirth, or sustained nursing.

maternal mortality rates: A statistic calculated on the basis of how many women die during pregnancy or while giving birth, expressed as the number of deaths per 100,000 births per year.

matriarchy: Technically this means rule by mothers. In folk beliefs, it is women's control over governments; the historic existence of matriarchies is widely debated. Anthropologists find no association between matriarchies and matrilineal descent. See **matristic** or **gynocracy.**

matrifocal: Mother-centered families, households, or genealogies; groups centered on the primary links between a mother and her children. The basic pattern in primate societies. A common pattern in human societies that may co-occur within a number of different marriage patterns and gender arrangements.

matrilineal, matriline, matriliny: Kinship systems and associated customs in which both males and females trace their descent and inheritance through their mothers and through a female line and female ancestors. Approximately one-third of the world's societies can be considered matrilineal; this pattern is often associated with horticultural societies. See **patrilineal.**

matrilocal residence patterns: A common system in the world where a young couple live with the bride's parents or family members after their wedding. This means the groom must move into his wife's household or nearby. Matrilocal may also mean the home territory of the matrilineal kin group, family, or tribe. See also **patrilocal** and **neolocal residence patterns.**

matristic, matristic society: A term for cultures that probably had matrilineal kinship and a kind of "partnership" with men; women are honored in various practical ways, but do not subjugate men. Believed to have existed in the past.

matron: The term used for senior Iroquois women who were leaders in clan, lineage, longhouse, and political affairs. In the United States, matron is a title for a type of work status often associated with discipline, order, and cleanliness.

means of production: The tools or resources a person or group needs to earn a living. These include but are not limited to land, education, bank loans, draft animals, tools, inheritance, or capital for investment.

medicalization of childbirth: A system of authoritative knowledge in which pregnancy and childbirth are believed to be a kind of illness, pathology, or medical problem, and in which women are "delivered" by specialists who use technology in hospitals.

menarche: The technical term for the first menstrual period and the beginning of monthly cycling. Menarche or first menses is marked in some ceremonial way in many cultures to indicate a girl's sexual or reproductive maturity.

menstrual hut: A practice in tribal cultures (largely precolonial) in which menstruating females were secluded in separate places for the duration of their periods. It is unclear from existing records how women evaluated or responded to this practice.

menstrual taboos: Widespread although not universal beliefs about the dangers that menstruating people represent to themselves and others. Also includes the precautions one must take to protect oneself and others. May also be called female pollution beliefs.

midwife, midwives, midwifery: From Anglo-Saxon meaning "wise woman" or "witch." Generally means women who serve as birth attendants. The most common kind of healer in traditional human societies.

missionary position: A popular term for beliefs about (or the practice of) a male-on-top position for vaginal intercourse. The term reflects the legal, jural, religious, and moral underpinning for defining culturally sanctioned sexuality.

monandry: The most common form of marriage in the world. It refers to the practice in which a woman takes a man as spouse or spouse emulator.

mother-right: An old-fashioned term for matrilineal descent. Popularized by Bachofen, who said that matrilineal kinship combined with matriarchy was the universal first stage of human development. Lewis Henry Morgan, Frederick Engels, and Karl Marx used mother-right for the stage of human history that preceded patrilineal descent and patriarchies. Bronislaw Malinowski used the term for Trobriand legal systems and matrilineal clans.

myth: For some, myth is a synonym for error, lie, or fallacy. In anthropology, however, this is a very important word for the sacred narratives that answer the all-encompassing questions about life and death. Such questions always include: Where does life come from and how is it created? Why do bad things happen to good people and good things happen to bad people? What is the spirit world like and how can we get in touch with it? Myths are a major element in the women's movements and women's spirituality.

natal family: The family into which we were born or adopted.

natural attitude: A common belief system marked by the idea that there are two and only two genders, indicated by genitals, assignment at birth, and identification in childhood. "Natural" means that religious, scientific, or other authoritative knowledge systems have provided irreducible categories believed to be based or found in nature.

neolithic: "New Stone Age"; Refers to the period of time after 10,000 B.C. when many human groups settled in villages, used ground stone tools, and produced food by cultivation of crops and the domestication of animals. Scholars often refer to it as a revolution because humans developed a radically new relationship to the environment.

neolocal residence patterns: Customs in which the newly married couple establishes a residence apart from either set of relatives. These independent and privatized households

are characteristic of industrial and postindustrial Western countries. They are the residence patterns typical of nuclear families in the United States. See **matrilocal** or **patrilocal residence patterns.**

Old Europe: The cultures that inhabited Europe from the seventh to the third millennia B.C. (between 6500 and 3500 B.C.); Neolithic Europe before the coming of the Indo-Europeans. Some scholars believe these cultures were **matristic, matrilineal,** and characterized by cults, temples, and sacred scripts centered on Goddess worship.

omnivorous: Animal species like humans who are known to eat virtually anything.

ovulation: The point in the monthly cycle of female mammals in which the eggs leave the ovary for a trip to the uterus.

Pagan Path, neo-paganism: These terms refer to new or redefined patterns of women-centered spirituality and religious expressions in contemporary Euro-American societies which find roots in ancient practices and beliefs as alternatives to world religions. See also **Goddess Path** or **feminist spirituality.**

pair-bond, pair-bonding: A term from primate studies for a female and a male who go off together for a while and form a temporary couple. See **consort** and **courtship.**

parental investment: Behavior toward one's offspring that increases their chances of survival. May include behaviors that favor some offspring at the cost of investing in other offspring. Assumed to differ from females and males in any given species, hence the terms male parental investment and female parental investment.

pastoralists, pastoralism: Societies that depend on herding and breeding animals like horses, cattle, sheep, goats, camels. Because they must move their herds in relationship to the environment, they are usually mobile or seasonally nomadic. Pastoralists generally have a bad reputation with settled agriculturalists, on whom they prey for harvested crops, and with feminists because their kinship systems are typically **patrilineal, patrilocal** or **patriarchal.**

patriarchy, patriarchal: Cultures in which males as fathers or husbands are assumed to be in charge, official heads of household, where descent and inheritance are traced through the male line and where men are generally in control of the distribution of family resources. Also refers to the extensions of kinship into **gender ideologies** and a world system of domination of men over women.

patrilineal, patriline, patriliny: Kinship systems and associated customs in which both males and females trace their descent and inheritance through their fathers and a male line and male ancestors. See **matrilineal.**

patrilocal residence patterns: A common system in the world, where a young couple lives with the groom's parents or family members after the wedding. This means the bride must move into the household of her husband's family. Patrilocal may also mean the home territory of the husband's family, kin or tribe. See **matrilocal** or **neolocal residence patterns.**

periods, periodicity: Menstruation and the relationship of time, the lunar calendar, and menstrual cycles to pregnancy and safe periods to enhance or avoid conception.

pink ladies, "in the pink": See **estrus, estrous cycles.**

pollution beliefs: See **menstrual taboos.**

polyandry, fraternal polyandry: From the Greek words for "many" and "men." A woman is wife to more than one man at a time. In fraternal polyandry, her husbands are two, three, or more brothers. Polyandry is the rarest system of getting married in the world.

polygamy: From the Greek words for "many" plus "mate." This is a general term for all forms of plural marriage in which a person has more than one spouse or spouse emulator at one time. This includes polyandry and polygyny, as well as systems of concubinage in which the legal standing of women differs from each other and from their husbands.

polygyny: From the Greek words for "many" and "women." A marriage custom in which a man has more than one wife at one time.

possession, spirit possession, possession cults: This is the idea that the human body can be entered and owned or used by a supernatural personality in addition to its own ordinary personality. Possession states are typically part of women's religions, women's resistance to organized religion and a characteristic form of expressing spirituality for women.

postmodern, postmodernism: Usually refers to the emotional, social and intellectual currents that began in the 1950s and 1960s in capitalist Western countries and are characterized by such concepts as pluralisms, multiplicity, differences, ambiguities, fragmentation, and discontinuities. Generally thought to be cultural-ideological domains in which older belief systems, often referred to as narratives, are unstable, disintegrating, or fail to explain the qualities of human existence. Postmodernist critiques and writings highlight issues about power, desire, ethnicity, gender, sex, and race.

postpartum sex taboo: A widespread custom in which women who have given birth (or men as new fathers) are forbidden to have intercourse for a culturally specific period of time and for an established set of reasons. Like other customs surrounding women, it is unclear if this is a restriction or a blessing.

production, productive work: Work for pay in cash or kind. This includes market production with a real or potential exchange value and subsistence, home, agricultural production with use-value.

prostitute, prostitution: A prostitute is a person, usually a woman, who exchanges goods or money for the service of sex. Some synonyms: call girl, streetwalker, hooker, courtesan, trollop, whore, harlot, hussy, strumpet. See **sex work.**

public space, private space: Cultural definitions about how physical and social spaces are defined: who is allowed where and under what circumstances. Usually, rules differ by gender and may involve a range of customs. See also **social space.**

purdah: This is a term from Hindi, Urdu, Persian, and related languages in South Asia that means "curtain." Today it refers to the practices of seclusion for women in Islamic and Hindu cultures, including harems or women's quarters, the screens placed in households to prevent men from seeing women, or the veils used for the streets and other public places or other forms for enforcing standards of female modesty.

reproduction, reproductive work: Childbearing/childrearing responsibilities and extended or associated domestic tasks done by women. This refers not only to sexual and biological reproduction, but the work of maintaining and caring for others.

residence patterns: Where a couple resides after marriage (or its local equivalent) has extremely important consequences for the status and life-trajectory of the bride. Postmarital residence patterns are strongly connected to gender ideologies and treatment of women in human cultures. See **matrilocal** and **patrilocal residence patterns** or **neolocal residence patterns.**

rites of passage: This term refers to the ceremonies and rituals that mark the passage of a person through life stages. Although cultures may recognize a variety of stages in life, the generally acknowledged ones are birth, puberty, marriage, and death.

sati: A set of customs in certain castes and areas of India that prescribed the burning of widows on their husband's funeral pyre.

second shift: A concept popular in the United States that refers to the entrenched division of labor by sex in which women are in charge of children, household, and domestic lifestyles, in addition to any full-time or part-time wage-labor jobs. See also **double day,** a term often used internationally.

sexual division of labor: A universal, pan-human, and time-honored practice of *Homo sapiens* in which necessary work and tasks are divided up according to gender. Men get some of the jobs and women get some of the jobs.

sexual segregation systems: See **gender separation systems.**

sexual selection, female sexual selection, male sexual selection: In all animal groups (including humans), potential partners are believed to be actively, rather than randomly, choosing each other from within a breeding population. This theory assumes that certain criteria for selecting a mate carry more weight than do others, that social competition and cooperation are at work, that these collective actions affect the evolving characteristics of the species, and that females and males have different strategies.

sexual slavery, female sexual slavery: This includes involuntary prostitution, incest, kidnapping, the sale of women through marriage contracts, or other circumstances where women or girls cannot change the immediate conditions of their lives, where they cannot get out of a captive state, and where they are subject to sexual violence and/or exploitation.

sex work, sex workers, sex industry: A form of productive work in marketing and selling sex. See **prostitute**.

shaman, shamanism: A shaman is a spiritual specialist adept at trance, divination, and curing. She or he derives power directly from a supernatural source, usually through mystic experiences and apprenticeships. An important part of their work is psychic journeying and performance of public ceremonials for healing.

social birth: The event, ceremony, ritual, or marked point in time when an infant child takes on or is given a cultural identity. This is usually different from biological birth.

social paternity: The ascription and assignment of the status of father to a male. May or may not be connected to biological fatherhood.

social space: Cultural definitions about social interactions, who may do what with whom and when; cultural definitions about roles and appropriate behaviors. See also **public space**.

spermicide: Any substance that kills sperm; a form of birth control.

spinsters: A common term for unmarried women in many cultures where making cloth

was a primary contribution to households. This is an example of work attached to marital status for females.

spiritualism, spiritualist: A set of beliefs and practices around the idea that spirits of dead people, surviving after their mortal life, can and do communicate with living people, especially through a person who is unusually sensitive to their influence. Such a person may be called a medium or channeler.

status hierarchy: A term used in primate studies to refer to ranking systems evident in the interactions of individuals. These complicated systems seem different for males and for females, and appear to require consistent negotiations, alliance formation, and social strategies. This is not the same thing as winner-take-all, dog-eat-dog, survival of the fittest, or pecking orders.

third sex: A convenient category to use in discussing structured, culturally patterned systems in various human cultures where men take on females' dress and work or where females take on males' dress and work, or where conventional and dichotomous gender systems cannot account for individuals or groups of people who live apart from them. See **two-spirits, hijras**.

Third World: A term adopted by post colonial and nonaligned nations of Asia, Africa, and Latin America after World War II to distinguish themselves from the "First World," the Western democracies and former colonial powers, and the "Second World," or the Soviet-bloc nations. See **Fourth World**.

transsexuals: Refers to individuals who somehow change into or move to the "opposite sex" or into a third sex; a type of border crossing. There is no firm agreement on the meaning of this term. For example, the term transsexuals may include anatomical males or anatomical females who believe that a person of the opposite sex lives in their bodies; it may include intersexed or transgendered individuals. Responses include cross-dressing, assumption of alternative lifestyles, and in some cases surgical, hormonal, or other body alterations. May include reassignment of biological sex or social gender.

two-spirits, two-spirited: This is a generic term for people who are lesbian, gay, transgendered, cross-dressers, transvestites, transsexuals, or otherwise have "marked" lives in the bands, tribes, or nations of Native North America where concepts of multiple genders occur.

use value: Services and products made and consumed within families that do not have a monetary value and are not sold. They have "value" only in private domestic settings.

Venus figurines: Three-dimensional sculptures of faceless and footless females with large breasts and hips, sometimes stomachs swollen with pregnancy, periods, or menopause. Most date to a narrow time period 25,000 to 23,000 years ago in western and central Europe and southern Russia. What they meant to the people who made them is not clear. Suggestions include fertility symbols, emblems of group identity, and statues of early goddesses.

virgin: *Random House Dictionary:* "1. a girl or woman who has never had sexual intercourse; 2. an unmarried girl or woman; 3. Ecclesiastical: an unmarried religious woman, especially a saint; 4. the Virgin, Mary the mother of Christ; 5. a female animal that has never copulated; 6. a boy or man who has never had sexual intercourse; 7. an unfertilized insect."

virginity complex: Widespread belief systems that center on the ideological and symbolic separation of female sexuality from motherhood and the requirement that a female cannot

have intercourse before her marriage ceremony. Often associated with the world religions, patriarchies, and belief systems centered on concepts anthropologists identify as honor and shame.

visiting relations: A term for a woman and a man in a relationship, often long-term or parental, who do not live together in the same household. See **consensual unions**.

wean, weaning: To accustom a child or other young animal to food other than its mother's milk; to withdraw or withhold suckling as a mark of a specific developmental stage in infant growth; to withdraw something pleasurable from a dependent creature.

Western culture: A practical shorthand term for European societies, European-derived, and Euro-American-centered cultural traditions that spread during colonial expansion of the last 500 years. Includes the cultural constructions inherited and reformulated from Greco-Roman cultures, Judeo-Christian traditions, and beliefs in personality, democracy, sexual division of labor, or other systems of thought and practice developed within these cultural systems.

wet-nurses, wet-nursing: A common set of customs in which parents place their newborn child into the care of a lactating woman not its biological mother.

wife battering: This is a category of abuse of women more severe than **wife beating**; it includes the possibilities of severe injuries, disabilities, and death. It does not matter whether or not the partners are officially married.

wife beating: Defined as a man deliberately inflicting physical pain on a woman within a male–female relationship. It does not matter whether or not the partners are officially married.

witch: From Anglo-Saxon and medieval English, meaning "to see or to know" or "knowing one." The word has complex and overlapping applications. (1) In anthropology the generic term witch refers to people believed to have the psychic power to cause harm, evil or death. (2) In western European traditions, witches were generally thought to be older women, often persecuted or killed by church or state, believed to possess powers or knowledge to hurt others even if they themselves are unaware of this power. (3) Contemporary witches, both female and male, who use older European traditions of knowledge, spirituality, rituals and healing; an example is Wicca.

Wok Meri: Neo-Melanesian word that means "the work of women." These female-centered groups operate savings, banking and exchange systems in both formal and informal economic sectors in the Highlands of New Guinea.

womanism, womanist movement: African American feminists use these terms for contemporary spiritual movements that draw on such sources as literature, African American folklore, Christianity, and feminism, and which look to adaptive and creative forms of partnerships with men.

women's culture: A term used to describe female-centered values, activities, and experiences apart from the general culture in which females and males both participate. Women's culture is not a subculture. See **bicultural.**

work: Any kind of labor or activity that has some recognizable or measurable social value, however these may be expressed. Includes work as production, reproduction, status enhancement, and moral-morale building. See **use value** and **exchange value work.**

world religions: Religions with a worldwide spread through military, economic, migratory, colonial, evangelical, or other forms of historic expansion. The main ones are Christianity (including Catholicism, Protestantism, and Pentecostalism), Islam, Buddhism, Hinduism, Confucianism, and Judaism.

#

Abu-Lughod, Lila 1993 *Writing Women's Worlds: Bedouin Stories.* Berkeley: University of California Press.

—— 1986 *Veiled Sentiments: Honor and Poetry in a Bedouin Society.* Berkeley: University of California Press.

—— 1985 "A Community of Secrets: The Separate World of Bedouin Women." *Signs* 10(4):637–57.

Adler, Margot 1986 *Drawing Down the Moon: Witches, Druids, Goddess-Worshippers, and Other Neo-Pagans in America Today.* Boston: Beacon Press.

Agostin, Marjorie (Ed.) 1993 *Surviving Beyond Fear: Women, Children and Human Rights in Latin America.* Fredonia New York: White Pine Press.

Albers, Patricia and Beatrice Medicine (Eds.) 1983 *The Hidden Half: Studies of Plains Indian Women.* Washington, D.C.: University Press of America.

Allen, Paula Gunn 1989 "Lesbians in American Indian Cultures." In Martin Duberman, Martha Vicinus, and George Chauncey (Eds.). *Hidden from History: Reclaiming the Gay and Lesbian Past.* New York: Meridian, 106–17.

—— 1986 *The Sacred Hoop.* Boston: Beacon.

—— 1991 *Grandmothers of the Light: A Medicine Women's Sourcebook.* Boston: Beacon Press.

Altmann, Jeanne 1980 *Baboon Mothers and Infants.* Cambridge MA: Harvard University Press.

Amadiume, Ifi 1987 *Male Daughters, Female Husbands: Gender and Sex in an African Society.* London: Zed Books.

Anagnost, Anna 1989 "Transformations of Gender in Modern China." In Morgan 1989:313–42.

Ardener, Shirley (Ed.) 1978 *Defining Females: The Nature of Women in Society.* New York: John Wiley and Sons.

—— (Ed.) 1975 *Perceiving Women.* London: Malaby Press.

Asian Women United Coalition of California (Eds.) 1989 *Making Waves: An Anthology of Writings By and About Asian American Women.* New York: Beacon Press.

Bachofen, J. J. 1967 *Myth, Religion and Mother Right: Selected Writings of J. J. Bachofen.* Introduction by Joseph Campbell. Translated by Ralph Manheim. Princeton New York: Princeton University Press.

Barry, Kathleen 1984 *Female Sexual Slavery.* New York: New York University Press.

Bateson, Gregory 1958 *Naven*. 2d ed. Stanford: Stanford University Press.

Bateson, Mary Catherine 1984 *With a Daughter's Eye: A Memoir of Margaret Mead and Gregory Bateson*. New York: William Morrow.

——— 1989 *Composing a Life*. New York: Plume.

Bell, Diane 1993 *Daughters of the Dreaming*. 2d ed. Minneapolis: University of Minnesota Press.

Bell, Diane 1987 "The Politics of Separation." In Strathern 1987:112–129.

Bell, Laurie (Ed.) 1987 *Good Girls/Bad Girls: Sex Trade Workers and Feminists Face to Face*. Toronto: Women's Press.

Bell, Shannon 1994 *Reading, Writing, and Rewriting the Prostitute Body*. Bloomington: Indiana University Press.

Bellman, Beryl 1979 "The Social Organization of Knowledge in Kpelle Ritual." In Jules-Rosette 1979:39–56.

Benedict, Ruth 1934 *Patterns of Culture*. New York: Mentor.

——— 1934 *Zuni Mythology*. 2 vols. New York: Columbia University Contributions to Anthropology No. 21.

——— 1923 "The Concept of the Guardian Spirit in North America." *Memoirs of the American Anthropological Association* No. 29.

Bennett, Lynn 1983 *Dangerous Wives, Sacred Sisters: Social and Symbolic Roles of High Caste Women in Nepal*. New York: Columbia University Press.

Bennholdt-Thomsen, Veronika 1988 "Why do housewives continue to be created in the Third World too?" In Mies et al. 1988:159-167.

Beyene, Yewoubdar 1989 *From Menarche to Menopause: Reproductive Lives of Peasant Women in Two Cultures*. Albany: State University of New York Press.

Blackwood, Evelyn (Ed.) 1985 "Anthropology and Homosexual Behavior." *Journal of Homosexuality* 11(3/4).

——— 1985 "Breaking the Mirror: The Construction of Lesbianism and the Anthropological Discourse on Homosexuality." In Blackwood 1985:1–15.

——— 1984 "Sexuality and Gender in Certain Native American Tribes: The Case of Cross-gender Females." *Signs* 10:27–42.

Bledsoe, Caroline 1980 *Women and Marriage in Kpelle Society*. Palo Alto: Stanford University Press.

Blumberg, Joan 1989 *Fasting Girls: The Surprising History of Anorexia Nervosa*. New York: Plume.

Boddy, Janice 1991 "Body Politics: Continuing the Anticircumcision Crusade." *Medical Anthropology Quarterly* 5(1):15–17.

Bolin, Anne 1988 *In Search of Eve: Transsexual Rites of Passage*. South Hadley MA: Bergin and Garvey.

Bornstein, Kate 1994 *Gender Outlaw: On Men, Women and the Rest of Us*. New York: Routledge.

Boserup, Ester 1970 *Woman's Role in Economic Development*. New York: St. Martin's Press.

Bouvard, Marguerite Guzman 1994 *Revolutionizing Motherhood: The Mothers of the Plaza de Mayo*. Scholarly Resources, Inc.

Brettell, Caroline and Carolyn Sargent (Eds.) 1993 *Gender in Cross-Cultural Perspective*. Englewood Cliffs NJ: Prentice-Hall.

Brown, Karen McCarthy 1991 *Mama Lola: A Vodou Priestess in Brooklyn*. Berkeley: University of California Press.

Brown, Paula and Georgeda Buchbinder (Eds.) 1976 *Man and Woman in the New Guinea Highlands*. Washington, D.C.: American Anthropological Association.

Browner, Carole and Ellen Lewin 1982 "Female Altruism Reconsidered: The Virgin Mary As Economic Woman." *American Ethnologist* 9:61–75.

Browner, Carole and Bernard Ortiz de Montellano 1986 "Herbal Emmenagogues Used by Women in Colombia and Mexico." In Nina Etkin (Ed.) 1986 *Plants in Indigenous Medicine and Diet: Biobehavioral Approaches*. Bedford Hills NY: Redgrave Publishing.

Buckley, Thomas and Alma Gottlieb (Eds.) 1988 *Blood Magic: The Anthropology of Menstruation*. Berkeley: University of California Press.

Budapest, Zsuzsanna 1979; 1980 *The Holy Book of Women's Mysteries*. 2 vols. Los Angeles: Susan B. Anthony Coven #1.

Bullough, Vern and Bonnie Bullough 1993 *Cross Dressing, Sex and Gender*. Philadelphia: University of Pennsylvania Press.

Bumiller, Elisabeth 1990 *May You Be the Mother of a Hundred Sons: A Journey Among the Women of India*. New York: Fawcett Columbine.

Bunch, Charlotte and Niamh Reilly 1994 *Demanding Accountability: The Global Campaign and Vienna Tribunal for Women's Human Rights*. New Brunswick NJ: Rutgers University Center for Women's Global Leadership.

Burbank, Victoria 1994 *Fighting Women: Anger and Aggression in Aboriginal Australia*. Berkeley: University of California Press.

———— 1988 *Aboriginal Adolescence: Maidenhood in an Australian Community*. New Brunswick NJ: Rutgers University Press.

Burgess, Lauren Cook (Ed.) 1994 *An Uncommon Soldier: The Civil War Letters of Sarah Rosetta Wakeman alias Pvt. Lyons Wakeman*. Pasadena MD: Minerva Center.

Busby, Margaret (Ed.) 1992 *Daughters of Africa: An International Anthology of Words and Writings by Women of African Descent from the Ancient Egyptians to the Present*. New York: Pantheon Books.

Buss, Fran Leeper (Ed.) 1993 *Forged Under the Sun: Forjada Bajo el Sol: The Life of Maria Elena Lucas*. Ann Arbor: University of Michigan Press.

Caffrey, Margaret 1989 *Ruth Benedict: Stranger in This Land*. Austin: University of Texas Press.

Callender, Charles and Lee Kochems 1983 "The North American Berdache". *Current Anthropology* 24(4):443–70.

Chang, Jung 1991 *Wild Swans: Three Daughters of China*. New York: Anchor Books.

Chodorow, Nancy 1978 *The Reproduction of Mothering.* Berkeley: University of California Press.

Christ, Carol and Judith Plaskow (Eds.) 1989 *Weaving the Visions: New Patterns in Feminist Spirituality.* San Francisco: HarperCollins.

———— (Eds.) 1979 *Womanspirit Rising: A Feminist Reader in Religion.* San Francisco: Harper & Row.

Claassen, Cheryl (Ed.) 1994 *Women in Archaeology.* Philadelphia: University of Pennsylvania Press.

———— (Ed.) 1992 *Exploring Gender Through Archaeology.* Monographs in World Archaeology No. 11. Madison WI: Prehistory Press.

Clark, Garcia 1994 *Onions Are My Husband: Survival and Accumulation by West African Market Women.* Chicago IL: University of Chicago Press.

Conly, Shanti and Sharon Camp 1992 *China's Family Planning Program: Challenging the Myths.* Washington, D.C.: Population Action International.

Counts, Dorothy, Judith Brown and Jacquelyn Campbell (Eds.) 1991 *Sanctions and Sanctuary: Cultural Perspectives on the Beating of Wives.* Boulder CA: Westview.

Dahlberg, Frances (Ed.) 1981 *Woman the Gatherer.* New Haven CN: Yale University Press.

Daly, Mary 1978 *Gyn/Ecology: The Metaethics of Radical Feminism.* Boston: Beacon Press.

Daly, Martin and Margo Wilson 1984 "A Sociobiological Analysis of Human Infanticide." In Hausfater and Hrdy 1984:487–502.

Dandekar, Hemalata (Ed.) 1993 *Shelter, Women and Development: First and Third World Perspectives.* Ann Arbor MI: George Wahr Press.

Davis, Dona 1993 "When Men Become "Women": Gender Antagonism and the Changing Sexual Geography of Work in Newfoundland." *Sex Roles* 29(7/8):457–75.

———— 1989 "The Variable Character of Nerves in a Newfoundland Fishing Village." *Medical Anthropology* 11:63–78.

———— 1983 "Woman the Worrier: Confronting Archetypes of Stress." *Women's Studies* 10(2):135–46.

Davis-Floyd, Robbie 1992 *Birth As an American Rite of Passage.* Berkeley: University of California Press.

Delacoste, Frederique and Priscilla Alexander (Eds.) 1987 *Sex Work: Writings by Women in the Sex Industry.* San Francisco: Cleis Press.

Devereaux, George 1976 *A Study of Abortion in Primitive Societies.* Rev. Ed. New York: International University Press.

Devor, Holly 1989 *Gender Bending: Confronting the Limits of Duality.* Bloomington IL: Indiana University Press.

di Leonardo, Micaela (Ed.) 1991 *Gender at the Crossroads of Knowledge: Feminist Anthropology in the Postmodern Era.* Berkeley: University of California Press.

Dobash, Russell; R. Emerson Dobash; Margo Wilson and Martin Daly 1992 "The Myth of Sexual Symmetry in Marital Violence." *Social Problems* 39(1):71–91.

Drakulič, Slavenka 1993 *How We Survived Communism and Even Laughed*. New York: Harper Perennial.

Dunham, Carrol 1991 *Mama Toto: A Celebration of Birth*. New York: Penguin.

Eck, Diana and Devaki Jain 1987 *Speaking of Faith: Global Perspectives on Women, Religion and Social Change*. Philadelphia: New Society Publishers.

Ehlers, Tracy Bachrach 1991 "Debunking Marianismo: Economic Vulnerability and Survival Strategies Among Guatemalan Wives." *Ethnology* 30:1–16.

Ehrenberg, Margaret 1993 "The Role of Women in Human Evolution." In Brettell and Sargent 1993:14–18.

Ehrenreich, Barbara and Deidre English 1978 *For Her Own Good: 150 Years of the Expert's Advice to Women*. New York: Anchor Doubleday.

——— 1973 *Witches, Midwives and Nurses: A History of Women Healers*. Feminist Press.

Eller, Cynthia 1993 *Living in the Lap of the Goddess: The Feminist Spirituality Movement in America*. New York: Crossroad.

——— 1991 "Relativizing the Patriarchy: The Sacred History of the Feminist Spirituality Movement." *History of Religion* 30/3:279–95.

El Saadawi, Nawal 1980 "Creative Women in Changing Societies: A Personal Reflection." *Race and Class* 22(2):159–82.

——— 1980 *The Hidden Faces of Eve*. London: Zed Press.

Engels, Frederick 1972 *The Origin of the Family, Private Property and the State*. Edited, with an introduction by Eleanor Leacock. New York: International Publishers.

Etienne, Mona and Eleanor Leacock (Eds.) 1980 *Women and Colonization: Anthropological Perspectives*. New York: Praeger.

Eyer, Diane 1992 *Mother-Infant Bonding: A Scientific Fiction*. New Haven: Yale University Press.

Falk, Nancy and Rita Gross (Eds.) 1980 *Unspoken Worlds: Women's Religious Lives in Non-Western Cultures*. San Francisco: Harper & Row.

Fedigan, Linda M. 1994 "Science and the Successful Female: Why There Are So Many Women Primatologists." *American Anthropologist* 96:529–40.

Fedigan, Linda M. and Laurence Fedigan 1989 "Gender and the Study of Primates." In Morgan 1989:41–65.

Fernea, Elisabeth 1988 *A Street in Marrakech*. Prospect Heights IL: Waveland Press.

Finkler, Kaya 1994 *Women in Pain: Gender and Morbidity in Mexico*. Philadelphia: University of Pennsylvania Press.

——— 1994 *Spiritualist Healers in Mexico*. Salem WI: Sheffield.

Fisher, Helen 1992 *The Anatomy of Love: The Mysteries of Mating, Marriage, and Why We Stray*. New York: Fawcett.

Fisher, Jo 1989 *Mothers of the Disappeared*. London: Zed Books.

Fossey, Dian 1983 *Gorillas in the Mist.* Boston: Houghton Mifflin.

Foucault, Michel *The History of Sexuality. Volume 1: An Introduction.* 1978. *The Uses of Pleasure. Volume 2.* 1982. *The Care of the Self. Volume 3.* 1986. Translated from French by Robert Hurley. New York: Random House.

Friedl, Erika 1989 *Women of Deh Koh: Lives in an Iranian Village.* New York: Penguin.

Friedl, Ernestine 1975 *Women and Men: An Anthropologist's View.* New York: Holt, Rinehart and Winston.

Frisbie, Charlotte 1967 Kinaaldá: *A Study of the Navaho Girl's Puberty Ceremony.* Middleton CN: Wesleyan University Press.

Gacs, Ute; Aisha Khan, Jerrie McIntyre, and Ruth Weinberg 1989 *Women Anthropologists: Selected Biographies.* Urbana: University of Illinois Press.

Gailey, Christine Ward 1993 "Equalitarian and Class Societies: Transitions and Transformations." In Sutton 1993:67–76.

Galdikas, Biruté 1987 Interview. *Omni* 9 (July):77 ff.

Garber, Marjorie 1992 *Vested Interests: Cross-Dressing and Cultural Anxiety.* New York: Harper Perennial.

Gelles, Richard and Jane Lancaster 1987 *Child Abuse and Neglect: Biosocial Dimensions.* New York: Aldine de Gruyter.

Gero, Joan and Margaret Conkey (Eds.) 1991 *Engendering Archaeology: Women and Prehistory.* Oxford: Basil Blackwell.

Gewertz, Deborah 1983 *Sepik River Societies: A Historical Ethnography of the Chambri and their Neighbors.* New Haven: Yale University Press.

—— 1981 "A Historical Reconsideration of Female Dominance Among the Chambri of Papua New Guinea." *American Ethnologist* 8:94–106.

Gill, Lesley 1994 *Precarious Dependencies: Gender, Class and Domestic Service in Bolivia.* New York: Columbia University Press.

Gimbutas, Marija 1991 *The Civilization of the Goddess: The World of Old Europe.* San Francisco: HarperCollins.

Ginsberg, Faye 1989 *Contested Lives: The Abortion Debate in an American Community.* Berkeley: University of California Press.

Ginsberg, Faye and Anna Lowenhaupt Tsing (Eds.) 1990 *Uncertain Terms: Negotiating Gender in American Culture.* Boston: Beacon Press.

Ginsberg, Faye and Rayna Rapp (Eds.) 1995 *Conceiving the New World Order: The Global Politics of Reproduction.* Berkeley: University of California Press.

—— 1991 "The Politics of Reproduction." *Annual Reviews in Anthropology* 20:311–43. New York: Annual Reviews Inc.

Gleason, Judith 1987 *Oya: In Praise of the Goddess.* Boston and London: Shambhala Publications.

Gmelch, Sharon 1986 *Nan: The Life of an Irish Travelling Woman.* Prospect Heights IL: Waveland.

Gonzáles-Wippler, Migene 1981 *Santeria: African Magic in Latin America.* New York: Original Products.

Goodale, Jane C. 1994 *Tiwi Wives: A Study of the Women of Melville Island, North Australia.* Prospect Heights, Illinois: Waveland Press. First published in 1971.

Goodall Jane 1990 *Through a Window: My Thirty Years with the Chimpanzees of Gombe.* Boston: Houghton Mifflin.

——— 1986 *The Chimpanzees of Gombe: Patterns of Behavior.* Cambridge MA: Belknap Press.

——— 1971 *In the Shadow of Man.* New York: Dell.

Gross, Susan Hill and Mary Hill Rojas 1989 *Family Configurations in the Third World: A Focus on Women As Single Heads of Households.* St. Paul MN: Upper Midwest Women's History Center.

Gutmann, David 1992 "Beyond Nurture: Developmental Perspectives on the Vital Older Woman." In Kerns and Brown 1992:221–33.

——— 1987 *Reclaimed Powers: Toward a New Psychology of Men and Women in Later Life.* New York: Basic Books.

Hahn, Robert (Ed.) 1987 *The Anthropology of American Obstetrics.* Special Issue of *Medical Anthropology Quarterly* 1(3).

Hale, Sondra 1989 "The Politics of Gender in the Middle East." In Morgan 1989:246–67.

Hanaway, Donna 1989 *Primate Visions: Gender, Race, and Nature in The World and Modern Science.* New York: Routledge.

Hardee-Cleaveland, Karen and Judith Banister 1988 "Fertility Policy and Implementation in China, 1986–1988."

Population and Development Review 14(2):245–85.

Harvey, Youngsook Kim 1980 "Possession Sickness and Korean Shamans." In Falk and Gross 1980:41–52.

——— 1979 *Six Korean Women: The Socialization of Shamans.* St. Paul MN: West Publishing.

Hausfater, Glenn and Sarah B. Hrdy (Eds.) 1984 *Infanticide: Comparative and Evolutionary Perspectives.* New York: Aldine.

Hawley, John Stratton (Ed.) 1994 *Fundamentalism and Gender.* New York: Oxford University Press.

——— (Ed.) 1994 *Sati: The Blessing and the Curse.* New York: Oxford University Press.

Herdt, Gilbert (Ed.) 1993 *Third Sex, Third Gender: Beyond Sexual Dimorphism in Gender and History.* New York: Zone Books.

——— 1987a *Guardians of the Flute: Idioms of Masculinity.* New York: Columbia University Press.

——— 1987b *The Sambia: Ritual and Gender in New Guinea.* HB Collins Pubs.

——— (Ed.) 1984 *Ritualized Homosexuality in Melanesia.* Berkeley: University of California Press.

——— (Ed.) 1982 *Rituals of Manhood: Male Initiation in Papua New Guinea.* Berkeley: University of California Press.

Herskovits, Melville J. 1938 *Dahomey: An Ancient West African Kingdom.* 2 vols. New York: Augustin.

Hill, Susan Gross and Mary Hill Rojas. 1990 *Women and Development Issues in Three World Areas: An Overview Workshop*. St. Paul MN: Upper Midwest Women History Center.

Himes, Norman E. 1970 *Medical History of Contraception*. 1936 Williams and Wilkins Co.: Baltimore. Republished Schocken 1970.

Hochschild, Arlie with Anne Machung 1990 *The Second Shift: Working Parents and the Revolution at Home*. New York: Avon.

Hogbin, Ian 1970 *The Island of Menstruating Men: Religion in Wogeo, New Guinea*. Scranton: Chandler Publishing Co.

Honigman, John 1954 *The Kaska Indians: An Ethnographic Reconstruction*. New Haven: Yale University Press.

Howard, Jane 1984 *Margaret Mead: A Life*. New York: Simon and Schuster.

Hrdy, Sarah B. 1981 *The Woman That Never Evolved*. Cambridge: Harvard University Press.

Inhorn, Marcia 1994 *Quest for Conception: Gender, Infertility, and Egyptian Medical Traditions*. Philadelphia: University of Pennsylvania Press.

Iwao, Sumiko 1993 *The Japanese Woman: Traditional Image and Changing Reality*. New York: Free Press.

Jelliffe, D. B. and E. F. Jelliffe 1978 *Human Milk in the Modern World: Psychological, Nutritional and Economic Significance*. Oxford: Oxford University Press.

Jenness, Valerie 1993 *Making It Work: The Prostitutes' Rights Movement in Perspective*. New York: Aldine de Gruyter.

Jordon, Brigitte 1993 *Birth in Four Cultures: A Cross-Cultural Investigation of Childbirth in Yucatan, Holland, Sweden, and the United States*. 4th ed. Revised and expanded by Robbie Davis-Floyd. Prospect Heights IL.: Waveland Press.

Jules-Rosette, Bennetta (Ed.) 1979 *The New Religions of Africa*. Norwood NJ: Ablex Publishing Corp.

Kahn, Miriam 1994 *Always Hungry, Never Greedy: Food and the Expression of Gender in a Melanesian Society*. Prospect Heights IL: Waveland Press.

Katchadourian, Herant A. (Ed.) 1979 *Human Sexuality: A Comparative and Developmental Perspective*. Berkeley: University of California Press.

Keesing, Roger 1982 "Prologue: Toward a Multidimensional Understanding of Male Initiation." In Herdt 1982.

Kendall, Laurel 1985 *Shamans, Housewives, and Other Restless Spirits: Women in Korean Ritual Life*. Honolulu: University of Hawaii Press.

Kerns, Virginia 1989 *Women and the Ancestors: Black Carib Kinship and Ritual*. Urbana: University of Illinois Press.

Kerns, Virginia and Judith K. Brown (Eds.) 1992 *In Her Prime: New Views of Middle-Aged Women*. Urbana: University of Illinois Press.

King, Ursula 1993 *Women and Spirituality: Voices of Protest and Promise*. 2d. ed. Pennsylvania Park PN: The State University Press of Pennsylvania.

Kitzinger, Sheila 1978 *Women As Mothers: How They See Themselves in Different Cultures*. New York: Vintage Books.

Koblinsky, Marge; Judith Timyan and Jill Gay 1993 *The Health of Women: A Global Perspective.* Boulder CA: Westview Press.

Koso-Thomas, Olayinka 1987 *The Circumcision of Women.* London: Zed Books.

Kramer, Heinrich and James Sprenger 1928 *Hammer of Witches. The Malleus Maleficarum.* Translated by Montague Summers. London: John Rodker. Reprinted 1971, New York: Dover Publications.

Krentz, Jayne Ann 1992 *Dangerous Men and Adventurous Women: Romance Writers on the Appeal of the Romance.* Philadelphia: University of Pennsylvania Press.

Kung, Lydia 1994 *Factory Women in Taiwan.* New York: Columbia University Press.

Lafitau, Joseph Francois 1724 *Moeurs des Sauvages Ameriquains comparées aux Moeurs des Premiers Temp.* 4 vols. Paris.

Lamphere, Louise 1972 "Strategies, Cooperation and Conflict Among Women in Domestic Groups." In Rosaldo and Lamphere 1972:97–112.

Lancaster, Jane 1973 "In Praise of the Achieving Female Monkey." *Psychology Today* 7(4):30–36, 99.

Lancaster, Jane, Jeanne Altmann, Alice Rossi, and Lonnie Sherrod (Eds.) 1987 *Parenting Across the Life Span: Biosocial Dimensions.* New York: Aldine de Gruyter.

Lancaster, Jane and Beatrix Hamburg (Eds.) 1986 *School-Age Pregnancy and Parenthood.* New York: Aldine de Gruyter.

Landes, Ruth 1994 *The City of Women.* Introduction by Sally Cole. Albuquerque NM: University of New Mexico Press.

Langness, Lew 1974 "Ritual Power and Male Domination in the New Guinea Highlands." *Ethos* 2(3):189–212.

Leacock, Eleanor 1993 "Being an Anthropologist." In Sutton 1993:1–32.

———— 1981 *Myths of Male Dominance: Collected Articles on Women Cross-Culturally.* New York: Monthly Review Press.

Leacock, Eleanor and Helen Safa (Eds.) 1986 *Women's Work: Development and the Division of Labor by Gender.* South Hadley MA: Bergin and Garvey.

Leavitt, Judith Walzer 1986 *Brought to Bed: Child-Bearing in America, 1750–1950.* New York: Oxford University Press.

Lee, Richard 1979 *The !Kung San: Men, Women and Work in a Foraging Society.* Cambridge: Cambridge University Press.

Lee, Richard and Irvin DeVore (Eds.) 1968 *Man the Hunter.* Chicago: University of Chicago Press.

Lepowsky, Maria 1993 *Fruit of the Motherland: Gender in an Equalitarian Society.* New York: Columbia University Press.

Lerner, Gerda 1986 *The Creation of Patriarchy.* Oxford: Oxford University Press.

Levack, Brian (Ed.) 1992 *Witchcraft, Women and Society.* Vol 10. in *Witchcraft, Magic and Demonology: A Twelve Volume Anthology of Scholarly Articles.* Brian Levack (Ed.) New York: Garland Publishing, Inc.

Levinson, Daniel 1989 *Family Violence in Cross-Cultural Perspectives*. Newbury Park CA: Sage Publications.

Levinson, David 1988 "Family Violence in Crosscultural Perspective." In Van Hasselt *et al.* 1988:435–55.

Levy, Marion Fennelly 1988 *Each in Her Own Way: Five Women Leaders of the Developing World*. Boulder CO: Lynne Rienner.

Levy, Robert 1971 "The Community Function of Tahitian Male Transvestism: A Hypothesis." *Anthropological Quarterly* 44:12–21.

Lewin, Ellen 1993 *Lesbian Mothers: Accounts of Gender in American Culture*. Cornell University Press.

Lewis, I. M. 1971 *Ecstatic Religion: An Anthropological Study of Spirit Possession and Shamanism*. New York: Penguin.

——— 1966 "Spirit Possession and Deprivation Cults." *Man* 1:307–329.

Lightfoot-Klein, Hanny 1989 *Prisoners of Ritual: An Odyssey into Female Genital Mutilation in Africa*. New York: Haworth Press.

Linnekin, Jocelyn 1990 *Sacred Queens and Women of Consequence: Rank, Gender and Colonialism in the Hawaiian Islands*. Ann Arbor: University of Michigan Press.

Lock, Margaret 1993 *Encounters with Aging: Mythologies of Menopause in Japan and North America*. Berkeley: University of California Press.

MacCormack, Carol (Ed.) 1982 *Ethnography of Fertility and Birth*. New

York: Academic Press. 1994 2d ed. Waveland Press.

——— 1979 "Sande: The Public Face of a Secret Society." In Jules-Rosette 1979:27–38.

MacKenzie, Maureen 1991 *Androgynous Objects: String Bags and Gender in Central New Guinea*. Cooper Station NY: Harwood Academic Publishers

McClain, Carol (Ed.) 1989 *Women As Healers: Cross-Cultural Perspectives*. New Brunswick: Rutgers University Press.

——— 1989 "Reinterpreting Women in Healing Roles." In McClain 1989:1–19.

McDowell, Nancy 1991 *The Mundugumor: From the Field Notes of Margaret Mead and Reo Fortune*. Washington D.C.: Smithsonian.

Maher, Vanessa (Ed.) 1992 *The Anthropology of Breast-Feeding: Natural Law or Social Contract*. Oxford: Berg.

Makhlouf, Carla 1979 *Changing Veils: Women and Modernization in North Yemen*. Austin: University of Texas Press.

Malinowski, Bronislaw 1929 *The Sexual Life of Savages in North-Western Melanesia*. New York: Harcourt, Brace and World.

Marshall, Mac and Leslie Marshall 1990 *Silent Voices Speak: Women and Prohibition in Truk*. Belmont CA: Wadsworth.

Martin, Emily 1992 *The Woman in the Body: A Cultural Analysis of Reproduction*. Boston: Beacon Press.

Martin, Kay and Barbara Voorhies 1975 *Female of the Species*. New York: Columbia University Press.

Marx, Karl 1948 *The Communist Manifesto*. U.S.: International Publishers, Inc.

Matthews, Glenna 1987 *"Just a Housewife": The Rise and Fall of Domesticity in America*. New York: Oxford University Press.

Mead, Margaret 1975 "Bisexuality: What's It All About?" *Redbook* (January): Pages 29–30.

——— 1974 *Ruth Benedict*. New York: Columbia University Press.

——— 1973 *Coming of Age in Samoa*. New York: William Morrow and Company. First published in 1929.

——— 1972 *Blackberry Winter: My Earlier Years*. New York: William Morrow.

——— 1967 Male and Female: *A Study of the Sexes in a Changing World*. New York: Dell Laurel. First published in 1949.

——— 1963 *Sex and Temperament in Three Primitive Societies*. New York: William Morrow Co.

——— 1959 *An Anthropologist at Work: The Writings of Ruth Benedict*. Boston: Houghton-Mifflin.

Medicine, Beatrice 1983 "Warrior women: Sex Role Alternatives for Plains Indian Women." In Albers and Medicine 1983:267–80.

Meggitt, Mervyn 1964 "Male-Female Relationships in the Highlands of Australian New Guinea." *American Anthropologist* 66(2/4):204–24.

Mencher, Joan and Anne Okongwu (Eds.) 1993 *Where Did All the Men Go? Female-Headed Households in Cross-Cultural Perspective*. Boulder CA: Westview Press.

Menchú, Rigoberta 1984 *I, Rigoberta Menchú: An Indian Woman in Guatemala*. Edited and introduced by Elizabeth Burgos-Debray. Translated by Ann Wright. London: Verso.

Mernissi, Fatima 1994 *Dreams of Trespass: Tales of a Harem Girlhood*. Reading MA: Addison-Wesley.

——— 1989 *Doing Daily Battle: Interviews with Moroccan Women*. Translated by Mary Jo Lakeland. New Brunswick NJ: Rutgers University Press.

——— 1975 *Beyond the Veil: Male-Female Dynamics in a Modern Muslim Society*. New York: Schenkman.

Messenger, John 1971 "Sex and Repression in an Irish Folk Community." In Marshall, Donald and Suggs, Robert (Eds.) *Human Sexual Behavior*. New York: Basic Books.

——— 1969 *Inis Beag*. New York: Holt, Rinehart and Winston.

Metraux, Rhoda 1979 *Margaret Mead: Some Personal Views*. New York: Walker and Co.

Mies, Maria 1986 *Patriarchy and Accumulation on a World Scale*. London: Zed Books.

Mies, Maria, Claudia Von Werlhof, and Veronika Bennholdt-Thomsen. 1988 *Women: The Last Colony*. London: Zed Books.

Miller, Casey and Kate Swift 1991 *Words and Women: New Language in New Times*. New York: HarperCollins.

Mills, Jane 1993 *Womanwords: A Dictionary of Words About Women*. New York: Henry Holt.

Minturn, Leigh 1993 *Sita's Daughters: Coming Out of Purdah*. New York: Oxford University Press.

———— 1989 "The Birth Ceremony As a Rite of Passage into Infant Personhood." In *Abortion Rights and Fetal Personhood*. Edd Doerr and James Prescott (Eds.). Long Beach CA: Centerline Press.

Mintz, Sidney. 1981 "Economic Role and Cultural Tradition." In Steady 1981:515–32.

Mitter, Sara 1991 *Dharma's Daughters*. Rutgers University Press.

Modell, Judith S. 1983 *Ruth Benedict: Patterns of a Life*. Philadelphia: University of Pennsylvania Press.

Momsen, Janet (Ed.) 1993 *Women and Change in the Caribbean*. Bloomington: Indiana University Press.

Morgan, Lewis Henry 1851 *League of the Ho-De-No-Sau-Nee or Iroquois*. 2 Vols. New York.

Morgan, Lynn 1989 "Where Does Life Begin: A Cross-Cultural Perspective on Personhood." *In Abortion Rights and Fetal "Personhood."* Edd Doerr and James Prescott (Eds.). Long Beach CA: Centerline Press.

Morgan, Sandra (Ed.) 1989 *Gender and Anthropology: Critical Reviews for Research and Teaching*. Washington, D.C.: American Anthropological Association.

Moser, Caroline 1993 *Gender Planning and Development: Theory, Practice and Training*. New York: Routledge.

Moses, Yolanda 1981 "Female Status, the Family and Male Dominance in the West Indian Community." In Steady 1981:499–514.

Mosher, Steven 1993 *A Mother's Ordeal: One Woman's Fight Against China's One-Child Policy*. New York: Harcourt Brace.

Mowat, Farley 1987 *Woman in the Mists: The Story of Dian Fossey and the Mountain Gorillas of Africa*. New York: Warner Books.

Muecke, Marjorie 1992 "Mother Sold Food, Daughter Sells Her Body: The Cultural Continuity of Prostitution." *Social Science and Medicine*. 35(7):891–901.

Murdock, George 1934 *Our Primitive Contemporaries*. New York: Macmillan.

Murphy, Yolanda and Robert Murphy 1974 *Women of the Forest*. New York: Columbia University Press.

———— 1985 *Women of the Forest*. 2d. ed. New York: Columbia University Press.

Musick, Judith 1993 *Young, Poor and Pregnant: The Psychology of Teenage Motherhood*. New Haven: Yale University Press.

Nanda, Serena 1990 *Neither Man nor Woman: The Hijras of India*. Belmont CA: Wadsworth.

———— 1985 "The Hijras of India: Cultural and Individual Dimensions of an Institutionalized Third Gender Role." In Blackwood 1985:35–54.

Narasimhan, Sakuntala 1990 *Sati: Widow Burning in India*. New York: Anchor Books.

Newman, Lucile (Ed.) 1985 *Women's Medicine: A Cross-Cultural Study of Indigenous Fertility Regulation.* New Brunswick NJ: Rutgers University Press.

Nielsen, Joyce 1993 *Sex and Gender in Society: Perspectives on Stratification.* 3d ed. Waveland Press.

Nowak, Barbara 1979 "Women's Roles and Status in a Changing Iroquois society." *Occasional Papers in Anthropology: Sex Roles in Changing Cultures.* Department of Anthropology SUNY-Buffalo. Ann McElroy and Carolyn Matthiasson (Eds.) No.1:95-110.

Nuss, Shirley. In collaboration with Ettore Denti and David Viry. 1989. *Women in the World of Work: Statistical Analysis and Projections to the Year 2000. Women, Work and Development Series #18.* Geneva: International Labor Office.

O'Brien, Denise 1977 "Female Husbands in Southern Bantu Societies." In *Sexual Stratification: A Cross-Cultural View.* Alice Schlegel (Ed.). New York: Columbia University Press.

Ong, Aihwa 1991 "The Gender and Labor Politics of Postmodernity." *Annual Reviews of Anthropology* 20:279–309.

Orion, Loretta 1994 *Never Again the Burning Times: Paganism Revived.* Prospect Heights IL: Waveland Press.

Ortner, Sherry 1993 "The Virgin and the State." In Brettell and Carolyn Sargent (Eds.) 1993:257–68.

Ortner, Sherry and Harriet Whitehead (Eds.) 1981 *Sexual Meanings. The Cultural Construction of Gender and Sexuality.* Cambridge University Press.

Overall, Christine 1992 "What's Wrong with Prostitution? Evaluating Sex Work." *Signs* 17(4):705–24.

Parker, Richard 1991 *Bodies, Pleasures and Passion: Sexual Culture in Contemporary Brazil.* Boston MA: Beacon Press.

Parsons, Elsie Clews 1939 *Pueblo Indian Religion.* 2 vols. Chicago: University of Chicago Press.

Patai, Daphne 1993 *Brazilian Women Speak: Contemporary Life Stories.* New Brunswick NJ: Rutgers University Press.

Pheterson, Gail 1989 *A Vindication of the Rights of Whores.* Seattle WA: Seal Press.

Potash, Betty 1989 *Gender Relations in Sub-Saharan Africa.* In Morgan 1989:189–227.

Potash, Betty (Ed.) 1986 *Widows in African Society: Choices and Constraints.* Stanford: Stanford University Press.

Powdermaker, Hortense 1933 *Life in Lesu: The Study of a Melanesian Society in New Ireland* New York: W.W. Norton.

Price, Sally 1993 *Co-Wives and Calabashes.* 2d. ed. Ann Arbor: University of Michigan Press.

Prior, Marsha 1993 "Matrifocality, Power, and Gender Relations in Jamaica." In Brettell and Sargent 1993:310–17.

Pulsipher, Lydia Mihelic 1993 "Changing Roles in the Life Cycle of Women in Traditional West Indian Houseyards." In Momsen 1993:50-63.

Radway, Janice 1984 *Reading the Romance: Women, Patriarchy and Popular Literature.* Chapel Hill: University of North Carolina Press.

Ragoné, Helena 1994 *Surrogate Motherhood: Conception in the Heart.* Boulder CA: Westview Press.

Raphael, Dana (Ed.) 1979 *Breast-Feeding and Food Policy in a Hungry World.* London: Academic Press.

———— 1975 "Matrescence, Becoming a Mother: A 'New/Old' Rite of Passage." In *Being Female.* Dana Raphael (Ed.). The Hague: Mouton.

Rapp, Rayna 1993 "Leacock's Contributions to the Anthropological Study of Gender." In Sutton 1993:87–94.

Reanda, Laura 1991 "Prostitution As a Human Rights Question: Problems and Prospects of United Nations Action." *Human Rights Quarterly* 13:202–28.

Reichard, Gladys 1928 *Social Life of the Navajo Indians.* New York: Columbia University Press.

Reiter, Rayna (Ed.) 1975 *Toward an Anthropology of Women.* New York: Monthly Review Press.

Riddle, John 1992 *Contraception and Abortion from the Ancient World to the Renaissance.* Cambridge: Harvard University Press.

Rodriquez, Jeanette 1994 *Our Lady of Guadalupe: Faith and Empowerment Among Mexican-American Women.* Austin: University of Texas Press.

Rogers, Barbara 1986 *The Domestication of Women: Discrimination in Developing Societies.* London: Tavistock.

Rosaldo, Michelle and Louise Lamphere 1974 *Women, Culture and Society.* Stanford CA: Stanford University Press.

Roscoe, Will 1991 *The Zuni Man-Woman.* Albuquerque: University of New Mexico Press.

Rose, Kalima 1992 *Where Women Are Leaders: The SEWA Movement in India.* London: Zed Books.

Rowell, Thelma 1972 *The Social Behavior of Monkeys.* Baltimore: Penguin Press.

Ruis (Eduardo del Rio) 1979 *Marx for Beginners.* Pantheon Books.

Sachs, Karen 1982 *Sisters and Wives: The Past and Future of Sexual Equality.* Urbana: University of Illinois Press.

Sacks, Karen 1992 "Introduction: New Views of Middle-Aged Women." In Kerns and Brown 1992:1–6.

Safa, Helen 1994 *The Myth of the Male Breadwinner: Women and Industrialization in the Caribbean.* Boulder CA: Westview.

Sanday, Peggy 1990 *Fraternity Gang Rape: Sex, Brotherhood and Privilege on Campus.* New York: New York University Press.

———— 1981 "The Socio-Cultural Context of Rape." *Journal of Social Issues* 35:5–27.

Sanday, Peggy and Ruth Gallagher Goodenough (Eds.) 1990 *Beyond the Second Sex.* Philadelphia: University of Pennsylvania Press.

Sanjek, Roger and Shellee Cohen (Eds.) 1990 *At Work in Homes: Household Workers in World Perspective.* Washington D.C.: American Anthropological Association. American Ethnological Society Monograph Series #3.

Sankar, Andrea 1985 "Sisters and Brothers, Lovers and Enemies: Marriage Resistance in

Southern Kwangtung." In Blackwood 1985:69–81.

Sargent, Carolyn 1991 "Confronting Patriarchy: The Potential for Advocacy in Medical Anthropology." *Medical Anthropology Quarterly* 5(1):18–24.

Schaeffer, Claude 1965 "The Kutenai Female Berdache: Courier, Guide, Prophetess, and Warrior." *Ethnohistory* 12:195–216.

Scheper-Hughes, Nancy 1992 *Death Without Weeping: The Violence of Everyday Life in Brazil*. Berkeley: University of California Press.

———— (Ed.) 1987 *Child Survival*. Dordrecht, Boston, Lancaster, Tokyo: D. Reidel Publishing Company.

Scrimshaw, Susan 1984 "Infanticide in Human Populations: Societal and Individual Concerns." In Hausfater and Hrdy 1984:463–86.

Segun, Mabel 1985 *Sorry, No Vacancy*. Ibadan: University Press.

Sered, Susan Starr 1994 *Priestess, Mother, Sacred Sister: Religions Dominated by Women*. New York: Oxford University Press.

Sexton, Lorraine 1986 *Mothers of Money, Daughters of Coffee: The Wok Meri Movement*. Ann Arbor, MI: UMI Research Press.

Sha, Janet 1990 *Mothers of Thyme: Customs and Rituals of Infertility and Miscarriage*. Minnesota: Lida Rose Press.

Shaaban, Bouthaina 1991 *Both Right and Left-Handed: Arab Women Talk About Their Lives*. Bloomington IL: Indiana University Press.

Shiva, Vandana 1989 *Staying Alive: Women, Ecology and Development*. London: Zed Books.

Shostak, Marjorie 1983 *Nisa: The Life and Words of !Kung Woman*. New York: Vintage Books.

Smuts, Barbara 1985 *Sex and Friendship in Baboons*. New York: Aldine.

Snow, Loudell 1993 *Walking Over Medicine*. Boulder CO: Westview Press.

Soranus. 1965 *Gynecology*. Trans. by Owsei Temkin. Baltimore: The Johns Hopkins University Press.

Spretnak, Charlene (Ed.) 1982 *The Politics of Women's Spirituality: Essays on the Rise of Spiritual Power Within the Feminist Movement*. New York: Anchor.

Spring, Anita 1978 "Epidemiology of Spirit Possession Among the Luvale of Zambia." In Judith Hoch-Smith and Anita Spring (Eds.) *Women in Ritual and Symbolic Roles*. New York: Plenum Press. Pgs. 165-190.

Stack, Carol 1974 *All Our Kin: Strategies for Survival in a Black Community*. New York: Harper & Row.

Starhawk 1987 *Truth or Dare*. New York: Harper & Row.

Steady, Filomina Chioma (Ed.) 1981 *The Black Woman Cross-Culturally*. Rochester VT: Schenkman.

Strathern, Marilyn 1992 *Women in Between: Female Roles in a Male World*. New York: Rowman. [Originally published in 1972].

———— 1988 *The Problem of the Gift: Problems with Women and Problems with*

Society in Melanesia. Berkeley: University of California Press.

—— (Ed.) 1987 *Dealing with Inequality: Analysing Gender Relations in Melanesia and Beyond.* Cambridge University Press.

Strum, Shirley 1987 *Almost Human: A Journey into the World of Baboons.* New York: Random House.

Sutton, Constance (Ed.) 1993 *From Labrador to Samoa: The Theory and Practice of Eleanor Burke Leacock.* Washington, D.C.: American Anthropological Association.

Tanner, Nancy 1981 *On Becoming Human.* Cambridge University Press.

Tanner, Nancy and Adrienne Zihlman 1976 "Women in Evolution, Part I: Innovation and Selection in Human Origins." *Signs* 1(3):585-599.

Thiam, Awa 1986 *Black Sisters, Speak Out: Feminism and Oppression in Black Africa.* London: Pluto Press.

Truong, Tranh-Dam 1990 *Sex, Money and Morality: Prostitution and Tourism in Southeast Asia.* London: Zed Books.

Tucker, Susan 1988 *Telling Memories Among Southern Women Domestics.* Baton Rouge: Louisiana State University Press.

Underhill Ruth 1979 *Papago Woman.* New York: Holt, Rinehart and Winston. Reissued 1985 Waveland Press.

United Nations 1991 *The World's Women: Trends and Statistics* 1970–1990. New York: United Nations.

Van Esterik, Penny 1989 *Beyond the Breast Bottle Controversy.* New Brunswick NJ: Rutgers University Press.

Van Hasselt, Vincent; Randall Morrison; Alan Bellack and Michel Hersen (Eds.) 1988 *Handbook of Family Violence.* New York: Plenum.

Van Willigen, John and V. C. Channa 1991 "Law, Custom and Crimes Against Women: The Problem of Dowry Death in India." *Human Organization* 50(4):369–77.

Walker, Alice 1992 *Possessing the Secret of Joy.* New York: Harcourt Brace and Jovanovich.

Walker, Alice and Pratibha Parmar 1993 *Warrior Marks: Female Genital Mutilation and the Sexual Blinding of Women.* New York: Harcourt Brace and Company.

Walker, Barbara 1990. *Women's Rituals: A Sourcebook.* San Francisco CA: HarperCollins.

—— 1988 *The Woman's Dictionary of Symbols and Sacred Objects.* San Francisco: HarperCollins.

—— 1985 *The Crone: Women of Age, Wisdom and Power.* San Francisco: Harper & Row.

—— 1983 *The Woman's Encyclopedia of Myths and Secrets.* San Francisco: HarperCollins.

Ward, Martha 1993 *The Hidden Life of Tirol.* Prospect Heights IL: Waveland Press.

—— 1989 *Nest in the Wind: Adventures in Anthropology on a Tropical Island.* Prospect Heights IL: Waveland Press.

—— 1986 Poor Women, *Powerful Men: America's Great Experiment in Family Planning* Boulder CO: Westview Press.

Waring, Marilyn 1988 *If Women Counted: A New Feminist Economics.* San Francisco: Harper & Row.

Warshaw, Robin 1988 *I Never Called It Rape.* New York: Harper & Row.

Washburn, Sherwood and Irvin DeVore 1961 "Social Behavior of Baboons and Early Man." In *Social Life of Early Man.* S. L. Washburn (Ed.) 91–103. Chicago: Aldine.

Webster, Paula 1975 "Matriarchy: A Vision of Power." In Reiter 1975:141–56.

Weiner, Annette 1976 *Women of Value, Men of Renown: New Perspectives in Trobriand Exchange.* Austin: University of Texas Press.

Weiner, Annette and Jane Schneider (Eds.) 1989 *Cloth and Human Experience.* Washington, D. C.: Smithsonian Institution Press.

Weston, Kath 1993 "Lesbian/Gay Studies in the House of Anthropology." *Annual Reviews of Anthropology* 22:339–67. New York: Annual Reviews Inc.

——— 1991 *Families We Choose: Lesbians, Gays, Kinship Between Men, Between Women.* New York: Columbia University Press.

Wheelwright, Julie 1989 *Amazons and Military Maids: Women Who Dressed As Men in Pursuit of Life, Liberty and Happiness.* London: Pandora.

White, Jenny 1994 *Money Makes Us Relatives: Women's Labor in Urban Turkey.* Austin: University of Texas Press.

Whitehead, Harriet 1981 "The Bow and the Burden Strap: A New Look at Institutionalized Homosexuality in Native North America." In Ortner and Whitehead 1981:80–115.

Whitehead, Tony and Barbara Reid (Eds.) 1992 *Gender Constructs and Social Issues.* Urbana: University of Illinois.

Whyte, Martin and S. Z. Gu 1987 "Popular Response to China's Fertility Transition." *Population and Development Review* 13(3):471–93.

Wikan, Unni 1982 *Behind the Veil in Arabia: Women in Oman.* Baltimore: The Johns Hopkins University Press. (1991 Ed. University of Chicago).

——— 1977 "Man Becomes Woman: Transsexualism in Oman as a Key to Gender Roles." *Man N.S.* 12:304–19.

Williams, Walter 1986 *The Spirit and the Flesh: Sexual Diversity in American Indian Culture.* Boston: Beacon Press.

Wolf, Margery 1992 *A Thrice-told Tale: Feminism, Postmodernism, and Ethnographic Responsibility.* Palo Alto CA: Stanford University Press.

——— 1985 *Revolution Postponed: Women in Contemporary China.* Palo Alto CA: Stanford University Press.

——— 1972 *Women and the Family in Rural Taiwan.* Palo Alto CA: Stanford University Press.

Womack, Mari and Judith Marti (Eds.) 1993 *The Other Fifty Percent: Multicultural Perspectives on Gender Relations.* Prospect Heights IL: Waveland Press.

Woodhouse, Annie 1989 *Fantastic Women: Sex, Gender and Transvestism.* New Brunswick NJ: Rutgers University Press.

Young, Serinity (Ed.) 1994 *An Anthology of Sacred Texts By and About Women.* New York: Crossroad.

Zihlman, Adrienne. 1989 "Woman the Gatherer: The Role of Women in Early Hominid Evolution." In Morgan 1989:21–40.

——— 1978 "Women in Evolution, Part II: Subsistence and Social Organization Among Early Hominids." Signs 4(1):4-20.

Index